THE CAMBRIDGE COMPANION TO DANIEL DEFOE

Daniel Defoe had an eventful and adventurous life as a merchant, politician, spy, and literary hack. He is one of the eighteenth century's most lively, innovative, and important authors, famous not only for his novels, including *Robinson Crusoe*, *Moll Flanders*, and *Roxana*, but for his extensive work in journalism, political polemic, and conduct guides, and for his pioneering "Tour through the Whole Island of Great Britain." This volume surveys the wide range of Defoe's fiction and non-fiction, and assesses his importance as writer and thinker. Leading scholars discuss key issues in Defoe's novels, and show how the man who was once pilloried for his writings emerges now as a key figure in the literature and culture of the early eighteenth century.

JOHN RICHETTI is A. M. Rosenthal Professor (Emeritus) of English at the University of Pennsylvania.

THE CAMBRIDGE
COMPANION TO

DANIEL DEFOE

EDITED BY
JOHN RICHETTI

CAMBRIDGE
UNIVERSITY PRESS

2/17/09
ww
$ 29.99

CAMBRIDGE UNIVERSITY PRESS
Cambridge, New York, Melbourne, Madrid, Cape Town, Singapore, São Paulo, Delhi

Cambridge University Press
The Edinburgh Building, Cambridge CB2 8RU, UK

Published in the United States of America by Cambridge University Press, New York

www.cambridge.org
Information on this title: www.cambridge.org/9780521675055

First published 2008

Printed in the United Kingdom at the University Press, Cambridge

A catalogue record for this publication is available from the British Library

Library of Congress Cataloguing in Publication data
The Cambridge companion to Daniel Defoe / edited by John Richetti.
p.   cm.
Includes bibliographical references (p. 237) and index.
ISBN 978-0-521-85840-3 (hbk.)
ISBN 978-0-521-67505-5 (pbk.)
1. Defoe, Daniel, 1661–1731 – Criticism and interpretation.   I. Richetti, John J.
PR3407.C36   2008
823'.5–dc22
2008030240

ISBN 978-0-521-85840-3 hardback
ISBN 978-0-521-67505-5 paperback

CONTENTS

ILLUSTRATIONS

NOTES ON CONTRIBUTORS

SRINIVAS ARAVAMUDAN is Professor of English at Duke University, Director of the John Hope Franklin Humanities Institute, and President of the Consortium of Humanities Centers and Institutes from 2007 to 2012. His *Tropicopolitans: Colonialism and Agency, 1688–1804* (1999) won the outstanding first book prize of the Modern Language Association of North America. He has also edited *Slavery, Abolition and Emancipation: Writings of the British Romantic Period: Volume VI Fiction* (1999), and William Earle's *Obi: or, The History of Three-Fingered Jack* (2005). His most recent monograph is *Guru English: South Asian Religion in A Cosmopolitan Language* (2006).

PAULA R. BACKSCHEIDER is Philpott-Stevens Eminent Scholar in English at Auburn University. Among her books is *Daniel Defoe: His Life* (1990), which won the British Council Prize in 1990 and was selected by *Choice* as one of the ten Outstanding Academic Books for 1990. She is also the author of *A Being More Intense* (1984), *Daniel Defoe: Ambition and Innovation* (1986), *Spectacular Politics: Theatrical Power and Mass Culture in Early Modern England* (1993), and *Reflections on Biography* (1999). She has edited *Selected Fiction and Drama by Eliza Haywood* (1999) and, with John Richetti, the anthology *Popular Fiction by Women, 1660–1730* (1997). She has recently completed *Inventing Agency, Inventing Genre: Eighteenth-Century Women Poets and Their Poetry* (2007).

HAL GLADFELDER is a lecturer in eighteenth- and nineteenth-century English literature and culture at the University of Manchester. He is the author of *Criminality and Narrative in Eighteenth-Century England: Beyond the Law* (2001) and has edited John Cleland's *Memoirs of a Coxcomb* (2005).

J. PAUL HUNTER is the Barbara E. and Richard J. Franke Professor Emeritus at the University of Chicago and now teaches spring semesters at the University of Virginia. His scholarly and critical work has mostly involved prose fiction (*Before Novels: The Cultural Contexts of Eighteenth-Century English Fiction* (1990) won the Gottschalk Prize of the American Society for Eighteenth-Century Studies in 1991), but he is now at work on a cultural history of the couplet, tentatively entitled

Sound Argument, and the ninth edition of the *Norton Introduction to Poetry* has recently appeared.

DEIDRE SHAUNA LYNCH is Chancellor Jackman Professor and Associate Professor of English at the University of Toronto. Her publications include the prize-winning *The Economy of Character: Novels, Market Culture, and the Business of Inner Meaning* (1998) and *Janeites: Austen's Disciples and Devotees* (2000). A 2007 Guggenheim Fellow, she is currently completing a manuscript titled "At Home in English: A Cultural History of the Love of Literature."

JOHN MCVEAGH is Emeritus Professor of English at the University of Ulster. His publications include *Tradeful Merchants* (1981), *Strangers to That Land* (1994, co-edited with Andrew Hadfield), and other books on travel writing, eighteenth-century British literature, and Restoration drama. He has contributed a number of volumes to the Pickering Masters edition of *The Collected Works of Daniel Defoe* (2000–ongoing) including a new complete and annotated edition of Defoe's *Review* (2003–ongoing).

MAXIMILLIAN E. NOVAK is Distinguished Professor of English and Comparative Literature, Emeritus, at the University of California at Los Angeles. In addition to having written books on Defoe, Congreve, and the eighteenth century in general, he has edited several volumes of the *California Edition of the Works of John Dryden* and *The Stoke Newington Edition of Daniel Defoe*. He is one of the general editors of the latter edition.

ELLEN POLLAK is the author of *Incest and the English Novel, 1684–1814* (2003), *The Poetics of Sexual Myth: Gender and Ideology in the Verse of Swift and Pope* (1985), and essays on Behn, Defoe, Haywood, Manley, Swift, and Dorothy Parker, among others. She is Professor of English at Michigan State University, where she teaches feminist theory and eighteenth-century literature and culture, and where she presently serves as Director of Graduate Studies.

JOHN RICHETTI is A. M. Rosenthal Professor of English, Emeritus, at the University of Pennsylvania. His most recent book is *The Life of Daniel Defoe: A Critical Biography* (2005). Among his other books are *Popular Fiction Before Richardson: 1700–1739* (1969; rpt. 1992), *Defoe's Narratives: Situations and Structures* (1975), *Philosophical Writing: Locke, Berkeley, Hume* (1983), and *The English Novel in History 1700–1780* (1999). He has also edited *The Columbia History of the British Novel* (1994), *The Cambridge Companion to the Eighteenth-Century English Novel* (1996), *Popular Fiction by Women, 1660–1730* (with Paula Backscheider, 1997), the Penguin *Robinson Crusoe* (2000), and *The Cambridge History of English Literature, 1660–1780* (2005).

PAT ROGERS is DeBartolo Professor in the Liberal Arts at the University of South Florida and the editor of *The Cambridge Companion to Alexander Pope* (2007).

Relevant previous works include *Defoe: The Critical Heritage* (1972; 1995), *Robinson Crusoe* (1979), and an edition of *Moll Flanders* (1993); two abridged editions of Defoe's *Tour thro' the Whole Island of Great Britain* (1971; 1989 and 1993), as well as the introduction to the Folio Society edition (1983), and a study *The Text of Great Britain: Theme and Design in Defoe's Tour* (1998). His current projects include a series of linked essays exploring the *Tour* in relation to antiquarianism, crime, demography, economic geography, politics, topographic and touristic writing, travel, and urban history.

MICHAEL SEIDEL is Jesse and George Siegel Professor in the Humanities at Columbia University. His books include *Epic Geography: James Joyce's Ulysses* (1976), *Satiric Inheritance: Rabelais to Sterne* (1979), *Exile and the Narrative Imagination* (1986), *Robinson Crusoe: Island Myths and the Novel* (1991), and *James Joyce: A Short Introduction* (2002). He is co-editor of the first two volumes in the *Stoke-Newington Works of Daniel Defoe*, and wrote the introduction and notes for the Barnes & Noble edition of *Moll Flanders* (2005).

CYNTHIA WALL is Professor of English at the University of Virginia. She is the author of *The Prose of Things: Transformations of Description in the Eighteenth Century* (2006) and *The Literary and Cultural Spaces of Restoration London* (1998) and has edited works by Defoe and Pope, and the Norton Critical Edition of Bunyan's *The Pilgrim's Progress*.

CHRONOLOGY

1660 or 1661	Daniel Foe born in London (exact date unknown), son of James and Alice Foe. Restoration of the Stuart monarchy as Charles II returns to England.
1662	Act of Uniformity passed, mandating conformity in religious services to the Church of England Book of Common Prayer and requiring office-holders to be members of the state church. The Foes followed the lead of their minister, Samuel Annesley, and left the Church of England to become Dissenters.
1663	Drury Lane Theatre in London reopens.
1664	The Conventicle Act outlaws Nonconformist worship in gatherings of more than five people. Second Anglo–Dutch War (to 1667). Dutch ships sail up the Thames and destroy much of the English fleet.
1665–66	The Great Plague (kills over 70,000 people in London) and the Great Fire of London (consumes most of the old wooden city).
c. 1671–79	Attends school of the Rev. James Fisher at Dorking, Surrey, and then the Dissenting Academy of Rev. Charles Morton, Newington Green, north of London.
1675	Greenwich Observatory established by Charles II.
1678	"Exclusion Crisis" as the Earl of Shaftesbury leads a movement to exclude James, Charles II's Roman Catholic brother from the succession to the throne.

c. 1683	Foe is established as a wholesale hosiery merchant, living in Cornhill, near the Royal Exchange.
1684	Marries Mary Tuffley and receives a dowry of £3,700.
1685	Death of Charles II – succeeded by his brother, the Catholic James II. Louis XIV revokes the Edict of Nantes, ending religious toleration in France.
1685	Foe participates in the unsuccessful rebellion against James II led by the Duke of Monmouth, one of Charles II's illegitimate sons.
1685–92	Becomes a prosperous businessman dealing in hosiery, tobacco, wine, and other goods. Seems to have travelled extensively on business in England and in Europe.
1688	The "Glorious Revolution": James II is forced to vacate the throne and Prince William of Orange in the Netherlands is invited to reign as William III of England, with James's daughter, Mary, as his queen.
1690	William III defeats James II at the Battle of the Boyne in Ireland.
1692	Foe declares bankruptcy for £17,000 and is imprisoned for debt.
1694	Founding of the Bank of England. Foe establishes a brick and tile factory at Tilbury, in Essex.
1695	Daniel Foe begins to call himself Defoe.
1697	Publication of Defoe's first book, *An Essay on Projects*, a series of proposals for radical social and economic change. Death of Queen Mary.
1697–1701	Defoe acts as an agent for William III in England and Scotland.
1701	James II dies in exile. Act of Settlement establishes Hanoverian succession. *The True-Born Englishman*, a poetic satire of English xenophobia and a defense of William III, who was Dutch by birth.

1702	Death of William III; accession of Queen Anne, James II's daughter. England declares war against France and Spain: the War of the Spanish Succession. John Churchill, Duke of Marlborough, is named Captain-General of the English army. *The Shortest Way with the Dissenters*, a satiric attack on High Church extremists.
1703	Defoe arrested for writing *The Shortest Way*, charged with sedition, committed to Newgate prison and sentenced to stand in the pillory for three days. He publishes the poem *A Hymn to the Pillory* and an authorized collection of his writings, *A True Collection of the Writings of the Author of The True-Born Englishman* (a second volume in 1705). Released through the influence of the powerful politician and Speaker of the House, Robert Harley, but his brick and tile factory fails while he is in prison. Bankrupt again.
1704	The English capture Gibraltar; Duke of Marlborough defeats the French at Blenheim. Defoe begins the *Review*, a pro-government newssheet appearing as often as three times a week (until 1713).
1704–13	Defoe acts as secret agent and political journalist for Harley and other ministers, travelling widely in England and Scotland, promoting the union of the two countries.
1707	Union of England and Scotland.
1710	Tories gain control of Parliament under leadership of Robert Harley (later Earl of Oxford) and Henry St. John (later Viscount Bolingbroke). Statute of Queen Anne passed by Parliament, limiting copyright to twenty-eight years and recognizing authors' rights.
1711	Founding of the South Sea Company.
1713	Treaty of Utrecht, ending the War of the Spanish Succession.
1713–14	Defoe arrested several times for debt and for his political writings but released through government influence.
1714	Death of Queen Anne; accession of George I, the Elector of Hanover. Fall of the Tory government.

1715	*The Family Instructor*, the first of his conduct books.
	Jacobite Rebellion in support of James II's son, "James III," the "Old Pretender."
	Death of Louis XIV of France.
	Robert Harley (Earl of Oxford) and Henry St. John (Viscount Bolingbroke) are impeached for high treason. Bolingbroke flees to France.
1719	*Robinson Crusoe, The Farther Adventures of Robinson Crusoe*.
1720	*Captain Singleton, Serious Reflections of ... Robinson Crusoe*.
	War with Spain declared.
	South Sea Company fails ("South Sea Bubble").
1721	Robert Walpole appointed First Lord of the Treasury and Chancellor of the Exchequer.
1722	*A Journal of the Plague Year, Moll Flanders*, and *Colonel Jack*.
1724	*Roxana, A General History of the Pyrates, A Tour thro' the Whole Island of Great Britain* (3 volumes, 1724–26).
1725	*The Complete English Tradesman*, volume I.
1726	*The Political History of the Devil*.
1727	*Conjugal Lewdness, An Essay on the History and Reality of Apparitions, A New Family Instructor, The Complete English Tradesman*, volume II.
	Death of George I.
1728	*Augusta Triumphans, A Plan of the English Commerce*.
1729	*The Compleat English Gentleman* (not published until 1890).
1731	Dies on 24 April in Ropemaker's Alley, London, in debt, hiding from creditors.

Introduction

Book II of Alexander Pope's *Dunciad* includes an uproarious parody of the games of strength and speed featured in classical epics. The presiding goddess, Dullness, presents as a prize to the victor, the notorious publisher, Edmund Curll, a "shaggy Tap'stry" depicting Pope's satiric targets in the poem, Grub Street authors and booksellers. And at the forefront of the picture is Daniel Defoe: "Earless on high, stood unabash'd De Foe" (II, 147).[1] Having one's ears cut off, as suggested by Pope's slanderous depiction of Defoe, was in those days a possible if rare punishment for seditious publication. Pope and the members of his elite literary circle viewed writers for hire like Defoe with contempt as nothing more than literary prostitutes who catered to degraded popular taste or produced political propaganda. Defoe had been pilloried (made to stand in humiliating and dangerous public view, hands and head in a locked frame, elevated on a pillar) for parts of three days in July 1703 for writing *The Shortest Way with the Dissenters* (1702), a pamphlet the government deemed incendiary. Swift, in a pamphlet in 1708, said that Defoe was "One of these Authors (the Fellow that was pilloryed, I have forgot his name) so grave, sententious, dogmatical a Rogue, that there is no enduring him."[2]

Three hundred years or so later, however, Defoe has had the last laugh on mandarins such as Pope and Swift. Thanks partly to contemporary redactions in film (*Castaway*) and television (*Survivor*), the *Robinson Crusoe* story remains an enduring archetype, just as the book itself is a world classic, translated into many languages. And thanks to the novel's dominance in modern times as a literary form, Defoe is these days a major figure in the history of its development in England, with *Moll Flanders* (1722), *A Journal of the Plague Year* (1722), and *Roxana* (1724) along with *Robinson Crusoe* read as standard texts for academic study, as founding moments in the emergence of modern fiction. Moreover, it is precisely by virtue of Defoe's career as the versatile professional writer (hack is the word they would have used) that Swift and Pope found so contemptible, that his writings have in the last three decades or so come to command increasing attention from literary, social, political, and cultural historians.

The bankrupt merchant turned writer and political propagandist, the object of abuse and condescension from traditionalists in his own day, Defoe is arguably the most important writer of the first thirty years of the English eighteenth century, and perhaps the one who is nowadays most widely read. As the thirteen essays in this volume will demonstrate, he was certainly the most prolific and one of the most versatile and effective writers of his time. A political and religious polemical journalist, a satirical and philosophical poet, an economic theorist, a moralist and social commentator, and of course late in life a writer of long narrative fictions, Defoe produced a richly varied body of work. His literary output was staggering, so much so that just how much and precisely what he actually wrote are matters of scholarly dispute.[3] He wrote in many genres, poetic and prose kinds, and he may be said to have inaugurated one characteristically modern mode of publication – the syndicated column, the periodical he called the *Review*, which he produced single-handedly (two and then three times a week) from 1704 to 1713. Defoe, in short, was a major force in the explosion of print and the founding of that free public exchange of political ideas that has been called the bourgeois public sphere in early eighteenth-century England. His restless and omnivorous intelligence, to say nothing of his talent for non-stop articulation, propelled him through a life of writing and political activism without real precedent in England.

As the *Review* especially makes clear, Defoe was a man of the world, deeply immersed in early eighteenth-century politics and economics. A public intellectual well before the phrase came into the English language, he was interested in everything, seemed to have strong opinions about everything, and wrote about almost everything in his world and his time. Brash, opinionated, "so grave, sententious, dogmatical" (in Swift's sneering phrase), Defoe is perhaps the most indefatigable and energetic author of his day: a veritable writing machine. And yet for all that unceasing torrent of language he produced, Defoe was not chained to his desk. He lived an eventful and indeed danger-filled existence, beginning as a wholesale merchant and entrepreneur and then thanks to bad luck as a businessman/writer – bankrupt after risky speculation and briefly imprisoned for writing *The Shortest Way with the Dissenters* (1702) – he was forced to gain his living by writing and as a secret political agent for the powerful Tory politician, Robert Harley, for whom he agitated to promote the proposed union of England and Scotland. From the wreckage of personal and financial disaster, Defoe constructed by virtue of sheer will and persistence a career that made him one of the best-known writers of his time.

The details of Defoe's life and its relationships with his multifarious writings are a recurring emphasis in some of the essays in this volume, which dramatize his intellectual range and literary versatility in the face of many hardships, trials, and setbacks. A majority of the essays deal, naturally, with the long narratives he wrote from 1719 to 1724, which are the works that will appeal most to contemporary readers and which are the most immediately available and pertinent of his works today. But it is worth noting that these "novels" represent only a small fraction of what Defoe wrote. Moreover, the novels are in fact enriched by being placed in the context of Defoe's non-fictional writings, those political, social, economic, and moral works that occupied him for many years. Defoe's novels, that is to say, encompass not only the lives of their individual actors but also their intersection and involvement with issues within the larger socio-historical world in which they acquire their identities; they are novels of ideas as well as of character. Defoe never stops thinking, questioning, and agitating, and some of the essays in this volume will ponder his provocatively original notions about key topics in his narratives such as money,[4] commerce, gender, psychology, politics, religion, empire, and crime that link his novels to the rest of his intellectual life.

Without minimizing the rough and tumble side of Defoe's career in the fractious literary and political marketplace of the early eighteenth century, or his self-aggrandizing and self-promoting tendencies, his often reckless, self-destructive, mendacious, and always radically contentious personality, the essays in this volume take Defoe with full seriousness as an engaged and committed writer and even as an important thinker, finding in his works a veritable encyclopedia of the issues central to his time. The journalist and polemicist without peer, the criminologist, the urbanist, the proto-feminist, the early theorist of globalism and imperialism, the poet and satirist, moralist and social critic, the promoter of Britain's mercantile power and prophet of its future imperial glories, to say nothing of the creator of memorable fictions – Defoe fits all these descriptions and works in all these fields. Much more so than Pope, Swift, and other elite writers of the time, Defoe is a representative of the spirit of his age: forward-looking and open to new ideas, enlightened and rationally pragmatic in the moderate eighteenth-century English sense, religious but not fanatical or exclusivistic in his views. As a religious Dissenter from the merchant classes, lacking the university education and the ruling-class connections or patronage other writers of the time enjoyed, Defoe was an outsider who was thereby able, thanks to sheer intelligence and drive, to offer in his works an overview of the age, biased, to be sure, but comprehensive in its ambition and inventive and revealing in its articulations. In a word, he is perhaps the first truly *modern* English writer.

NOTES

1. *The Poems of Alexander Pope*, ed. John Butt (London: Methuen & Co, 1963), p. 741.
2. Cited in Pat Rogers, ed., *Defoe: The Critical Heritage* (London: Routledge & Kegan Paul, 1972), p. 38.
3. The most recent and thorough (and for many convincing) reconfiguration of the canon of Defoe's works can be found in a number of books by W. R. Owens and P. N. Furbank: *Defoe De-Attributions: A Critique of J. R. Moore's Checklist* (London and Rio Grande, Ohio: The Hambledon Press, 1994) and *A Critical Bibliography of Daniel Defoe* (London: Pickering & Chatto, 1998), and P. N. Furbank and W. R. Owens, *The Canonisation of Daniel Defoe* (New Haven: Yale University Press, 1998). Owens and Furbank are the general editors of the ongoing edition of Defoe's (selected) works, *The Works of Daniel Defoe*, 44 vols. (London: Pickering & Chatto, 2000–8). But no one will ever know exactly what Defoe wrote. Many Defoe specialists disagree with at least some of Furbank and Owens's de-attributions. Some texts they designate as only "probably" by Defoe in *The Works of Daniel Defoe*, such as *Due Preparations for the Plague Year* and *Conjugal Lewdness*, are widely accepted as Defoe's.
4. Money is a crucial subject in all of Defoe's works, and it is important for readers to have some notion of what these sums might be worth in early twenty-first-century purchasing power. There are a number of web sites that will provide an approximation of contemporary monetary equivalents. I would recommend http://measuringworth.com/calculators/ppoweruk.

I

PAULA R. BACKSCHEIDER

Defoe: the man in the works

One of Daniel Defoe's contemporaries, Eliza Haywood, opens *The Invisible Spy* (1755) by taunting the reader: "I have observed that when a new book begins to make a noise in the world ... every one is desirous of becoming acquainted with the author; and this impatience increases the more ... he endeavors to conceal himself." Shortly before her death, Haywood "laid a solemn injunction" to keep her secrets on the person who knew her life best, because she believed "improper liberties [would be] taken with her character after death, by the intermixture of truth and falsehood."[1] Almost from the beginning of his writing career, Defoe could serve as proof of these statements. Although his contemporaries often wanted to "become acquainted with the author" in order to get him arrested, many of his modern-day biographers and critics have dedicated themselves to scrutinizing the works to find the man.

Most people think that a writer can be found in the works and that "writing was his/her life." The writer, however, was a material body, a mortal body. Defoe stood in the rain in the pillory and could not brush the water off his nose. Although he obviously had an excellent constitution and unusual stamina, he had colds, bruises, and surgery. People responded to his material body in ways that affected his behavior and self-perception; they remembered his hooked nose, his habit of crooking his little finger, and his foppishness. Writing was not Defoe's life. Unlike most writers, for whom "life" and its demands are obstacles to writing, except for the brief period of Defoe's poetic aspirations, he preferred life and resorted to writing when enraged, unoccupied, or in economic need. Taken without external evidence, much that he (or any other biographical subject) "revealed" should not be believed. It has been demonstrated by those who study biography writing that the memories of biographical subjects, their relatives, and friends are the most unreliable sources of "facts." Even a private diary can be delusional. Indeed, one found and taken to have been personal can, in fact, have been intended to be read by a sneaking, suspicious spouse.

Unlike Haywood, who successfully suppressed details of her life, Defoe tried rather repeatedly to control the story of his life. In *An Appeal to Honour and Justice* (1715) he wrote, "I should *even Accounts* with this World before I go, that no Actions (Slanders) may lie against my Heirs, Executors, Administrators, and Assigns, to disturb them in the peaceable Possession of their Father's (Character) Inheritance."[2] *An Appeal* is usually granted the status of a defense of Defoe's life, if not quite of autobiography. Some biographies of Defoe, for instance, give it quite different degrees of reliability,[3] and I remember the exact moment as I reread it for my *Daniel Defoe: His Life* when I stopped believing Defoe, when I "knew" he was prevaricating.

Defoe lived a long time, he was secretive and tricky and had a lot to hide, and he was an exceptionally skillful writer. This last fact is the most complicating; as John Richetti has observed, even as a young writer Defoe had a "striking" ability to slip "easily into narrative mimicry of a persona at variance with his own reality."[4] Although biographers and critics have taken "improper liberties," or at least gone too far in reading some of Defoe's printed statements as autobiography, as biographers we believe that our most accurate insights about writers come from cumulative experience with their total *oeuvre*. Over a lifetime, a writer's recurring opinions about society, human behavior and relationships, and politics emerge, as does some understanding of their personality and "reality." The languages of law and business funnel into the conflation of "character" and "inheritance" in the sentence I quoted from *An Appeal*, which reveals the way Defoe thought and the reality he believed in. Like many people of his time, and especially those with a Puritan heritage, he kept "accounts" of his conduct on earth with an eye on a reckoning in Heaven. Judgments of moral character were always figured into assessments of achievement. Defoe's focus here is on what he is leaving, his inheritance, which is his "character." Throughout *An Appeal* he writes about sources of credit, reputation, and perceptions of him and his conduct. As Catherine Ingrassia remarks, property shifted from the material to "fluid, immaterial, and multiple" forms, and they "could be realized only imaginatively."[5] Just as he speculated on all kinds of investments in the new credit economy, he speculated on a wide variety of kinds of self-representation in publications; his goal was the same – the amassing of credit that would improve his personal and economic status. All kinds of paper and material credit are conflated in the culture and in Defoe's writings about himself. His awareness of the power and also the volatility of established authorial personae is evident. His credit as a man, as a former tradesman, as an employee of the queen (he insists it was she for whom he worked), and as a writer are all at issue in *An Appeal*, mutually reinforcing a person and a life story that he cannot quite sustain.

How free writers ever are from genre conventions, from their own horizons of expectation for the forms in which they write, and from the pressures exerted on them can never be known, but writers have agency, and traces of the mind that created the texts linger. In this chapter I will define some of the places where I find Defoe's mind and reality insistently and dramatically revelatory of his personality. Identity is the meeting point of biological characteristics, who a person wants to be, historical circumstances, and what the world will allow him or her to be. For example, a man may have the tactical mind and physical strength to be a great general, but he must want that destiny, have a war in which to exercise these abilities, and be allowed by the culture to advance to that position. Defoe was one of the most embattled public figures in history. He lacked any of the sources of power – position, family, wealth, charisma. His life was a struggle to hang on to what he wanted to be and thought he was, and he faced frequent, very harsh confrontations with contradicting facts. In Defoe's case, political, religious, and economic forces were especially strong, as were, as we will see, the pressures of his sense of himself.

Defoe's life is a monumental contradiction. He helped create modern counterintelligence and opinion-sampling and virtually invented modern political propaganda. He was a tireless fighter for freedom of the press and religion, single-handedly wrote the first essay periodical for nine years,[6] and published beautiful economic geographies of his own nation and the world. His novels still intrigue and entertain us. Yet he was also pardoned by two monarchs, jailed repeatedly, suffered the ignominious pillory *three* times, and died in hiding from a creditor who was so tenacious that she took her case to the mighty Court of Exchequer. Who was he? What was Defoe like? How did he perceive himself and his place in the universe? Through a series of quotations, I will offer a few conclusions.

> But in the Middle of all this Felicity, one Blow from unforeseen Providence unhing'd me at once.   Robinson Crusoe in *Farther Adventures*

> And now I began to think my Fortunes were settled for this World ... But an unseen Mine blew up all this apparent Tranquility at once, and tho' it did not remove my Affairs there from me, yet it effectually remov'd me from them, and sent me a wandring into the World again ...   *Col. Jacque*

> In the middle of what she thinks is her Happiness and Prosperity, she is ingulph'd in Misery and Beggary.   *Roxana*[7]

These quotations describe one of the ways Defoe experienced his life. Once he turned away from the dissenting ministry, he followed a well-marked career path that should have led to economic and even political success. He became a wholesale hosier, a merchant who bought stockings from the districts that produced various kinds and redistributed them around the kingdom for profit. He prospered with his wide selection of stockings of different thicknesses, lengths, textures, colors, prices, and especially patterns in a time when even the poorer people were beginning to want fashion hosiery. He had a home and a warehouse in Freeman's Yard, Cornhill, an area known for high quality woolen manufacture and for the attractive residences of substantial tradesmen.

By necessity, Defoe practised his trade traveling all over England. Indeed, the travel was one of his reasons for choosing this occupation. As an opinion-gatherer in 1705–1711, and as a merchant-investor and the writer of the *Tour* in the 1720s, he would re-create this life on horseback. One of the most revealing ways to understand a life is to search for the things the person works to keep stable. In his life of arrests, turmoil, and change, what Defoe fought to recreate and maintain tells us as much about him as studies of how he changed over time. In the weeks before he was apprehended for publishing *The Shortest Way*, he described himself to several people as having "a Mind Impatient of Confinement"; that he so consistently created employment for himself that involved travel poignantly glosses that statement.[8]

At the same time that Defoe was building his trade, he began to build the reputation he would need to be elected to, for instance, the Court of Aldermen or even Lord Mayor. The Sheriff appointed him to the petty (or trial) jury in 1684, an unusual responsibility conferred on such a young man. In 1687 he became a livery man of the City, a member of the group allowed to vote for the highest City of London offices, such as auditors, Lord Mayor, and Members of Parliament. He served on the petty jury in 1685–86 and again in 1688, and in 1689 was a member of the eleven-member governing board of Cornhill ward. He paraded as one of the "chief Citizens, who being gallantly mounted and richly accoutred" formed a "volunteer regiment" to welcome and support King William upon his arrival in London. He served in the right offices, joined the right groups, and signed the right documents, including some to protect trade with North America.

His marriage to Mary Tuffley with her £3,700 dowry led to his expansion into the export–import business and trade in wine, spirits, cloth, and other commodities (in today's currency, her dowry would be £400,000 or about $800,000). He speculated in investments in such risky ventures as diving bells and civet cats. One of the ships in which he invested was captured by a French man-of-war, and there were unexpected losses on cargoes to New England and Ireland. In 1692, he was committed to the Fleet Prison on the complaint of numerous, ordinary citizens, some owed as little as £33; the complaints kept being filed, and as soon as he was released, he would be re-committed.

Rather than mingling with the first citizens of London, he was housed in squalor with felons and shoplifters.

Defoe would sometimes describe this bankruptcy for the enormous sum of £17,000 as one of the unseen mines that exploded his plan for his life. In *An Appeal to Honour and Justice* he writes, "Misfortunes in Business having unhing'd me from Matters of Trade ..." (194). "Unhing'd" is defined by the *Oxford English Dictionary* as "to unsettle, unbalance, disorder (the mind)"; "to deprive of stability or fixity; to throw into confusion or disorder." As a young man, he had elected to turn away from the ministry, but now he had lost both the credit and the means to carry on in his chosen profession. In the years to come, he would sometimes describe going bankrupt as a horrendous, extended process that led him to do "many little, mean, and even wicked things" that even "the most religious tradesman" will stoop to when harassed beyond endurance, even as he continued to describe prosecutions for debt as surprises initiated by his malicious and insignificant enemies.[9] Both descriptions highlight the contradiction between his self-image and the actual experience in a very public world.

The Shortest Way with the Dissenters (1702) was the second major "unseen Mine." In an autobiographical account requested by his powerful employer, Robert Harley, who would rise to the highest offices in government, Defoe explained: "I began to live, Took a Good House, bought me Coach and horses a Second Time." "But I was Ruin'd *The shortest way* ..." (*Letters*, p. 17). Many of his private and published explanations and defenses sound a note of surprise. "That the Govornment, whom I Profess I Did not foresee would be Displeas'd .... I had it not in my Thoughts That the Ministers of State would Construe That as Pointing at Them, Which I Levell'd Onely at Dr. Sachavrell," he writes, and "it seems Impossible to imagine it should pass for any thing but a Banter upon the High-flying Church-Men."[10] A few of the changes in power during Queen Anne's reign caught Defoe off guard and unsettled his affairs, and he was arrested in 1713 for publishing three pamphlets, including the provocatively titled *And What If the Pretender Should Come*. Defoe, like the characters in his novels, would think his "Fortunes were settled for this World" only to find himself "unhing'd." In his petition for pardon to Queen Anne, he describes what happened as meanings "wrested against the true design" and finds himself "to his great Surprize ... Misrepresented, and the said Book Misconstrued."[11] In *An Appeal*, he writes, "I leave it to any considering Man to Judge, what a Surprise it must be to me to meet with all the publick Clamour that Informers could invent ..." (*Appeal*, p. 213).

Again in the 1720s Defoe's fortunes seemed settled, and he lived in a lovely home with a beautiful garden. He wrote books such as *A General History of*

Discoveries and Improvements (1725–26) that were his favorite kind of book to write and that speak of an unhurried occupation. He hoped to propagate useful knowledge and encourage the present age to invent and improve discoveries. His language is expansive and highly figurative: "*Tyre* was the Daughter of *Sidon*, and she dwelt so near her Mother, that they went on hand in hand in the Improvement of their Navigation, as well as of their Commerce" (Tyre and Sidon were the two leading commercial ports of ancient Phoenicia).[12] He draws entertaining and instructive examples from Greece, Carthage, Rome, Phoenicia, Egypt, from the past and America, Africa, and Russia in his own time and suggests, with lists of specific benefits, such things as Great Britain taking and re-building the North Africa of Carthage. After lingering on expositions of world history, he compares Great Britain and its strengths to the great nations throughout time and space, and then he recommends immediate action for Britain's attainment of world domination. He also editorializes against war and tyranny, which, he says, beggar the world. He takes the time to extend lyrical comparisons; of the age of Renaissance exploration, he writes, "Now the adventurous Mariner confin'd himself no more to the meanness of coasting along the Shores .... Immediately like young Swimmers grown expert, and who scorn any longer to keep within their depth, and in shallow Waters, but boldly swim off into the Channels of the largest Rivers; so have the Mariners." "Meanness," "coasting," and "scorn" give way to the image of the strong, bold, free explorers. But this situation is analogous to the opportunities offered by Africa and America in his own time: "How little then of this newly discover'd World is yet known, compar'd to what there is yet left to know?"[13] At the same time his imagination was sailing free, he was over-investing and speculating as he had in the 1690s, and old creditors were stirring. He began to write compulsively about the costs of everyday items and even recommended the regulation of prices charged by sellers of common wares including tallow chandlers, his dead father's occupation. Into this world of expansive dreaming and proposing, new lawsuits for debts intruded, and Defoe was driven into hiding, his life, like Roxana's, "ingulph'd in Misery and Beggary again" (*Roxana*, p. 149).

> **I Do allready Find Tis No Very Difficult Thing for me to Get my Bread.**

> **He that gave me Brains, will give me Bread.**

> **I Never Despaird and In the Worst Condition allways believ'd I should be Carryed Thro' it.**[14]

Displaying another consistent aspect of his personality, resilience, Defoe set about rebuilding his life after each disaster. Over a number of years, he repaid more of his debts from his first bankruptcy than seems possible, published his immensely popular poem, *The True-Born Englishman* (1701), received some government positions from acquaintances at the fringe of King William's government, and began to write in support of the king and his initiatives, such as the controversial maintenance of a "standing army." He also advocated religious tolerance and, some believed, began the debate over occasional conformity, a provision in the Test Act of 1673 that allowed men willing to take communion in the Church of England to hold civil, military, and crown offices. These causes had a high profile and were bitterly contested. The debate over whether England should have a large standing army awakened memories of Oliver Cromwell and continued for three years. Members of Parliament, the Lord Chancellor, the poets Richard Blackmore and Matthew Prior, and other equally prominent people published about it, and Defoe began to be called a "party tool."[15] Occasional conformity was an accepted practice within his own denomination, and to many it seemed a benign benefit for large numbers of people. In fact, it had originally been practised as a gesture of "brotherly love" among Protestant churches. Defoe's language was extreme and vivid, and he divided the Dissenters into "religious" or "politic." In one memorable moment, he described the Lord Mayor, Sir Humphry Edwin, as "bantering with Religion" and "*playing Bo-peep* with God Almighty."[16] His opponents and even some who agreed with him commonly characterized him as "rash," "immoderate" and "foul mouthed."

A poem written to support William, *The True-Born Englishman*, sold better than any poem had since John Dryden's *Absalom and Achitophel*, and the notoriety of his *Legion's Memorial* and other pamphlets about the imprisoned Kentish petitioners led him to begin claiming to be "the voice of the people." In 1701 he also wrote the great *Original Power of the Collective Body of the People of England*, and he began to see himself as a poet using verse to champion right. Passage that year of the Act of Settlement, which guaranteed a Protestant succession to the throne and attempted to limit some of the powers of the monarch, made timely Defoe's writings on the "contract" between a monarch and the people and on mixed government built on checks and balances between branches. He set up at this apparently auspicious moment as the propagator and celebrant of the principles growing from the Glorious Revolution of 1688, thus identifying himself as a "revolution man," his third controversial step.[17] It seems fair to say, in short, that Defoe was in these opening years of the eighteenth century, well before he had to face public humiliation in the pillory, a notorious and controversial figure.

Once committed to a line of action, Defoe characteristically worked to establish two lines of credit. Analogous to his parallel development in investments in a career as factor/merchant and as a city politician, he began to devote more time to writing elite as well as public poetry, each career offering him, he believed, different potential payoffs. For example, he wrote the poem *The Pacificator* (1700) as part of the ancients–moderns controversy. He began the poem that would, he hoped, establish his preeminence as a poet and a defender of revolution principles: *Jure Divino* (1706), an ambitious twelve-book verse essay clearly drawing upon the ideas in *Original Power*. These two texts and the Legion's Memorial writings assert that the purpose of government is "public good" and that the supreme power is in the people, and explain many of the major principles in John Locke's *Second Treatise on Civil Government*. As a young man, Defoe's ambitions were to be a great poet and to be Lord Mayor. Nonconformists had become Lord Mayors, as Sir Humphrey Edwin and Sir Thomas Abney had. The pillory ended that hope. Part of the poem that would have established that reputation had to be destroyed; as he said in the Preface, coming from him at that time and after the death of William, he had reason to fear it would "give Offense." Writing poetry requires leisure and tranquility of mind; it would be fifteen years before Defoe had that again.

Instead, his mantra became, "The God who gave me brains will give me bread," a line from *Elegy on the Author of the True-Born Englishman*, the poem he had written to be handed about as he stood in the pillory in July 1703. In April, before he was apprehended, he wrote to an acquaintance that he was finding "Tis No Very Difficult Thing for me to Get my Bread," and less than a year after the pillory wrote to Robert Harley, who would shortly become his patron, that he always believed he would be carried through his troubles. Every other avenue at least temporarily closed to him, he began to write thousands of journalistic and propagandistic words, "history writing by inches" in the *Review*, and energetic defenses of himself, including his *A True Collection of the Writings of the Author of the True-Born Englishman*, a careful crafting of himself as a man and a writer.

> Alas, *Poor De Foe*! what hast thou been doing, and for what hast thou suffer'd?
>
> My Case may, without any Arrogance, be likened to that of the Sacred Prophet[18]

One of the places where Defoe's voice is most insistent is in the passages in which he represents himself as suffering, then questions why, and then reconstructs the reason in his favor, in a maneuver that shows him clinging to and shoring up his self-image as an admirable man. In *More Reformation*, a poem he wrote to vindicate himself, he concludes with poignant, morose dignity, "'tho I have been a Man of Misfortunes ... I have not been a Man of Vice."[19] In those frantic days of economic collapse during which he squandered his wife's enormous dowry and cheated his friends and mother-in-law, during the disaster of Newgate and the pillory, and again during the terror of the 1713 arrest, he insists that he was misunderstood, and the misunderstanding is not just of his writing but of the kind of moral man he is. In *An Appeal to Honour and Justice*, Defoe writes, "I hear much of Peoples calling out to punish the Guilty; but very few are concern'd to clear the Innocent." He describes himself as falling "a Sacrifice for writing against the Rage and Madness of that High Party, and in the Service of the Dissenters" (*An Appeal*, pp. 191, 199).

Defoe's self-image was constantly contradicted, and he often responded, "Alas, poor De Foe." In 1703, he begged for the punishment of a "gentleman," but abuse was heaped on him; Newgate and the pillory made him confront the reality of a man made "despicable" (*Letters*, pp. 2, 12). *More Reformation* includes a remarkable list of the epithets hurled at him and his equally remarkable effort to cling to what he thought he was. In like manner, *An Appeal* is an extended exercise in Defoe confronting the contradictions to his sense of himself, exploring why he suffers, and, until it breaks down as an unsustainable fiction, using that suffering to reinforce his moral superiority. These narratives often begin with an egregiously wrong act to which Defoe (and in his opinion all ethical people) would respond with outrage: he explains that John Tutchin's *The Foreigners* "fill'd me with a kind of Rage against the Book and gave birth to ... *The True-Born-Englishman*." He makes it clear that, rather than party zeal, it was King William's support for the Protestant religion and the injustice of attacks on William that motivated him (*An Appeal*, pp. 195, 197). In endlessly reiterated statements, he explains that *The Shortest Way with the Dissenters* was also born in reaction to un-Christian and inhumane attacks on his persecuted fellow Dissenters. After laying out at length how mistaken about him and his cause those who attack him are, he often ends with a typological parallel to the Bible: "But such is my present fate," he writes in *An Appeal*, "and I am to submit to it, which I do with meekness ... and am practising that duty which I have studied long ago, of *forgiving my enemies*, and *praying for them that despitefully use me*" (*An Appeal*, 235–36). Quoting key phrases in Jesus's charge to his disciples (Luke 6:27–28), Defoe claims to be true to their Christian ideal of forbearing love and suffering for moral acts.

The book of the Bible that Defoe quoted most frequently was that of Jeremiah, that fascinating young man who left both a record of remarkable prophecies, many against his own people, and, more arresting, an unparalleled insight into the inner life of a prophet. Jeremiah prophesied during the forty years that preceded the destruction of Jerusalem in 586 BC. In his *Family Instructors* alone, Defoe quotes Jeremiah more than twenty times. In his earliest known manuscript, Defoe used Jeremiah's parable of the potter and his clay from 18:1–10, perhaps to address his change of vocation.[20] As Defoe says in the above excerpt from *An Appeal*, his case can be likened to Jeremiah's life, and at that point he quotes, "I heard the Defaming of many ... Peradventure he will be enticed, and we shall prevail against him, and we shall take our Revenge on him" (Jeremiah 20:10). The chapter that Defoe is quoting includes this passage as well: "Now Pashur ... chief governor in the house of the Lord ... smote Jeremiah the prophet, and put him in the stocks that *were* in the high gate of Benjamin, which *was* by the house of the Lord" (Jeremiah 20:1–2). Defoe stood in the pillory in equally prominent places, beside the Royal Exchange (almost within sight of his home and warehouse), at Cheapside Conduit, a major shopping area and home of many of the city guilds, and at Temple-Bar, a gateway to the city where the heads of traitors were displayed.

In other places, Jeremiah complained that he was considered "A man of strife and a man of contention to the whole earth!" (15:10) and that he was treated unjustly: "Then said they, / Come, and let us devise devices against Jeremiah ... And let us not give heed to any of his words" (18:18). Defoe was often taunted for using the tone and rhetoric of prophecy. The title page of *The Proceedings at the Tryal Examination, and Condemnation of a Certain Scribling, Rhyming, Versifying, Poeteering, Hosier* includes the phrase, "*Commonly known by the Name of Daniel the Prophet*," and another attack is *Daniel the Prophet No Conjuror* (both London, 1705). Nearly ten years later, the lead story in *The Flying Post* began, "'Tis very well known that *Mr. Foe* has set up for Daniel the Prophet a long while" (14 April 1713). Another of the most frequent charges against Defoe was that he exacerbated strife. As the anonymous author of *Reflections upon some Scandalous and Malicious Pamphlets* wrote of Defoe, his "invenom'd Libel ... is writ on purpose to set the Nation in a Flame."[21]

Defoe not only read the Bible, but he used such common study aids as Matthew Poole's *Annotations upon the Holy Bible*, which he quotes in *An Appeal* and elsewhere. In his introduction, Poole writes of Jeremiah, "He setting himself against the Torrent of the Corruptions of the Times, was always opposed and unjustly treated by his ungrateful Countrey men." The commentary on the passage Defoe quotes in *An Appeal* reads, "The Prophet here rendreth a reason why he thought of giving over his work as a Prophet, his ears were continually filled with ... Obloquies and reproaches ... he was afraid on all hands there were so many Traps laid for him."[22] Defoe's identification with Jeremiah's experiences is revealing. Jeremiah's first prophecies were critical of his own people, as were many of Defoe's early publications. He laid into his people for practising Occasional Conformity (that is, attending Church of England services and taking the sacrament once a year in order to qualify for offices from which Dissenters were excluded), and, more exasperatingly, lectured them on how they should conduct themselves in every situation. Jeremiah was imprisoned in a cistern, and his prophecies were once formally torn to pieces in the temple, parallels to Defoe's prison experiences and the time his pamphlets were burned by the common hangman. Both denounced the social ills and religious hollowness of contemporary life – in religious terms, they were called, in their opinions, to speak to their time. Jeremiah more than most of his contemporaries grasped the significance of his era's international turmoil, and Defoe demonstrated the same kind of grasp from at least the first decade of the eighteenth century. Jeremiah was also a great poet, and, like Defoe, often expressed dismay, sorrow, and resentment because of the way he was treated.

Even in an age of vicious *ad hominem* attacks, the number and ferocity aimed at Defoe are extraordinary. The purpose of the pillory was to stigmatize and discredit, and the public nature of bankruptcy proceedings did the same. In *More Reformation* (1703), he writes that "the whole World ... reckon up all the Faults of his Life, and Ten Thousand more than ever he Committed, to be the common Places of their general Discourse."[23] Eight years after the pillory, William King wrote jovially, "I never saw a *Whigg* with Satisfaction before, unless it was *D — l d'Foe* in the Pillory": Defoe was identified as "render'd *infamous* by *Law*" and "a broken *Hosier*" fifteen years later, and twenty years later as "DEF-E in the Pillory."[24] As late as 1735, a fellow journalist, John Oldmixon, could identify him casually: "the same who afterwards was Pillory'd for writing an ironical Invective against the Church, and did after that list in the Service of Mr. *Robert Harley*." These humiliations could be endlessly thrown in Defoe's face, and each time his moral self was threatened. As early as the late 1690s opponents were attempting to argue a contradiction between Defoe's self-representation and the content and consequences of what he published. They began to accuse him of being a "tool" of a political party and a trouble-maker and played on "Legion" being a kind of devil in the New Testament; at that time, he began to insist endlessly that no one ever told him what to write, that he was an independent mind and wrote selflessly for the benefit of others. During the time he wrote for King William and especially in *The True-Born Englishman*, Defoe represented himself as the fearless defender of "inalienable rights," contract government, and the king. At the same time, the author of *A Reply to the New Test of the Church of England's Loyalty* mused, "'Tis your way to make bold with Princes."[25] Their image of him and the real consequences of things he wrote – increased controversy and bitter exchanges – conflicted with his belief that he was a champion of moderation.

Moreover, many of the politicians with whom he was associated were, at one time or another, accused of malfeasance, and by association or by defending them he became vulnerable to the same charges. Of course, by defending them, he was also defending himself. In attempting to create and maintain a political platform of "moderation" in a time of extreme party division, Harley put himself in an untenable position, and Defoe, who sincerely believed in that policy, opened himself up to charges of having no principles and writing on both sides of questions (which he sometimes did deliberately).

Defoe left a record of intense suffering, which is often forgotten because of his astonishing resilience. All of the writings around the time of his 1703 imprisonment, various scattered comments in the *Review*, and his late publications written under the pseudonym Andrew Moreton reveal such admissions. A line from *Robinson Crusoe* suggests the shock he felt: "At this surprising Change of my Circumstances from a Merchant to a miserable Slave, I was perfectly overwhelm'd."[26] His final known letter confesses to "a Mind Sinking under the Weight of an Affliction too heavy for my strength." But immediately he alludes elliptically to why he suffers ("Wicked, Perjur'd, and Contemptible Enemy" and "Inhuman Dealing of my Own Son") and begins to spin out a resilient scenario. He outlines a fantasy of having secret lodgings near his favorite daughter Sophia and her husband, "But just to come and look at you, and Retire Imediately, tis a Burthen too Heavy. The Parting Will be a price beyond the Enjoyment" (*Letters*, pp. 473–76). As so often in Defoe's life, he discloses genuine suffering that would break a lesser man and the almost immediate ability to imagine an evasion of a seemingly intractable problem. Some of the most memorable parts of Defoe's novels are about partings, and many of them are exceptionally painful. Moll's with Jemy is famous, but those even of minor characters are often vividly and painfully rendered. Few, however, are permanent unless death intervenes, as it did shortly after Defoe wrote this letter.

Of the Fleet ...

As to Poland   (*Letters*, pp. 20, 48)

These are headings for advice to Robert Harley, Speaker of the House of Commons. Harley had spent his life in government and would rise to be Lord Treasurer. Defoe was released from Newgate prison at the beginning of November 1703 and by the end of May 1704 was having regular meetings with Harley, who had recently acquired the office of Secretary of State for the Northern Division, which included northern Europe and Scotland. "Of the Fleet," probably written in early June, thus less than a month after his employment commenced in earnest, begins, "It will Easily be Allow'd the Fleet May be Made more Usefull Than it is."[27]

What could this recently-pilloried tradesman know about the British Navy? He implies that he is making an absolutely obvious statement, and he goes on to recommend the dismissal of Sir George Rooke, Commander of the Fleet! He concludes the lengthy position paper: "The Nations Safety, the Publick Reputation, and the Creditt of the Ministry, Calls for a Suspension at least of this Obnoxious Suspected Man" (*Letters*, p. 25). The hyperbolic rhetoric that sweeps from a big picture ranging over history ("The Grecians, the Romans, and the Carthaginians Allwayes Laid by Unfortunate Generlls ..."), through modern Europe ("The French Presume ..."), to details ("the relief of Niza [Nice, then a small Savoyard port] ...") is typical, as are the revealing references to "reputation" and "credit." Over and over, he will appeal to Harley to amass credit and invoke the Secretary's duty to accept and maintain the image Defoe is creating for him and his ministry.

When Defoe writes "As to Poland," probably in late summer of that year, he demonstrates sophisticated knowledge of diplomatic maneuvering and the movements of European armies – and the same amazing self-confidence. Defoe obviously had a very high opinion of himself. As he demonstrates in these papers to Harley, he consistently believed that he was the best informed and most insightful person in any gathering or in any dispute. In his writing, he often slipped into pedantic, condescending, arrogant tones and implied that other writers or advisers were short-sighted, stupid, or even "incompetent bigots."[28]

He lectured everybody as he did Harley without regard for their status, experience, or knowledge. He assumed an authoritative posture as he wrote about alcoholism, angels, commerce, crime, corruption, economics (local, national, and global), education, farmers, foundling hospitals, gambling, history (of apparitions, of conflicts (personal, local, national, European), of the devil, of inventions, of Scotland), insurance, marriage, old age, pickpockets, pirates, plague, the press (how it worked, what it contributed, what was wrong with it), refugees, religion, rights (civil, human, natural), seamen, sex, slavery, strumpets, taxes, treaties, volcanoes, wars, watermen, women – and more. He wrote on all of these subjects and more with deep, specific information and broad grasp.

Defoe was undoubtedly a genius, and he knew it. His reading was encyclopedic; his memory prodigious; his comprehension of context and immediate and long-term issues instantaneous; his reasoning powers formidable. These powers are evident in his first substantial publication and in many of his last books. In "Of the High-Ways" in *An Essay upon Projects* (1697) he gives tedious directions for building the roads (men, horses, carts, drainage, enclosures) and presented the result as the foundation of a great inland trade and, by extension, of England's establishing itself as the premier trading nation. He takes up the immediate issues, such as objections likely to be raised to his methods, and then stretches the benefits far into the future. As he would do in one of his last books, *A General History of Discoveries and Improvements*, he distinguishes between "New Inventions and Projects" and "Improvements" and encourages English people to devise and take advantage of anything that may be "of publick Advantage."[29] In between, he wrote the *Review*, and as its editor, John McVeagh says, "for the first time a writer of genius used the new freedom [of the press] to instruct, entertain and help shape the new reading public." McVeagh points out that none of his contemporaries could match "the intellectual range and energy of the *Review*, its insinuating dexterity in argument, its fund of stories, its appeal to common sense or common life, its witty, salty style."[30]

A Testimony of my good Will to my Fellow Creatures[31]

Defoe wrote *Augusta Triumphans*, from which this quotation comes, when he was sixty-eight. By writing "testimony of my good will," Defoe puts the emphasis on himself, the writer, rather than on the people whose situation he is describing and whom his plans will benefit. This sixty-page tract is one of six written from the point of view of Andrew Moreton, a man of Defoe's own age. Along with two other tracts featuring Moreton, *Every-Body's Business is No-Body's Business* (1725) and *The Protestant Monastery* (1727), *Augusta Triumphans* was surprisingly popular, and Defoe attributed the second edition of *A Compleat System of Magick* (1730) to Moreton in an attempt to sell more books. These books swing from tirades against the kinds of people that make life in cities unpleasant, to sensitive discussions of the need for foundling hospitals and the abuse of confining wives in private madhouses to original, forward-looking proposals, such as one for a university in London that would be more democratic and modern than Oxford and Cambridge. Some of the proposals are insane. He wants the shoe cleaners, who allegedly cheat people and gamble and steal, forced to be wool combers, miners, or sand hill removers in the Thames – all occupations in need of laborers. The shoe cleaners would be replaced with "ancient Persons, poor Widows, and others" who get inadequate support from the parish.[32] His genuine concern for the poor, for women, for the mentally ill and incompetent (he once proposed a tax on books to support such people), and the miserable is as often behind his plans for a better-run city and nation as his somewhat compulsive drive to tell people how to fix everything.

Were his fellow creatures to take his advice in these and a number of other books such as *The Great Law of Subordination* and *Conjugal Lewdness* (1727), they would devote themselves to demanding copies of marriage certificates before renting rooms and to fighting street robberies and prostitution, but they would also be kinder to each other and, especially, better husbands and wives. Some of Defoe's most amusing and most intimate anecdotes are in these lengthy effusions of moral outrage and of distress at a poorly administered society. Such scenes as the shop run by the slothful person in *The Complete English Tradesman*, the watchman with "one Foot in the Grave, and t'other ready to follow," and the bedroom scenes in *Religious Courtship* punctuate complaints and proposals.[33]

His desires to warn, reform, and put his readers to work are the services he is offering as evidence of his goodwill. The language is as vivid and lively as any Defoe ever wrote. His warnings are especially memorable: "Moreton" in *Every-Body's Business* complains of servant "wenches": "If you send 'em with ready Money they turn Factors, and take 3d or 4d in the Shilling."[34] He explains that unwed, pregnant girls leave their parishes, where they would be easily identified and punished, and pour into London, which is "like the Ocean, that receives the muddy and dirty Brooks, as well as the clear and rapid Rivers, swallows up all the scum and filth of the Country."[35]

This metaphor of London as the ocean into which the population flows has a remarkable existence in the great global visions he was creating at the same time for Great Britain. Somehow the world seemed small to him; he easily grasped continents, distances, products, and the state of their commercial advancement. Space and time presented no obstacles. As he portrayed the ancient world, he remarked that the Moors and Turks entered the stage as upstart "Vagrants and Thieves."[36] As he described his own time, he identified all of the countries where coffee or raisins or sugar were available and most inexpensive in almost off-hand ways. He created a spoke and hub model through a survey of the present state of England (*A Tour*) and the world (*Atlas Maritimus* and other books) and through guides (*Plan of the English Commerce, Complete English Tradesman, Great Law of Subordination Consider'd*). Every part of Great Britain and the world had things to ship to London, and London would re-distribute them to the world.

These books and their tone suggest that Defoe saw himself not as a visionary but as eminently practical. He observes of North America, "In a word, fitted by Nature for Commerce, it affords the best Product for Trade, and the best Harbours for Shipping, of any other Part of the World."[37] In a time when many maps showed rivers rather than roads as the transportation routes, Defoe's consistent attention to water was, indeed, practical, and the same arrogance that led him to write "Of the Fleet" deludes him into thinking he can persuade his countrymen to build colonies in America and Africa and standardize wages for servant girls. Twenty-five years after he wrote "Of the Fleet," he complained that a proposal for the reduction of street robberies before Parliament was really his, for he published a plan "for the total

Suppression and Prevention of Street Robberies" six months earlier. He has now improved it, he says in *Second Thoughts are Best* (1729), and quotes large sections of *Augusta Triumphans* verbatim. This time, he dedicated the work to George II, and sent it to the king, queen, "Lords Spiritual," and many MPs.[38] His opinion of himself and faith in his insight into everything are obviously a "reality" he never doubted.

As in *An Appeal*, Defoe refers to his mortality in *Augusta Triumphans*: "if like *Cato*, I enquire whether or no before I go hence and be no more, I can yet do anything for the Service of my Country."[39] Defoe still considered himself morally superior and perfectly suited to be adviser, censor, and legislator for the nation. Shortly after the pillory, he wrote of something he had learned: "Preaching of Sermons is Speaking to a few of Mankind: Printing of Books is Talking to the whole World."[40] He lectured away on innumerable subjects for the rest of his life. The best thing people could do for themselves and their country was to do what he told them.

To assemble the writings by Defoe that might be called autobiographical is to become intensely aware of the ways he could dramatize, reinterpret, obscure, falsify, and mask his life. As biographies show, we can follow his interests, rhetorical and literary strategies, and developing persuasive and narrative powers through a long series of titles and dates of publication. A wealth of external evidence allows us to follow the man and opinions about him year by year, sometimes day by day. Even his printers tell a story, as they vary in prestige, specializations, and party alignments. But what can we know of *him*, of Defoe? At that meeting point that is identity, we know that he struggled for most of his life to buttress his image of what he wanted to be and sometimes believed he was. We know what he did, how he reacted to many experiences, and which parts of his culture most influenced him.

The meeting point of historical circumstances and what the world would allow him to be, combined with his innate abilities, determined that he was often frustrated and his life was not what he imagined and repeatedly chose. That he began trading actively in such things as anchovies, timber, cheese, and oysters in his old age argues that trade was indeed the whore he "doated upon,"[41] and that was trade he personally carried out, not just wrote about, regardless of the range and mastery of his grasp and writing. He rented rich farm lands in Colchester and planned to breed cattle and raise corn; he could sell some of the corn and market cheese, butter, veal, and beef, all established Essex products. He would be a merchant again; as he said in *Roxana*, "a true-bred Merchant is the best Gentleman in the Nation; that in Knowledge, in Manners, in Judgment of things ... out-did many of the Nobility ... able to spend more Money than a Gentleman of 5000 l. a Year Estate ... [for] an

Estate is a Pond; but … a Trade was a Spring."[42] He was part of a persecuted minority; many opportunities and occupations were closed to him. His ambitions and his rage, but also his clear-sightedness, lured him into religio-political controversy, first to support a king who was expanding toleration and then to attempt to expose the extremism that would further oppress the Nonconformists. His extravagant, old-fashioned poet-portrait printed with *Jure Divino* made him ridiculous, a kind of cosmic joke that punctuated what the pillory had writ: he would never again ride with the chief citizens of London.

The quotation in the first of my subheads concludes, "one Blow from unforeseen Providence unhing'd me." Defoe's relationship to God was both dutiful and deeply adversarial. Novels are revelatory of more than the political unconscious, and as Defoe spun out his stories he created characters who thought and said unspeakable things. Robinson Crusoe is at war with God. He, like Defoe, has been interrupted, had his plans destroyed, and been disordered mentally. Crusoe reflects: "I had great Reason to consider it as a Determination of Heaven, that in this desolate Place, and in this desolate Manner I should end my Life … Why Providence should thus compleatly ruine its Creatures, and render them so absolutely miserable, so without Help abandon'd, so entirely depress'd …" (p. 47). During the two years he lives in fear because of the footprint, he pettishly snipes, "I seldom found my self in a due Temper for application to my Maker" (p. 128). Defoe makes Crusoe angrier than Job, closer to another quotation from the same chapter of Jeremiah used in *An Appeal*, one that also analogizes Defoe's experiences: "O Lord, thou hast deceived me, and I was deceived: / Thou art stronger than I, and hast prevailed: / I am in derision daily, / Every one mocketh me." "Wherefore came I forth out of the womb / To see labor and sorrow, / That my days should be consumed with shame?"[43] "Providence" is responsible in *Robinson Crusoe* and invoked as Defoe does in his letters. He writes Harley in 1710 that "Providence Sir Seems to Cast me back Upon you." Although, as he wrote earlier, he sometimes has to trust that Providence will bring him through, how "Remaines a Mystery of Providence Unexpounded" (*Letters*, pp. 273, 17). The "mystery" determines that Defoe's fiction, and his life, will be a pilgrimage, a psychologizing search for explanations and meanings that make events acceptable, perhaps even bearable.[44]

Later Defoe would write books in which he attempted to sort out superstition, religion, and science, and that endeavor is a theme in *Robinson Crusoe* and an obsession in *Journal of the Plague Year*. Much of Defoe's writing is so compelling because he was poised at the moment in time when religious certainty gave way to modern skepticism and empiricism, when fideism yielded to an obligation to test and question. As Leo Damrosch points out, "When the myth itself is under strain, its tensions are particularly visible in narratives that purport to reflect the coherence of reality."[45] The sentence describes *Crusoe*, and it becomes the subject of *Plague Year*. Books with very old-fashioned titles, such as *The Political History of the Devil* (1726) and *An Essay on the History and Reality of Apparitions* (1727), are part of Defoe's thinking on these topics and also on criminal motivation and culpability. He plays with questions such as "Can the Devil make people commit crimes?" and "What do dreams, as the one the desperate tradesman has in which he imagines killing a child with a bag of gold and a diamond necklace, really mean about the individual and humankind?"[46]

Defoe's life created paradoxes. In novel after novel as well as in his non-fiction, for instance, he insisted that everyday practices were evil and actually gave rise to evil in people who wanted to be good. By the end of the century, some of his novels were considered unfit to be read. His life was like that of many of his characters – contingent, picaresque, eager for experience, and in tension with "God's story." Like those who would read Defoe's life, those who read his books are challenged to determine how much weight circumstances and motives should have. Who was Defoe? He was the embattled genius who created new subjects, new concepts, and new literary forms to embody them.

NOTES

1. Respectively, Eliza Haywood, *The Invisible Spy* in *Selected Fiction and Drama of Eliza Haywood*, ed. Paula R. Backscheider (Oxford: Oxford University Press, 1999), p. 245; quoted in Christine Blouch, "Eliza Haywood and the Romance of Obscurity," *SEL*, 31 (1991), 545.
2. Daniel Defoe, *An Appeal to Honour and Justice, Tho' it be of his Worst Enemies*, in *The Shortest Way With the Dissenters and Other Pamphlets by Daniel Defoe* (1715; Shakespeare Head Edition. Oxford: Basil Blackwell, 1927), p. 192. All further references in the text are to this edition.
3. Most biographers find this text more unproblematically autobiographical than I do; James Sutherland and John Richetti call it an *apologia*: Sutherland, *Daniel Defoe: A Critical Study* (Boston: Houghton Mifflin, 1971), 19, and used as autobiography, 67, 68, 133; Richetti, *The Life of Daniel Defoe* (Oxford: Blackwell, 2005), 17, and see 10, 19, 341, for use of it as autobiography; Maximillian E. Novak, *Daniel Defoe: Master of Fictions* (Oxford: Oxford University Press, 2001); P. N. Furbank and W. R. Owens call it "autobiographical," although noting at least one lie, *A Political Biography of Daniel Defoe* (London: Pickering & Chatto, 2006), 15, 145–46.
4. John Richetti, *The Life of Daniel Defoe: A Critical Biography* (Oxford: Blackwell, 2005).
5. Catherine Ingrassia, *Authorship, Commerce, and Gender in Early Eighteenth-Century England* (Cambridge: Cambridge University Press, 1998), p. 5, and see pp. 6, 11, 13, and 172.

6. John McVeagh credits Defoe with inventing "a new genre, the eighteenth-century periodical essay," and his *Review* with inaugurating "the modern press," in McVeagh (ed.), *Daniel Defoe: "Introduction"* to *A Review of the Affairs of France, Volume 1: 1704–1705* (London: Pickering & Chatto, 2003), respectively xiv, xiii.

7. Defoe, *Farther Adventures of Robinson Crusoe* (1719; Shakespeare Head Edition, Totowa, NJ: Rowan and Littlefield, 1974), II, 116; *The History and Remarkable Life of the Truly Honourable Col. Jacque*, ed. Samuel Holt Monk (1722; London: Oxford University Press, 1965), pp. 263–64; *Roxana, The Fortunate Mistress*, ed. Jane Jack (1724; London: Oxford University Press, 1964), p. 149.

8. George Harris Healey, *The Letters of Daniel Defoe* (Oxford: Clarendon Press, 1955; rpt. 1969), pp. 1, 3, 6. All further references in the text are to this edition.

9. Defoe, *The Complete English Tradesman in Familiar Letters*, 2 vols. (1727; New York: Augustus M. Kelley Publishers, 1969), I, 79.

10. Healey, *Letters*, p. 4; Defoe, *A Brief Explanation* in *A True Collection of the Writings of the Author of the True Born Englishman* (London, 1703), p. 435.

11. National Archives, SP 34/37; the indictment is KB 10/15, pt. 2.

12. Defoe, *A General History of Discoveries and Improvements*, 4 vols. (London, [1725–27]), I, 30.

13. Defoe, *General History of Discoveries*, IV, 259, 286.

14. Healey, *Letters*, p. 6; Defoe, *Elegy on the Author of the True-Born Englishman* (London, 1704), p. 33; Healey, *Letters*, p. 17.

15. See J. A. Downie, *Robert Harley and the Press* (Cambridge: Cambridge University Press, 1979), pp. 29–33.

16. Quoted in Paula R. Backscheider, *Daniel Defoe: His Life* (Baltimore and London: Johns Hopkins University Press, 1989), p. 88.

17. He says in *An Appeal*: "I never once deviated from the Revolution Principles, nor from the Doctrine of Liberty and Property, on which it was founded," p. 232.

18. Daniel Defoe, *A New Test of the Church of England's Honesty* (London, 1704), p. 19; and *An Appeal*, p. 236.

19. Defoe, Preface, *More Reformation* (London, 1703), A3v. See Richetti, *Life of Defoe*, pp. 67–68.

20. Defoe, "Meditations" (1681), n.pag. The Meditations are the last twenty-three pages of a manuscript in which Defoe transcribed sermons.

21. *Reflections upon some Scandalous and Malicious Pamphlets* (London, 1703), p. 10.

22. Matthew Poole, *Annotations upon the Holy Bible* (London, 1685), vol. II; the text is unpaginated, as readers could follow books, chapters and verses.

23. Defoe, *More Reformation*, A3v.

24. [William King], *A Vindication of the Reverend Dr. Henry Sacheverell* (London, 1711), p. 2; *Remarks on the Letter to the Dissenters*. By a Churchman. (London, 1714), pp. 4, 28; and *The Art of Railing at Great Men* (London, 1723), p. 12.

25. *A Reply to the New Test of the Church of England's Loyalty* (London, 1687), p. 8.

26. Defoe, *The Life and Strange Surprizing Adventures of Robinson Crusoe*, ed. J. Donald Crowley (London: Oxford University Press, 1972), p. 19.

27. The speculative dates of these two advices are Healey's; quotation, *Letters*, p. 20.

28. The last phrase is McVeagh's description of what even the subtitle of the *Review* did, "Introduction," p. xiii.

29. Defoe, *An Essay upon Projects* (1697; Menston, Yorkshire: Scholar Press, 1969), p. 15.

30. McVeagh (ed.), *Daniel Defoe: A Review of the Affairs of France, volume I*, pp. xiv, xv.

31. Defoe, *Augusta Triumphans* (London, 1728), p. 4.

32. Defoe, *Every-Body's Business* (London, 1725), pp. 24–32. He goes into considerable detail about the misuse of funds by parishes in *Parochial Tyranny* [1727].

33. Defoe, *Complete English Tradesman*, I, 46–47; *Augusta Triumphans*, p. 47.

34. Defoe, *Every-Body's Business*, p. 8.

35. Defoe, *Great Law of Subordination* (London, 1724), p. 86.

36. Defoe, *General History of Discoveries*, I, 97.

37. Defoe, *Atlas Maritimus and Commercialis* (London, 1728), p. 277.

38. Defoe, *Second Thoughts are Best* (London, 1729), p. v.

39. Defoe, *Protestant Monastery* (London, 1727), [iii]-iv. In *An Appeal*, he writes, "By the Hints of Mortality ... I have Reason to think that I am not a great way off from ... the great Ocean of Eternity," p. 192.

40. Defoe, Preface, *The Storm: A Collection of Casualties and Disasters* (London, 1704), n. pag.

41. Defoe, *Defoe's Review*, ed. Arthur Wellesley Secord, 22 vols. (New York: Published for the Facsimile Text Society, by Columbia University Press, 1938), I: 213.

42. Defoe, *Roxana*, p. 170.

43. Jeremiah 20:7, 18; other passages showing alienation from God are 14:8–9; 15:18; 17:17, and 20:7.

44. See Leo Damrosch, *God's Plot and Man's Stories: Studies in the Fictional Imagination from Milton to Fielding* (Chicago: University of Chicago Press, 1985), p. 15, and for the modernity of Defoe's thinking compared to earlier Puritan thought, see N. H. Keeble, *The Literary Culture of Nonconformity in Later Seventeenth-Century England* (Athens: University of Georgia Press, 1987), pp. 268–82.

45. Damrosch, *God's Plot*, p. 8.

46. An incident very much like this is one of the best-known scenes in *Moll Flanders*. It is noteworthy that Damrosch speculates, "One may well suspect that this desperate and guilty tradesman was Defoe himself," *God's Plot*, p. 194.

2

MAXIMILLIAN E. NOVAK

Defoe's political and religious journalism

In his book on *The Invention of the Newspaper*, Joad Raymond remarks that in the early part of the seventeenth century it was customary to greet people with the expression "What News?" He argues that such a greeting is suggestive of a society that was eager to be informed about the events of the time and maintains that this was a development that led to the numerous newsletters that circulated during the period between 1642 and 1660 known as the Interregnum.[1] Indeed, although Ben Jonson's satirical comedy *The Staple of News* (1626) mocked the notion of an office that distributed news and showed it going belly up, like so many projects of the time, he clearly saw the need for news and the willingness to pay for it as a developing element in society.[2] This scepticism about the value of news was later reflected in *Spectator* essay no. 452, by Addison and Pope. On 8 August 1712, they wondered about "half a Dozen Ingenious Men, who live very plentifully upon this Curiosity of their Fellow-Subjects," especially since, with the end of the War of the Spanish Succession, there appeared to be a dearth of news. They then provided a list of trivial stories – happenings of no significance – that might fill up the newspapers.[3] In fact, as newspapers grew in size, there was a need for such filler. But for all such criticism, as Raymond argues, an active press might succeed in creating a coherent nation in England.[4] When large parts of the population shared knowledge of what was happening within England and abroad, there was a possibility of communication among those in the country and those in the towns. Such a system of news had been fully achieved by the early eighteenth century, when writers such as Daniel Defoe and Jonathan Swift were to struggle for command of the kind of public opinion that might influence elections or votes in Parliament.

In many ways, Daniel Defoe was one of the quintessential newsmen of his time – one of those "half a Dozen Ingenious Men" of whom Addison and Pope complained. At one point in his life he had an office that translated and distributed the news from abroad much in the manner of the news office in Jonson's *Staple of News*.[5] Yet his specialty was not news. Rather it was opinion. Others might report on the events happening around the world and particularly in Europe. The *London Gazette* had been issuing its single sheet of official news from 5 February 1666, and during the Restoration a variety of newspapers were issued three times a week. With the *Daily Courant* of 11 March 1702, Londoners could read announcement of the events of the day.[6] But Defoe's role was different. He was there to argue about the events of the time – to satirize the wrong view and to assure his readers that his interpretation of events was the proper one. One attack upon him linked him with the Daniel for whom he was named, the biblical prophet who (Daniel 5:25–28) could read the words on the wall, "Mene Mene Tekel Upharsin," that no one else could decipher, words that predicted the fall of Belshazzar, king of the Chaldeans. In fact, Defoe had his prophetic moods, but his specialty was a powerful rhetoric in prose and poetry.

Defoe was imprisoned for his opinions on three occasions. Distributing the news had always been difficult. At various times during the seventeenth century, the government attempted to suppress all kinds of newspapers, and several of the publishers were not merely shut down but put in jail.[7] During Defoe's early life, there was a Licensing Act that gave control of the press to the government. Satires were often circulated successfully in manuscript form, but for those opposed to the government, print publication was generally available mainly to the friends of the government. During the time of the Popish Plot and the Exclusion Crisis, the first a period of hysteria over a supposed Roman Catholic conspiracy to take over the state, the second an attempt to exclude King Charles II's brother, James, Duke of York, from succeeding him, roughly 1679–82, the weakness of the government created an opposition press, but after Charles II's triumph over his opponents at Oxford in 1681, and during the reign of James II, control was reasserted. Although the Licensing Act was allowed to lapse in 1695, this did not mean that writers were not punished for their publications. If articles in newspapers might contain dangerous materials, commentary was even more subject to punishment by the government.

Defoe had his predecessors in this effort to shape opinion in the direction of Whig ideals. He admired the poetry and prose of Andrew Marvell and John Oldham. Henry Care's *Weekly Pacquet, Or Advice from Rome* (1678–83), delivered a steady diet of Whig propaganda, and Defoe wrote that he felt complimented by a reader who suggested he was borrowing from him, since Care "discovered such a Spirit; such Learning, such Strength of Reason, and such a Sublime Fancy," he would value his *Review* "so much the more as it resembles his."[8] And if the lapse of the Licensing Act failed to protect journalists, it did produce the print publication of satiric poetry that had been written over thirty-five years in a series of volumes generally titled *Poems on Affairs of State*. Some of these works had been suppressed or had a limited circulation in manuscript. Defoe's poetry will be discussed elsewhere in this volume, but it should be noted that poetry often functioned as a form of journalism, both from the standpoint of news carried in ballads and through the expression of opinion, often in the form of satire. Beginning in 1695, then, the publication of political poetry in the many volumes with the title *Poems on Affairs of State* provided a running history on the corruptions of the Stuarts and the Restoration. Many of Defoe's poems were to appear in some of the later volumes.

Nevertheless, it was mainly through prose – through the pamphlet and the newspaper – that Defoe managed to influence his audiences. And we have to be aware of the volatility of the time. England was divided between various factions. Whigs (proponents of toleration and the power of Parliament) opposed Tories (politically conservative) and Jacobites (followers of James II and his heirs). The Church of England was divided between the Low Churchmen, who were mainly Whigs, and the High Churchmen, who were mainly Tories and often tended toward Jacobitism. Outside the Church were the Nonjurors, who refused to support any monarch but the descendants of James II, the Roman Catholics, and the Dissenters, who were Protestants but could not in good conscience swear to some of the provisions of the Thirty-Nine Articles of faith required by the Church of England. Other groups dissatisfied with the status quo included the Country Party, which was suspicious of the Court and the very notion of a government centralized in London, and the poor, especially the poor of London, who felt (and indeed were) disenfranchised by the system of government. If Swift was to satirize the disagreements of the time as equal to the question of whether to break an egg on the pointed or round end or whether to wear high heels or low heels,[9] most did not see it that way. The population was, as Holmes and Speck appropriately called it, a *"Divided Society."*[10] Opinions ran high, and to most partisans there seemed no way toward reconcilement. Into such tinder, powerful propagandists such as Defoe and Swift threw their fiery rhetoric, and with their wit and their mastery of language they succeeded in inflaming public opinion.

In his earliest writings Defoe appears to have functioned mainly as a defender of the Dissenters and as a "Court Whig," as a supporter of the policies of the government of William III. These works are often distinguished by an ironic tone. In one of his earliest (1688) pamphlets, urging the Dissenters to reject James II's proposal to repeal the Test Act as a subterfuge for turning England into a Catholic nation, Defoe remarked sarcastically that James revealed "such an effect of a great passion for Liberty of Conscience as was never known before."[11] As William Minto observed, Defoe "was a great master of the language of sarcasm and abuse."[12]

Defoe begins to pick up the pace of his productions with the Standing Army Controversy, a disastrous attempt to get England to scale back its army after the victory over France in the Nine Years War. It was disastrous because, despite the Treaty of Ryswick in 1697, after nine bloody years of war, France's king had not abandoned his attempt to control Spain. In supporting William's need to keep an army to defend against the aggressive and expansionist tendencies of France's Louis XIV, Defoe began by attacking a pamphlet by the Whigs John Trenchard and Walter Moyle, using the familiar device of the fable – the story of the sheep who requested that the wolves be deprived of teeth – to make the point about living in a dangerous world.[13] His remark that "War is become a Science, and Arms an Employment,"[14] implicates his first book, An Essay upon Projects (1697), in this propaganda endeavor, since, in that work, he argues for the importance of a Military Academy, on much the same basis.[15] In producing so many works, Defoe's notion was to flood the press with works on the need for a standing army, thereby giving the impression that a tide of public opinion existed.

Of course the key to such a project was anonymity. During this period, anonymity was the rule rather than the exception. Defoe placed his initials, "D.F." before some works, but such relatively open admission of authorship became increasingly rare in Defoe's publications. When The True-Born Englishman, an attack upon pride of birth and nationalism, was published in 1701 and enjoyed enormous popularity, none of those who replied, defending, as they thought, the honour and purity of the English race, knew who the author was. Defoe subsequently adopted the mask or persona, "By the Author of the True-Born Englishman," as he would later become "Mr. Review." Even after everyone who kept attuned to current controversies knew who Defoe was, he preferred concealing his identity under such transparent masks, and, of course, he frequently had recourse to complete anonymity. For all the problems with such a stance, it created a distance between the author and his public that helped foster genuine debate. It has been argued that this very practice created the "public sphere" that flourished during the eighteenth century.

When he published the pamphlet, The Shortest Way with the Dissenters in December 1702, he was pursued by the government for "libel" or for writing what was equivalent to a publication that resulted in a disturbance of the peace. He was eventually captured, imprisoned, and sentenced to stand in the pillory three times. There could be no more obvious public exposure. The mob often threw rocks and feces at the victim, and the pillory had sometimes proved fatal. Defoe apparently organized a counter demonstration and sold his poem, *A Hymn to the Pillory* (1703), accusing those who had sentenced him of far worse crimes than any of which he was accused.

The narrative surrounding this event might be read as a triumph of journalistic integrity over the forces of government repression, a narrative that still resonates for us today. But *The Shortest Way with the Dissenters* had an element of hoax as well as irony. Defoe assumed the mask of a vicious High Church clergyman seeking to take revenge against the Dissenters by hanging their leaders and forcibly converting the rest. Since the Act of Toleration (1689) was still in effect, Defoe had created a monstrous personality, who advocated breaking that law and violently turning against a minority. Ian Watt has suggested that Defoe's pamphlet was closer to fiction than irony and that the power of the character had escaped his control.[16] But Defoe wanted to do this. He wanted to confront the innuendos of High Church clergymen such as Henry Sacheverell, whose *Political Union* (1702) advocated hanging out the "*Bloody Flag*" of defiance against the Dissenters.[17] And he wanted to make it close enough to the writings of such preachers of intolerance so that a few readers would believe that at least one of those many writers of sermons against the Dissenters for 30 January, the anniversary of the execution of Charles I, would have had the courage to advocate violence. Since such an act would have subverted the law, one would have thought that, after two decades in which irony was a prevailing mode, every reader would have seen that the intent of the work was to awaken the readers to how close to an impermissible savagery these preachers were coming.

Defoe claimed that his was "an *Irony not Unusual.*"[18] But every teacher of literature knows that there are some readers who are immune to irony. And even the many who recognized the irony would have felt uncomfortable. Among those who considered the work dangerous were Defoe's fellow Dissenters. Queen Anne insisted that Defoe be punished severely. Some suspected a plot of some kind and tried to get him to turn over his fellow conspirators.[19] Defoe refused. He was ruined financially, but the ruin of the tradesman, small-time merchant and brick manufacturer had its advantages, at least from the standpoint of his future readers. His career as a journalist was just beginning.

Recognizing Defoe's talent, the Secretary of State, Robert Harley, put him on the government's payroll. He used Defoe as a kind of adviser, spy, and as a writer who might, at times, be used to advocate positions that Harley favored. But he knew that Defoe had a reputation as a radical Whig and a gadfly and so far as it is possible to determine, at least at the beginning, he did not prevent Defoe from advocating his political, social, and religious positions. Defoe continued publishing pamphlets, and some of them were collected in two volumes as *A True Collection of the Works of the Author of the True-Born*

Englishman (1703, 1705). Anonymity gave him the possibility of opposing the views of Harley or later Godolphin when he felt strongly on certain issues. But from the standpoint of journalism, the great work that came out of his release from prison was the *Review*, a journal that began as a weekly, then bi-weekly, and after 22 March 1705 was usually published three days a week. It ran from 19 February 1704 to 11 June 1713. When the nine original volumes were published in reprint form by Arthur Secord in 1938, they came to twenty-two volumes and revealed a writer with a seemingly endless fund of knowledge about the contemporary world, a lively imagination, a powerful, satiric wit along with a sense of humor that some of his less perceptive followers might have found surprising.

The full title of the first issue was:

A Review of the Affairs of France: and of All Europe, as Influenc'd by that Nation: Being, Historical Observations, on the Publick Transactions of the World; Purg'd from the Errors and Partiality of News-Writers, and Petty-Statesmen of All Sides, with an Entertaining Part in Every Sheet, Being, Advice from the Scandal Club, to the Curious Enquirers; in Answer to Letters Sent Them for that Purpose.

The title varied greatly after this initial claim to be writing on practically everything. Nevertheless, there was something cheeky about a journal devoted to the nation with which England was at war. Most people simply wanted to find reasons for hating the enemy and hoped to defeat them. They hardly wanted to learn how powerful the French were and how they had dominated Europe since the middle of the seventeenth century. To many, the king of France, Louis XIV, was somewhat like Hitler during the twentieth century – a persecutor of the minority Huguenots, an absolute monarch intent on expanding his nation at the expense of his neighbors. Defoe also claimed to be an impartial observer, which he certainly was not, and that he would provide some form of entertainment in each issue. In the "Preface" to the first volume, he noted that this would be an "Innocent Diversion," which would be necessary because "this Age has such a Natural Aversion to a Solemn and Tedious Affair, that however Profitable, it would never be Diverting and the World would never Read it."[20] In fact, the entertaining part, "Advice from the Scandalous Club," proved to be popular enough so that Defoe could complain about having to reply to what he considered to be too many letters from his readers.

At the beginning, Defoe used his "Advice from the Scandalous Club" section to comment ironically on the errors of other newspapers, a practice which surely did not endear him to his fellow journalists. But the initial heading, *Mercure Scandale*, suggested that more personal problems might appear in this section. He dropped this heading in the issue for 6 May 1704 but defended his use of it on the basis of a book published in 1681 that was suppressed for "making a little too free with their Superiors."[21] Defoe wanted to give his readers the impression that he was a muckraker, someone who might dare to speak out against the powerful. His punishment for publishing *The Shortest Way* stood him in good stead on this point. Thus, on 23 May 1704, he laid out his agenda on improving behavior:

> But, Gentlemen, if all we have said can be made out, if when we have told of a drunken Justice fallen into the Mill-pond, or an eminent Citizen taken with a Twelve-penny Whore, if when we have told of a Magistrate stabbing a Man into the Back in the Dark, or a Man of Letters corresponding with our Enemies abroad. If these things are true, and can be made out; if these Men have Names and are to be found out by their Characters; if writing Nonsence, or translating Foreign Nonsence into *English* Nonsence; if false Geography and false History be to be Found among our News-writers; why then, Gentlemen, with all our Hearts to a Court of Honour with us, as soon as you please ... Now if ye can take our Society there, Gentlemen, we are content.

The "Society" or "Club" sat in judgment on all kinds of reports of citizens doing this or that wrong. These included husbands betraying loyal wives by going to prostitutes; the masters of an apprentice attempting to declare his marriage void; and fathers complaining of the disobedience of their children. In an attempt to answer the many letters he received, Defoe found it necessary to publish five supplements to the *Review*. Defoe eventually had enough of adulterous wives and wandering husbands. He turned the scandal club into a section titled "Miscellanea," brief essays that dealt with whatever interested him at the moment.

Although "Advice from the Scandal Club" was an important journalistic innovation, Defoe's true interest lay in giving his opinion on the events of the day. Though it came in the form of a "Peny Paper," he argued that he was actually "writing History sheet by sheet, and *letting the World see it as I go on.*"[22] He filled the pages of the *Review* with poems celebrating the victories of Marlborough in France along with one of his favourite topics – advocating for a change in the bankruptcy laws that, by putting the debtor in prison, prevented him from earning the money that would enable him to pay off his debts. And he fought the efforts of the High Church to impose new disabilities upon the Dissenters. In 1706, he even devoted a number of issues to a debate on political theory with Charles Leslie, author of a competing Tory and High Church journal called *The Rehearsal*. Defoe restated the Whig position on the basis of government: the rights of the people were based on an original contract; kings and queens did not rule by divine right but by the consent of Parliament and a legal constitution; the rights of the people to their property was inviolable.[23]

It is interesting to speculate how such a debate was carried on in the public arena, and how many people who may not have read John Locke's *Two Treatises* on government absorbed Whig ideas through this popular medium. It would have been possible to stop by a coffee house and read what Mr. Review had to say about the most recent issues of the day.[24] Defoe reported on these matters with a genuine sense of urgency. Writing in 1706, John Dunton explained that he was prejudiced against Defoe for having stolen some of his ideas, but despite this, he praised Defoe as a "Master of the English Tongue," capable of framing an argument "upon any Subject" and admitted somewhat grudgingly, "I can't but own, His Thoughts upon any Subject are always *Surprizing, New*, and *Singular*."[25]

But politics was only one of the many tasks that Defoe undertook in the *Review*. He established a fund for the poor on the lines of the *New York Times*'s annual drive to aid the "neediest cases." He attacked middle men who raised the prices of grain and caused food shortages in order to enrich themselves. He supported the keel men (highly skilled boatmen, who handled the movement of coal from the riverside to ships on the River Tyne in small vessels called keels) in Newcastle in their effort to obtain a decent wage from the wealthy coal miners. He argued that the thief who is motivated by necessity is not the worst person in society and relative to those who got their wealth by corrupt means might be considered innocent. He urged the government to pardon the pirates in Madagascar for a price. And he lectured his readers on economics, frequently resorting to fables to explain the economic development of society, the role of invention, or the role of credit. He used dialogues with a character named Mad Man, who would present seemingly strange perspectives on European politics. And at one point, in speaking of the possibility of capturing some Spanish galleons with their treasure, he broke out (" O Money, Money") in a paean to the ways in which money shapes the world:

> Thou art the Test of Beauty, the Judge of Ornament, the Guide of the Fancy, the Index of Temper, and the Pole Star of the Affections; Thou makest Homely Things Fair, Old Things Young, Crooked Things Straight; Thou has the great Remedy of Love, thou can'st give the Blind an Eye, the Lame a Leg, the Froward a Temper, and the Scandalous a Character; Thou Makest Knaves honest, Whores chast, and Bullies Justices of the Peace; Thou creepest into all our Towns, Cities, Corporations Court Houses, ay, and Churches too; Thou makest the Differences there between the Great and the Small, the High and the Low, and to thy Charge it is justly lay'd, why Sotts lead, Blockheads preach, Knaves govern, and Elected Fools make Aldermen and Mayors.[26]

Despite this attack upon the way money may twist the values of society, Defoe concludes that money encourages ambition and is the reward of virtue and honesty.

In some ways he felt it his duty to educate his audience about economic and social theory. One of his allegories shows his interest in keeping his audience amused while informing them of how society worked. Defoe began with Necessity as the daughter of her father Pride and her mother Sloth. After spending her entire estate, she married Poverty. Her children were a son, Invention, and Wit, a daughter. The sons of Invention – Industry, Ingenuity, and Honesty – do very well. From them come agriculture and the handicrafts. Honesty's granddaughter, Mrs. Punctual, marries Barter and their child is Credit.[27] On the other hand, there is a certain cyclic pattern in this allegory, since Necessity is produced by parents who have false values, spending money wastefully without laboring to replenish what they have. A combination of regularity in business along with a voluntary exchange of goods eventually produces Credit, which allows business to expand. Defoe may have been influenced by Bernard Mandeville, whose *Grumbling Hive* (1705) argued a *laissez-faire* attitude toward the emergence of new wealth and the fall of old. But Mandeville's concept was more static, proposing that it was in the interest of the wealthy to keep down the poor; whereas Defoe saw the continual success of merchants and tradesmen and their transformation into members of the upper-middle class and gentry as signs of a healthy society. It is an economic reading of the workings of society, and, in his last issue, he argued that every person has his "Whore" – an individual hobby-horse – and that "Trade was the Whore ... [he] doated on."

When the Union between England Scotland became, in his opinion, the most significant event of the time, he filled the pages of the *Review* with news about the progress of the negotiations. He went up to Scotland as a spy for the government, but he was also a reporter, providing his audience with a blow-by-blow account of the proceedings. Before leaving for Scotland on 13 September 1706, Defoe embarked on an ambitious series of pamphlets intended to promote the Union to the Scots, beginning with *An Essay at Removing National Prejudices against a Union with Scotland*, Part 1 (London, 1706), and he continued that work once he was there. His real commitment hinged on the notion that once England was joined to a state which had Presbyterianism as its official religion, the toleration of Dissent would have to be acknowledged. But he threw himself into the work of making the Union, both as a kind of consultant to the committees engaged in creating the Union and in writing about it. The great work that came out of these efforts was his *History of the Union* (1709), which combines a collection of documents – an ideal of adherence to truth by supplying original materials – with a journalistic account of the events leading to the Union. The length of the work gave Defoe a chance to do some of his best descriptive accounts of the riots and popular unrest that accompanied the approval of the Treaty. After describing the violent action of the crowds in Edinburgh, he turned to the scenes in Glasgow:

> The Rabble was now fully Master of the Town, they ranged the Streets, and did what they pleased; No Magistrate durst show his Face to them, they challenged People as they walk'd the Streets with this Question, *Are you for the Union?* And no man durst own it, but at their extremest Hazard.
>
> The next thing they did, was to search for Arms in all the Houses of those, that had appeared for the union; And first they went to the Dean of the Guild, and, upon his refusing to give them Arms, they took them away by Force; They stopt here a little, but having given out, that they would search the Houses of all that were for the Union, the Magistrates Assembled, and, Considering, that, if the Citizens were Disarmed, and the Rabble possest of their Weapons, they might, in the next place, possess their Houses, Wives and Wealth at their Command; and that it was better to Defend themselves now, then be Murdered and Plundered in cold Blood; They resolved therefore to raise some Strength, to oppose this Violence.[28]

Although Defoe probably thought he was writing the best kind of history in the form of first-hand accounts of events, he strove to achieve a kind of immediacy and particularity that, at least today, we associate with journalism.

Defoe lost some of his audience when, in 1710, with the fall of the Whig ministry, he decided to support Robert Harley's new Tory government. The battle between Whig and Tory that informed the last few years of Anne's reign put enormous stress on Defoe's ability to maintain a degree of credibility with his readers. The situation is reminiscent of 1938 when, at the time of the pact between Hitler and Stalin, editor after editor of leftist journals, which had accommodated themselves to the Communist Party line, resigned their posts. But Defoe was in the employ of the government, and he believed that he could accept some changes. He believed in the war against France, but he argued for the benefits of peace. He considered Britain's abandoning her allies to be dishonorable, but he began attacking the Dutch as willing to fight to the last Englishman. He believed that France would be the clear gainer in an open trade with England, but he found himself arguing for the Commercial Treaty that was supposed to be part of the Peace of Utrecht in 1712. It was the difficulty of this last task that caused him to abandon the *Review* and begin writing for a new journal, *Mercator: or, Commerce Retrieved* on 26 May 1713.

Mercator was not the only newspaper that Defoe had toyed with. In 1704, the first year of his *Review*, he had started a short-lived journal called the *Master Mercury*. Although *Master Mercury* was supposed to be "An Abstract of the Publick News," as its subtitle stated, and stayed closer to the happenings of the day than did the *Review*, the two journals often overlapped. Perhaps Defoe thought there would be some advantage to controlling at least two angles of vision in the press. As we shall see, at one point in the future he was to be controlling about five different journals at one time. In his semi-official capacity, Defoe was able to gain access to the records of trade between Britain and France, and, through juggling the figures a bit, he was able to argue that history showed England to have been the gainer in trade to France. Unfortunately for Defoe, his misuse of statistics was caught by *The British Merchant*, one of the journals set up to oppose his arguments. *Mercator* limped to its end on 20 July 1714.

During this period of newspaper publication, Defoe never ceased writing pamphlets of between twenty-four and forty-eight pages on various subjects. In 1710, he wrote a number of pamphlets attacking his old nemesis, the opponent of the Dissenters, Henry Sacheverell. Sacheverell's sermon of 1709, *The Perils of False Bretheren*, delivered with what Geoffrey Holmes called a "frenzy of invective,"[29] suggested that there was a conspiracy among rationalists and unbelievers to undermine both the Church of England and the British constitution. The government felt that he had to be put on trial for such an accusation, but the trial ended in triumph for him, followed by a procession through England. This trial helped to turn the electorate against the government of the Whigs, Godolphin and Marlborough, and brought in Robert Harley, a Tory, to head the government. Interestingly enough, a number of Defoe's more radical statements about Parliament's power to select the nation's monarch were quoted at the trial to demonstrate how seemingly anti-monarchical the Whigs could be. Later in that year, having in a sense switched his loyalty to the moderate Tories, he published his *Essay upon Publick Credit* (1710), an attempt to argue that Harley's new government would not mean a revolution in the nation's credit. As with many pamphlets, he varied his manner of writing to suit his purpose, and in this case chose a more formal style. In their cautious estimate, W. R. Owens and P. N. Furbank credit Defoe with thirty works during 1711 to 1712,[30] and although some of these, such as his *History of Trade* (1713), are on general topics, most are pamphlets for the Harley administration.

In 1713, he reverted to his ironic posture in three pamphlets that succeeded in getting him in prison once more. They were *Reasons against the Succession of the House of Hanover*; *And What if the Pretender Should Come?*; and *An Answer to a Question that No Body Thinks of, Viz. What if the Queen should die?* They show Defoe insisting on raising questions that were extremely delicate. The queen was old and ailing. Some proposed that the heir to the throne, George Augustus, might be brought over from Hanover to safeguard the succession to the throne. But many were hopeful that Anne would opt for the Jacobite cause and choose her brother's son, James III, who was living in exile in France. Anne did not want the subject raised; so it was up to Defoe to speak the unspeakable. Although the irony of the pamphlets was obvious enough, his Whig enemies claimed that they were libellous, and, according to the contemporary definition of libel, they were, since they were intended to awaken the public to the possible dangers before them and create a degree of turmoil. In response to Defoe's defense that the pamphlets were ironic, one of the justices remarked that men had been hanged for such irony.[31]

Defoe was pardoned by the intervention of the queen through her government. Many years later, *The Whitehall Evening Post* instanced the way in which Defoe managed to escape punishment for writing three Jacobite tracts as an example of how the government flouted the law.[32] Surely neither Harley nor Henry St. John, first Viscount Bolingbroke, who now shared considerable power with Harley and who would eventually replace him, could have been happy with what Defoe did, but he was too valuable a writer to lose. What these pamphlets suggest is that the possible return of the family of James II to the throne – the hope of the Jacobites – may have been the one point at which he would have been impelled to abandon his lucrative employment by the Tory government. Anne died on 1 August 1714, and, by approving the appointment of the Duke of Shrewsbury as Lord Treasurer, she assured the Protestant Succession with George I as the next ruler. Defoe was no longer drawing pay from the government, and he would have to find a way of earning a living purely on his writings.

It is possible that Defoe was still receiving some secret remuneration from Harley, since he published three parts of *The Secret History of the White Staff* (the "white staff" was the symbolic token of his office carried by the monarch's first minister) between 1714 and 1715 in defense of Harley's actions. From the standpoint of their reasoning and arguments, these were among the best pamphlets Defoe ever produced. Defoe has sometimes been accused of mistaking his audience in failing to keep Harley out of prison, but in fact, no defense would have been adequate, since the Whigs were eager for revenge against Harley. Defoe also thought it necessary in February 1715 to publish a fifty-eight-page pamphlet in his own defense with the hopeful title, *An Appeal to Honour and Justice, Tho' It Be of His Worst Enemies*. The purport of Defoe's defense was that he always remained true to his principles and that it was the times that changed, not he. It ended with a "Conclusion by the Publisher," stating that Defoe was seriously ill and could not finish. It is impossible to avoid the conclusion that Defoe was manipulating his audience, especially since, in his *Mercator*, he had staged a similar sickbed scene by way of propping up the lie that he had nothing to do with that newspaper. It seems likely that Defoe suffered a minor stroke at around this time, but it does not appear to have disabled him in any significant way.[33]

To use Defoe's own formula, during 1715 necessity forced him to invent some clever approaches to writing pamphlets. He assumed the voice of a Quaker in *A Friendly Epistle by Way of Reproof from One of the People Called Quakers* on 19 February. It was one of several pamphlets in which he used the Quaker's speech mannerisms (especially "thee" and "thou") to achieve a comic effect. The pamphlet went into six editions, but forced Defoe to apologize to the Quakers, who were offended by what they considered to be a satire against them. Defoe softened some of his remarks by the sixth edition and wrote a public apology in which he stated his respect for their beliefs. Another scrape was more difficult to escape. As he explained it to Harley on 31 August 1714, he had been trying to get control of another newspaper, the *Flying Post*, after its editor, George Ridpath, had been forced to flee abroad to avoid government prosecution. Defoe explained how he had tried to soften the tone of a letter containing an attack upon Arthur Annesley, fifth Earl of Anglesey, for Jacobite activity in Ireland and in the process had been charged with responsibility for writing the letter. Since Anglesey was one of the Regents chosen to welcome George I to the throne, such an apparent insult would demand punishment. Harley was not able to help, and on 12 July 1715, after a trial in the King's Bench, Defoe appeared to be on his way to a severe punishment, when he wrote what was apparently a moving letter to Justice Parker offering his services to the new Whig government. He was pardoned and took on a new role – which *Read's Weekly Journal* was to name sarcastically "*Corrector-General* of all the News-Papers, excepting his own."[34]

His letter to Harley of 31 August 1714 revealed that Defoe was attempting to control an opposition paper, and in his *Checklist* Moore has Defoe writing for the *Flying Post and Medley* for part of July and August. Indeed, the issue for 17 August has some passages praising George I that appear to be in Defoe's style.[35] Defoe was now to take up the task of controlling the press for the new Whig government. He wrote of his work in a letter to Charles de la Faye, an official in the office of the Secretaries of State, which attempted to explain the degree to which he could control certain newspapers.

> … with his Ldpps [Sunderland's] Approbation, I Introduced my Self in the Disguise of a Translator of the Forreign News to be So farr Concerned in This Weekly Paper of *Mists*, as to be able to keep it within the Circle of a Secret Mannagement, also, prevent the Mischievous Part of it, and yet Neither Mist or any of those Concerned with him have the least Guess or Suspicion By whose Direction I do it.[36]

Defoe may have been a brilliant secret agent, but it is difficult to believe that Mist had no suspicion of Defoe's motives. On the other hand, Defoe was an excellent writer and would attract readers. Mist may have been willing to accept having a spy around if he sold newspapers. However doubtful his method, at least Defoe was working for causes in which he believed, including the Protestant Succession and toleration for the Dissenters.

Between 1716 and 1730, one year before his death, Defoe wrote for and controlled for periods of time about twelve newspapers.[37] Between June 1716 and October 1720 he ran *Mercurius Politicus*, a monthly with a distinct High Church and Tory slant, and between January 1718 and March 1719 *Mercurius Britannicus*, supposedly by a Scot with the name Walter Cambell, which had a Whig bias. He started *The White-Hall Evening Post* on 18 September 1718, a newspaper with a Whig slant, which lasted into the 1790s. Defoe edited it for two years, until 14 October 1720. One way of controlling the press was for Defoe to set the limits of political opinion by writing all of it himself. Of course, he could not control everything, but until the publication of the genuine opposition paper, *The Craftsman*, in 1726, he succeeded in muting criticism of the government.

One of the more specialized papers was *The Manufacturer*, which ran from 30 October 1719 to 17 February 1720. It was established to support the workers who had been protesting the import of calicoes by the East India Company. The workers felt that such imports were undercutting their weaving of wool and other materials, enriching the East India Company and impoverishing British workers. This was a cause that Defoe found easy to support, and, in addition to the paper itself, Defoe published some pamphlets on this subject.[38] During a time when there was a lull in the actions of Parliament on this issue, Defoe took time out to contemplate the situation of the journalist in his time, comparing him to a "Manufacturer":

> it is inconceivable, what a Number of Poor, we that are Masters and Undertakers *in the Pen and Ink Manufacture*, do daily employ: For Example, *poor* Authors, *poor* Publishers, *poor* Printers, *poor* Paper-makers, and above all *poor Readers*; without whom indeed, the Manufacture would be in great Danger of being ruin'd, and the Nation of being depriv'd of so eminent a branch of her Commerce. For it is by these last that we *Writing Manufacturers* are chiefly supported, to the manifest Encouragement of the whole Trade, and the immediate creating of News-houses, Coffee-houses, *etc.* by whome the King's Revenues of Excise are considerably increas'd, and the Poor kept, in the Country.

Defoe's amusing parody of an economic argument for the benefits of industry should not disguise his image of the journalist as part of an important enterprise. The comparison that he was to make between the rhetoric of the writer composing dialogues and allegories with the woof and warp of the weavers may stretch his point, but Defoe was in one of his familiar guises, the prophet of the future. At the end of the century, in books describing the various industries in Britain, writers were finally listed among those who might be regarded as part of a genuine profession.

In writing for *Mist's Weekly Journal* and what came to be called *Applebee's Original Weekly Journal*, Defoe was influenced by the expectations raised by *The Spectator* of Joseph Addison and Sir Richard Steele. Steele's *Tatler*, which ran from 12 April 1709 to 2 January 1711, had been influenced by Defoe's *Review*, especially in its personal observations in the section titled "From My Apartment," in its defense of satire, and in its strong moral judgments. *The Spectator*, which ran from 1 March 1711 to 20 December 1714, insisted on a combined tone of politeness, wit, and morality. The satire was lighter and it carried the suggestion that the discussions of poetry, aesthetics, and social customs embodied a set of ideas to which the readers might aspire. For the most part Addison and Steele avoided direct involvement in politics, except occasionally when they derided party strife. *The Spectator*'s most recent editor described it as having the major influence on behavior in Britain aside from the Bible.[39] When, in 1728, Defoe wrote the opening essay in *The Universal Spectator* edited by Henry Baker (his son-in-law), he praised *The Spectator* as the model for contemporary journalism and argued that there was still much to be done in the manner of *The Spectator*.

> Let no Man envy us the celebrated Title we have assumed, or charge us with Arrogance, as if we bid the World expect great Things from us. Must we have no Power to Please, unless we come up to the full height of those Inimitable Performances? Is there no Wit or Humor left, because they are gone? Is the Spirit of the *Spectators* all lost, and their Mantle fallen upon no Body? ... Has the World offered no Variety, and presented no new Scenes, since they retired from us? Or did they leave off, because they were quite exhausted, and had no more to say? We think quite otherwise.[40]

Many of the essays in *The Spectator* appeared in the form of letters to the editor, and in his contributions to *Mist's* and *Applebee's* Defoe followed that practice. He had long experience writing through a mask and the method served his purposes.

He wrote one letter to *Mist's* arguing for the relief of imprisoned debtors and signed his own initials to it on 28 December 1717, but most of the letters provided a slightly wry view of contemporary politics. He followed stories such as that of Peter the Great and his cruel treatment of his son, the approaching plague and John Law's economic experiments in France. He got into some trouble by writing a letter under the name of Sir Andrew Politick that displeased the government. Defoe was also involved in writing on the crime wave that hit Britain in the wake of the South Sea Scandal. He appears to have done some of this in *Applebee's Original Weekly Journal* as well as in separate pamphlets on individual criminals, such as Jonathan Wild and John (Jack) Shepherd. Although Defoe's authorship of these works, which carried into the middle of the 1720s, has been challenged, his involvement with writing on crime is clear from novels such as *Moll Flanders* and *Colonel Jack* as well as tracts such as *Augusta Triumphans*.

A typical essay in *Applebee's* is one on the subject of fools and folly, a subject that he was to develop fully in his *Mere Nature Delineated* (1726). The occasion was the publication of Edward Young's satire on the passions that dominated society, *Love of Fame, the Universal Passion* (1725–28). Defoe considered this a particularly bad work and posed the ironic possibility that new examples of folly were as important as new discoveries in science:

> But I wonder much, that notwithstanding this Curiosity, we do not find them equally diverted with the various new Species and Kinds of Fools which the Age supplies us with; and yet, we find the Times are very fruitful in that kind of Production too. Wherefore I think we cannot do Mankind a great Piece of Service, than now and then to enlarge upon the wonderful Productions of this kind which have assisted to make the present Age particularly Remarkable, more than all that went before it; and which might, in the due Improvement of New Discoveries, serve to Instruct us, as much as any New Butterfly, or new Insect, which had never been seen before.[41]

Young deserved better, but Defoe had apparently liked some of Young's earlier verse and thought his poetry was getting worse. What is important about this and similar essays in *Applebee's Journal* is that, following the lead of *The Spectator*, Defoe was turning toward a wider frame of reference, including the criticism of contemporary literature.

Defoe may have lost some interest in the grind of writing for the newspapers, and he began to produce some important pamphlets on social issues. For example, in 1725, under the pseudonym of Andrew Moreton, Esq., he produced a pamphlet called *Every-Body's Business, Is No-Body's Business*, an attack on the high wages of servants. This was the first of a series of such criticisms of contemporary society using this pseudonym and probably the most popular, going into five editions and provoking a number of replies. In *The Protestant Monastery* (1727), he attacked the mistreatment of the aged in contemporary society, and in *Second Thoughts Are Best* (1728), he proposed improving street lighting in London as a way of preventing robberies. Defoe wrote a number of such pamphlets advocating social improvements at this time. The Andrew Moreton pseudonym gave him the view of society from the standpoint of an old man impatient with the social and moral direction of his world, and it was an effective rhetorical device.

At the end of his life, he briefly assumed control of a monthly summary of the news that had been run by Abel Boyer until his death on 16 November 1729. He turned the journal in the direction of economic subjects and some of his other favorite themes. He looked back to the time of King William and even further back to the plague of 1665. He insisted that the trade to the Spanish colonies that went through Spain was preferable to the dream of trading directly to those colonies, but he reminded Spain that it was unwise to attack the English sloops that carried on an illegal trade to those colonies during a time of peace. And he reminisced about how, in 1686, one of the Barbary Pirates captured a ship bound from London to Amsterdam and carried off the entire cargo. He commented on crime including Newgate prison, "that dismal Place," as he called it here and in *Moll Flanders*.[42] And of course, he praised one of his own works as "Extraordinary."[43] It was Defoe's last fling at periodical journalism.

The German political philosopher Jürgen Habermas has argued that the creation of the "public sphere" through this combination – papers such as the *Review* and the coffee houses where the citizens could debate the issues of the time – created a unique kind of democratic atmosphere in Britain:

> Compared to the press in the other European states, however, the British press enjoyed unique liberties.
>
> Harley was the first statesman to understand how to turn the new situation to his advantage. He engaged authors like Defoe (who has been called the first professional journalist), who defended the cause of the Whigs not only in the pamphlets in use up until then but also in the new journals. Indeed, he was the first to make the "party spirit" a "public spirit." Defoe's *Review*, Tutchin's *Observator*, and Swift's *Examiner*, were discussed in clubs and coffee houses, at home and in the streets. Walpole and Bolingbroke themselves addressed the public. Men like Pope, Gay, Arbuthnot, and Swift combined literature and politics in a peculiar fashion comparable to Addison's and Steele's combination of literature and journalism.[44]

Habermas proceeds to lament the ways in which public opinion is manipulated in the modern world where the "integrity of the private sphere" becomes an "illusion."[45] There is little question that Habermas tends to idealize somewhat the journalism of Defoe's period as uniquely free.[46] As has been suggested, Defoe tried his best to control opinion.[47] He once spoke of an ideal style as one in which a man speaking to a crowd would be understood in exactly the way he wished to communicate his ideas. The ideas for which he fought – progress in science, trade, and the arts, the Protestant Succession, toleration of religious and political dissent, and a Whig form of government in which Parliament would speak for the people and have the strongest say in government – were all advances that he thought would benefit Britain, and he was willing to do anything to see them come about. And "anything" might mean a degree of control of those writings for the press that, to his mind, were on the wrong side of these issues.[48]

The Tory opposition eventually succeeded in getting its ideas out so well that between 1726 and 1728, with the Tory *Craftsman*, Swift's *Gulliver's Travels*, Gay's *Beggar's Opera* and Pope's *Dunciad* , it was possible to create a Tory ideology that would influence the rest of the century. That only one of the works on the Tory side was a journal devoted to politics suggests that the indirection of literature (as opposed to journalism) might have certain advantages. Between 1711 and 1714 Addison and Steele had used *The Spectator* to present essays on literature and society with a subtly Whiggish point of view and which continued to be widely read for close to three centuries. But Defoe was ever a controversialist. Whether as the True-Born Englishman or Andrew Moreton, he appears to have felt a necessity to remind people about the right way to think and to behave, and he did this as a true journalist, covering issue by issue, ephemeral crisis after ephemeral crisis. He is fascinating to read as a mirror of his age, and because he was intent on keeping the interest of his audience, he is still worth reading. But as with that other journalist, his antagonist, Jonathan Swift, it was through his literary efforts, through *Robinson Crusoe* and some of his other fictions, that his journalism would be remembered.

NOTES

1. *The Invention of the Newspaper: English Newsbooks 1641–1649* (Oxford: Clarendon Press, 1996), especially pp. xiii, 16–17.
2. See the wonderful list of false news provided by the news office to satisfy the curiosity of the people. *Complete Plays*, 2 vols. (London: Dent, 1942), II, 384–88 (III.i).
3. See *The Spectator*, ed. Donald Bond, 5 vols. (Oxford: Clarendon Press, 1965), IV, 90–94.
4. See Raymond, *Invention of the Newspaper*, p. 16.
5. For the physical conditions involved in the distribution of the news – how it was distributed, by whom and the relationship between the printers and the journalists, see James R. Sutherland, *The Restoration Newspaper and its Development* (Cambridge: Cambridge University Press, 1986), especially pp. 1–43, 185–232.
6. Defoe appears to have believed that the development of the newspaper signified an important divide between a time when news circulated in an unreliable, oral fashion and his period, when news and its sources might be verified . Thus he has his protagonist, H.F., in his account of the plague of 1665, *A Journal of the Plague Year* (1722), complain about the ways in which the lack of reliable newspapers at that time permitted the dissemination of false rumors about the plague, both those

circulated orally and those printed from oral sources in the "Bills of Mortality," and how this would sometimes lead to the deaths of citizens. See Paula McDowell, "Defoe and the Contagion of the Oral: Modeling Media Shift in *A Journal of the Plague Year*," *PMLA*, 121 (2006), 87–106.

7. See for example, Sutherland, *Restoration Newspaper*, p. 14.

8. *Defoe's Review*, ed. Arthur Wellesley Secord (New York: Published for the Facsimile Text Society by Columbia University Press, 1938), I, sup. 1, 5–6.

9. See *Gulliver's Travels*, Book I, Chapter 4.

10. See the collection of documents put together by Geoffrey Holmes and W. A. Speck, *The Divided Society* (New York: St. Martin's Press, 1968).

11. *A Letter to a Dissenter from His Friend at the Hague, Concerning the Penal Laws and the Test* (The Hague [London?], 1688), p. 3.

12. *A Manual of English Prose Literature* (Boston: Ginn, 1901), p. 351.

13. *Some Reflections on a Pamphlet lately Publish'd, entituled, An Argument Shewing that a Standing Army Is Inconsistent with a Free Government* (London, 1697), p. 11.

14. Ibid., p. 16

15. See *An Essay upon Projects*, ed. Joyce Kennedy, Michael Seidel, and Maximillian Novak (New York: AMS Press, 1999), pp. 97–108. Defoe called this project "the most Noble and Useful Proposal in this Book" (p. 97).

16. *The Rise of the Novel: Studies in Defoe, Richardson, and Fielding* (Berkeley and Los Angeles: University of California Press, 1957), p. 126.

17. (Oxford, 1702), p. 59.

18. *A Brief Explanation of a Late Pamphlet, Entituled, The Shortest Way with the Dissenters*, in *A True Collection of the Writings of the True-Born Englishman*, 2 vols. (London, 1703–5), I, 436.

19. Defoe may have expected an outpouring of pamphlets against the attitudes expressed in *The Shortest Way with the Dissenters* – a controversy to which he and some other Whigs, such as John Tutchin, might contribute a number of pamphlets. A large number of copies were sent to Holland, perhaps to make the Dutch aware of the attitudes of the High Church. See Alsop, "Defoe, Toland and *The Shortest Way with the Dissenters*," *Review of English Studies*, ns. 43 (1992), 242.

20. *Review*, ed. Secord I, sig. A3v.

21. Ibid., I, 88.

22. Ibid., I, 49.

23. Defoe began his arguments on 13 July 1706. See the *Review*, III, 334–50.

24. John Richetti quotes Defoe's contemporary and opponent, Charles Leslie, to the effect that the *Review* was often read aloud in the street to an eager, often illiterate audience. Leslie complained that by these means the populace are taught "the principles of rebellion" and hatred of the clergy, opinions which they "suck in greedily." See *The Life of Daniel Defoe: A Critical Biography* (Oxford: Blackwell, 2005), p. 88.

25. *Dunton's Whipping Post: or, a Satyr upon Every Body* (London, 1706), p. 90.

26. *Review*, IV, 423.

27. *Review*, VIII, 153–56.

28. "Of the Carrying on of the Treaty in Scotland," *The History of the Union of Great Britain* (Edinburgh, 1709), p. 64.

29. See *The Trial of Doctor Sacheverell* (London: Eyre Methuen, 1973), p. 49.

30. See *A Critical Bibliography of Daniel Defoe* (London: Pickering and Chatto, 1998), pp. 103–29. J. R. Moore's *Checklist of the Writings of Daniel Defoe*, 2nd edn. (Hamden: Archon Books, 1971), pp. 82–100, has seventy-two pamphlets by Defoe listed for 1711 and 1712.

31. See my *Daniel Defoe: Master of Fictions* (Oxford: Oxford University Press, 2001), pp. 425–26. John Oldmixon ascribed the remark to judge Powis. See *The History of England* (London, 1735), p. 510.

32. *The Whitehall Evening Post*, 25–27 January 1728.

33. See Novak, *Daniel Defoe: Master of Fictions*, p. 467.

34. 24 August 1717.

35. See Novak, *Daniel Defoe: Master of Fictions*, p. 459.

36. *The Letters of Daniel Defoe*, ed. George Harris Healey (Oxford: Clarendon Press, 1955), p. 453.

37. See Moore, *Checklist of the Writings of Daniel Defoe*, pp. 233–35. Some of these, such as *The Director*, 5 October 1720 – 14 May 1721, were intended for a specific purpose, in this case to deflect criticism of the government for the South Sea Scandal. Others, such as *The Commentator*, 1 January 1720 – 16 September 1720, were more general publications in the mode of *The Spectator*.

38. *The Just Complaint of the Poor Weavers* (London, 1719); and *A Brief State of the Question between the Printed and Painted Callicoes, and the Woollen and Silk Manufacture* (London, 1719).

39. *The Spectator*, ed. Donald Bond, 5 vols. (Oxford: Clarendon Press, 1965), I, xcvi–cvi.

40. William Lee, *Daniel Defoe: His Life and Recently Discovered Writings*, 3 vols. (London, 1869), III, 466.

41. Lee, *Recently Discovered Writings*, III, 393.

42. *The Political State* (March 1730), p. 326.

43. *The Political State* (March 1730), p. 315.

44. *The Transformation of the Public* Sphere, trans. Thomas Burger (Cambridge, MA: Massachusetts Institute of Technology Press), p. 59.

45. Ibid., p. 171.

46. Lloyd Kramer considers his idealization of the free exchange of ideas "utopian." See "Habermas, History and Critical Theory," in *Habermas and the Public Sphere*, ed. Craig Coulhoun (Cambridge, MA: MIT Press, 1993), p. 254.

47. Defoe frequently stated his belief that some regulation of the press was legitimate. See, for example, *An Essay on the Regulation of the Press* (London, 1704).

48. For an excellent discussion of Defoe's arguments concerning the balance between authorial ownership and responsibility in regard to freedom of the press, see Jody Greene, *The Trouble with Ownership* (Philadelphia: University of Pennsylvania Press, 2005), pp. 107–49.

3

SRINIVAS ARAVAMUDAN

Defoe, commerce, and empire

A True-Bred Merchant is a Universal Scholar; his Learning Excells the meer
Scholar in Greek and Latin as much as that does the Illiterate Person, that cannot
Write or Read: He Understands Language, without Books, Geography without
Maps, his Journals and Trading-Voyages delineate the World, his Foreign
Exchanges, Protests and Procurations, speak all Tongues; he sits in his
Counting-House, and Converses with all Nations, and keeps up the most exqui-
site and extensive part of human Society in a Universal Correspondence.

Daniel Defoe, the *Review*[1]

As the eighteenth-century geographer Herman Moll asserted, "no one Man
can possibly view the whole Earth in a Life-Time."[2] Reading Defoe's extensive writings, one might be excused for thinking that Moll underestimated the
singular imaginative powers of one of his acquaintances who wrote as if he
had first-hand knowledge of the entire globe. While Defoe was not a genuine
globetrotter, he had an expansive global perspective on trade. He was a
spokesperson for the new world order of the English Enlightenment – its
scientific, political, and financial revolutions – and his commercial curiosity
and colonial projections involved domains as far-flung as China, the South
Seas, and the Americas. Defoe's extensive writings covered the viability of
commerce and colonization in all four major continental landmasses, and the
still uncharted "South Seas," or Pacific Ocean. Defoe thought about the
commercial world as one complex interactive entity, and he wrote many
thousands of words about it.

Defoe began to explore adventure themes very late in his career (the first
volume of *Robinson Crusoe* appeared when he was fifty-nine years old). For
Defoe, adventure stories were like thought-experiments. In his hands, the
adventure novel is a means of diagnosing global positioning for national
domestic advantage. Adventure leads to empire in Defoe's writings. And yet
imperial acquisition seems merely incidental to the adventure tale. As one
scholar puts it, Defoe's imperialism can be termed "mundane rather than
ideological."[3] Colonial acquisition, in all of Defoe's writings, is a much more
unreliable process than it has sometimes been portrayed. All the same, he
often appears enthusiastic for opportunistic colonial exploitation despite its
multiple reverses and difficulties, which he readily acknowledges. Crusoe's
"native Propensity to rambling" lets slide the hard-earned territory of the

island in *The Farther Adventures*, illustrating how colonies that can take several decades to consolidate can also be lost in a moment. Given that an older Crusoe abandons his West Indian island property in favor of reconnoitering the East Indies, trading and vandalizing along the way, the sequel teaches us that the first volume was a stage in a more complex process.[4] Colonies are never just independent ends in Defoe's thought-processes; colonial acquisition plays a functional role in bolstering national competitive leverage and assaying the newer possibilities of commercial success that present themselves.

The epigraph to this chapter demonstrates the profit-oriented justifications that lie beneath Defoe's global vision of the merchant scholar's disinterested universality. The image of the merchant in his counting house is strange and fascinating. It suggests an unconventional erudition amidst isolation, an almost monastic detachment rather than the typical hurly-burly of the marketplace that one might have associated with the merchant profession. The practical knowledge of the merchant is as superior to that possessed by the theoretically learned scholar as the lettered person is to the illiterate. The merchant's activities perform crucial mapping functions, which supplement current knowledge and enlarge its global scope. However, the merchant's solitude corresponds to Crusoe's loneliness, and also to the alienation Defoe claimed to have experienced personally in the City, the financial center of London. Solitude might be necessary for the objectivity of the merchant's decision-making, but it comes with the price of generating a social isolation that might also turn out to be disadvantageous in multiple ways.

Within the Baconian framework of empirical science that greatly influenced Defoe, the merchant-traveler is also explorer, observer, technological innovator, and experimentalist. Such praise of merchants is constant throughout Defoe's writings: in *An Essay Upon Projects* (1697), Defoe argues that voyages and travels make "a True-Bred Merchant the most Intelligent Man in the World."[5] In *Atlas Maritimus* (1728), probably written by Defoe, an important passage argues very clearly for the commercial objectives of all forms of global mapping, which integrate the functions of the geographer and the historian with that of the tradesman and the seaman; it is for this reason that "we do not describe thousands of little Creeks and Coves upon the Coast, and ten thousand nameless and useless Islands."[6] There is something almost mystical about the merchant's solitary absorption of learning, where language is learned without books and geography without maps. However, this mysticism is dissolved by the commercial power and purposefulness of the merchant, whose transactions with all nations generate the "universal correspondence" of the Baconian and Royal Society ideals by combining elite and popular knowledge. In Defoe's expansive evocation, the merchant's contact with "the most exquisite and extensive part of human society" links commerce to the modern project of scientific management of the world and nature. In his unpublished *The Compleat English Gentleman*, Defoe reiterates this ideal for the gentleman-merchant who is encouraged to "make the tour of the world in books" and "make himself master of the geography of the Universe in the maps, attlasses [*sic*] and measurement of our mathematics."[7] At the same time, Defoe's nationalism fits well with his universalism. In his poetic paean to the mongrel origins of the English nation, *The True-Born Englishman* (1701), Defoe represents the locals as the product of multiple races and nations; in fact, at his fullest, the native-born Englishman is, "[A] metaphor invented to express/ [A] man akin to all the universe."[8]

While commerce, adventure, and imperial designs are thoroughly intertwined in all of Defoe's writings, we can separate them in order to see how they interact. A central thread in Defoe's writings – Protestant Christianity – also threatens to undermine significantly the symbiosis of these three terms. As a religious Dissenter, Defoe was at odds with some Church of England doctrines, but in their foreign settings his narratives feature a crusading Christian intolerance. Extreme, often unmotivated violence is a prominent aspect of Defoe's voyaging narratives, featuring primitive accumulation alongside the massacre of those deemed savage. We therefore encounter an unprocessed mixture of attitudes as different as cosmopolitan detachment and crude xenophobia, a cool tolerance of human difference and also a hotheaded demonization of indigenous others, all issuing from the viewpoint of the same fictional character. Defoe's Puritan English nationalism can perhaps be singled out as the culprit, the most volatile element in his otherwise rational repertoire. Some historians indeed see this testosterone-infused Protestantism as the essence of modern Englishness, providing a violent surplus that justifies the interconnections of commerce, adventure, and colonialism through the darker fantasies of Christian dominance over the non-Christian world.

Global commerce

Defoe was born in 1660, just when the English monarchy was restored. By 1731, the year of his death, Great Britain (which now formally included Scotland and the colony of Ireland) had defeated or undercut Spain, France, and Holland to occupy the position of pre-eminent maritime and commercial power in Europe. London had displaced Amsterdam as Europe's financial center. While Spain and Portugal held vast colonial dominions in the Americas, Britain had been learning to "encrease [her] Treasure by Forraign Trade" as Thomas Mun had presciently suggested as early as 1630.[9] Despite her wealth, Spain was perceived as feudal and indolent in comparison with Britain, hence the damning charge about Spain summarized in *The True-Born Englishman*: "Never was nation in the world before, / So very rich, and yet so very poor" (Part I, lines 94–95).

While Defoe was not a follower of Mun's mercantilist doctrines for national economic advantage to the letter (for instance, bitterly opposing the East India Company, whereas Mun was a great proponent of that monopoly), his support of foreign trade allowed monopoly and antimonopoly to play off against each other. For example, Defoe defended the privileges of the Royal African Company against private traders. There was perhaps a venal motive behind this as well, as Defoe had invested in the monopoly. All the same, in works such as *A General History of Trade* (1713), Defoe plugs free trade with France and other nations, and the promotion of free trade with France is even more strident in *Mercator: Or, Commerce Retrieved* (1713–14). Often, it appears that trade preoccupies Defoe as a matter of global scale. The Asian demand for gold and silver is counteracted by the goal of a favorable balance of trade for Britain, and Europe, as Mun and other mercantilists had advised. In Defoe's view, God had wisely separated various goods and services so that mankind could reunite them again through a judicious mercantile circulation: "England thus converses with India and enjoys all that India can give, Returns what ever India wants."[10] His organicist metaphors of trade render the globe as an immense vitalist body: "Trade, like the Blood in the Veins, Circulates thro' the whole Body of Fraternities and Societies of Mankind." Trade has succeeded with the "help of Miracle and supernatural Operation," and "even Religion itself has been Propagated by Trade" (*A General History of Trade*, Part I, pp. 5, 24). However, when the balance of trade goes awry, with the transfer of money rather than manufactures to Asia, it results in a religious and cultural catastrophe: "*Europe*, like a Body in a warm Bath, with its Veins open'd, lies bleeding to Death; and her Bullion, which is the Life and Blood of her Trade, flows all to *India*, where 'tis amassed into infinite Heaps, for the enriching the Heathen World at the Expence of the Christian World."[11]

Defoe anticipated that trade would prosper with population increase. Society, he says in *A General History of Trade*, should pay attention to infrastructural investment: improving land, creating transportation links, ensuring the availability of cheap labor, and putting aside capital for further investment into technology and inventory (Part III, pp. 22, 45). Holland and England manage to dominate trade, in Defoe's view, not because of geographical positioning but through advances in navigation. Shipping largely enabled the increase in eighteenth-century global trade. As a result, since the 1660s, the ocean becomes a proxy for British power and, in the words of one scholar, "the sea becomes the national rhetorical element."[12] Poets such as Edward Young wrote *Ocean* (1728) and *Imperium Pelagi* (1729) celebrating Britain's new found oceanic empire. The historians Nathaniel Crouch, in *The English Empire in America* (1685), and John Oldmixon, in *The British Empire in America* (1708), had laid out the potential of the mainland American settlements followed by the Caribbean island possessions. Those who attacked the colonies on account of their depopulation of the metropolitan country were not aware of how rich and productive they could indeed become. Oldmixon asserts that "there are no Hands in the British Empire more usefully employ'd [than American colonists] for the Profit and Glory of the Commonwealth." [13] Defoe represents a universalist interpretation of this new national confidence when he asserts in the *Review* that "the Sea seems to be the great Common of all the Creation; all have a Right to Range in it; none have an Exclusive Right to any part of it." Furthermore, "Rivers and Roads, are as the Veins and Arteries that convey Wealth, like the Blood, to all the Parts of the World" (vol. VIII, no. 149, 24 April 1711); and vol. III, no. 2, 3 January 1706). It is understood that British naval power guarantees the reliability of the shipping lanes. France would have destroyed Britain's colonies if not for Britain's superior naval power (the *Review*, vol. I, no. 30, 17 June 1704, 133–36).

Defoe's globalism, therefore, is a network theory inflected by his mercantilism, which seeks national economic advantage over other areas. It was the absence of natural resources that paradoxically stimulated the desire to trade: "the Merchant makes a wet Bog become a populous State" (the *Review*, vol. III, no. 2, 3 January 1706, 7). Trade takes precedence over everything: "Trade ought always to be Safe, and that let Nations Fight, Quarrel, and make War as they please, they should never make War with Trade" (*A General History of Trade*, Part II, p. 37). Trade is portrayed as disinterested, enlightened, and cosmopolitan: "no private circumstances, prejudice or hatred has any concern in trade" (Part III, p. 46). Furthermore, "Trade is the Universal Advantage of Mankind" and Defoe, when arguing on behalf of his Tory patron, Robert Harley, inveighs against proposed plans to destroy Dunkirk as a freeport in the peace negotiations with France, instead suggesting that "the Peers [Piers], Harbour, and Channel, belong to all the World; they are like a strong Man with his Arms spread out receiving a Child running from a Thief; like a Door for a distress'd Mariner" (Part II, p. 38). *A General History of Trade* represents moderate free trade ideology well before David Hume and then Adam Smith took it up as a philosophical doctrine. Defoe, however, was not an unrestricted free trader. He favored the promotion of English advantage, and he would always support a globalizing trade through private enterprise and ingenuity, with or without governmental backing. For him, trade is the reasonable and persuasive solution to governmental coercion and force. In a 1728 pamphlet on the problem of providing gainful employment to sailors after their demobilization following peace treaties, Defoe suggests that "the Government uses Force, and takes the Seamen by Impress and Arrest; the Merchants use a Force also, tho' of a different Kind, and that is the Force of Persuasion, I mean the powerful Persuasion of Money, giving higher Wages."[14] The gentler action of merchants' need for labor tempers the instabilities of a state structure that makes military demands on its able-bodied seamen but that cannot support them during a time of peace. In contrast to many of his contemporaries, Defoe's sensibility took into account laborers' needs for social security, job insurance, medical care, disability compensation, widows' pensions and the like – attitudes that originate in a pre-capitalist resistance to brutal aspects of capitalist growth.

With his immense powers of sympathetic projection, Defoe saw trade from all sides, taking into account the concerns of governmental regulators, speculating merchants, and the laboring poor, and uniting the multifarious actors into a universal correspondence. Defoe took major trading risks himself: going bankrupt twice, and being involved in business projects from breeding civet cats to manufacturing bricks and tiles. He traded New World tobacco for English wool, and marketed a diving machine as well as a lottery "adventure" scheme. He dabbled in linen manufacture, horse dealing, and the timber and wine trades. Towards the end of his life, Defoe was still an active merchant, dealing on a wholesale level in products such as wine, cheese, anchovies, and oysters. As a globalist, Defoe saw the world as composed by trade in the form of several overlapping circles of continuity. *A Plan of the English Commerce* (1728) discusses how, amongst the clothier, merchant, and seaman, "Every Man knows his own Affairs, moves in his own Circle," whereas "the Merchant on the other Hand moves in another Sphere"; "Captains, Masters, Owners, and Navigators of Ships ... move in another Orb but still act in the same Round of Business." The ultimate impact of all these ascending concentric commercial activities is that the "Commerce of the World ... [is] carried on in an unbounded Ocean of Business; Trackless and unknown."[15] These metaphors of fluidity, circularity, and global interconnectivity – "infinite and incessant Circulation" as Defoe puts it – are but one aspect of the author's profound belief in trade as the vehicle for global improvement (the *Review*, vol. III, no. 2, 3 January 1706). In this same vein, Defoe looks approvingly on the influx of foreigners into Britain, as this would be likely to increase trade, personal wealth, and liberty (the *Review*, vol. v, no. 143, 24 February 1709, 572).

At the same time, Defoe could also be a partisan for those most hurt by unrestricted trade. A particularly interesting case is the polemical spirit of the journal called *The Manufacturer; or, The British Trade Truly Stated*, which

Defoe authored between 1719 and 1721 to support English weavers hurt by the East India Company's importation of cheap calico. Here, Defoe is against globalization. His antipathy to cotton and support of wool takes a decidedly xenophobic turn: "All this is owing to the Custom, or Fashion, of wearing Calicoes instead of Stuffs, Cotton instead of Wool and Silk, and employing *Pagans* and *Indians*, *Mahometans* and *Chineses* instead of *Christians* and *Britains*."[16] This protectionist sentiment continues over several numbers lamenting the inroads on the wool trade made by "interloping Callicoes" that create potential English starvation at the hands of "*Negroes, Savages, Chineses,* and I know not how many Sorts of Barbarians" (no. 2, Wednesday 4, November 1719). These pamphlets espouse a strident economic nationalism. English weavers (many of whom Defoe knew intimately at Spitalfields from childhood and as a wholesaler of woolen cloth) became the model for a long-suffering Everyman. Christians were being starved for the advantage of Muslims, who were being fed (no. 65, Thursday 13 October 1720).

In this phase, global commerce also involves the threat of rampant international speculation, which can destroy various national economies, as has often been the case in Defoe's time and ours. In one number, the narrator's hope for Parliamentary legislation to regulate the stockmarket and prevent scams is disdainfully parried by "Mr. Sharp, a Bubble-Broker":

> Do you think we mind Acts of Parliament here, or do you not know where you are? Sir, you are in the City, just at the corner of *Exchange-Ally*. Here we settle Nations, buy Parties, make War and Peace, form Alliances, and break and dissolve them; and all the great Affairs of the World are rated by us in the Price of Stock. (no. 45, Wednesday 25, May 1720)

The attack on "Bubble-Masters" continues through several numbers in this journal. Defoe's mercantilism opposed monetism (a very strict control of the money supply). Restrictions on the money supply (paper instruments as well as bullion) squeezed credit to the detriment of trade. At the same time, Defoe was equally very skeptical of unbridled financial speculation. Stockjobbing, his contemptuous term for buying and selling shares in an open market, threatened to inflate money out of all proportion to goods. Defoe systematically attacked stockbrokers in *The Anatomy of Exchange Alley* (1719) and *The Director* (1720–21). He also criticized English consumption of luxury goods, which depleted gold and silver reserves, showing that he was a moderate bullionist (taking the position that precious metal reserves enhanced economic advantage). Sometimes monetist, and at other times bullionist, Defoe is at other times a proto-capitalist free trader. At some brief moments in the fictions and moral writings he even floats a medieval canonist's position, that is to say, he condemns superfluous economic activity beyond that needed to maintain already assigned social status. For these reasons, Defoe's economic thought might be judged as doctrinally incoherent, or, in the words of one critic, by a "theoretical fragmentariness."[17] Defoe's flexible globalism imports the useful theological technique of casuistry, or arguing for context-driven ethical and moral principles, to the economic realm. Defoe's mercantilism in a global frame involves complex balances and adjustments among the attitudes and behaviors of a large number of individual actors. Despite some incoherence and inconsistency in his statements, in the main Defoe aims to enhance the British economy first, even while anticipating the exploitation of all others in a zero-sum game.

A colonial world

As Leslie Stephen put it, we find Defoe's men of commerce "shoving their intrusive persons into every quarter of the globe."[18] Crusoe's shipwreck and deliverance in *Robinson Crusoe* is followed in the sequel by his return to the island and departure for other destinations. Crusoe detaches himself from the colony, revealing a thirst for global knowledge over narrow self-interest. In the *Farther Adventures*, Crusoe insists that he didn't "plant in the Name of any Government or Nation, or to acknowledge any Prince, or to call my People Subjects to any one Nation more than another" (p. 217). Some colonies, it appears, are exempt from national partisanship when they are founded, and can also involve, as Crusoe's colony does, multinational thought-experiments. Crusoe populates his island with Spanish Catholics, renegade Englishmen, and Carib women brought to reproduce the labor force and thereby make the enterprise viable. It is perhaps this type of social experiment that Defoe has in mind when he recommends in *A Plan of the English Commerce* that the English colonists need "to civilize and instruct the Savages and Natives of those Countries wherever they plant, so as to bring them by the softest and gentlest Methods to fall into the Customs and Usage of their own Country, and incorporate among our People as one Nation" (p. 341).

However, to expect imperialist success as a matter of course would be wishful thinking. Crusoe's colony could very well be an example of mercantile export such as he had evoked in *An Essay upon Projects* when "all Foreign Negoce … is in its beginning all Project, Contrivance and Invention" (p. 8). Within this context, a colonial project could resemble "a vast Undertaking, too big to be manag'd, and therefore likely enough to come to nothing" (p. 20). In a commercial age, all projects and schemes relied on money raised from the stockmarket: "Stock-Jobbing nurs'd Projecting, and Projecting in return has very diligently pimp'd for its Foster-Parent till both are arriv'd to be Publick Grievances" (p. 30). Technological improvements need a money supply even while the share market exploits this demand to hoodwink customers "to part with their Money for Shares in a *New-Nothing*" (p. 12). In *The Manufacturer*, Defoe continues this complaint against instantaneous commoditization of new ideas: "our Projects are all Bubbles, and calculated for *Exchange-Ally* discoveries, not for enlarging our Commerce, settling Colonies, and spreading the Dominions of our Sovereign from Pole to Pole" (no. 56, 10, Aug. 1720). However, even though he explicitly shies away from calling a colony a project, colonies are some of the most complex long-term commercial projects imaginable. To be able to succeed, a colony has to maintain the initial conquest of land, organize supplies, and procure labor to keep the enterprise going. Floating a mere stock issue, in comparison, would be small potatoes (*An Essay on Projects*, p. 28). Of course, with something like the South Sea venture, itself a result of "the forward Humor of the Age in New Adventures," colonial projections blended seamlessly into stock-market futures, and the creative financing of state-incurred budgetary deficits.[19]

Defoe promoted his own interpretation of the South Sea venture to Harley in a letter on 23 July 1711, much before the stock-market fiasco from over-valued shares of this company took place in 1720–21. He claims to have personally promoted the South Sea venture even earlier to King William III, although some biographers have speculated that Defoe might have been making a self-aggrandizing claim in lieu of his friend William Paterson, who verifiably promoted a similar scheme to the king. Defoe's *An Essay on the South-Sea Trade* (1711) argues for a separation of colonization from trade, decrying the speculators, and analyzing objections by critics who were calling the fledgling venture a "Buccanier Company" (p. 34). Starting in 1711, the Tory scheme was intended to ease the shortage of credit in Britain by making the national debt (incurred by the War of the Spanish Succession) liquid, that is to say, the government proposed to convert the vast sum of £9.5 million into equivalent shares in the South Sea Company, which promised annuities of anywhere between 5 per cent and 8 per cent. This strategy, it was thought, would have the effect of reducing the huge government debt and making credit more easily available in the economy. Through this venture, the Tories were avoiding the Whig-dominated Bank of England and East India Company while attempting to raise capital from alternative sources. In his pamphlet, Defoe hopes trade will triumph over politics, and criticizes the entry of unprofessional first-time speculators into the fray:

> Butchers, Grasiers, Cheesemongers, Ship-chandlers, Carpenters, Smiths (and other Handicrafts,) Brewers, Bakers, Coopers, and the like, and an infinite

Number of these; to talk to these of a *South Sea* Trade is to talk *Hebrew* and *Arabic*: Like Esop's Cock, they spurn the Diamond with Contempt, and will sell Two of them for an Handful of Barley. (p. 34)

The danger spelled out here and elsewhere is that chaotic decision-making by inexperienced speculators can sink any market. The absence of regulation inflated the market beyond sustainability. The national debt went up from £14 million in 1714 to nearly £50 million in 1720, even as the capitalized value of the London stock exchange went from £20 million in 1717 to £50 million in 1720. Paper was chasing paper without proper collateral. Looking back after the fiasco, Defoe continued to argue for the genuine profitability of colonial investment schemes.

A New Voyage Round the World (1724), Defoe's last major narrative, involves an actual South Sea venture with an open propaganda function, as the book advertises on its title page a colonial scheme for settlement in South America. Yet another global fiction in its scope, *New Voyage* describes a ship's legitimate trading that is commingled with piracy. Led by a nameless English captain who is the narrator, the novel's ship sails under the pretended command of a French captain, Jean-Michel Mirlotte, to enable transactions in areas of Spanish control of the Americas where English shipping was considered hostile. In the East Indies, the ship trades under Spanish imperial colors at English or Dutch ports. After travels around the Cape of Good Hope to Madagascar, Arabia, India, Ceylon, Borneo, and the Philippines, all of which lead to a series of skirmishes, windfalls, and discoveries, some of the ship's sailors disembark to start a new colony in Oceania, proudly commending their desire for "*English* Women, to raise a new Nation of *English* people; in a Part of the World, that belongs neither to *Europe*, *Asia*, *Africa*, or *America*."[20] At the same time, the narrator describes all these incipient colonialists as "Madagascar Men," a euphemism for pirates and rogues. The desire to explore new lands dominates the narrative. Conquest and settlement come up as possibilities, but are never sustained. As in the second volume of *Robinson Crusoe*, or the bulk of the narrative of *Captain Singleton* (1720), the propensity for rambling overrides all other impulses (p. 176). Whoever goes via the southern hemisphere of the globe "shall never fail to discover new Worlds, new Nations, and new inexhaustible Funds of Wealth and Commerce, such as never were yet known to the Merchants of *Europe*." A colonial imagination anticipates trading surpluses without worrying about the competition. Colonization of new areas becomes a fantasy alternative to actual trade with its existing drawbacks (p. 178).

This newfound globalism was based on a realizable dream of "new inexhaustible Funds of Wealth." Defoe's fixation on "new Worlds" is nowadays described in more prosaic fashion as emerging markets.[21] In the second half of *A New Voyage*, Defoe imagines the creation of a cross-Andean trading route from Baldivia to Camarones that could prove lucrative if developed by venture capitalists. In floating this trial balloon, he was following predecessors such as John Narbrough and Amédée Frézier.[22] However, the project was wishful thinking based on Defoe's study of an erroneously angled map of South America by Herman Moll, which suggested non-existent valleys and rivers. The novel's propaganda is to suggest that the colonial exploitation of these areas lacks a proper follow through. Defoe's energies are focused on boosting the discovery phase of colonial adventure, but the realities of territorial consolidation and expansion were starker. All the same, narratives such as *A New Voyage* demonstrate the planetary links among travel, trade, and colonization. Defoe's fictionalized travel narratives imitate the extensive recording of natural phenomena by actual seamen like William Dampier and Woodes Rogers, who reported to the Royal Society. Defoe acknowledges these connections in *A Plan of the English Commerce*, commending both "the diligent Seamann," and "the adventurous Merchant" (p. 35) as "pushing on Discoveries, planting Colonies, and settling Commerce, even to all Parts of the World" (p. xii). These parallel activities allow the respective parties to egg each other on: "the Planter … fires the Merchant with the Desires of enlarging his Adventures, searching out new Colonies, forming new Adventures, and pushing at new Discoveries for the Encrease of his Trading Advantages" (p. 366). Simply put, the more the colonies, the greater the accumulated trade, and the consequent circulation. Colonies are attractive to Defoe's mercantilism because they were the most efficient way of generating inventory without having to pay for the goods across national boundaries. While remaining part of the national economy, symbiotic relationships obtain among the colonies, which are said to "depend upon one another, as the Belly and the Members" (the *Review*, vol. 1, no. 30, 17 June 1704, 133).

An Essay on the South-Sea Trade defines adventuring as the process of colonial acquisition with commerce as its objective. Defoe doesn't mince words, claiming that the Pacific trade will be enabled when the British "shall, under the Protection, in the Name, and by the Power of Her Majesty, *Seize, Take*, and *Possess*, such Port or Place, or Places, Land, Territory, Country or Dominion, *call it what you please*." This land will be kept for the exclusive use of the British, and keeping "implies Planting, Settling, Inhabiting, Spreading, and all that is usual in such Cases." Colonialism without excuses, and all the ensuing violence against indigenes is at stake. The British will need to establish themselves by force or fraud. The means of that exercise are baldly stated and not even rationalized, and ethical compunctions seem to be in very short supply (p. 39). A global approach to colonies cannot be without the headache of garnering competitive advantage in relation to economic and imperial rivals, no matter what Crusoe might claim about his colonists who are supposedly citizens of the world. Defoe laments that Britain's superciliousness about foreign trade and her inability to organize a reliable supply chain had allowed her European competitors to forge ahead. While the Portuguese laughed at the British traders and the French insulted them, "the *Dutch* come Home Freighted with Gold, Elephants Teeth, and the Rich Goods of the Country; and [the British] come Loaden with the Wretched Accounts of what they could do if they had been supplied, and what they have lost for want of it" (the *Review*, vol. VIII, no. 52, 25 July 1710, 203. See also the *Review*, vol. VII, no. 54, 29 July 1710, 210).

Defoe's imperial aspirations for Britain are not undifferentiated. He discriminates against some regions even as he promotes others. If the South Seas and the Pacific coast of America represented attractive futures for trading and colonization, perhaps not surprisingly, the negative pole of the commercial world for him was Africa. "Mahometan Superstition" is blamed as detrimental to commerce in Africa in *A General History of Trade* (Part II, July, p. 7). Robinson Crusoe's early skirmishes with natives of the African coast and Captain Singleton's long overland trek across the continent yield negative images of African barbarity and primitivism. The *Atlas Maritimus* is even more vehement about the continent, excoriating Africa's lack of agriculture and civilization. Intriguingly, Africa's central geographical location gives it the greatest potential of all continents, by virtue of "a much nearer communication with all the other Parts of the World." Its rivers are easily navigable and if only its people were "qualified for business that understood Trade, and furnish'd with a genius for Improvement, they would be the Medium of an endless Correspondence" (p. 236). However, Africa is deemed to have lost her past glory as the center of all world trade (p. 263). Denigrating adjectives about the inhabitants pile up. "Unpolish'd, vile, and degenerate," Africans are also "brutal, savage, untractable." The indolence in Africa is supposedly worse than that in Spain. Egyptians, deemed more civilized than the rest, are nonetheless "a perfidious, thievish and murdering Race." Blaming the victims, the observer of the slave trade judges Africans as willing to "barter Baubles for the Souls of Men" (p. 237). Yet, the worst result combined with the greatest potential alludes to a history of earlier failed attempts to make Africa the first site of global interconnectivity. The Suez was "the Spot which the *Romans*, as reported, attempted to cut thro', so to join the Mediterranean and the Indian Ocean together; but they could not render it practicable" (p. 238). At the same time, Defoe ferociously defends the Royal African Company monopoly (and his own undisclosed investment in that enterprise), inveighing against the separate traders as interlopers (the *Review*, vol. V, no. 158, 31 March 1709, 629–32). In "A Brief Account ... of the African Trade," his calculation was that a monopoly would lead to cheaper prices of slaves needed for the plantations in the Americas (p. 45).

Defoe's negative views of China and India are tinged with worry about the unequal balance of trade with such nations, as well as mercantilist resentment of the danger that trade for manufactured goods from those countries would drain the English treasury of precious metals such as gold and silver. The bullion and trading profits brought into Europe by the American colonies were being squandered in the East: "all the Trade of *Europe*, he says in *Atlas Maritimus*, is but a Bag with Holes, and that which goes in at the Top runs out at the Bottom" (p. 220). Ultimately, the doctrine of infinite circulation in which goods move to the advantage of all concerned from country to country was beset by anxieties that Britain was losing out by paying in gold and silver. The vast national debt, almost £50 million in 1720, could have contributed to such bullionist concerns.

Adventure fiction

Defoe's late forays into fictional narrative provide further indications of his global perspective. Defoe's fictions are set on a world stage, making his contributions to the history of the novel perhaps even more far-reaching than his economic and political journalism. Defoe composed his fiction, in a sense, as a series of thought-experiments, representing projects as well as projections. Let us consider the geographical coverage of Defoe's major fictions serially, in order to identify their overall scope. By proceeding chronologically, we can discern a "world-picture" that develops cumulatively.

The Life and Strange Surprizing Adventures of Robinson Crusoe of York, Mariner (1719) features Crusoe's departure from England, his Barbary captivity, escape, and eventual success as a Brazilian planter, followed by his shipwreck and long isolation on a Caribbean island, and his eventual return home. Crusoe's Mediterranean and then transatlantic circuit in the original is balanced by an eastward ramble in *Farther Adventures* (1719). The sequel commences with Crusoe going back to the Caribbean, and then on to Madagascar, the Persian Gulf, and the Indian Ocean, and then ending in his overland voyage through China and Tartary to Archangel, from where he returns to England. Defoe's next fiction, *Memoirs of A Cavalier* (1720) takes place a century earlier on the European continent rather than in exotic places. Set during the reign of Swedish king Gustavus Adolphus, the novel features the Cavalier-narrator from Shropshire seeing military action in Vienna and Magdenburgh. This European jaunt is followed immediately by another rest-of-the-world narrative. *The Life, Adventures, and Pyracies, of the Famous*

Captain Singleton (1720) covers both land and sea in one volume, in two neatly composed halves. The first half of the novel includes a remarkable overland trek across Africa after the characters are stranded in Madagascar, and the second half is almost entirely at sea, involving piratical heists in the East Indies. Eventually, Captain Bob and his close friend William Walters return to England with their spoils via Venice, disguised as Armenians. *Serious Reflections during the Life and Surprizing Adventures of Robinson Crusoe* (1720), takes a more contemplative perspective on the preceding descriptions of global travel. "Robinson Crusoe's Preface" retrospectively argues that Crusoe's overseas adventures in the first two volumes are to be taken allegorically, at least in part. But Puritan allegory was always there in good measure in the earlier fictions. The spiritual reflections interrupt and recast the meaning of the global commercial activities pursued by economic- ally motivated planters and pirates.

Following this first phase of masculine fictions, Defoe's next novel turns to a fictional female criminal case history. *The Fortunes and Misfortunes of the Famous Moll Flanders* (1722) tracks an economic individualist over a colo- nial double circuit from London to Virginia and back again, twice. Defoe's turn to a London-based fiction through *Moll Flanders* is continued by his next major fiction, *A Journal of the Plague Year* (1722). The latter is unique, the only novel by Defoe that does not involve international travel. Sharing the chaos of urban life during a major epidemic, the narrator, H. F., is an observer-anthropologist more than a half-century before the time of writing, when Londoners were victims of a contagion that nearly decimated the city. *A Journal of the Plague Year* features the intersection of biomedical and eco- nomic circumstances alongside a religious framework. Published on the heels of this work is a *Bildungsroman, The History and Remarkable Life of the Truly Honourable Col. Jacque* (1722), which several critics have appropri- ately described as a male *Moll Flanders*. A pickpocket like Moll, Jack is also made to follow the colonial circuit, going through multiple spouses and forced travel from London to Virginia before a happy ending.

Following the developing stability of this pattern, we reach the fiction that blows these romances apart, *The Fortunate Mistress* (1724), more commonly known as *Roxana* after the nickname adopted by the female protagonist. *Roxana* has been seen by some as a *roman à thèse* (a novel of ideas) for bourgeois ideology despite its dark and controversial ending.[23] Roxana's rise from kept mistress to independently wealthy proprietor is a primer for emulation with respect to financial management. Of French Huguenot origin, Roxana travels freely between Europe and England. Her affectation, later in the novel, of a Turkish persona, thanks to a pretended Turkish dance learned from an Italian dancing master, intriguingly touches on Middle Eastern sources and interests that are otherwise lacking in Defoe's fictions, except for the brief Barbary captivity in the first volume of *Robinson Crusoe*. However, the spectacular unraveling of Roxana's elaborately crafted identity in the last quarter of the novel points to this novel's deliberate experimentalism. Defoe refuses to stay with a tried and tested pattern, and the world portrayed in his fiction is never straightforward. Allegorical interpretation can be brought to bear on literal-sounding travels, lives, fortunes and misfortunes, and memoirs. The self-aggrandizement made possible for Roxana by the swelling of her capital is suddenly confronted by the self-destructive personal elements of Roxana's family life.

Defoe's last fiction, *A New Voyage Round the World* (1724), entirely lacks the occasional if slapdash interiority tacked on to external actions in most of the others. While *Roxana* features Defoe's deepest, almost abyssal subjective characterization of the dark nightmares of the protagonist, *New Voyage* contains Defoe's flattest portraits of human beings involved in financial, piratical, and colonial adventures where action is almost purely impersonal. The unmapped blankness of the Pacific dominates the first half of this text in the way that the overland expedition of an unmapped African continent was featured in *Captain Singleton*. *Captain Singleton* brings its characters to pirating voyages in the second half, while the characters in *New Voyage* make an overland trek across South America from the Pacific to the Atlantic coast. Defoe also published the first volume of *A Tour thro' the Whole Island of Great Britain* (1724) between *Roxana* and *New Voyage*. It is intriguing that the impulse to describe rural Britain in copious detail in *A Tour* was satisfied entirely under the rubric of a non-fictional survey, within the genre of social history and economic geography, but without any parallel fictional work that explored the English countryside in relation to the city. *Robinson Crusoe*, *Captain Singleton*, and *Memoirs of a Cavalier* take place largely outside England. Most of Defoe's novelistic protagonists originate in England, but they treat the world as their bailiwick. Especially interesting is that Defoe does not feature the English countryside in fictional form – despite what was clearly his deep knowledge of it.

This brief redaction emphasizes the resolutely experimental nature of Defoe's forays into adventure fiction. The global novelist provides multiple perspectives on London, the world at large, various continents, and the transatlantic colonial circuit, even as he appears willfully to avoid treating the English countryside. Defoe's global fictions are intersectional exercises that allow commercial, colonial, and adventuring impulses to collide in the context of large trans-national spaces. When social topography is analyzed, it is in the context of the newly developing urban conglomeration of London (in *Moll Flanders* and *A Journal of the Plague Year*). As he proceeds from colonial to urban circulation, Defoe places the global as the connective tissue between the overseas and the urban, replacing any potential naturalization of the rural in relation to the urban in the context of the nation. This move emphasizes global mercantilist contexts rather than domestic agricultural ones. It is as if Defoe is indicating that the true economic hinterland of eighteenth-century London as metropolis was the world, rather than the immediate countryside. In this regard, Defoe points in the direction of a global transnational realism, one that the English novel ultimately did not end up taking, instead favoring the closed-door domestic fiction that in fact is "an evasion or even an occlusion of the historical realities that were creating much of the wealth and leisure that support the social world depicted in the novel."[24] England's sustaining domestic agriculture is ignored, whereas Crusoe's tobacco cash crops, or Moll's Virginia plantations merit greater fictional representation. Most important, though, are the ways in which Defoe's adventure fictions record exchange functions of agriculture or manufacture or primitive accumulation, made possible through a series of transactions, whether they involve voluntary exchange, theft, or piracy. Furthermore, texts such as *Robinson Crusoe* participate in the genre of science fiction, in that they stage competitive technological rivalry in relation to the perceived superiority in the manufacturing and quality of goods such as the ceramics emanating from Asia.

These deft moves in Defoe's fiction simultaneously denaturalize and defamiliarize any organic-cultural understanding of England or Britain as a nation. Instead, the implicit definition of the nation in Defoe's worldwide context makes it an artificial and constructed entity, rather like English national character in *The True-Born Englishman*. The British nation is decidedly not the economic and political outcome of internal activities alone; rather, it is a retroactive result of a series of global mercantilist and credit-granting frameworks that facilitates and profits from colonial traffic, technological competition, piratical crimes on the high seas, and discovery, exploration, genocide, slavery, and colonization. Defoe's fictions generate a sense of multiple transnational, oceanic and global settings for England, rather than the comforting if false idea of a little island nation constricted by its political boundaries and internal obsessions. Adventure appears to be a way of investigating the global, and its financial and commercial implications. At its outer limit, however, adventure can produce terrible results, which shut down the very idea of the global as an epistemological perspective. As mother hen, Roxana lays and multiplies her golden nest eggs, but her financial rise is literally destroyed by one of her very own biological chickens coming home to roost. In parallel fashion, the globally effective unnamed narrator of *New Voyage* becomes so faceless as to lose all English specificity altogether. The unnamed English captain is an adventurer lacking interiority, even though his cold-bloodedness, like William Walter's in *Captain Singleton*, might well represent the idea of a true-born Englishman as an universal, but more specifically, financial placeholder. The universal man as projected by Defoe's fiction turns out to be coldly calculating economic man. Credit, profit, and class mobility find their home in colonially and globally inflected fictions that appeal to the literary imagination, and that tend to confuse truth, falsehood, creative license, and fictionality.

However, there is still one turn of the screw left regarding these well-documented tendencies that allow commerce, empire, and adventure to collide, interanimate, and progress to another level. The Christian elements in Defoe have often been wheeled into functional affirmations of the affinity between Puritan Christianity and the rise of financial capitalism. This element rings true when we consider the thrift practised by a range of Defoe's characters, and the attitudes recommended in a number of his prescriptive manuals about commerce. In this context, the excessive and unmotivated violence that bubbles over in some of Defoe's fictions is still shocking and explosive. What do we make of those episodes such as Crusoe's hot-blooded massacre of the cannibals in *Robinson Crusoe*, or his destruction of the idol of Cham-chi-thaungu in *Farther Adventures*? Another jaw-dropping episode, but this time of a different, cold-blooded sort of cruelty, occurs in *Captain Singleton*, in the southern hemisphere somewhere between New Guinea, the south-eastern coast of Australia, and Tasmania. When Singleton and his crew land to restock their shipboard supplies, they find out that the natives are hostile and suspicious. The natives keep away from the sailors but shoot arrows at their white flag of truce and at a hunting party. Following some violence that leads to losses on both sides, the sailors find that the natives are barricaded inside a large tree-trunk, a natural obstacle that turns out to be a secret entrance to a larger cavern. With hostilities abated as the natives hide, the confrontation turns into a coldly executed massacre. Relying on the military ingenuity of William Walters, the Quaker, the sailors attack the native garrison over several days with smoke bombs, hand grenades, and other incendiary devices. Captain Bob urges William to give up on the exercise, and the latter acknowledges "that there was nothing but our Curiosity to be gratified in this Attempt ... [but] he would [still] have this Satisfaction of them."[25] Bringing in two barrels of gunpowder from the ship, William decides to kill all the natives, resulting in a charnel-house conclusion to the episode: "we saw what was become of the Garrison of *Indians* too, who had given us all this Trouble; for some of them had no Arms, some no Legs, some no Head, some lay half buried in the Rubbish of the Mine ... and, in short, there was a miserable Havock made of them all."[26]

Adventure is not just about self-aggrandizement through financial motives, but the sadistic pleasure that can come from the wanton destruction of other people and places. It might be possible to read such incidents as expressing an atavistic "Protestant revenge fantasy" or stemming from amoral scientific detachment combined with the Baconian experimental motives discussed earlier, leading to an "Universal Correspondence for the Advancement of Knowledge both Natural and Civil." While such perspectives may help contextualize this episode's shocking violence, our modern sensibilities cannot fully plumb the psychic depths of Defoe's exploration of genocidal violence as also part and parcel of the *topoi* of adventure, commerce, and empire. Perverse cruelty in excess of the profit motive is at stake here, rather than just bourgeois ideology.

Crusoe doesn't flinch from calling for a new "Crusadoe" to convert the heathens and civilize the barbarians at the end of *Serious Reflections*. Defoe's first published (but now lost) text was an attack on the Muslim Ottomans for their invasion of Christian Vienna in 1683. The many modern aspects of adventure are also connected with residual notions of holy war and the extermination of Islam and the heathen. It is important to recognize that these kinds of episodes also participate in Defoe's notion of adventure, well beyond the merely acquisitive motivations behind bourgeois ideology.

NOTES

1. *Defoe's Review*, ed. Arthur Wellesley Secord, 22 vols. (New York: Published for the Facsimile Text Society by Columbia University Press, 1938), vol. III, no. 2 (3 January 1706), 6–7. All further references in parenthesis in the text are to this edition.

2. Herman Moll, *The Compleat Geographer* (London, 1723), n.p.

3. J. A. Downie, "Defoe, Imperialism, and the Travel Books Reconsidered," in *Critical Essays on Daniel Defoe*, ed. Roger Lund, (New York: G. K. Hall, 1997), p. 85.

4. *The Farther Adventures of Robinson Crusoe* (London, 1719), p. 1. All further references in parenthesis in the text are to this edition.

5. *An Essay Upon Projects* (London, 1697), p. 8. All further references in parenthesis in the text are to this edition.

6. *Atlas Maritimus and Commercialis, Or, A General View of the World So Far as Relates to Trade and Navigation* (London, 1728), p. ii. All further references in parenthesis in the text are to this edition.

7. *The Compleat English Gentleman*, ed. Karl D. Bülbring (London: David Nutt, 1890), p. 225. All further references in parenthesis in the text are to this edition.

8. *The True-Born Englishman* (London, 1704), Part I, lines 376–77. All further references in parenthesis in the text are to this edition.

9. Thomas Mun, *England's Treasure By Forraign Trade* (1664; New York: Macmillan, 1895), p. 7. Mun's text was composed around 1630 but first published

by his son in 1664. Adam Smith suggests that Mun's mercantilist doctrine dominated English economic thought until well into the eighteenth century, when Hume and later Smith make the argument for free trade.

10. *A General History of Trade*, Part II (London, 1713), p. 25. All further references in parenthesis in the text are to this edition.

11. *A Brief Account of the Present State of the African Trade* (London, 1713), p. 39. All further references in parenthesis in the text are to this edition.

12. Laura Brown, "Oceans and Floods: Fables of Global Perspective," in *The Global Eighteenth Century*, ed. Felicity A. Nussbaum (Baltimore and London: Johns Hopkins University Press, 2003), p. 110.

13. See R. B. [pseudonym of Nathaniel Crouch], *The English Empire in America* (London, 1685), and John Oldmixon, *The British Empire in America*, 2 vols. (London, 1708), I, xxxvii.

14. *Some Considerations on the Reasonableness and Necessity of Encreasing and Encouraging the Seamen* (London, 1728), p. 13.

15. *A Plan of the English Commerce* (London, 1728), pp. iii, iv, v, vii. All further references in parenthesis in the text are to this edition.

16. *The Manufacturer* no. 1 (Friday, 30 October 1719). All further references in parenthesis in the text are to this edition.

17. John McVeagh, *Tradefull Merchants: The Portrayal of the Capitalist in Literature* (London: Routledge and Kegan Paul, 1981), p. 53.

18. Leslie Stephen, "Defoe's Novels," *Hours In A Library* (London: Smith and Elder, 1909), I, 63.

19. *An Essay on the South-Sea Trade* (London, 1712), 31. All further references in parenthesis in the text are to this edition.

20. *A New Voyage Round the World* (London, 1724), vol. I, 175. All further references in parenthesis in the text are to this edition.

21. For an interesting discussion of the contours of these fantasies, see Robert Markley, " 'So Inexhaustible A Treasure of Gold': Defoe, Capitalism, and the Romance of the South Seas," *Eighteenth-Century Life*, 18.3 (November 1994), 114–28.

22. See Amédée Frézier, *A Voyage to the South-Sea and Along the Coast of Chili and Peru* (London, 1717).

23. See for instance, Bram Dijkstra, *Defoe and Economics: The Fortunes of Roxana in the History of Interpretation* (Basingstoke: Macmillan, 1987), n. 35.

24. John Richetti, *The Life of Daniel Defoe* (Oxford: Blackwell, 2005), p. 217.

25. *Captain Singleton*, ed. Shiv K. Kumar (Oxford and New York: Oxford University Press, 1990), p. 213.

26. *Captain Singleton*, pp. 213–14. Martin Green suggests that, "explosions producing human debris are a motif in much adventure fiction," and indeed, Defoe himself was fascinated by explosion throughout his life. Martin Green, *Dreams of Adventure, Deeds of Empire* (New York: Basic Books, 1979), p. 86.

4

HAL GLADFELDER

Defoe and criminal fiction

On the morning of his death, the celebrated housebreaker and prison escape artist John Sheppard bequeathed his life story to the press. According to one source, at the scene of his impending execution Sheppard "sent for Mr. *Applebee*, a printer, into the Cart, and, in view of several thousands of People, delivered to him a Pamphlet, entitled, *A Narrative of all his Robberies and Escapes*."[1] Then, according to a later account, Sheppard "said in a loud clear voice that this was his authentic confession and that he wished Mr. Applebee to print it for him. It was an effective advertisement. That night thousands of copies of the pamphlet were sold for a shilling in the streets."[2] The pamphlet in question, *A Narrative of all the Robberies, Escapes, &c. of John Sheppard*, was attributed to Daniel Defoe by the Victorian Defoe connoisseur William Lee in 1869, and in fact Lee added an interesting twist to the tale: the man to whom Sheppard handed his manuscript was not Applebee at all but an imposter – none other than Defoe himself.[3]

Lee devised an elaborate story of deceit to place Defoe at the scene of Sheppard's death. He held that Defoe, impersonating Applebee (with Applebee's consent), had visited Sheppard in prison to obtain his life story firsthand, and that Sheppard had thus been tricked into telling that story to an author he imagined, if there's any truth to Lee's hypothesis, to be somebody else. As Applebee was the leading publisher of criminal lives in the period, perhaps Defoe meant to flatter Sheppard's vanity by pretending that the great man himself took a personal interest in his case. Or perhaps he simply took pleasure in impersonation. Both as an author and as a political agent, Defoe made the assumption of false or alternate identities the very essence of his working method, and this propensity connects him to the protagonists of his major criminal fictions: *Moll Flanders*, *Colonel Jack*, *Roxana*, and, as I will suggest, *Robinson Crusoe*. While Lee's evidence for Defoe's dramatic impersonation of Applebee at the scaffold is tenuous, anonymity and disguise – the concealment and falsification of his own authorial name – were integral to Defoe's manner of writing. And the effect of his imitation of the speech of others is to induce us as readers to identify with alien subjectivities, to judge the degree of our own likeness to the crew of outcasts, adventurers, and delinquents that populate his fiction.

In his work of the 1720s, Defoe exhibits an uneasy mixture of fascination and panic in the face of what was widely felt to be a sharp and widespread increase in levels of violent crime, especially in London. Such a divided response to the threat of crime may have been commonplace, but it takes an aggravated form in Defoe's writing because of his assumption of distinct and often rhetorically extremist personae. In some texts, such as the 1724 *Great Law of Subordination Consider'd*, crime is seen to originate in a breakdown of customary relations of class deference: "when once Servants are brought to contemn the Persons and Authority of their Masters, or Mistresses, or Employers, they soon come to despise their Interests; and at last to break into their Property; and thus they become Thieves, in a manner insensible."[4] The persona Defoe adopts here is that of a blustering patrician, given to absurd claims ("In *England*," he writes earlier in the tract, "the Poor govern, and the Rich submit"), and nervously protective of his own vulnerable authority (*The Great Law of Subordination*, p. 105). By contrast, in *Roxana*, published just three weeks earlier, murderous violence is seen to arise from "a secret Hell within," the effect of guilt that can be neither acknowledged nor expunged because of the heroine's relentless desire to maintain her social respectability.[5] Roxana herself is haunted by bloody apparitions and evil spirits, projections of her own tormented psyche, while in the fiction bearing *her* name, Moll Flanders vacillates between blaming her fall into crime on the lack of provision for the poor and laying it to the account of devils whispering at her ear. Defoe had no overarching or unifying theory of crime; rather, his criminal texts move between the social and the subjective, between crime as a threat to political and domestic order and crime as the product of ill-suppressed longings and terrors, evincing an especially strong interest in the inward experience of transgressive women and children. In the remainder of this essay I want to trace the impact on Defoe's work of the contemporary social climate as well as the popular tradition of criminal narrative from the seventeenth and early eighteenth centuries, and then to explore his engagement with criminal impulses and acts in the longer fictions for which he is best known. Focusing his attention on the experience (both inward and in the world) of characters marked by circumstances and their own desires as deviant, and drawing us as readers into complicity with them, Defoe exposes the delinquency at the heart of the modern individualist subject.

London in the 1720s seemed, to contemporaries, to be in the grip of a crime wave; and Defoe has been called its "mythologist."[6] The label is telling because it leaves open the question of whether, or in what sense, the crime wave was real. The historian John Beattie has written that "a great deal of concern was expressed through the 1720s in pamphlets and in the press and by the authorities about the extent of crime in the capital."[7] But from the surviving court records it is impossible to know whether this reflected an increase in the rate of prosecution – which might or might not reflect the real crime rate – or to what extent this anxiety was a product of the press itself. "Even a small number of incidents reported in the press," as Beattie notes, "can create an impression of extreme danger" (p. 218). Beattie writes that later in the century, when court records are more complete, "the bulk of the evidence seems to me to suggest that when prosecutions declined during wars it was because the numbers of offenses actually had gone down ... and that when they rose with the peace it was because the number of offenses had increased" (p. 218). My concern, however, is with the ways in which crime was represented and explained, rather than with the raw numbers.

Some at the time recognized that sensational reporting could play havoc with the truth, as is evident in the anonymous 1726 *Lives of Six Notorious Street Robbers*, ascribed to Defoe by James Crossley. The author of that text complains that

> on a sudden we found street-robberies became the common practice, conversation was full of the variety of them, the newspapers had them every day, and sometimes more than were ever committed; and those that were committed were set off by the invention of the writers, with so many particulars, and so many more than were ever heard of by the persons robbed, that made the facts be matter of entertainment, and either pleasant or formidable, as the authors thought fit.[8]

This is not to deny that street robberies were a real problem, or that in the wake of the military demobilization of 1713 and the financial crash of 1720 there may have been a surge in the incidence of economically motivated crime; rather, the author's complaint pertains to the potential dangers of representation itself. If crime is made "matter of entertainment," this might mean readers are induced to laugh off a real problem or, conversely, that they are so bombarded with exaggerated scenes of street violence they fear to go out. Either way, such fictional (or fictionalized) accounts influenced readers' perceptions of the social world, and so carried political and psychological implications. Consider this passage from a text published during an earlier crime wave, in the 1670s:

> Notwithstanding the severity of our wholesome Laws, and vigilancy of Magistrates against Robbers and Highway-men, 'tis too notorious that the Roads are almost perpetually infested with them; especially of late, Tidings daily arriving from several parts of fresh Mischiefs committed in that kind: and

having done their wicked Exploits, they commonly retire to, and lurk up and down in this great and populous City, undoubtedly the best Forest for such Beasts of Prey to shelter in.[9]

The intended effect of such rhetoric is to create or reinforce a climate of fear and uncertainty, so that readers who live in "this great and populous City" no longer feel confident of their safety, but are driven to seek the protection of ever more vigilant magistrates and ever more severe laws. Those who rob are not desperate or poor but wicked, not pitiable fellow creatures but savage beasts of prey: dehumanizing the outlaw, the pamphlet's author denies any kinship with or responsibility for the vermin who infest our roads and lurk up and down in our city.

Not all those who wrote on crime adopted such a severe stance. Instead, criminal literature of the seventeenth and early eighteenth centuries was marked by considerable ideological diversity and psychological variety, even if not always intentionally. Amidst the various criminal genres that proliferated in the period – from picaresque romps to officially sanctioned trial reports, from the "last dying speeches" of the condemned at the gallows to broadsides reporting bloody murders – a vast range of competing explanations for and political responses to crime can be found, articulated in an equally vast range of real or imagined voices. Some genres, such as the *Accounts* written by the Ordinary (chaplain) of Newgate prison of the final days of the condemned, concluding with the prisoner's penitent last words at the gallows, aimed to reinforce the political and moral legitimacy of the law by dramatizing the criminal's grateful endorsement of the verdict against him; but in practice the message was often not so straightforward, as the very public nature of the prisoner's last speech provided an opportunity for resistance and protest.[10] There were sometimes several competing versions of the convict's life in circulation, each one proclaiming its authenticity, and even in the most authoritarian versions the presumed malefactor might contest official readings of his or her life history, soliciting the reader's sympathy or protesting against legal injustice. Just as, at the scene of execution, the crowd of spectators often demonstrated, even violently, their support for the condemned and their rage against the executioners, so were readers often encouraged or at least allowed to sympathize with the outlaw. In one of the several pamphlets chronicling John Sheppard's prison-escape exploits, for instance – a work often (if debatably) attributed to Defoe – the author validates the account's authenticity by declaring that it is based on the testimony of "divers Justices of the Peace," the shopkeepers Sheppard robbed, and "the principal Officers of *Newgate* and *New Prison*," as well as "the Confession of *Sheppard* made to the Rev. Mr. *Wagstaff*, who officiated for the Ordinary of Newgate."[11] Yet despite these ideologically unimpeachable sources, the mocking, dissident voice of Sheppard himself comes increasingly to dominate the text, so that the final pages are given over to his written and spoken quips. When the Reverend Mr. Wagstaff comes to offer him Christian counsel and pump him for information (as a sign of genuine repentance), Sheppard "would passionately, and with a Motion of striking, say *ask me no such Questions, one* File's *worth all the* Bibles *in the World.*"[12] The text produces a split effect: at the same time enjoining its readers (addressed as "the Citizens of *London* and *Westminster*") to help "bring to Justice this notorious Offender," and inciting them to look on with wonder and amusement at the hero's daring escapes and witty ripostes.

This internally conflicted response to the simultaneous threat and allure of criminal lives runs through all the genres of seventeenth- and eighteenth-century crime writing, from the ghost-written autobiographies of penitent or impenitent rogues to sermonizing histories of "God's Revenge, against the Crying, and Execrable Sinne of Murther" (the title of a 1621 collection by John Reynolds, which had a powerful influence on authors through the end of the eighteenth century).[13] Whether they aimed to entertain their readers or to terrorize them into lawful conduct – or, often, both at once – authors played on a sense of affinity between reader and outlaw that was grounded in Christian doctrine as well as an emergent secular individualism. If "crimes were sins, yet sinning was universal," as Cynthia Herrup suggests, then "the threat of criminality was both internal and external; the criminal could not be defined simply as something alien and other."[14] At the same time, the criminal might be understood as the perfect representative of a newly dominant ideology of the individual: one who acts on impulse to get ahead at any cost, to win status, property, sex, money, or power over similarly acquisitive rivals. Even though these Christian and capitalist mentalities may be incompatible, both contributed to shaping the preconceptions authors brought to the subject of crime, and each in different ways invited readers to regard the outlaw as a figure in whom they could see themselves: "observing, and seeing herein, as in a Christall mirrour, the variety of the Devills temptations, and the allurements of sinne."[15]

No author was more aware of the potential dangers of this sort of identification than Defoe, and no one exploited its ambiguities more cunningly. In his work Defoe articulates a complex, ironic, morally conflicted understanding of the self as inescapably transgressive, which was already implicit in much criminal writing of the period. The avowed aim is that the reader will recognize his own faults and urges in the "Christall" or criminal "mirrour" of Defoe's protagonists and draw the relevant moral lesson from that recognition. As Colonel Jack puts it at the end of his text: "I recommend it to all that read this Story, that when they find their Lives come up in any degree to any Similitude of Cases, they will enquire by me, and ask themselves, Is not this the time to Repent? perhaps the Answer may touch them."[16]

Or perhaps, as Defoe complains time and again, it may not. Readers, he laments, seem perversely inclined to relish the wickedness against which the narrative means to sound a warning. "Vitious Readers," he asserts in the preface to *Moll Flanders*, will always find pretexts to turn virtuous texts to their own ends. "It is suggested," he writes, that "there cannot be the same Life, the same Brightness and Beauty, in relating the penitent Part, as is in the criminal Part: If there is any Truth in that Suggestion, I must be allow'd to say, 'tis because there is not the same taste and relish in the Reading, and indeed it is too true that the difference lyes not in the real worth of the Subject so much as in the Gust and Palate of the Reader."[17] In another work, *Conjugal Lewdness; Or, Matrimonial Whoredom* (1727), Defoe declares that "if a vicious Mind hears the Vice reproved, and forms pleasing Ideas of the Crime ... the fault is in the Depravity of the Mind, not in the needful and just Reprover."[18] Such readerly depravity, however, is the basis for identification with the pre-penitent outlaw; and this identification, as I have suggested, is indispensable to Defoe's moral aims of self-recognition and self-reproof.

Yet the moral implications of Defoe's criminal fictions are really not as clear-cut as he maintains in their anxious, defensive prefaces. In practice, he continually smudges and obscures the boundaries separating licit from illicit, reckless criminal from respectable man (or woman) of business. For example, in the 1728 crime-prevention tracts *Augusta Triumphans* and *Second Thoughts Are Best* Defoe presents himself (under the pseudonym Andrew Moreton) as a spokesman for the law-abiding and prosperous, concerned with the threat posed by the outlaw poor to their security and comfort. As Michael Shinagel has argued, in these works Defoe appears "anxious to discover ways of curtailing the crime rate and alerting the citizens of London on how to protect themselves and their property" – a stance in keeping with the ideological aims of such major works as *The Compleat English Tradesman* (1726), which celebrates "the Dignity and Honour of Trade."[19] Yet even in this latter work, Defoe observes that "Trade is almost universally founded upon Crime," and so the moral gulf that ostensibly separates economic virtue from economic predation turns out to be a self-serving lie on the part of the propertied.[20] *All* forms of individualist self-assertion are transgressive: that is, all are marked by wilful deviation from prescribed social norms or passive accommodation to one's "station." For tradesman and thief alike, success depends on a willingness to risk everything and to cut oneself loose from the stultifying comforts of the familiar – a willingness to defy the law, whether this be the law of the father, of the state, or of divine authority.

Nowhere is this virtual compulsion to transgress more feelingly evoked than in the first of Defoe's fictions, *Robinson Crusoe*. Crusoe is not, of course, in legal terms an outlaw, but part of my argument here is that neither Defoe nor his narrators really draws a distinction between crime and other sorts of adventurism and rebellion – whether defiance of parental or patriarchal authority, or putting to sea in search of "immense Treasure" (*Colonel Jack*, p. 296). All of these are expressions of a spirit of restlessness and discontent, an unquiet will, which for Defoe was at once sinful and necessary to life itself – and for which, accordingly, his protagonists are at once punished and rewarded. Take, for example, the opening pages of *Crusoe*, in which the young Robinson wrestles with his own "rambling Thoughts," trying to restrain these in obedience to his father's injunctions to rest content with "a Life of Ease and Pleasure" in "the middle State, or what might be called the upper Station of *Low Life*."[21] In this station, his "wise and grave" father declares, one is "not expos'd to so many Vicissitudes as the higher or lower Part of Mankind"; instead, "this way Men went silently and smoothly thro' the World, and comfortably out of it" (pp. 4, 5). Such a life, of course, is devoid not only of distress but also of narrative interest: to go silently and smoothly through the world is the antithesis of a *novelistic* career, which depends (as the word itself suggests) on novelty, on vicissitude, conflict, opposition, chance, aspiration, loss, and danger. But for Robinson, despite his resolution "to settle at home according to my Father's Desire" (p. 6), an irresistible impulse pulls him away from home and pushes him, against his own conscience and reason, into open if unintended war against parental and divine authority. "I would be satisfied," he writes, "with nothing but going to Sea, and my Inclination to this led me so strongly against the Will, nay the Commands of my Father" that finding himself one day, as if by chance, at a port, he boards a ship bound for London "without asking God's Blessing, or my Father's" (pp. 3, 7). A classic generational conflict, the rebellion of son against father, is replayed in these opening pages, and the pairing of father and god as blessing-givers evokes a pattern that stretches back in the Judeo-Christian tradition to the series of rebellious sons in Genesis – to Jacob, Cain, Adam. Even in his own family, Robinson is not the first: both his elder brothers were prompted by "young Desires" (p. 6) to leave home, one to die in war and one to disappear; but the family pattern had already been set by their father, who as we learn in the novel's first paragraph is "a Foreigner of *Bremen*" (p. 3) who abandoned his own "Father's House and [his] Native Country" (p. 4) in search of fortune. So while he warns his third son that "it was for Men of desperate Fortunes on one Hand, or of aspiring, superior

Fortunes on the other, who went abroad upon Adventures, to risk by Enterprize, and make themselves famous in Undertakings of a Nature out of the common Road" (p. 4), Kreutznaer (for such is their real name) unwittingly grounds his son's transgression in a history of sins against the father, which is also the history of heroic adventure.

But Robinson's filial crime is not just a re-enactment of family and universal history: it is also the expression or symptom of a specifically modern form of restlessness felt by all of Defoe's protagonists, a by-product of the new world of colonial expansion and capitalist venture. The "Undertakings of a Nature out of the common Road" by which Robinson will assert his autonomy and freedom as a subject are tied to the slave and tobacco trades of the mid-seventeenth century: indeed by his own account he is something of a pioneer in urging his fellow plantation owners in Brazil, where he first establishes his fortune, to increase the numbers of slaves imported from Africa in defiance of restrictions imposed by "the Kings of *Spain* and *Portugal*" (p. 39). The well-financed voyage to buy and then smuggle into Brazil a shipload of slaves, which leads directly to Crusoe's shipwreck and solitary confinement to his island, is thus piratical, a breach of the colonial law to which he is subject, just as his first setting foot on a ship was "a Breach of my Duty to God and my Father" (p. 8). And he is punished – repeatedly, providentially – for his crimes: on his first short sea voyage his ship is twice assailed by storms and ultimately destroyed; on an early trading voyage he is seized by Moroccan pirates and enslaved; on his slaving expedition he is shipwrecked. But he is just as providentially and extravagantly rewarded, as he tirelessly reminds us: earning £300 from a stock of £40 worth of "Toys and Trifles" (p. 17) on his first trading voyage; selling his faithful fellow slave Xury and two animal skins for enough gold to start a plantation (pp. 33–34); ending his shipwreck years with £5,000 "in Money" and "an Estate" of "above a thousand Pounds a Year" (p. 285), not to mention a flourishing island colony of his own. Robinson has the good luck, and the bad luck, too, to live in a world where fortunes could be made from colonial, speculative ventures, for if this allows him to become unimaginably rich by the novel's end, it also means he can never be satisfied with his state, but is endlessly driven by discontent.[22]

The pattern of conflict Defoe establishes in the opening pages of *Robinson Crusoe* between benevolent authority and rebellious energy was a staple of criminal biographies of the period, and in its focus on the adolescent defiance of authority this work adheres more closely to the conventions of criminal biography than such later fictions as *Moll Flanders* or *Colonel Jack*, even though these are more obviously concerned with crime as such. Crusoe's "rambling Thoughts" affiliate him with a recurrent figure in criminal biography of the period, the rebellious apprentice, whose actions, according to

John Richetti, embody "furtive and unnatural longings for disruptive revolt" which the biographies' intended readers are presumed at least potentially to share.[23] In the 1725 *True and Genuine Account of the Life and Actions of the Late Jonathan Wild* (often, and I think plausibly, attributed to Defoe), the criminal subject, who would one day become the notorious "Thief-Taker General" of Great Britain, is first seen as a young man, the son of "Honest and Industrious People," educated in a manner "suitable to his Father's Circumstances" before being apprenticed, by his father, to "a Hardware Man."[24] Although, as his biographer writes, he "very honestly work'd for some time at his Trade" of buckle-making, Wild has an aspiring spirit: "his Thoughts, *as he said*, being above his Trade, tho' at that time he had no Tast of the Life he afterwards led, yet he grew uneasie in the Country, was sick of his Work, and in short, after a few Years came away to *London*, to see if he could get into any Business there" (p. 237). There is no suggestion of financial hardship; instead, Wild's dissatisfaction is portrayed as a kind of sickness or uneasiness arising from the gulf between his low trade and his loftier thoughts. Once in London, he applies himself desultorily to his trade, but he is "not enclin'd to sit very close to his Work" (p. 237), and so falls into debt and jail. Crusoe, too, before sailing away "continued obstinately deaf to all Proposals of settling to Business" (p. 7), not, as his later life shows, out of indolence, but wanderlust. Both Crusoe and Wild are in fact prodigiously energetic, as are Moll and Colonel Jack, but all of them bridle at the dullness and constraint of workaday life, and at any form of subservience or confinement.

Wild soon becomes a ruthless and repressive master himself, a corrupter of "poor wretched Creatures, like himself; who he having first led them on in the Road of Crime for several Years, as long as they would be subservient to him, and put all their Purchase into his Hands, abandon'd as soon as they offer'd to set up for themselves, and leaving them to the mercy of the Government, made himself the Instrument of their Destruction" (p. 264). In his capacity as crime boss, Wild fences the goods he organizes his underlings to steal, but at the same time he acts the part of public servant, turning in those thieves who rebel against his authority for the £40 blood money paid out by the state. In this respect he is an extreme or grotesque version of Crusoe and Colonel Jack, both of whom undergo similar reversals, from anti-paternal rebel to paternalist master, slave to slave owner. But if the author of the *True and Genuine Account* deplores the mature Wild's inhumanity, he treats his youthful discontent and striving sympathetically: who would want to settle for a life of buckle-making in the country? And yet his rebellion has also to be punished. All Defoe's criminal fictions are charged with this same internally conflicted energy, at once sharing in their protagonists' restive ambition and condemning their disruptive insubordination. But the forms that their individual life histories take, and the moral implications of those lives, are strikingly diverse.

Moll Flanders and *Colonel Jack* were published eleven months apart in 1722 and together constitute a kind of experiment in narrative voice: what happens when the same material is presented from the perspectives of a female and a male narrator? Both Moll and Jack are orphans; marry five times; turn to crime because (at first) of poverty; are at one time wrongly arrested (though guilty of other crimes); are transported as indentured servants to America; become rich plantation owners in their turn; profit (in different ways) from the advice of a teacher (Moll's Governess, Jack's Tutor); reunite after many years with a lost spouse, with whom they live out their last days; report, in their texts' final sentence, their return to London. Both aspire to a state of gentility (Moll to be a gentlewoman like others she sees as a girl, Jack to be the gentleman he's told he is by birth) and both achieve this longed-for state, so that their tales, for all their low-life harshness, also offer the gratification of romance. Yet each of these plot elements occupies a very different place in the respective histories, the moral and social progress, of the two protagonists. The criminal phases of each character's life, for example, share many specific details of incident and setting, but practically and imaginatively Moll and Jack *experience* criminality in almost contrary ways. The guileless street urchin Jack is ignorant of money or property and thus of any notion of what crime means: on his first outing as partner to the pickpocket Will, when they come to divide the spoils, Jack asks, "*must we have it all? we have it! says [Will], who should have it? Why says I, must the Man have none of it again that lost it*"; which prompts this from Will: "He Laught at me, you are but a little Boy *says he*, that's true, but I thought you had not been such a Child neither" (p. 21). As he is inducted into the criminal trade, Jack gains skills but never picks up "the hardness, and wickedness of the Company I kept" (p. 60), and when first brought face to face with the agony his actions cause, he resolves to give over thieving for good. While he later expresses remorse for "the Wickedness of my younger Years" (p. 119), Jack's is a relatively straightforward progress from ignorance to knowledge, so that when the wealth he acquired as a thief is all lost in a shipwreck, he is glad: "for I look'd on it as none of mine, and that it would be fire in my Flax if I should mingle it with what I had now, which was honestly come by" (p. 157). His eventual gentility is not defiled by crime.

Moll's moral consciousness, by contrast, is both more complex and more opaque, as much to herself as to us. When she falls into crime she is a fifty-year-old widow with two young children to feed, impelled to her first theft by a mixture of desperation and fatality as she finds herself involuntarily repeating her mother's life history. Moll is born to crime, her mother having given birth to her in Newgate prison while awaiting execution (her death sentence later commuted to transportation to Virginia). When, at sixty, Moll is arrested and taken back to Newgate, she calls it "that horrid Place! ... the Place where my Mother suffered so deeply, where I was brought into the World, and from whence I expected no Redemption, but by an infamous Death: To conclude, the Place that had so long expected me, and which with so much Art and Success I had so long avoided" (p. 273). Yet despite her low birth in prison, and her complaint about the lack of provision for the children of criminals in the form of a "*House* of *Orphans*, where they are Bred up, Cloath'd, Fed, Taught, and when fit to go out, are plac'd out to Trades, or to Services, so as to be well able to provide for themselves by an honest industrious Behavior" (p. 8), Moll actually receives all the benefits of such a provision without the institutional miseries Dickens would convey a century later in the workhouse of *Oliver Twist* (1837), and seems to be set on a wholly different course of life from her mother's.

Brought up by "a very sober pious Woman" in Colchester, Moll is indeed, as she writes, "Bred up" to go into service, but the prospect terrifies her, "for I had a thorough Aversion to going to Service, as they call'd it, that is to be a Servant" (p. 10). Moll's aversion to "that terrible Bug-bear *going to Service*" (p. 13), like Robinson's to the middle state or Wild's to buckle-making, is the first sign of a more general discontent with her station: for if at first she only aspires "to be able to get my Bread by my own Work" (p. 13), a week spent at a local Lady's house gives her "such a Tast of Genteel living ... that I was not so easie in my old Quarters as I us'd to be, and I thought it was fine to be a Gentlewoman indeed" (p. 16). The term "Gentlewoman," in fact, runs as a leitmotif through the novel's early scenes, signalling Moll's developing consciousness of her unstable (for good and for ill) social position, which is the source of both her vulnerability and her freedom. Her first childish understanding of the term is of a woman who gains an independent living by work; but when she points to an example of what she means, a woman who mends ladies' lace caps, her guardian warns that she "may soon be such a Gentlewoman as that, for she is a Person of ill Fame, and has had two or three Bastards" (p. 14). The warning means nothing to Moll at the time, but it serves as both an ironic foreshadowing of her later sexual transgressions and an indirect comment on the difficulty, for women, of ever gaining an independent life. For in due course, at seventeen, she is seduced by the elder son of the genteel family with whom she now resides, and so enters into a series of relationships with men (some marital, some not; but the distinction is flimsy anyway, since most of her five marriages are simultaneous) whose main object is to secure a social identity above the criminal taint and insecurity of her birthright.

Even her love for the elder brother in the house at Colchester, which she presents as the most sexually and emotionally fervid of all her amours, is fired more by gold than eros, or rather by the erotic glamour of gold itself, as when he gives her, at their first tryst, a silk purse containing a hundred guineas: "My Colour came, and went, at the Sight of the Purse, and with the fire of his Proposal together; so that I could not say a Word, and he easily perceiv'd it; so putting the Purse into my Bosom, I made no more Resistance to him, but let him do just what he pleas'd; and as often as he pleased" (pp. 28–29). Moll berates herself for being a whore, but her narrative suggests that this is not so much a case of moral turpitude as the necessary consequence of the structure of heterosexual relationships in the period (and perhaps not only in that period), embodied in that common but revealing phrase, the marriage market. As one of her lover's sisters notes, "the Market is against our Sex just now; and if a Woman have Beauty, Birth, Breeding, Wit, Sense, Manners, Modesty, and all these to an Extream; yet if she have not Money, she's no Body, she had as good want them all, for nothing but Money now recommends a Woman; the Men play the Game all into their own Hands" (p. 20). This "Game" is the one Defoe called "Matrimonial Whoredom" in a later work, by which he means not just the sale of sex for money but the marketing of the self in exchange for social or financial gain. "Marriages," Moll writes when she comes to London, "were here the Consequences of politick Schemes, for forming Interests, and carrying on Business, and ... Love had no Share, or but very little in the Matter" (p. 67). She and the other women she meets have been terrorized by "the fear of not being Marry'd at all, and of that frightful State of Life, call'd *an old Maid*" (p. 75) into accepting a state of dependency in relation to men, but even when she recognizes this she can only try to raise her value on the market, rather than take herself off it, for she sees herself as what the market ideology constructs women to be: an available commodity. While "Men can be their own Advisers, and their own Directors," a Woman alone "is just like a Bag of Money, or a Jewel dropt on the Highway, which is a Prey to the next Comer; if a Man of Virtue and upright Principles happens to find it, he will have it cried, and the Owner may come to hear of it again; but how many times shall such a thing fall into Hands that will make no scruple of seizing it for their own" (p. 128). It is hard to imagine a more desolate image of the condition of women under an emerging capitalism: "Bag[s] of Money" that more or less scrupulous men can own, advertise, or steal. And it is all the more desolate for the underlying recognition that her relationships with men, through which she aimed to achieve a degree of social and financial security, have only made her status more insecure, as, for example, when her fifth husband goes bust, dies of grief, and leaves her with no money and two children. It is only when she ventures forth alone into the London streets, prompted by poverty and a "diligent Devil" (p. 199) to seek out other people's bags of money to steal, that she finds her real calling, and wins a measure of autonomy and even delight in her own resourcefulness and skill.

Not that crime is without its own forms of insecurity. Moll is continually tormented by the fear of being caught, even when she knows herself to be out of danger; and there are practical issues as well, such as how to dispose of the goods – bolts of fabric, jewellery, silver plate – she has stolen. The pages in which she recounts her exploits as pickpocket and thief are dense with the sort of detail that is only very rarely found in criminal biographies or trial reports of the period, as when, after her first, opportunistic theft "at an Apothecary's Shop in *Leadenhall-street*," Moll writes,

> When I went away I had no Heart to run, or scarce to mend my pace; I cross'd the Street indeed, and went down the first turning I came to, and I think it was a Street that went thro' into *Fenchurch-street*, from thence I cross'd and turn'd thro' so many ways and turnings that I could never tell which way it was, nor where I went, for I felt not the Ground, I stept on, and the farther I was out of Danger, the faster I went, till tyr'd and out of Breath, I was forc'd to sit down on a little Bench at a Door, and then I began to recover, and found I was got into *Thames-street* near *Billingsgate*. (p. 192)

There are a number of similar passages elsewhere in *Moll* and *Colonel Jack*, involving an excess of topographical detail whose effect is both to locate events in a precise, recognizable public space – and thus to reinforce the text's verisimilitude – and to evoke the protagonist's state of mind or soul in an almost allegorical way. Here the tortuous twists and turns imitate Moll's own distracted, fearful, desperate mood, her sense of physical and moral *lostness* or unfamiliarity, just as the mazelike, breathless construction of the sentence itself captures the adrenaline rush of her first, panicky getaway from the scene of a crime. This imaginative fusion of inner and outer worlds – projecting his narrator's psychic anguish onto a detailed map of the city – is characteristic of Defoe's criminal fictions, and while it owes something to the documentary realism of legal depositions and newspaper reports, his writing goes much further than anything to be found in these forms, piling up details in "discordant profusion" and registering the disorienting rush of his characters' sensations. In this way Defoe is able to both create "the effect of the real," in Roland Barthes's phrase, and solicit our readerly complicity with Moll's (or Jack's, or Roxana's) wayward thoughts.[25]

In the course of her ten-year career as a criminal, Moll vacillates between feelings of horror and remorse, on the one hand, and pride in her reputation as "the greatest Artist of my time" (p. 214), on the other. Her greatest satisfaction derives from her independence: "for I was seldom in any Danger when I was by my self, or if I was, I got out of it with more Dexterity than when I was entangled with the dull Measures of other People … for tho' I had as much Courage to venture as any of them, yet I used more caution before I undertook a thing, and had more Presence of Mind when I was to bring my self off " (p. 220). Her boasting is a sign of vanity, of course, and so far sinful, but the autonomy, energy, and bravado she exhibits in her "Adventures" (p. 195) are plainly traits Defoe admires. Moll is most fully alive, most fully herself, when disentangled from "the dull Measures of other People"; amidst the stir and tumult of London she achieves a degree of emotional isolation almost as complete as Robinson's on his island. She does have an adviser and accomplice, whom she calls her "necessary Woman" (p. 198) or Governess, but while there are glimmers of affection between them, their relationship is based on a severely pragmatic calculation of benefits and risks, as Moll notes when she reports her Governess's reaction to the hanging of another criminal:

> [she] was for a while really concern'd for the Misfortune of my Comerade that had been hang'd, and who it seems knew enough of my Governess to have sent her the same way, and which made her very uneasy … It is true, that when she was gone, and had not open'd her Mouth to tell what she knew, my Governess was easy as to that Point, and perhaps glad she was hang'd … But on the other Hand, the loss of her, and the Sense of her Kindness in not making her Market of what she knew, mov'd my Governess to Mourn very sincerely for her: I comforted her as well as I cou'd, and she in return harden'd me to Merit more completely the same Fate. (pp. 207–8)[26]

Moll does not comment on the glaring ironies of this passage – the juxtaposition, for one, of "perhaps glad she was hang'd" and "mov'd … to Mourn very sincerely" – presumably because she takes it for granted that kind thoughts and fellow feeling, no matter how sincere, cannot be allowed to obscure the principle of self-interest. Moll's avoidance of entanglements is in part a necessary, self-protective response to the dangers of the criminal milieu, as Ian Watt has observed, and this would have been especially so in Defoe's time, when, in the absence of a regular police force, law enforcement depended on a system of betrayals and rewards (*Rise of the Novel*, p. 111). But it also exemplifies a quality common to all of Defoe's protagonists, which lies at the heart of his conception of the pleasures and costs of individualist self-assertion: an irremediable sense of apartness which is, for better and for worse, the corollary to his characters' restless pursuit of "a little more, and a little more" (p. 207). Just as Moll's Governess mourns very sincerely yet is glad her comrade's death has put her out of danger, so Robinson promises the slave boy Xury "if you will be faithful to me I'll make you a great Man"

(p. 23) only to sell him back into slavery ten pages later. He invests the profit in a Brazilian plantation that will make him rich, and only regrets Xury's loss when he finds he needs help with the harvest. The point is not, or not only, that these are a parcel of greedy hypocrites but that the individualist spirit they each embody tends, in its pure and most enterprising form, to set the self against all others. Crime, of the thieving and shoplifting sort in which Moll and Colonel Jack engage, is wicked, and frays the social fabric, but is no more wicked in its motives and no more disruptive in its effects than the self-interested fortune-hunting and status-seeking by which all Defoe's protagonists, from tradesman to slave-dealer to courtesan to wife, claw their way to comfort.

Unfortunately, for all their respectability and riches, they are never really comfortable. Returned to England after thirty-five years away, aging, married, and rich, Robinson feels a gnawing "Inclination to go Abroad" that can only be deferred, not denied: the moment his unnamed, unmourned wife has died, he sails off with his nephew as "a private Trader to the *East Indies*," promising "some very surprizing Incidents in some new Adventures of my own" (pp. 305–6) in the novel's now little-read second volume (published later in 1719). Just when he has abundance for a quiet and happy ending to his life, he has "a great Mind to be upon the Wing again" (p. 304), even if in giving way to it he repeats the original sin of defiance of his father's will. The rich plantation owner Colonel Jack, too, has "a wandring kind of Taste" (p. 233), and when, near the end of his story, he reflects that "now was my time to have sat still contented with what I had got," nevertheless "I Dream'd of nothing but Millions and Hundred of Thousands; so contrary to all moderate Measures, I push'd on for another Voyage" (pp. 296–97). For both characters, restlessness might be seen as a function of avarice, as Moll notes of her own inability to give up the "horrid Trade" of theft, which has made her rich: "Avarice join'd so with the Success, that I had no more thoughts of coming to a timely Alteration of Life; tho' without it I cou'd expect no Safety, no Tranquility in the Possession of what I had so wickedly gain'd" (207). Enough is never enough – not just because of greed, but because safety and tranquillity, the very things promised by the happy endings of fiction, are inimical to the kind of life Defoe's characters seek, as they are to a flourishing economy in the new world of capitalist enterprise. That world's principles are those of the crime boss Jonathan Wild, of whom his biographer observes that "had he contented himself with the same Cautious wary Way of Acting, which his first Instructor introduc'd him by, he might have grown Rich, and been safe too; but as he was of a pushing, enterprizing Nature, he could content himself with nothing but every thing he could get" (pp. 251–52). It is their inability to rest content with what they are and have that makes Defoe's criminal narrators typical of their "pushing, enterprizing" age, even as it marks them as renegades living outside the laws that others dully obey.

In criminal biography, trespass usually leads to punishment; and if the biographer's aim is moral instruction, the criminal's repentance transforms punishment into expiation of guilt, so that the end of his or her wicked life is redemption. Defoe's criminal fictions broadly adhere to this pattern while calling its moral certainties into question. For his acts of filial rebellion, Robinson is chastised by shipwreck: as he expresses it, "I was a Prisoner lock'd up with the Eternal Bars and Bolts of the Ocean" (p. 113).[27] Yet if his time on the island can be interpreted as morally transformative – "now I chang'd both my Sorrows and my Joys; my very Desires alter'd, my Affections chang'd their Gusts, and my Delights were perfectly new" (pp. 112–13) – he hankers after rambling and gold no less at the novel's end than at its beginning; and though he castigates himself later for "the Breach of my Duty to God and my Father" (p. 8), it cannot be overlooked that this defiance has led to a fortune so great that he compares it to God's reward to His most faithful servant Job (p. 284). Similarly, Moll is thrown into Newgate for her crimes, and comes to "look back upon my past Life with abhorrence" so that "the things of Life ... began to look with a different Aspect, and quite another Shape, than they did before; the greatest and best things, the views of felicity, the joy, the griefs of Life were quite other things ... It appear'd to me to be the greatest stupidity in Nature to lay any weight upon any thing tho' the most valuable in this World" (p. 287). Yet in her case the gap between words and actions is even greater, for she is soon scheming to shorten her sentence, buying her way out of indentured servitude; and she is only too happy to retire on profits she has made from stolen goods. Like Crusoe and Colonel Jack, ever sailing off for one more "enterprizing" adventure, she is governed by the same wayward and acquisitive impulses after her "conversion" as before, but is never able to shake the feeling that she has not truly expiated her crimes. Desire is never satisfied; guilt is never appeased.

Roxana, the protagonist of Defoe's last, most tortuous fiction, is also haunted by a sense of implacable guilt; yet even if "Crime" is the last word of her text, she is not in any straightforward sense a criminal. She calls herself a "Whore," but as always in Defoe this crude term masks a complex, ambiguous critique of conventional gender relations and roles, and Roxana's repeated insistence that marriage is for women a form of enslavement implies a corollary claim that other, transgressive forms of sexuality might thus be integral to the realization of female autonomy or freedom. Urged to marry, she protests that "I knew no State of Matrimony, but what was, at best, a State of Inferiority, if not of Bondage ... and seeing Liberty seem'd to be the Men's Property, I wou'd be a *Man-Woman*; for as I was born free, I wou'd die so" (p. 171). Though she has the best of the argument, her male listener's mocking reply, that "I talk'd a kind of *Amazonian* language," suggests that Roxana's imagined breach of gender boundaries as a Man-Woman marks her as alien, even monstrous. This defiance of sexual norms – at one point she claims that "if [a woman] had a-mind to gratifie herself as to Sexes, she might entertain a Man, as a Man does a Mistress" (p. 149) – sets her so radically at odds with conventional expectations of woman's nature that it is almost unsurprising, if deplorable, that she is finally led to commit the most unnatural of crimes: a mother's murder of her own daughter in order to maintain her façade of respectability.

Defoe sets up this harrowing last act with unusual care, tracing the tangled sequence of events that lead Roxana's abandoned daughter Susan to learn of her career as mistress to a series of powerful men, and then to track her down just when Roxana has "put an End to all the intrieguing Part of my Life" (p. 243) and married a baronet, launching into a new life her daughter's exposure threatens to undo. But having drawn together all the plot strands that seem inexorably to drive her to murder, Defoe leaves Roxana's confession frustratingly incomplete: that is, she never reveals what has happened to Susan. No one can come to the end of the story in much doubt that Roxana's violent, inhumanly loyal servant Amy has somehow managed to "make her away" (p. 302), or that in doing so she has acted as Roxana's criminal shadow-self, carrying out her inadmissible desires. Outwardly, Amy leaves Roxana in the clear, offering her the perfect alibi: for whatever happens to Susan happens when Roxana is living abroad, and Roxana repeatedly emphasizes her geographical distance from the crime she imagines with such horror. Moreover, as she (also repeatedly) avows, "I had always express'd myself vehemently against hurting a Hair of her Head" (p. 311). Yet this very vehemence is the most damning sign of Roxana's guilt, for as she well knows, the more harshly she represses Amy's murderous urgings, the more she winds her up, to a pitch of homicidal frenzy. When Amy, irritated by Susan's persistence, blurts out that "she began to think it wou'd be absolutely necessary to murther her" (p. 270), Roxana, rather than take this for what it surely is, a heated rhetorical outburst, takes it literally, and conjures up an image of herself murdering Amy in retaliation: "I shou'd cut your Throat with my own Hand; I am almost ready to do it, *said I*, as 'tis, for your but naming the thing" (p. 271). Roxana turns Amy's hollow remark into a vivid scene of bloodshed, just as later, when she has gone abroad (leaving Amy to handle Susan), she writes that Susan "was ever before my Eyes ... Sometimes I thought I saw her with her Throat cut; sometimes with her Head cut, and her Brains knock'd-out; other-times hang'd up upon a Beam; another time

drown'd in the Great Pond at *Camberwell*" (p. 325). All these gory fantasies –
for nothing, as yet, has happened to Susan – give the lie to Roxana's assertion
that she "was not arriv'd to such a Pitch of obstinate Wickedness, as to
commit Murther, especially such, as to murther my own Child, or so much
as to harbour a Thought so barbarous, in my Mind" (p. 302). Her mind
harbours many such thoughts, indeed overflows with them. She is haunted,
but not by Susan's ghost, for Susan is not dead (at least not yet); she is
haunted, instead, by her own imagining of the many deaths Susan might
suffer at her behest.

Roxana is the author of these imagined crimes, Amy merely their vehicle.
And this makes Roxana guilty of murder, whatever befalls Susan. She has
already said she would cut Amy's throat not for actually killing Susan but
"for your but naming the thing": to name the crime – that is, to imagine, and
by imagining to desire it – is as wicked as to carry it out. As she upbraids Amy
later, "why you ought to be hang'd for what you have done already; for
having resolv'd on it, is doing it, as to the Guilt of the Fact; you are a
Murtherer already, as much as if you had done it already" (p. 273). In
Roxana's tortured confession, guilt comes before crime. If in one sense this
gives Amy license to kill – since if she is already guilty, what has she to lose by
doing the deed? – it is also an admission of guilt on Roxana's part, and an
accusation levelled against the reader: for who more than the reader of
Roxana longs for Susan's murder? And who is more compelled, by
Roxana's (and Defoe's) twisted, bewildering plot, to try to "name" the
crime Roxana never reports? Defoe, in the last of his criminal fictions, denies
us any sense of narrative completion or closure: Roxana ends the novel
suspended between worldly success and criminal guilt, splendor and shame,
fear of exposure and compulsion to confess. She can neither rid herself of the
past nor allow it to become known, neither deny herself the pleasure of being
called "Ladyship" nor live with the guilt she incurs to hold on to that name.
Although not a criminal in the eyes of the law, she carries, like readers who
relish tales of wickedness, "a Heart loaded with Crime" (265).

NOTES

1. Quoted in William Lee, *Daniel Defoe: His Life, and Recently Discovered Writings*
   (London: John Camden Hotten, 1869), 1, 387. The source is unidentified.
2. Christopher Hibbert, *The Road to Tyburn: The Story of Jack Sheppard and the
   Eighteenth-Century Underworld* (London: Longmans, Green, 1957), p. 145.
3. Lee, *Daniel Defoe*, 1, 383–89. Lee's attribution of this and other criminal texts
   published by Applebee to Defoe has been contested by P. N. Furbank and
   W. R. Owens in "The Myth of Defoe as 'Applebee's Man'" in the *Review of
   English Studies*, New Series, 48: 190 (May 1997), 198–204 and in W. R. Owens

and P. N. Furbank, *The Canonisation of Daniel Defoe* (New Haven and London: Yale University Press, 1988), pp. 72–74.

4. Defoe, *The Great Law of Subordination Consider'd* (London, 1724), p. 211.

5. Defoe, *Roxana: The Fortunate Mistress*, ed. Jane Jack (Oxford: Oxford University Press, 1964), p. 260. All references in the text are to this edition.

6. Maximillian E. Novak, *Realism, Myth, and History in Defoe's Fiction* (Lincoln, NE: University of Nebraska Press, 1983), p. 123.

7. Beattie, *Crime and the Courts in England, 1660–1800* (Princeton: Princeton University Press, 1986), p. 216.

8. Defoe (attrib.), *A Brief Historical Account of the Lives of Six Notorious Street Robbers*, in *Romances and Narratives by Daniel Defoe*, ed. George A. Aitken (London: J.M. Dent, 1895), XVI, 371.

9. *News from Newgate: or, a True Relation of the Manner of Taking Seven Persons, Very Notorious for Highway-men, in the Strand* (London, 1677), pp. 3–4.

10. J. A. Sharpe, " 'Last Dying Speeches': Religion, Ideology and Public Execution in Seventeenth-Century England," *Past and Present*, 107 (1985), 144–67; Peter Linebaugh, "The Ordinary of Newgate and His *Account*," in *Crime in England, 1550–1800*, ed. J.S. Cockburn (London: Methuen, 1977), 246–69; Hal Gladfelder, *Criminality and Narrative in Eighteenth-Century England* (Baltimore and London: Johns Hopkins University Press, 2001), pp. 50–57.

11. Defoe (attrib.), *The History of the Remarkable Life of John Sheppard* (1724), printed with *The Fortunate Mistress* (Oxford: Basil Blackwell for the Shakespeare Head Press, 1928), II, 161.

12. Ibid., p. 202.

13. John Reynolds, *The Triumph of God's Revenge, against the Crying, and Execrable Sinne of Murther* (first published London, 1621). William Godwin cites Reynolds in the 1832 preface to his novel *Caleb Williams* (1794).

14. Cynthia Herrup, "Law and Morality in Seventeenth-Century England," *Past and Present*, 106 (1985), 110 and 112.

15. Reynolds, *The Triumph of God's Revenge*, p. iv. On the impact of political and economic individualism, and the conflicted relationship between it and the values of Dissenting or Puritan Christianity, see Ian Watt, *The Rise of the Novel: Studies in Defoe, Richardson, and Fielding* (Berkeley and Los Angeles: University of California Press, 1957), esp. pp. 124–30; and John Richetti, *Defoe's Narratives: Situations and Structures* (Oxford: Clarendon Press, 1975), esp. pp. 14–15, 23–31.

16. Daniel Defoe, *The History and Remarkable Life of the Truly Honourable Col. Jacque, commonly call'd Col. Jack*, ed. Samuel Holt Monk, intro. by David Roberts (Oxford: Oxford University Press, 1989), p. 309. All references in parenthesis in the text are to this edition.

17. Defoe, *Moll Flanders*, ed. G. A. Starr (Oxford: Oxford University Press, 1981), pp. 1, 2. All references in parenthesis in the text are to this edition.

18. Defoe, *Conjugal Lewdness; Or, Matrimonial Whoredom* (1727; reprint with intro. by Maximillian Novak, 1967), p. 9. A similar passage appears in the preface to *Roxana*, p. 2.

19. Michael Shinagel, *Daniel Defoe and Middle-Class Gentility* (Cambridge, MA: Harvard University Press, 1968), p. 170; Defoe, *The Compleat English Tradesman, volume I* (London, 1726), title page.

20. Defoe, *Compleat English Tradesman, Volume II* (London, 1727), part 2, p. 108.

21. Defoe, *Robinson Crusoe*, ed. J. Donald Crowley (Oxford: Oxford University Press, 1972), pp. 3, 4. All references in parenthesis in the text are to this edition.

22. See Watt's discussion of this "dynamic tendency of capitalism itself, whose aim is never merely to maintain the *status quo*, but to transform it *incessantly* [my emphasis]" in *Rise of the Novel*, p. 65.

23. John Richetti, *Popular Fiction before Richardson: Narrative Patterns, 1700– 1739* (Oxford: Clarendon Press, 1969; rpt. with a new introduction by the author, 1992), p. 56. See also Lincoln B. Faller, *Turned to Account: The Forms and Functions of Criminal Biography in Late Seventeenth- and Early Eighteenth-Century England* (Cambridge: Cambridge University Press, 1987).

24. Defoe (attrib.), *The True and Genuine Account of the Life and Actions of the Late Jonathan Wild* (1725), reprinted with *Colonel Jack* (Oxford: Basil Blackwell for the Shakespeare Head Press, 1927), II, 236. All references in the text are to this edition. The best study of Wild's career is Gerald Howson, *Thief-Taker General: The Rise and Fall of Jonathan Wild* (New York: St. Martin's, 1971).

25. Roland Barthes, "The Reality Effect," in *The Rustle of Language*, translated by Richard Howard (New York: Hill & Wang, 1981). "The effect of the real" is my translation of Barthes's "l'effet du réel." On "discordant profusion," see John Bender, *Imagining the Penitentiary: Fiction and the Architecture of Mind in Eighteenth-Century England* (Chicago: University of Chicago Press, 1987), p. 48; and Lincoln B. Faller, *Crime and Defoe: A New Kind of Writing* (Cambridge: Cambridge University Press, 1993).

26. Watt writes of Defoe's characters, "essentially solitary, they take a severely functional view of their fellows" (*Rise of the Novel*, p. 112).

27. On Defoe's use of prison imagery in *Crusoe*, see Bender, *Imagining the Penitentiary*, pp. 52–61.

5

DEIDRE SHAUNA LYNCH

Money and character in Defoe's fiction

As they tell their stories, the protagonists of Defoe's fictions may alert modern readers to the older meanings of the verb "to tell," reminding us that, in the eighteenth century, stories and money alike were things that (along with ships' cargoes and tradespeople's stock) required *telling*. The *Oxford English Dictionary* in fact cites Defoe three times in its entry enumerating the twenty-six meanings of *tell*. Attending to these citations and the usage that the *OED* uses them to reconstruct can make visible the deep affinities, ones especially fruitful for Defoe's novels, that link the human activities of narrating and counting – just those affinities that still make "account" both another designation for a narration and a word for the computations, the reports on moneys paid and received, that comprise, for instance, a bank statement. To tell about *tell*, the *OED* draws first on Robinson Crusoe's reference to his Carib man Friday's inability to "tell twenty in English." The *OED* moves next to the eponymous Colonel Jack's recollection of an episode from his youth, when he claimed a reward from a gentleman whose associate he and his mentor in the thieving trade had robbed earlier: the gentleman, Jack states, "told the money into my hand." Then comes Jack's statement, from a subsequent moment in his criminal career, that when he disposed of the stolen goods abandoned by his foster brother (Captain Jack), he prudently took pains to know nothing about the bundle's content: "what his cargo amounted to, I knew not, for I never told it."[1]

No reader of *Crusoe* or *Colonel Jack* or any other of the Defoe fictions in which ragged orphans, castaways, and abandoned women start from nothing, make their fortunes, and turn gentlemen and gentlewomen will be surprised to learn that lexicographers found his works a handy source of quotations to illuminate how telling can be a synonym for counting, counting out, and reckoning up. After all, no other eighteenth-century novelist is quite so willing to put the recounting of a sequence of events on hold, so as to make time for counting, pure and simple. Defoe's narrators like to tally up and take stock. Robinson Crusoe famously adopts the methods of double-entry book keeping to itemize the "Comforts" of his situation on the island and measure them against the "Miseries," and other Defoe narrators appear to share Crusoe's conviction that such stock-taking can make manifest not just the state of one's finances but also one's moral and spiritual condition.[2] In these narratives, accordingly, "books of accompts" are regularly opened up for readers' inspection. Invoices get transcribed, as the narrators record the fruits of their mercantile or piratical fortune-hunting. Even at almost forty years' distance, Colonel Jack recalls with preternatural vividness his first experience of how crime pays: he provides from memory an inventory of the booty that his other foster-brother, Major Jack, brings home after a sortie to Bartholomew Fair to pick pockets. That inventory is too lengthy to reproduce in full, but it begins like this:

I. A white Handkerchief from a Country Wench, as she was staring up at a *Jackpudding* [a clown], there was 3*s*. 6*d*. and a Row of Pins, tyed up in One End of it.
II. A colour'd Handkerchief, out of a young Country Fellow's Pocket as he was buying a *China* Orange.
III. A Ribband Purse with 11*s*. 3*d*. and a Silver Thimble in it, out of a young Woman's Pocket, just as a Fellow offer'd to pick her up.[3]

Minute particulars like these, details involving pocket-sized things and petty cash, selected seemingly at random by a prosy narrator, endow Defoe's fictions with their slice-of-real-life feel. They also underwrite readers' sense that even as the page count of one of these fictions mounts, so does the character's net financial worth.

The *OED* editors' association of his fiction with enumeration and calculation reinforces premises traditional to Defoe criticism since the nineteenth century. It is a commonplace, for instance, to identify the style favored by Defoe's narrators with the sort of medium that Thomas Sprat touted in his 1667 *History of the Royal Society* as he lauded the Society for avoiding, in their scientific reports, the language of "Wits and Scholars" and adopting instead the style of "Merchants." (Merchants for Sprat represent the maestros of a prose plain-dealing, "delivering so many *things* almost in an equal number of *words*.") And the stories Defoe's plain-speakers deliver have often seemed to critics to exemplify what is ethically and aesthetically deplorable about the modern mercantile attitude: to exemplify, in particular, a myopic, self-satisfied materialism that (as Dorothy Van Ghent put it, writing of *Moll Flanders* in 1953) converts "all subjective, emotional, and moral experience ... into pocket and bank money, into the materially measurable."[4] Defoe has few rivals as a chronicler of the era in economic history in which, suddenly, money could do more, travel greater distances along global trade routes, and extend its powers of measurement to more arenas of human life, than ever before. Still, many who admire such skill have wondered whether an excessive enthusiasm for the materially measurable might be Defoe's character flaw in addition to his protagonists', a symptom of his complacency in addition to theirs.

Even as it reviews this way of reading Defoe, this essay aims, as well, to reorient it – for a start, by highlighting how the expansion of the market economy also engendered new sorts of ignorance and uncertainty, placing new impediments in the way of individuals who aspired to take the measure of their circumstances. Indeed, in the episode in *Colonel Jack* from which the *OED* takes its first quotation, Jack is forced to admit that he has no way to determine whether the reward money the gentleman has told into his hand is equal to the sum promised: "I *did not know* how to tell money ... I *did not know* how much a Guinea was" (p. 36, emphasis added). The admission underscores the fourteen-year-old character's naiveté and poverty. It also brings to view a possibility that this chapter will examine at length as it takes a second look at the way Defoe narrates his characters' affinities for money and (as we shall see) their affinities *with* it. This is the possibility that there may in fact be nothing plain about either the pocket or bank money that preoccupies Defoe's plain-speaking narrators. In Defoe's day money was increasingly a heterogeneous and perplexing thing. The historian Deborah Valenze has noted how negotiating the chaos of England's currency during this period required on the part of all those with things to buy or sell "a particular form of technical virtuosity." Money's adepts had to learn not simply the "art of making payments" but also how to argue at the point of purchase for their own particular money's worth. They had to reckon from "different standards of value," while approaching their acts of exchange with an eye to past and future values of the currency they proffered and received.[5] Monetary transactions presented these challenges because – as this chapter will outline – there was so little agreement, in either British markets or global ones, about what might and might not count as money, about what gave money its capacity to stand in or substitute for things beyond itself (bushels of corn, hours of labor power), and about what difference there was between the way that units of currency did that representing and the way that the words of a language did it. (Reinforcing that difference became urgent in Defoe's lifetime. After the Promissory Notes Act of 1704 confirmed that individuals' drafts on their goldsmith-bankers could be treated as transferable, so that these promises to pay could be legitimately circulated to third parties, money began, in its new guise as a paper currency, to look as if it might even be *written* into being.)

"Your Business is money." This is the mantra William the Quaker repeats throughout *Captain Singleton*, as he guides the remarkably easy transition that Defoe's eponymous hero makes from bloody-minded buccaneering to peaceable trade. Many readers have identified William's creator with William's bullish worldview, as, too, with Sprat's confidence that British society's way to certain knowledge would be through the true "trading style."[6] But that conventional reading of Defoe might be usefully offset by an investigation of the period's contentions over money's meaning. It might be usefully offset, additionally, by an investigation of the *un*certainties engendered at this time by new habits of speculation – by ways of playing the market (ways of using loans and stocks to make money from money) that were inimical to those measures of worth that from time immemorial had been founded on landed property. This essay therefore sets out to supply the historical contexts that might prompt modern readers to wonder anew how money may be told. As this discussion proceeds, we will move outward, from pocket to bank money, from individuals' pockets and purses to the financial networks that had begun to connect creditors and debtors across the seven seas.

Let us begin with coins – since, eminently touchable, smooth and shiny, they often sponsor the pleasure that the protagonists intermingle with their business. Telling money can be a deeply sensuous activity. In recalling their many romantic entanglements Defoe's heroines tend to linger lubriciously over the moments when their lovers deposit guineas in their hands and more gold still in their laps. From Moll Flanders' adventures we might single out, for example, the scene marked by a strange mix of charitable and erotic impulses, affection and coercion, in which her fellow lodger at Bath invites her into his bedchamber, has her bring him a drawer from a box in the room, and then "held my Hand hard in his Hand, and put it into the Drawer, and made me take out as many Guineas almost as I could well take up at once."[7] Moll's way in this passage of calling attention to the physicality both of the other person and of the other person's guineas – the way, too, that she melds the two together – bear out observations that anthropologists, historians, and sociologists make about money's capacity, when materialized as specie, to establish a particularly intimate relation with its possessor. In 1900 the sociologist Georg Simmel wrote of how, before money was money, it was the precious metals and gemstones that people wore next to their skin, as jewelry. His observation might make us think both about Bob Singleton's condescension toward the Africans he encounters in his travels who use gold to ornament themselves but not to trade with and also, contrariwise, about how Moll and Roxana often mention gold and pearl necklaces in ways that suggest that these Englishwomen are quite open to wearing their economic resources in the manner in which Singleton's "savages" do. Through the heightened thinginess that distinguishes them from our paper currency, our coins, Simmel implied, preserve this memory of money as something that can meld notions of self and notions of the economy, the adornments and investments, that we nowadays usually distinguish. Deborah Valenze proposes, to similar effect, that "coins bear a special affinity to people" and explains that affinity by noting that coins are things with *faces*: "they usually display the image of a head or body." Specifying "the old attitude to coins" that persists even in an age of paper money, Elias Canetti noted that "people like imagining the coin as an individual."[8]

Indeed, thoroughly entangling ideas of personal character and current coin, moralists and preachers of Defoe's day often made the piece of metal a symbol for the person: working from an understanding of *character* as a designation first and foremost for "a mark; a stamp; a representation" (to cite the definition proffered by Johnson's *Dictionary* in 1755), they aligned the inscriptions that identify coins as legal tender, with the traits that composed the individual's personality, and with the lineaments on those persons' physiognomies (stamped by time and events or stamped by God, who was conceptualized in sermons operating in this tradition as a Supervisor of a celestial Mint).[9] This understanding of identity as something outwardly oriented, as a documentary matter existing for others' readings and for exchanges in the market of public life, could be deeply reassuring for those intent on preserving social hierarchy. (Defoe's contemporary, John Gay, has a character in *The Beggar's Opera* explain, "A wife's like a guinea in gold, Stamp'd with the name of her spouse" – although Mrs. Peachum does undercut the conservatism of that metaphor for domestic subordination when she adds that the stamp actually enables married women to circulate, be "current in every house.")[10] And, naturalizing the social constraints on individuals' powers of self-definition and self-alteration, the idea that bodies should tell tales about their owners' real characters even informed criminal penalties in Defoe's day. Consider, for example, the English judiciary's branding of criminals – memorialized in the episode in which Moll's mother peels off the glove that declares her a genteel lady to show Moll, beneath the glove, the scar that declares her an old offender. The Crown that claimed exclusive control over the stamps that converted metal into money also claimed the power to write out character in indelible marks on the bodies of its subjects. To govern was to force specie and flesh alike into tell-tale legibility.

Early modern culture's ready joining of the self with the self's money had its dark dimensions. Moll's harsh description of the lot of the single woman – "she is just like a Bag of Money, or a Jewel dropt on the Highway, which is Prey to the next Comer" (p. 128) – calls attention to some others. The conception of the person exposed by Moll's simile makes personification (the process that endows coins with faces) and objectification (the process that makes people thing-like, like their coins) look eerily the same. Roxana's description of herself as "a standing Mark of the weakness of Great Men in their vice ... [who] raise the Value of the Object which they ... pitch upon, by their Fancy" works to similar effect, with its flinty assessment of the inflationary trends that have pushed up her market value.[11] As Defoe's protagonists account for their lives, they participate in what Valenze calls a "tendency to create equivalencies between people and prices" – "a recognized feature of the age," the historian asserts, that bespeaks a "complex psychological involvement with money very different from our own."[12] These narratives make volatile the opposition between individual persons and marketable, exchangeable things. Thus Crusoe's and Colonel Jack's acquaintance with human exchange value is established not just through their slave-owning (referred to with disturbing matter-of-factness) but also through experiences of being the objects of exchange themselves. Before he owns slaves, Jack is shipped as human cargo across the Atlantic, where he adds a body to a Virginia planter's work crew. The same role reversal structures the episode early in Crusoe's career that begins with his capture and enslavement by Algerine pirates and ends with his sale, for sixty pieces of eight, of the boy who assisted him in his escape. And Captain Singleton's origins, as far as he knows his pedigree, lie not with biological generation but in an act of purchase. The gypsy woman whom he calls Mother "told me at last, she was not my Mother, but that she bought me for Twelve Shillings" (p. 2).

Such conflations of persons and commodities are ubiquitous in *Moll Flanders* and *Roxana*, where the financial security that makes the protagonists' self-assertion possible is so often purchased by an objectification of self. Their faces are these heroines' fortunes. Roxana thus seems to view her body from the outside, as an article of alienable property, seeing it accordingly in just the way one lover does when he asks (having led her to the mirror and pointed at her reflection), "Is it fit that Face ... should go back to *Poictou?*" (p. 60). Trafficking in themselves, whether in prostitution or on the marriage market, represents almost the only route to economic survival open to these characters, and, as each discovers, "the Market is against our Sex just now" (pp. 20, 21). Feminist critics have ably analyzed Defoe's depiction of this market, underlining, for example, as an instance of how Defoe insists on making his female capitalists *embody* their capital, that Moll Flanders acquires the surname we know her by during the period of her life when, on the lam from her second husband's creditors, she conceals herself in the neighborhood of "the Mint," then a debtors' sanctuary ("I went into the Mint ... drest me up in the Habit of a Widow, and call'd myself Mrs. *Flanders*" (p. 64)). The detail about location suggests the strength of the identification between Moll and money. It also suggests that this re-birth, the debut performance in a career of quick-change artistry in which Moll will forever be taking up "new Figures" and appearing "in new Shapes" (p. 262) depends on something like a recoinage (an identity melt-down, as it were).[13]

As noted above, the material qualities of coins – their graspability, their resemblance to jewelry – provide a basis for their perceived affinity to persons. These qualities make possessing *this* money form seem a particularly intimate affair. And yet during Defoe's lifetime there was much the matter with the matter of money. It was increasingly the case that a coin's material substance (its weight) might indicate one thing about its value and/or validity, while its "tale" (the stamp on its surface betokening its worth) might indicate something quite different. For all their perceived affinity to persons, in other words, in the context of the chronic currency crises of the era, coins appear treacherous – possessions that are wont to betray their owners' convictions about their worth.

Several factors had contributed to this situation. The primary cause was probably the Crown's reluctance, dating back to the Tudor period, to mint a quantity of small-denomination silver coins sufficient to cover the commercial transactions of ordinary, wage-earning people. Because of the resulting shortage of specie (which occurred at a time, too, when the velocity and volume of commerce were increasing), the sixpences, shillings, and crowns that people could manage to preserve from thieves like Jack were often worn thin through the wear and tear of their prolonged circulation. That physical diminution – and attendant diminution of the intrinsic value of specie – was hastened by clippers, who, skimming off value, shaved off coins' edges and either passed on the metal so acquired to their partners-in-crime, the counterfeiters, or themselves sold it as bullion. (The crude stamping process by which seventeenth-century coins were manufactured was almost absurdly easy to duplicate, in lead, brass, or silver alloys, and counterfeiting was rampant.) Another factor contributing to coins' scarcity and debasement was the existence of a commodities market in precious metal. Clippers were incited in their crimes, and the law-abiding were incited in their hoarding of full-weight coins, by their knowledge of the profit opportunities awaiting those "money-jobbers" who sent money to markets across the seas; through much of the seventeenth century, in fact, the rate the London Mint paid for silver had been less than the market rate for bullion. By the opening of the 1690s, perplexity over the fact that the relation of coins to their metallic substance had changed and was changing, while the coins' names remained the same (as the very phrase "pound sterling" continues to suggest) was widespread. Early in that decade a sampling of the currency demonstrated that £57,200 in silver coin, a sum that officially should have contained 220,000 ounces of pure silver, in reality contained only 141,000 ounces. Officially, twenty silver shillings counted, as the decade opened, as the equivalent of one *guinea* – the gold coin introduced into circulation in 1663, named to commemorate financiers' excitement about the gold of West Africa, and playing so conspicuous a role in Roxana's and Moll's stories of amorous exchange.[14] The trading price bounced around, however, rising in 1695 to thirty shillings. (Even after the Crown had adjusted the official rate upward, the diarist John Evelyn was still in 1696 grumbling of how, nevertheless, "great summs" of "Guinnys" were "daily transported into Holland, where it yeelds more.")[15]

Under these conditions, in which nominal and intrinsic value were so often at odds, a piece of silver could pass as (for instance) a half-crown, exert the purchasing power of a half-crown, and yet in some sense – measured by bullion value – not *be* a half-crown. That indeterminacy bespeaks the multiform nature of metallic money (an indeterminacy compounded in England by the extra opportunities for speculation engendered by that country's adherence to a bi-metallic system). Metallic money is currency *and* tangible treasure, both the measure of price and a commodity that varies in its price as other commodities do. And, by extension, money was during Defoe's lifetime simultaneously a thing that certain tradespeople might *count* ("reckon by the tale" was the technical term) *and* a thing that certain other tradespeople, mistrusting the tale, might *weigh* (or bite, or strike against the shop counter so as to listen to its chink). All determinations as to whether prices would refer to tale or weight, whether the money proffered to match those prices would be judged good or bad, enough or too little, were willy-nilly left to individuals' discretion. This made the point of purchase a scene of contention – the arena of a commercial athleticism that put the cunning of both those receiving money and those disbursing it to the test.

The Treasury did attempt to bring order to this confusion when it undertook a large-scale recoinage in 1696. In defense of the idea of intrinsic value, it called in the old, deteriorated silver, reminted it at value, and endowed the new coins with milled edges that were supposed to deter counterfeiting and make clipping easier to discern. And yet the continuing scarcity, through the entirety of the eighteenth century, of small-denomination coin meant that for expediency's sake the British state had to turn a blind eye to its populace's persistence in those monetary experiments in which they disregarded intrinsic value and counted a motley assortment of instruments as good money: foreign coin; underweight and/or clipped English coin; "trade tokens" (turned out in reams by independent manufacturers who sold them in packages to petty shopkeepers, giving them and their clientele the small change that they needed to carry on as economic agents); and the money-substitute embodied by the promissory notes of an emerging system of paper credit. All these forms of money might lodge together in early eighteenth-century pockets.

In the epistle in his conduct-book *The Complete English Tradesman* (1725–27), which Defoe devotes to frauds in trade, he writes of the bad old days when "people were daily on the catch to cheat and surprise one another" as they looked out for dupes with whom to make dubious money pass as bonafide currency. Thank goodness, he comments, the recoinage of 1696 made such cunning unnecessary and so delivered tradesmen "from a vast accumulated weight of daily crime." (However, Defoe also observes signs of a relapse, in a line suggesting just how motley the money supply remained: "we see the current coin of the kingdom strangely crowded with counterfeit money again, and especially we have found a great deal of counterfeit foreign money, as particularly Portugal and Spanish gold, such as moydores and Spanish pistoles.")[16] If Defoe the business consultant decries the swindles it facilitates, the indeterminacy of money seems, by contrast, to inspire Defoe the fiction-maker. This is in part, arguably, because that indeterminacy chimes so well with his protagonists' evasion of determinate character, the flexibility, or escape artistry, which enables them to pursue their self-interest in the face of unfavourable odds. The teasing way that Moll and Roxana admit to using aliases while withholding their real names has made many readers wary. And what about Captain Singleton, who turns his back on his piratical past and returns incognito to England, disguised as a mustachioed Greek who is never heard speaking English in public? He declares himself penitent, made honest by his awareness that the "Time of Account" approaches, but don't we suspect some cooking of the books and that the bluff candour and plain English that Singleton adopts as he breaks cover and tells all to *us* might simply represent his latest way of baffling inquiries? (p. 265). Perhaps in the strange bargain that a Defoe narrator strikes with readers, a compact licensing the narrator to both "*give*" us her character and withhold it, be both verbose and tight-lipped, we are seeing an especially sophisticated example of the sharp-dealing that was the rule in the early modern marketplace.[17] By extension, one way to specify how Defoe reworks the coin-character analogies of his age would be to notice that his characters' self-representations – these characters' *tales* – are as shifty as the self-representations of coins, whose display of their respective "characters" (which they wear forthrightly on their faces) might in the early modern context have been the most misleading thing about them.

One other aspect of Defoe's refashioning of the numismatic metaphor for character is noteworthy. Crusoe ascribes to himself a moral failing that is typical among Defoe's protagonists when, early in his time on the island, he deplores how his gratitude to God for his preservation has repeatedly proved fleeting, and how his conversion has never quite taken: "as soon as ever … [the evidence of God's hand in his preservation] was removed, all the

Impression which was rais'd from it, wore off also." Tellingly, to describe his lumpishness, he uses language that conceives of the mind as a printable surface, set up to receive a stamp, as the disk of metal receives the inscription by which the Mint renders it current coin. To restore the dead metaphor in "Impression" to the life it enjoyed in the early eighteenth century reveals Crusoe as a coin devoid of the characters that are supposed to identify its value and provenance (pp. 89–90).

Crusoe regrets this condition. But, as a group, Defoe's socially mobile, resilient protagonists will use all their powers of invention and talents of impersonation to outrun the characters that other people might try to fix on them, to avoid, that is, being ensnared by other people's representations of who they are. (Think of Moll taking up "new Figures" and appearing in "new Shapes" to carry on her thieving. Even the reform [re-form] brought about by her penitence at Newgate appears, in the closing pages, less than conclusive.) The protagonists' aim is to evade the indelible brand that would, as with the scar Moll's ex-convict mother carries to her grave, reconnect them to their pasts and the associates, spouses, and offspring they seek to leave behind.

In ways the remainder of this chapter will examine, money (bank or credit money especially) plays a key role in those escapes. That role is complicated, since, as we are beginning to see, money too escapes its past during the eighteenth century, an escape that discloses the ambiguities lodged within the semantic complex that linked character, countenance, and coin. Deborah Valenze's vivid example of that escape is the semantic drift that alters the meaning of "quid" – as an abbreviation of "quiddity" (the real nature of a thing, the essence, that which makes a thing what it is) – by the close of the century. Early in the century, the English use "quid" to identify their guinea coin specifically (so called because gold is ostensibly the essence, the quiddity, that makes money what it is). By the century's close, "quid" can also name cash in general, a usage in which ideas of intrinsic value and essence are discounted, and in which the abstracting power that money exercises, in its guise (in Karl Marx's terms) as a universal equivalent capable of the "compounding and confounding of all things," is turned on money itself. "O Money, Money, who can form thy Character!" Defoe asks. The epithets he tries out in his 1707 essay, such as "Mighty *Neuter*" and "great *Jack-a-both sides* of the world," do not pin it down.[18]

"Wherever there is money there is money to be lost," the critic James Thompson remarks, summing up the anxieties that money's escape artistry often produces in Defoe's world. For all his enthusiasm over rags-to-riches transformations – witness Roxana's declaration that "it was not a strange thing for young Women to go away poor to the *East-Indies*, and come home vastly rich" (p. 193) – Defoe associates the windfall with fear as well as joy.

Having obtained almost £5 – four guineas and fourteen shillings – in his first outing as a thief, the fourteen-year-old Colonel Jack is sadly perplexed about where to put those spoils, since he has "no Box or Drawer to hide" the money in, "no "Pocket but such ... was full of Holes" (p. 22). His scheme of carrying the shillings in one hand while he stores the guineas inside his shoe does not work: now his gain inflicts pain ("but after I had gone a while, my Shoe hurt me so, I could not go," p. 23). Learning on his long-delayed return to Europe that his Brazilian plantation has been earning steadily during his absence on the island (thanks to its slave labour), and that he is therefore master of £5,000 and of an estate that earns £1,000 per annum, Crusoe's reaction resembles Jack's, despite the discrepancy between the sums involved: "I had now a great Charge upon me ... I had ne'er a Cave now to hide my Money in [a comment sounding a note of nostalgia for his castaway condition] ... I knew not where to put it" (p. 286). Jack sits down and cries; Crusoe falls ill as a consequence of scarce knowing "how to understand, or how to compose [his] self, for the Enjoyment" of his riches (p. 285).[19] If riches are the object of Defoe's protagonists' ardent identifications, the precariousness of their possession also renders money something alien and even hurtful to the self. To have a fortune fall into one's hands is in some sense to suffer a dispossession (that "great Charge" to which Crusoe, ever the accountant, refers).

Of course, even Defoe characters have guilty consciences, and even with them – figures in the vanguard of what Valenze calls the eighteenth-century detoxification of riches – premodern worries about the sin of avarice die hard. But the association of riches (and not just ill-gotten gains) with threat and loss also derives from Defoe's habit of arranging for his protagonists to be schooled, often the hard way, in asset conversion and liquidity ratios. After Roxana's first lover, the jeweller, is murdered in France by thieves, she takes advantage of the rumors that his diamonds were taken by the assailants and secures the jewels for herself (forestalling the jeweller's lawful wife from staking her rather more legitimate claim to his wealth). But when, later in her story, another lucrative love affair under her belt, she seeks to leave France and dispose of the diamonds ("convert them into Money, and so get me Bills for the Whole," p. 112), they are recognized as the murdered jeweller's wares. The treasure that she means to take away with her threatens to become the evidence that will land her in prison, immobilizing our freewheeling heroine. (In miniaturized form, Jack's story demonstrates this same transformation of asset into burden, when the money concealed in his shoe brings him to a standstill.)

Situations like Roxana's allow Defoe to usher onstage a figure for whom he has a soft spot, the benevolent financial adviser. This is the role of the Dutchman (later Roxana's husband), who spirits her away from the French authorities and helps her transfer her wealth into bills of exchange payable in Holland and, then, on Roxana's return to England, the role of Sir Robert Clayton (an actual participant in the world of Restoration high finance), who further tutors her in "the Arts of improving Money"(p. 169). Moll has her "honest friend at the Bank" (p. 160), and Jack has that gentleman who gives him the reward money he cannot tell and who then relieves Jack of his anxieties about losing that money by securing it with a bill of exchange. Taught by these figures, Defoe's protagonists learn to esteem the capacity this negotiable paper has to waft value across long distances – how, as paper, value takes a much easier and more theft-proof journey than the one it endures when housed in bulky coins. They also learn how the long-distance operations of this bank money obscure (as the "primitive money" of Roxana's tell-tale jewels does not) the *origins* of the wealth that this paper symbolizes.[20] The forgetfulness that negotiable paper facilitates becomes apparent when Jack himself is wafted to Virginia, victim of the shady labor contractor who, stealing the former thief, has sold him as an indentured servant. In his first interview with his master, he finds, when he produces another bill of exchange (confirming a second deposit), that he has in hand something like a letter of reference – a *character* (in Johnson's sense of "representation") that certifies Jack's identity as a man of worth. He has credit and has a new face to show the world. It is no longer an issue that behind the bill stand the takings from Jack's time as housebreaker, and not, as he told the gentleman, honest gain. As if by magic, Jack is set on the road toward a gentlemanly identity.

Issued by an individual banker rather than a government mint, Jack's bill only faintly resembles our dollars and pound notes. It is more akin to a certificate of deposit or IOU, an IOU set up, however, as an instrument for the transfer of funds, and so redeemable when presented to third parties. Much as an IOU would, Jack's bill raises questions about the trustworthiness of the issuer and about the risks involved in making one's own worth hostage to the conjecture one has made about another's. (Since the individuals and corporations issuing bills of exchange calculated that their depositors would not all want their money back at the same moment, they issued more bills than they had the money to cover.) Or it would raise these questions, if, as a group, Defoe's protagonists, although unlucky in love, were not uncannily fortunate in their choice of money managers.

Earning him interest, this bill of exchange also enrolls Jack as a participant in the central drama of early modern economic history, that transition in which *wealth* – hoarded, idle, stagnant – becomes *capital*: money put to work, money that flows (to use the metaphorical language of liquidity that Defoe favours in his economic writings). Capital – Defoe's characters learn as they become financially literate – is money expended to make more money still, breeding itself out of itself in what moralists since Aristotle had deemed a form of unnatural increase. But Credit, the mechanism responsible for setting money in motion, can "Out-do Nature," Defoe asserts in his poem *Jure Divino*. Credit can "Mines of Gold prepare, / And fleets of Coins from Paper and from Air." Of course, the questions about value that clipped silver shillings pose recur for users of bills of exchange, since this money – fashioned of paper made of rags – possesses value only so long as people continue to believe in it and believe in others' belief. And yet "Air Money," floating free of notions of intrinsic value, was becoming the wealth of nations: though constantly at war, France and Britain agreed about the convenience of deficit financing.[21] Thus, in 1711, when Defoe's patron and Chancellor of the Exchequer, Robert Harley, needed to refinance those war debts, London money men incorporated as the South Sea Company to assist him, motivated by the trading privileges in the South Pacific that Harley dangled before them. Debt was repackaged as company stock, which was offered as repayment to the government's creditors, with the assurance that the stock's future appreciation made theirs a win-win situation. The South Sea Bubble is the name given to the crash that happened nine years later, when, as dreams of the infinite profits to be had in the southern hemisphere evaporated, and suspicions about the overvaluation of Company stock became widespread, investors' confidence that "Paper would ... prove real Money, when they wanted it" collapsed.[22]

The most famous statement on money in Defoe's writings acknowledges that in certain contexts even gold might be as worthless as Company paper. Having salvaged from the ship that founders near his island provisions, timber, knives, forks, and books, Robinson Crusoe talks to the mingled heap of Spanish and English coin that he also finds on board to affirm to it that it does not merit his attention: "Said I aloud ... Thou art not worth to me, no not the taking off of the Ground" (p. 57). Crusoe's disdain is the product of his slightly self-congratulatory conviction that, since commerce is irrelevant to his society of one, he is no longer taken in by the value determinations generated out of exchange. He sees that the *true* value of things derives from their utility. ("All that was valuable" was what "I could make use of," p. 129.) This is, notoriously, a conviction that Crusoe does not always act up to. He does move the money from the wreck to his island cave, and finally, years later, from the island back to Europe. Indeed, the chief of the survival skills enabling Defoe's characters to keep in motion themselves might be their capacity to capitalize on value's contextual nature, on the fact that different value systems operate in different parts of the world. It is precisely because in some places gold and diamonds are, as Crusoe declares them to be at a moment of utmost enthusiasm for the utility of things, nothing more than dirt under our feet that the merchant adventurers of Defoe's age succeed in exchanging "the meanest Export … for the richest Return."[23] The uneven development of the global economy allows stupendous fortunes to be made simply by conveying goods from one economic zone to another. The golden adventure of Captain Singleton and his crewmates in Africa – which begins when these would-be mutineers are suddenly turned ashore on Madagascar – proves an exercise in such exchange. After an inauspicious beginning, when the Africans from whom they seek to purchase food refuse their money as "meer Trash," the company acquire the wherewithal to trade their way westward across the continent as they learn to make their *own* money. When their cutler hammers out their few silver coins and cuts the metal into the shape of birds, elephants, and civet cats ("so many Devices of his own Head, that it is hardly to be exprest"), they discover that "that which when it was in Coin was not worth Six-pence to us, when thus converted … was worth an Hundred Times its real Value, and purchased for us any thing" (pp. 27–28). Even the gold bullion they finally cart back to Europe from Guinea is included in this multiplication of value, since they purchase it with silver trinkets.

Have Singleton and crew indeed exchanged – as they believe – nothing for something (for "real Value")? Knowing what to think of those coinings of the cutler's fancy – knowing how the goods his African clientele obtain in these exchanges measure up against the fortunes that are the making of the Defoe protagonists – poses some difficulties for modern interpreters uncertain about the limits of Defoe's irony. In fact, a 1706 number of his *Review* zeroes in on the Guinea coast of Africa as Defoe discusses how, in the inter-cultural transactions of global trade, concepts of the matter most appropriate to money and concepts of how to justly rate it prove difficult to translate. Initially, Defoe acknowledges that it is local custom, rather than the quiddity of things, that determines value, but ultimately his essay casts Africans' choice of a trading medium of shells over one of gold as "Folly" – a manifestation of the unbridgeable gap that separates savagery from civility. But in 1721 that polarity might have seemed less stable, and readers pondering the ready money that Singleton's crewmate creates through his monetary experiment might have recalled exchange media closer to home. Britons' dealings in paper credit, their speculations on South Sea Stock particularly, struck many as incompatible with "solid Traffick."[24] And against Singleton's account of Africans' seduction by trinketry, we might pose the stories that Roxana tells of her countrymen's perverse readiness to be infatuated by what is strange, shiny, and ersatz. After all, Roxana's stock as a courtesan mounts to its highest level on the night that she performs, while in her Turkish costume (the one "set with Diamonds, only they were not true Diamonds," p. 174), a French dance that her audience credits as authentically Turkish; "nay, one

Gentleman had the Folly ... as to say ... that he had seen it danc'd at *Constantinople*" (p. 176).

This "fortunate mistress" 's account of the stupendous success she met with in her wicked courses (and her investments) has appeared to many readers an acerbic commentary on the new financial markets' capacity to defy rational assessments of the worth of things. This account has also been read as a self-conscious interrogation of the practice of fiction-making by a master counter-feiter, Defoe himself, so skilled at giving shape to the devices of his own head that he disappears behind them. In fact, the questions of credit and of fiction get intimately linked in the strange Preface that somebody called "the Relator" appends to *Roxana* (Defoe never put his name to the book during his lifetime). This Relator declares his certainty that the narrative has a grounding in solid truth, since he himself was "acquainted with the Lady's First Husband, the Brewer." He cannot vouch for the parts of her history that "lay Abroad," but hopes, he continues, in terms suggesting the promissory structure of the bills of exchange and stock certificates of eighteenth-century finance capitalism, that this acquaintance will serve "as a Pledge for the Credit of the Rest." The Relator has selected a strange character reference to shore up his Lady's narrative credit and, by extension, this fiction's claim not to be fiction. Since the gentleman in question is a bankrupt businessman and con-man, *caveat emptor*. And the Relator's prevarication about how invested he individually is in the veracity of this account gets restaged across *Roxana*, a book that repeatedly broods on the limits of both authentication and accountability. "If the Reader makes a wrong Use" of the tale, the Relator notes as he concludes this Preface, that is unfortunately outside his control: "the Wickedness is his own" (p. 2). If her dance performance got valued more highly than it merited, Roxana protests, how is she culpable? Blame that audience member who vouched for its Turkishness if it began to be credited as the real thing. Misrepresentation is not to be laid to the account of the author or narrator exclusively; it is the readers' problem too, their desires that are implicated, if it should prove more marketable than solid truth.[25] Think, too, of the episode in *Moll Flanders* in which the fortune-hunting suitor to whom Moll addresses her verses on her poverty, prefers, given a choice of accounts, to trust to the truth of the rumours of her wealth that are being whispered around the marriage market. Only when they compare stocks, the wedding performed, does Moll's reader inside the text realize the imprudence of his gamble.

This is all a bit disorienting, as is the way with irony: perhaps Defoe is teaching us a kind of financial literacy too, helping us perceive the resem-blance that links reading – the reading of character especially – to other sorts of speculations involving negotiable paper and investor confidence. And character is a complicated text to read, not least because credit transactions structured in the terms delineated by Roxana and her Relator both *preserve* the agency of the individual and *dislocate* it. The rhetorical slipperiness that prevents us from pinning the Relator down or placing a just value on his narrative might enable him to remain his own man. But it is also the case that (as the Relator's reference to the Brewer's testimony suggests) his credit is hostage to another's. It is vulnerable therefore to the kinds of domino effects *The Complete English Tradesman* often attempts to trace: "sad examples" of the contagious nature of ruin, in which the people the tradesman trusts fail to honor their debts to him and leave him unable to honor his to others, or in which the poor shopkeeper is forced by an importunate creditor to promise a payment by a certain date, knowing that he will be unable to perform. This extorted promise is, Defoe acknowledges, a white lie – a little like "poetical license" – but, still, this way of conducting business "multiplies promises, and consequently breaches," so that soon "there is no such thing as every man speaking truth with his neighbor."[26]

Money is the making of Defoe's self-seeking fortune-hunters, the secret and measure of their success. Without it, there is no escape from the past or a fixed station in life, no going it alone, nothing to tell, no interest generated for us readers. But during Defoe's lifetime the volatility of value on which these adventurers capitalize so deftly began to make it strangely difficult to apprehend economic affairs as a story in which individuals are straightforwardly the authors of their deeds and in which causes lead smoothly to effects. In his *Anatomy of Exchange Alley* Defoe marvels at the mercurial way that investor confidence and money's worth fluctuate and how those fluctuations flout the logic of narrative progression, so that "with so little regard to Intrinsick Value, or the circumstances of the Company ... when the Company has a loss, Stock shall Rise; when a great Sale, or a Rich Ship arriv'd, it shall fall."[27] Defoe's readers have sometimes taken early modern money at face value and believed its tale to have been a plain one. He knows better, knowing that sometimes it is a devil of a job to tell it.

NOTES

1. *Oxford English Dictionary*, 2nd edn. (1989), s. v. *tell*.
2. *Robinson Crusoe*, ed. J. Donald Crowley (London: Oxford University Press, 1976), p. 66. All further references in parenthesis in the text are to this edition.
3. *Colonel Jack*, ed. Samuel Holt Monk (London: Oxford University Press, 1965), pp. 13–14. All further references in parenthesis in the text are to this edition.
4. Sprat, *The History of the Royal-Society of London*, 2d edn. (London: Scot, Chiswell, Chapman, and Sawbridge, 1702), p. 113; Van Ghent, *The English Novel: Form and Function* (rept. New York: Harper and Brothers, 1961), p. 38.

5. *The Social Life of Money in the English Past* (Cambridge: Cambridge University Press, 2006), pp. 39; 49.

6. *Captain Singleton*, ed. Shiv K. Kumar (Oxford: Oxford University Press, 1990), p. 219. All further references in parenthesis in the text are to this edition. The "trading style" is Defoe's topic in *The Complete English Tradesman* (London: Charles Rivington, 1726 [1725]), Letter 3.

7. *Moll Flanders*, ed. G. A. Starr (Oxford: Oxford University Press, 1981), p. 112. All further references in parenthesis in the text are to this edition.

8. Simmel, *The Philosophy of Money*, trans. Tom Bottomore and David Frisby (London: Routledge Kegan Paul, 1978), p. 142, and see also Annelies Moors, "Wearing Gold," in *Border Fetishisms*, ed. Patricia Spyer (New York: Routledge, 1998), p. 209; Valenze, *The Social Life of Money*, p. 51; Canetti, excerpt from *Crowds and Power* (1960), in *The Oxford Book of Money*, ed. Kevin Jackson (Oxford: Oxford University Press, 1995), p. 109.

9. Deidre Shauna Lynch, *The Economy of Character* (Chicago: University of Chicago Press, 1998), pp. 30–38.

10. *The Beggar's Opera*, I, v, in *Eighteenth-Century Plays*, introd. Ricardo Quintana (New York: Modern Library, 1952), p. 188.

11. *Roxana*, ed. John Mullan (Oxford: Oxford University Press, 1996), p. 74. All further references in parenthesis in the text are to this edition.

12. Valenze, *The Social Life of Money*, p. 223.

13. For Moll's re-minting of her character, see Ann Kibbie, "Monstrous Generation: The Birth of Capital in Defoe's *Moll Flanders* and *Roxana*," *PMLA*, 110 (1995), 1024 and Ellen Pollak, "*Moll Flanders*, Incest, and the Structure of Exchange," *Eighteenth Century: Theory and Interpretation*, 30 (1989), 15.

14. Pierre Vilar, *A History of Gold and Money*, trans. Judith White (London: Verso, 1976), pp. 219; 214.

15. Quoted in James Thompson, *Models of Value: Eighteenth-Century Political Economy and the Novel* (Durham: Duke University Press, 1996), pp. 52–53.

16. *Complete English Tradesman*, pp. 293; 292; 294.

17. "Being to give my own Character, I must be excus'd to give it as impartially as possible" (*Roxana*, p. 6).

18. Valenze, *The Social Life of Money*, p. 43; Marx, "Economic and Philosophical Manuscripts of 1844," in *The Marx–Engels Reader*, ed. Robert C. Tucker, 2nd edn. (New York: W. W. Norton, 1978), p. 105; Defoe, *Review*, vol. IV, no. 106 (16 October 1707), p. 422; I follow William L. Payne's editorial emendation of this passage in *The Best of Defoe's Review* (New York: Columbia University Press, 1951), p. 131.

19. Thompson, *Models of Value*, p. 95.

20. See Thompson, *Models of Value*, p. 89.

21. *Jure Divino*, Book XII, lines 212–13; on "Air Money," see *Review*, vol. VI, no. 30, 11 June 1709.

22. Anon., *Considerations on the Present State of the Nation*, cited in Sandra Sherman, *Finance and Fictionality in the Early Eighteenth Century: Accounting for Defoe* (Cambridge: Cambridge University Press, 1996), p. 22.

23. Defoe, *A Plan of the English Commerce*, cited in Wolfram Schmidgen, *Eighteenth-Century Fiction and the Law of Property* (Cambridge: Cambridge University Press, 2002), p. 120.

24. *Review*, vol. III, no. 3 (5 January 1706), p. 9; Viscount Bolingbroke, *The Craftsman*, quoted in Jonathan Lamb, *Preserving the Self in the South Seas* (Chicago: University of Chicago Press, 2001), p. 64.
25. Insightful discussions of this Preface and Defoe's relationship to accountability may be found in Sherman, *Finance and Fictionality*, and John F. O' Brien, "The Character of Credit," *English Literary History*, 63 (1996), 603–31.
26. *Complete English Tradesman*, pp. 77; 275; 285.
27. *Anatomy of Exchange Alley*, in *Political and Economic Writings of Daniel Defoe*, vol. VI, ed. John McVeagh (London: Pickering & Chatto, 2000), p. 151.

6

PAT ROGERS

Defoe's *Tour* and the identity of Britain

The whole circuit

At the start of the second volume of his *Tour thro' the Whole Island of Great Britain* (1724–26), Defoe reflects on the progress of his circuit to date. His supposed journey had got as far as Land's End, the extreme tip of the British landmass as it juts out into the Atlantic Ocean.

> My last letter ended the Account of my Travels, where Nature ended her Account, when she meeted out the Island, and where she fix'd the utmost *Western* Bounds of Britain. (*Tour* II, 9)[1]

The syntax equates Defoe's own narrative with the "Account" of nature herself, and prepares us for a ceremonial beating of the national bounds conducted by the author as he carries forward his description of the country's imagined corners. This sentence continues:

> ... being resolv'd to see the very Extremity of it, I set my Foot into the Sea, as it were, beyond the farthest Inch of dry Land *West*, as I had done before near the Town of *Dover*, at the Foot of the Rocks of the *South-Foreland* in *Kent*, which, I think, is the farthest Point *East* in a Line; And as I had done, also, at *Leostoff* in *Suffolk*, which is another Promontory on the *Eastern* Coast, and is reckon'd the farthest Land *Eastward* of the Island in general; Likewise I had used the same Ceremony at *Selsy* near *Chichester*, which I take to be the farthest Land *South* ... so, in its Place, I shall give you an Account of the same Curiosity at *John a Grot*'s House in *Caithness*, the farthest Piece of Ground in *Great Britain, North*. (*Tour* II, 9)

In time Defoe does fulfil his last promise here – not something that applies to all the claims and protestations scattered through the text. Very near its end, the narration reaches northern Scotland and the antipodal point on the mainland from Land's End:

> Here is the House so famous, call'd *John a Grot*'s House, where we set our Horses Feet into the Sea, on the most northerly Land, as the People say, of

Britain, though, I think, *Dungsby-Head* is as far North … The Dominions of *Great Britain* are extended from the *Isle of Wight*, in the Latitude of 50 Degrees, to the Isle of *Unsta* in *Shetland*, in the Latitude of 61 Degrees, 30 Minutes, being Ten Degrees, or full 600 Miles in Length; which Island of *Unst* or *Unsta* being the most remote of the Isles of *Shetland* to the North East, lyes 167 Leagues from *Winterton Ness* in Norfolk. (*Tour* III, 273)

Even into the last pages of his book, Defoe is intent on charting limits, extent, dimensions. It is as though the subject exists only if it is defined by measurement.

Why should Defoe have made such a fuss about the gesture of dipping feet – his own, or his horse's – into the sea? The question grows more urgent if we recall that almost certainly he had never once ventured far into the Scottish Highlands, let alone into the remote fastnesses at the extremity of the northern peninsula. (The purported correction regarding nearby *"Dungsby-Head"* is a characteristic sleight of hand, drawing on material filched from maps and gazetteers.) Several explanations might suggest themselves, involving for example the need to give his narrative a shape by placing emphasis on these moments of arrested motion and recoil. But in the first place, the author was mimicking the ancient rites of "beating the bounds," when local officers, accompanied often by children, would make a compete circuit of the parish. Before accurate mapping or surveying existed, this was a way in which a community could establish its borders and proclaim its identity. The ritual, commonly performed on Ascension Day, had its religious and mystical functions, and when he projected the ceremony on a national scale Defoe carried out his own piece of sympathetic magic, as though placing feet into the water would absolve him from error, and thus confirm the claims he is making on behalf of Britain.

His first impulse as a writer was to convey a sense of precision – hence all the details about the time and place of robberies, or the charting of the relentless march of the plague, day by day, through London, with careful documentation of the mortality figures on a parochial basis in *A Journal of the Plague Year*. Such attention to the minutiae of experience has been codified by critics as the "formal realism" of his fiction. But it has its equivalent in the specificity of his political pamphlets, which regularly cite particular treaties and dates; and in the factual density of many of his historical and biographic works. Above all, his contributions to the literature of commerce are built around elaborate displays of statistics: books such as *A Plan of the English Commerce*, published soon after the *Tour* in 1728, rest on a bewildering array of facts and contentions with regard to economic history. Sometimes, in fact, his claims were quite inaccurate, as we shall see in the case of the *Tour* itself, but Defoe brandishes his evidence with an air of confidence that can easily hoodwink the reader.

So with the spatial data we have been looking at. When the *Tour* stops at London, in the fifth of its ten English sections, the principal aim of the treatment is to inscribe the centrality of the capital within the nation – politically, socially, culturally, but above all economically. In characteristic fashion, Defoe begins by taking a "Measure" of the "mighty" body of London. Several pages are devoted to "A LINE of Measurement, drawn about all the continued Buildings of the City of *London*, and Parts adjacent, including *Westminster* and *Southwark*, &c." (*Tour* II, 67). Nine numbered paragraphs cover the area north of the Thames, five to the south: each gives a minute street-by-street account of the city limits, accompanied by an estimate of the ground traversed in miles, furlongs, and rods (as with Washington and Jefferson, it looks as if Defoe would have been happy to spend his life as a surveyor). There is even a running tally of distances carried over from page to page, testifying equally to the accountant *manqué* in Defoe. Several of the many guides to London in this period have maps of the city: but apart from the *Tour* only one gives a precise account of the extent of the boundaries – the parish clerks' survey, *New Remarks of London* (1732), a work that is organized entirely by parishes and sticks to the official lines of the municipal map. Uniquely, Defoe charts more than the virtual lines of civic responsibility, though he is aware of these. He traces instead the actual margins of built-up London, and hence modern historians have sometimes used his data to compile their own models of the growth of the city, taking 1725 as their baseline. As with the macrocosm, so with the microcosm of the nation which is the capital: to circumscribe the area is to define the topic. All Defoe's claims about the size and grandeur of Britain, its spectacular growth, its economic power, its competitive advantages, its opportunities for further increases in commercial and civic development, as well as personal prosperity – all these start from a vivid bird's eye view of the *whole* island. As we know, he had not really visited every part of the country, and some of his optimistic projections would not ever match the facts. But most of what he said about the way the nation was developing was true, insightful and even prescient.

The fictional journey is an extrapolation from Defoe's own restless peregrinations during his early years, especially the traveling he did on behalf of two patrons, the important politicians Robert Harley and Lord Godolphin. Significantly, it takes Robinson Crusoe more than five years to "make a tour round the island" (*Robinson Crusoe*, p. 109[2]): Defoe himself would have found it impossible to hang around in this way for such a long period. In fact, the narrator of the *Tour* tells us that he had planned a more substantive sea voyage around the coast:

> I had once, indeed, resolved to have coasted the whole Circuit of *Britain* by Sea, as 'tis said, *Agricola* the *Roman* General did; and in this Voyage I would have

gone about every Promontory, and into the Bottom of every Bay, and had provided myself a good Yatch, and an able Commander for that Purpose; but I found it would be too hazardous an Undertaking for any Man to justify himself in the doing it upon the meer Foundation of Curiosity, and having no other Business at all; so I gave it over.   (*Tour* II, 9)

He explains that his project was deterred by the difficulties of finding pilots who would allow him to enter all the bays, creeks, and estuaries around the coast. As a result, he satisfied himself with making "the Circuit very near as perfect by Land" (*Tour* II, 10). In reality the disparate trips that Defoe took over many years follow a pattern and did not join up into any kind of circle. The symmetrical design of the book is entirely a matter of artifice, intended to express the fullness of the author's grasp of Britain in its variety and plenitude.

Sixty years ago G. M. Trevelyan gave eloquent tribute to Defoe's value as a witness to the significant historical processes of his time. His comments on Defoe as one who "first perfected the art of the reporter" come from one who had compiled what is still the most complete survey of England under Queen Anne:

> So then, the account that this man gives of the England of Anne's reign is for the historian a treasure indeed. For Defoe was one of the first who saw the old world through a pair of sharp modern eyes. His report can be controlled and enlarged by great masses of other evidence, but it occupies a central point of our thought and vision.[3]

Since these words, we have had the benefit of more than half a century of increasingly sophisticated research into early eighteenth-century Britain. Recent authorities continue to quote Defoe, to cite his information, and to debate his conclusions. But nothing has emerged that invalidates the central thrust of Trevelyan's comments. In the remainder of this chapter I shall explore the ongoing relevance of the *Tour* for anyone who wishes to get a full grasp of many aspects of the age and assess the worth of the book in the light of modern research. In turn I shall consider the significance of London in the life of the nation; the demographic issues charted in the *Tour*; the use Defoe makes of historical and topographic sources in his library; the importance of the system of transport, by land and water; and finally the vision of nationhood expressed in the book.

London

The *Tour* contains one notorious gaffe. This occurs when Defoe attempts to estimate the size of London:

The Guesses that are made at the Number of Inhabitants, have been variously form'd; Sir *William Petty*, famous for his Political Arithmetick, supposed the City, at his last Calculation, to contain a Million of People, and this he judges from the Number of Births and Burials; and by his Rule, as well by what is well known of the Increase of the said Births and Burials, as of the prodigious Increase of Buildings, it may be very reasonable to conclude, the present Number of Inhabitants within the Circumference I have mentioned, to amount to, at least, Fifteen Hundred Thousand, with this Addition, that it is still prodigiously increasing. (*Tour* II, 72)

This is an absurdly high figure. London, as then defined, had grown at an astonishing rate in the seventeenth century, from 200,000 people at the start of the century to almost 575,000 at the end. By 1750 it reached 675,000, and by 1800 not far short of a million. The demographic area covered by the "bills of mortality" included the historic city within and without the walls, together with adjoining parishes in Middlesex and the city of Westminster, and together with Southwark on the other side of the river. The boundaries of Defoe's "Line of Circumvallation" stretch a little way into outlying villages which had not yet been assimilated into the official returns. He observed with a certain alarm "That *Westminster* is in a fair way to shake Hands with *Chelsea*, as St. *Gyles*'s is with *Marybone*; and *Great Russel Street* by *Montague House*, with *Tottenham-Court*: all this is very evident, and yet all these put together, are still to be called *London*" (*Tour* II, 66). The image of shaking hands seems benign enough, but despite Defoe's feelings of wonder at this explosive growth there is something sinister, too, about the "joining" of these tentacles.

For one thing, he could see the process of urban sprawl working itself out beneath his nose, at the level of just one or two blocks:

The Town of *Islington*, on the north Side of the City, is in like manner joyn'd to the Streets of *London*, excepting one small Field, and which is itself so small, that there is no Doubt, but in a very few Years, they will be entirely joyn'd, and the same may be said of *Mile End*, on the *East* End of the Town. (*Tour* II, 66)

To the south of the river, Newington "is so near joining to *Southwark*, that it cannot now be properly called a Town by itself, but a Suburb to the Burrough, and if, *as they now tell us is undertaken*, St. *George*'s *Fields* should be built into Squares and Streets, a very little Time will shew us *Newington, Lambeth*, and the *Burrough*, all making but one *Southwark*" (*Tour* II, 66). Suburbs made up a largely new phenomenon in European cities, but it is as though Defoe might also have had access to a roadmap from the 1800s. In a daring rhetorical move, he asserted that the boundaries of the city now spread further still:

> The Town of *Greenwich*, which may, indeed be said to be contiguous with *Deptford*, might be also called a Part of this Measurement; but I omit it, as I have the Towns of *Chelsea* and *Knights-Bridge* on the other Side, tho' both may be said to joyn the Town, and in a very few Years will certainly do so. (*Tour* II, 72).

Such a claim amounts to a radical reconceptualization of London, as it had been defined up till now. This unplanned growth presented so many challenges that Defoe was even led to propose restrictions on future building in some districts.

The serious inaccuracy of Defoe's estimate can be explained partly by a reliance on the undependable registers of births and deaths, a parochial rather than a municipal responsibility. The miscalculation also reflects Defoe's strong sense of the way London was creeping remorselessly away from its old nucleus. In fact, the map of the city fifty years later would show that the kind of process he describes, with the assimilation of surrounding communities into the main urban mass, had already taken place. Villages such as Bethnal Green, Wapping, Chelsea, Paddington, and even Hammersmith had come to be regarded as part of the metropolis. As often happens, Defoe was just a little in advance of reality. But what matters most here is the nature of his exaggeration. He always tends to round figures up, but he does so most recklessly when he witnesses a process of rapid growth. His coverage of London is dominated by an awareness of the changes that had taken place in his own lifetime, and so he lays the principal emphasis on the dynamic and accelerating pace of the transformations, which were going on under his very eyes. This means that his account of *relative* size (between two cities, or a city in two stages of development) is nearly always correct, even though he falsifies the *absolute* figures by rounding them up to an implausible total.

A prime rhetorical aim of the *Tour* is to draw attention to the centrality of the capital in national life. Defoe had it altogether right here: London made up about a tenth of the population of England and Wales, whereas only one in forty of French nationals lived in Paris. Among major European cities only Amsterdam had anything remotely approaching a similar dominance, with 7 percent of the much smaller Dutch population. Modern demographers have calculated that a sixth of the adult population (again these counts relate to England and Wales only) would reside in London at some stage of their life. The metropolis was an irresistible magnet for people of all sorts and conditions: heavy immigration took place from nearby continental countries, from Scotland and Ireland, and from further afield. (A large number of Protestants fled from France in the 1680s, like Defoe's fictional heroine Roxana.) But the main agency was internal migration, with a steady stream of mostly young men and women flowing in from the provinces. As a result, around 1700, a net total of some 8,000 immigrants swarmed into the city each year, a process which would continue unabated for the rest of the century and help to create a steady rise in population despite a relatively stable birth-rate and initially little decline in the death-rate. The high incidence of young people in search of a work had consequences which are reflected in the cautionary tales found in the works which Defoe wrote on social topics, such as *The Complete English Tradesman* (1725–27), and on the plight of London itself, such as *Augusta Triumphans* (1728).

However, the significance of London in the nation went a long way beyond its mere size. Admittedly, the city stood out as a colossus in a predominantly rural society, where only Norwich and Bristol reached over 20,000 inhabitants, with a further six towns whose population exceeded 10,000, and perhaps twenty-five with over 5,000 people. The key fact that Defoe grasped was that London served as the main engine of economic activity in Britain. He saw "the general Dependence of the whole Country upon the City of *London* ... for the Consumption of its Produce commented." This is quoted by E. A. Wrigley, in the definitive modern discussion, "A Simple Model of London's Importance in Changing English Society and Economy, 1650–1750." First published in 1967, but often reprinted and endlessly cited, Wrigley's article documents the ways in which the capital came almost to monopolize some crucial aspects of national life around the time that Defoe was writing. Wrigley identifies ten economic, demographic, and sociological changes over the period. These range from "the creation of a single national market" and a better transport network to "the spread of the practice of 'aping ones' betters'," that is aspirational and emulative behavior.[4] Defoe's works have much to say on this last topic, as in *The Compleat English Gentleman* (written *c.*1730), while another of Wrigley's categories, the provision of more commercial and credit facilities, underlies much of the *Review* and the pamphlets Defoe wrote at the time of the Harley administration from 1710–14.

Defoe concerns himself principally with London as a centre of trade and industry. He dilates upon the various markets for commodities such as meat, fish, herbs, corn, leather, coal, and much more. He has a long section on the port: "The whole River, in a Word, from *London-Bridge* to *Black Wall*, is one great *Arsenal*, nothing in the World can be like it" (*Tour* II, 95). He describes the dock facilities in detail, and emphasizes the scale of shipbuilding down the river. These sections actualize the notion of London as the great emporium of the world, expressed in terms of a mythical aspiration in works such as John Dryden's *Annus Mirabilis* (1667). The Thames was, after all, the busiest thoroughfare in the city. Apart from its international shipping, London served as the base for a huge volume of coastal trade, with a high proportion of the mercantile fleet occupied in transporting coal from the northern mines around Newcastle to keep the wheels of the capital turning. In addition,

Defoe writes admiringly of the supply of piped water recently introduced, and discusses various support systems for business, including the customs house, the stock exchange, and the insurance companies (also a new innovation).

But even for Defoe, trade was not everything. At the same time he celebrates the great public buildings – architectural monuments such as St. Paul's Cathedral and Westminster Abbey. He gives an elaborate account of the palace of Whitehall, which had been the impressive centre of government before fire had destroyed most of its structures. He even sets out a fully documented proposal, occupying several pages, to erect a new palace on the site, something which would never be realized. Along with the court and the parliamentary buildings around Westminster Hall, he mentions one nearby black spot, the only street that gives the area "a Communication with *London*." This was King Street, "a long, dark, dirty, inconvenient Passage" from Westminster to the city (*Tour* II, 112). But then he lists the public gaols, totaling almost thirty, and along with these the schools, charities, and hospitals, including the foundation just set up by Thomas Guy, whose progress he carefully monitors throughout the text in appendices and addenda. Defoe's Britain, and not least the capital, is a work in progress.

London is the fulcrum of a machine that engages in a whirl of perpetual motion, where the spectacular growth in population and prosperity is matched by the renown of the cultural institutions and the noble edifices which fill the skyline of the capital: "But the Beauty of all the Churches in the City, and of all the Protestant Churches in the World, is the Cathedral of St. *Paul*'s" (*Tour* II, 81). Aesthetic appreciation goes with ideological fervour: the physical grandeur of the city expresses the emergent power of the nation, which had been locked for generations in a struggle for domination with its Catholic neighbors.

Vital statistics

We can see the same tendency to exaggerate population figures, where they are high and rising, in other sections of the book. The most extreme case occurs in Defoe's account of the wool towns of the West Riding of Yorkshire, where he describes Halifax as the most populous "country Parish" in England. He cites a dubious source, not quite committing himself to endorsing the information: "It is some Years ago that a Reverend Clergyman of the Town of *Hallifax*, told me, they reckoned that they had a Hundred thousand communicants in the Parish, besides Children" (*Tour* III, 67). This calculation is preposterously inflated, even granting the shock which must have come to a previously remote community on the slopes of the Pennine hills as the wool trade expanded. (Defoe had visited the place for Robert Harley in 1705, and knew a local dissenting minister, so his credulity is just about explicable.) The literal statement is wildly wrong: Halifax itself would not have had many more than 5,000 inhabitants, and the cluster of villages in the surrounding valleys can barely have doubled this total. But there is a poetic truth locked up in the claim: Halifax certainly was one of the largest parishes in the nation, along with Manchester, and one of the most densely populated communities outside a large conurbation. Defoe's over-statement dramatizes a real social dynamic which was just getting under way. Population moved from the south and west to the north as industrialization gradually shifted the main locus of manufacturing, to the detriment of the older centers of the textile trade, in East Anglia and the south-western counties. A century later, the biggest cities in the country after London would no longer be Norwich or Bristol, but places like Liverpool, Leeds, and Manchester, all dependent on the textile industry. What has puzzled economic historians is that Defoe sometimes writes as if this process had already reached an advanced stage, if not practically achieved completion, whereas in fact it had only just begun. Like his figures, Defoe's observations bizarrely appear more accurate if we project them forward a few decades.

We can generally rely on the comparative scale of numbers that the *Tour* provides. Defoe likes to take the instance of the tiny "city" of Wells in Somerset, a place where he could find only a small share in the stocking industry. Wells owed its status to the presence of the cathedral, so that civic life went on around the "dignified Clergy" in their "very agreeable Dwellings" round the close (*Tour* ii, 30). Elsewhere he observes that Deptford, on the eastern fringe of London, "is no more a separated Town, but is become a Part of the great Mass, and infinitely full of People too … were the Town of *Deptford* now separated, and rated by itself, I believe it contains more People, and stands upon more Ground, than the City of *Wells*" (*Tour* ii, 66). This time the claim is justified: Wells probably had fewer than 2,000 inhabitants with a static population, a figure eclipsed by the rapid growing Deptford.[5] A similar comparison is used to define Frome, a nearby Somerset town engaged in clothing manufacture that had seen a spectacular growth in the last few decades:

> The Town of *Froom* … is so prodigiously increased within these last Twenty or Thirty Years, that they have built a New Church, and so many Streets of Houses, and those Houses are so full of Inhabitants, that *Frome* is now reckoned to have more People in it, than the City of *Bath*, and some say, than even *Salisbury* itself, and if their Trade continues to increase for a few Years more, as it has done for those past, it is very likely to be one of the greatest and wealthiest Inland Towns in *England*. (*Tour* ii, 32–33)

This time the comparison was not quite so solidly based, and it would be falsified in the course of time. Salisbury continued to have a fairly small and static population, but Bath (which had little more than 1,000 residents in 1660) had begun to climb as the resort grew more fashionable. The big take-off occurred in the late 1720s, immediately after Defoe was writing, with important new building developments by John Wood the elder, so that by 1741 the town had reached 6,000. By contrast the meteoric rise of Frome spluttered to a halt, as the clothing industry migrated northwards, and it climbed only slowly to 9,000 late in the century. Though Defoe picked some unlucky examples, his calculation may just have been valid for a tiny window of time around 1710, soon after he himself made at least one visit to Frome on his electioneering trips.

Moreover, we can place complete reliance on Defoe's descriptive terms, such as "a Town of good Figure, and has in it several eminent Merchants" (of Lyme Regis, taking one example out of scores of similar epithets, *Tour* I, 246). Where he observes signs of decline, as with the shipping industry at Ipswich, we can always find contemporary documents to support the allegation of a decay in trade and prosperity. Where he notes a swing in the competitive position of two neighboring towns, such as the gains of Bideford at the expense of its rival Barnstaple, the archival evidence always confirms what Defoe had picked up, very often by first-hand observation. The detailed account he gives of the layout of some cities, such as Chester, provides a concrete basis for the assertions he makes about their size and prosperity. The facts were sacrosanct, when it came to matters pertaining to trade, even if he sometimes played fast and loose with the more striking and hyperbolic of his figures.

History and topography

Defoe's version of contemporary Britain owed much to his lifelong absorption in two allied branches of literature and knowledge. These are respectively the study of antiquity, especially the earlier history of England and Scotland (he does not seem to have been well versed in Welsh antiquarian matters), and the literature of travel and topography. At the start of his career he compiled a volume of *Historical Collections*, never published and lost since the eighteenth century. After this he wrote a number of books in the area of biography and historiography, and he maintained a close interest in everything connected with travel, exploration, and geography. He was evidently a close student of maps. Plenty of evidence for these obsessive concerns can be found within the text of his *Tour*.

However, our best guide to the range of Defoe's reading comes in the catalogue of his books, sold after his death. Unfortunately the list also embraces the collection of Dr Phillips Farewell, a High Church clergyman who died at the age of forty-two in late 1730, a few months before Defoe, too, went to his grave. We know little of Farewell, and many scholars have pointed to the risks we take if we assume that any given book in the catalogue belonged to either man. However, it seems wholly prudent to make a few, carefully chosen presumptions. The areas in which we may very reasonably suppose Defoe to be by far the likelier candidate for ownership are books on history, especially those on England and Scotland (where Defoe had many links, Farewell none at all), and those on travel. From sources identified by Defoe himself in the *Tour*, we can be absolutely certain that he had access to a number of titles on the list.

More than once in the *Tour*, the narrator makes much of his lack of interest in antiquarian lumber, and his refusal to follow previous travelers in swelling out his text with irrelevant gobbets of historical information. One passage explains his attitude more fully and openly:

> I cannot but say, that since I entred upon the View of these Northern Counties, I have many times repented that I so early resolved to decline the delightful View of Antiquity ... for the Trophies, the Buildings, the religious, as well as military Remains, as well of the *Britains*, as of the *Romans, Saxons*, and *Normans*, are but, as we may say, like Wounds hastily healed up, the *Calous* spread over them being remov'd, they appear presently, and though the Earth ... which naturally eats into the strongest stones, Metals, or whatever Substance, simple or compound, is or can be by Art or Nature prepared to endure it, has defaced the Surface, the Figures and Inscriptions upon most of these Things, yet they are beautiful, even in their decay. And the venerable Face of Antiquity has something so pleasing, so surprising, so satisfactory in it, especially to those who have with any Attention read the Histories of pass'd Ages, that I know nothing renders travelling more pleasant and more agreeable.
>
> But I have condemn'd my self (unhappily) to Silence upon this Head, and therefore, resolving however to pay this Homage to the Dust of gallant Men and glorious Nations, I say therefore, I must submit and go on.   (*Tour* III, 121)

In reality, Defoe stuffed the text with materials from earlier writers, especially his primary source, William Camden's *Britannia*, first published in Latin in 1586. Two versions came out in Defoe's lifetime of a new augmented translation and edition by Edmund Gibson, later Bishop of London (1695 and 1722). The earlier edition duly appears in the sale catalogue as item 186, along with a reply to Camden, reissued in 1724. Investigation reveals that it was the 1695 version that Defoe referred to. Scores of borrowings from *Britannia*, often quite lengthy, can be detected in the *Tour*; some are acknowledged, but rather more of them are not. The presence of Camden's great book in such a dense concentration within the text provides a clue to Defoe's aims: he wished to create not just a storehouse of antiquities, but a hymn to the nation, with its roots, development, and structure considered under the historical aspect. Using *Britannia* in this way enabled Defoe to give the surface of his narrative a kind of historical undercoat on which to paint in his own observations.

We can trace many of the other sources from which Defoe took his information, and from which he derived his sense of the nation's past. He used books such as Elias Ashmole's *History of the Order of the Garter* (1715), John Aubrey's *Miscellanies* (1721), Richard Carew's *The Survey of Cornwall* (1723), and the work mentioned in an earlier citation, Sir William Petty's *Political Arithmetick* (1691). Other books on the list, not acknowledged in the text, but possibly used in compiling the *Tour*, were antiquarian works by Richard Rawlinson, Jodocus Crull, Sampson Erdeswicke, Bulstrode Whitelocke, and many others. When the narrative reaches Stonehenge (*Tour* I, 229–31), abundant evidence demonstrates that Defoe had consulted not just Camden on this topic, but also other speculations on the origins of this monument. A volume containing the writings of Inigo Jones, Walter Charleton, and John Webb appears in the catalogue as item 192, dated 1725 – a year too late to be of use. Taken together, these facts show conclusively that it is impossible to take Defoe at his word, as critics and historians used to do, and imagine that he had a limited interest in the history of places he visited on his imaginary journey.[6]

Rather easier to spot is Defoe's fascination with topography and cartography. We can be sure that he availed himself of books in the collection such as John Ogilvie's *Britannia* (1696); while Farewell would not have preserved *A Book of the Names of all the Parishes, Market Towns, Villages* (1668). Surveys of Middlesex, Hertfordshire, and Northamptonshire, reprinted in 1720 and 1723, would have been highly germane to Defoe's task. As for previous British travels, one item stands out above all others. Item 950 contains John Macky's *A Journey through England in Familiar Letters*, together with its sequel *A Journey through Scotland* (1722–23). At regular intervals Defoe peppers the text with contemptuous references to his rival Macky's alleged blunders, but always under the guise of "a late author" or some variant which scornfully denies Macky a name. Unquestionably he wrote the *Tour* with one eye on the *Journey*, with at once a corrective but also an acquisitive gaze. Almost certainly Defoe knew, and perhaps carried with him on some trips, at least one of the roadbooks which gave detailed itineraries for travelers, even though none of these was sold with the collection. The works of Emmanuel Bowen, for example, had started to appear in time to be of use in plotting routes and calculating distances. Moreover, these guides show enough detail about the nature of the countryside (listing open fields, woods, hills, small streams, and so on) for an astute author to be able to stitch together a convincing description of the scenery, just as if he had recent memories of the landscape in question. Finally, the catalogue records "A map of Middlesex, Essex, and Hertfordshire, done by actual survey, six feet by four, with 728 coats of arms round the map." Middlesex and Essex were the two counties he knew best, with Hertfordshire also high up on the list. We might easily think that, granted some skill in draughtsmanship (and Defoe's handwriting is exceptionally neat), he could have run off such maps himself without too much trouble.[7]

The transport system

In Wrigley's model, we find categories such as agricultural change – a topic on which Defoe had less expertise than on trade, especially, and manufacturing, but which he does highlight in places, as for example when he discusses sheep husbandry, something with obvious relevance to the clothing trade he knew so well. But the category which stands out for a reader of the *Tour* is that relating to "the creation of a better transport system to reduce the cost of moving goods from place to place; to make it possible for goods to move freely at all seasons of the year."[8] Few had a closer knowledge than Defoe about the rigours of eighteenth-century travel, and his book describes the scorching reflections blinding the weary summer-time traveler on the Hogs Back in Surrey, along with the deep mud through which carts sank like stricken ships in Sussex each winter. He gives us the perils of crossing the high Pennines in a snowstorm, and (most likely pure invention) the hazards of negotiating a route past the towering precipices of Penmaenmawr on the coast of North Wales. The *Tour* actualizes the experience of travel. This makes for a sharp distinction from Macky and his breed, since they simply list successive towns and appear to be magically wafted from one stopping-place to another. Defoe's method here owes much to his invention of separate "circuits," closed systems which yet form a coherent pattern, radiating out from London and Edinburgh respectively in the English and Scottish sections.

As with the course of industry and agriculture, the full transport revolution had barely begun in Defoe's time. The building of the great canals had not yet begun, and railways would not start to sweep across the land for another hundred years. Even in the case of roads, the most important technological advances came with the road-surfacing and bridge-building methods of John McAdam, John Smeaton, and Thomas Telford later in the century. But the first whiff of change was in the air, and quite simply Defoe had the most sensitive nostrils to pick up this scent. He saw that better transport was the key not just to improvements in trade, but also to the creation of a more united kingdom. Indeed, the modern double sense of "communications," with a kind of pun on two meanings (transportation/personal interaction) could have been invented to explain the underlying message of the *Tour*, with its constant emphasis on the interdependence of different regions, cities, trades, and employments. At this date transport of heavy goods by water was far cheaper than land-carriage, often by a factor of three or four. Before the canals emerged, this situation placed great responsibility on natural water systems, and Defoe was quick to spot the importance of the "navigation" acts, which enabled communities to open up links to other parts of the country, both close at hand and distant. Many examples could be given; but it will suffice to cite just one, since Defoe's first impulse when he comes to a river is to ask whether it is navigable, by nature or by artifice:

> The *Trent* is navigable by Ships of good Burthen as high as *Gainsbrough*, which is near 40 Miles from the *Humber* by the River. The Barges without the Help of Locks or Stops go as high as *Nottingham*, and farther by the Help of Art, to *Burton* upon *Trent* in *Staffordshire* ... This, and the Navigation lately, reaching up to *Burton* and up the *Derwent* to *Derby*, is a great Support to, and Encrease of the Trade of those Counties which border upon it, especially for the Cheese Trade from *Cheshire* and *Warwickshire*, which have otherwise no Navigation but about from West *Chester* to *London*; whereas by this River it is brought by Water to *Hull*, and from thence to all the South and North Coasts on the East Side of *Britain* ... especially in Time of the late War, when the Seas on the other Side of *England* were too dangerous to bring it by long-Sea. (*Tour* III, 14–15)

We see from this how local measures could have regional and even national consequences. All the river improvements mentioned here had happened quite recently, and the Derwent navigation act had been passed only in 1719. These facts enable us to scotch a persistent canard, to the effect that Defoe's real work had all been done years before he actually wrote the *Tour*. The truth is that the book is marvelously up to the minute on several topics, and nowhere more so than in the case of matters relating to transport. In one section this sense of contemporaneity rises almost to the quality of visionary insight. It comes in the famous appendix to the second volume, devoted almost entirely to the state of the English roads and to the major hope for a better future, that is the new system of turnpikes. These devices took the responsibility for maintenance of major highways from the antiquated and inefficient mechanism in use (unpaid labour by a gang of reluctant locals at long intervals) in favour of new trusts, operating to make a profit from the tolls charged but discreetly monitored by the presence of men like justices of the peace among the trustees. Though one or two isolated turnpikes had been set up earlier, the trend gathered momentum only in the second decade of the eighteenth century, with a rapid acceleration in the 1720s. The instances cited by Defoe include one pioneering venture in 1696, and a number of trusts which had sprung up in the ten years prior to the appearance of the *Tour*. But what is just as striking, along with the freshness of Defoe's information, is the clarity with which he envisions the issues at stake. Overwhelmingly, these early projects were carried out on the major trunk roads leading out of London, and it was only gradually that the network spread to the minor routes scattered round the provinces. This fact suits Defoe's purposes, in emphasizing the crucial position of the capital in the business of the nation. He also points out that these improvements themselves constituted "an infinite Improvement to the Towns near *London*, in the Convenience of coming to them, which make Citizens flock out in greater Number than ever to take Lodgings and Country Houses." Such were the advantages now that "such Tolls are erected now on very Side of *London*, or soon will be," but he did not doubt that "in Time it will be the like all over *England*" (*Tour* II, 243).

Writing of the turnpikes, the historian Paul Langford has observed that "Defoe was excited by their galvanizing effect."[9] The writing in this appendix does indeed have an extraordinary energy, whether Defoe is lamenting the sad state of the old road system or greeting the arrival of the new promised land, fed and watered thanks to the revolutionary changes he saw in progress. Thus, he deplores the condition of the road from London to the West Midlands:

> Suppose you take the other *Northern* Road, namely, by St. *Albans*, *Dunstable*, *Hockley*, *Newport Pagnel*, *Northampton*, *Leicester*, and *Nottingham*, or *Darby*: On this Road ... you enter the deep Clays, which are so surprisingly soft, that it is perfectly frightful to Travellers, and it has been the Wonder of Foreigners, how considering the great Number of Carriages which are continually passing with heavy Loads, those Ways have been made practicable; indeed the great Number of Horses every Year kill'd by the Excess of Labour in those heavy ways, has been such a heavy Charge to the Country, that new Building of Causeways, as the *Romans* did of old, seems to be a much easier Expence.   (*Tour* II, 234)

And now the prospect in store:

> Upon this great Road there are wonderful Improvements made and making, which no Traveller can miss the Observation of, especially if he knew the Condition these Ways were formerly in; nor can my Account of these Counties be perfect, without taking Notice of it; for certainly no publick Edifice, Almshouse, Hospital, or Nobleman's Palace, can be of equal Value to the Country with this, no nor more an Honour and Ornament to it.   (*Tour* II, 239)

This was quite a new way of defining the state of the nation. Others were dubious about the value and profitability of turnpikes, but Defoe understood that most users would find tolls preferable to plunging into "Sloughs and Holes" (*Tour* II, 238): he was right in the long run. He saw, too, something we might miss, that better roads would facilitate not just speedier passage for passengers and goods vehicles, but also the driving of cattle and sheep over long distances, an essential part of the annual cycle in agriculture.

"Improvements made and making." This phrase sums up Defoe's attitude to Britain, as a country in the process of rapid and mainly beneficent change. He did not get everything right, but he was certainly among the very first to perceive that a more efficient transport network was vital to any advance in the commercial and manufacturing sphere, and by extension to wider possibilities for the nation's inhabitants in terms of their way of life. One of Wrigley's categories, we may recall, concerned new habits of consumption. Defoe saw very clearly the role which markets play in economic activity, and the need to encourage consumers to find producers, and producers to satisfy consumers. He hymned the traditional activity at Stourbridge Fair near Cambridge, but he also described with a hint of reserve the new leisure resorts and spas such as Bath and Bury St Edmunds. "I left *Tunbridge*," he records drily, "for the same Reason that I give, why others should leave it, when they are in my Condition; namely, that I found my Money almost gone" (*Tour* I, 166).

A vision of the nation

Humor is one of the key ingredients in the book, expressing Defoe's amused and frequently sceptical take on the world he saw around him. But at other moments the work attains a plangent and even tragic tone, most notably perhaps in his threnody for the losses suffered by some great mercantile figures as a result of the South Sea Bubble, just four years distant when he wrote:

> I shall cover over as much as possible the melancholy part of a Story, which touches too sensibly, many, if not most of the Great and Flourishing Families in *England*: Pity and matter of Grief is it to think that Families, by Estate, able to appear in such a Glorious Posture as this, should ever be Vulnerable by so mean a Disaster as that of Stock-Jobbing: But the *General Infatuation of the Day* is a Plea for it; so that Men are not now blamed on that Account: and if my Lord *Castlemain* was Wounded by that Arrow shot in the Dark, 'twas a Misfortune. (*Tour* I, 131)

This "Story" in fact recurs as a main thread in the plot of the book, as it represents a perilous moment when the march of Britain towards peace and plenty nearly hit a sudden roadblock. One other recent event had similarly jangled the alarm bells, but the Jacobite rising of 1715–16 was still too delicate a subject to be treated head on. Instead, the author generally tiptoes around the episode, except where he comes to the site of a major encounter such as Preston, scene of "the late bloody Action with the Northern Rebels" (*Tour* iii, 135). In his Scottish sections, he is forced to acknowledge the existence of Jacobites and their fate. But he nearly always chooses to write without undue edge or emphasis: thus, the Duke of Gordon "has been embroil'd a little in the late unhappy Affair of the *Pretender*; but he got off without a Forfeiture, as he prudently kept himself at a Distance from them till he might see the Effect of Things" (*Tour* iii, 264).

For the most part, Defoe provides adequate coverage of lowland Scotland, though never quite as convincingly as in his treatment of south and west England. His lack of firsthand knowledge of the Highlands shows up clearly: but then the mountains and glens had not yet really been brought under the remit of the Hanoverian government, despite the Union of parliaments in 1707. (And Wales, for that matter, is given almost as sketchy a treatment.) In that earlier phase of his life, Defoe had been retained as an agent for Godolphin and Harley, nominally as "a person employed for the queen's service in Scotland for the revenue, etc.," but really to promote the Union. He strongly supported the measure, but recognized that it could achieve success only with the willing consent of the Scottish people. The terms certainly satisfied the needs of the political class in the Lowlands, where Defoe was operating. In addition, he insisted that Scotland needed to develop its economy along the lines England had followed, so as to introduce improvements in trade, manufacturing, shipping, fishery, and agriculture.

Already, Defoe had explored these issues in the pamphlets he wrote during the time he spent in Edinburgh between 1706 and 1712; but he returns to them with fresh energy in the *Tour*. At Glasgow he sets out the ways in which the Scottish export trade could be boosted, despite the fact that it had been held back by the absence of profitable trade with the colonies, especially America (iii, 201–4). On the coast of Fife he takes up a different aspect of the problem, and recommends that more of Scottish production should be applied to consumption at home:

> I know ... that *Scotland* is now established in a lasting Tranquility; the Wars between Nations are at an End, the Wastings and Plunderings, the Ravages and Blood are all over; the Lands in *Scotland* will now be improv'd, their Estates doubled, the Charges of defending her Abroad and at Home lies upon *England*; the Taxes are easy and ascertain'd, and the *West-India* Trade abundantly pours in Wealth upon her; and this is all true; and, in the End, I am still of Opinion *Scotland* will be Gainer.

The answer is simple:

> I must add, that her own Nobility, would they be true Patriots, should then put their helping Hand to the rising Advantages of their own Country, and spend some of the large Sums they get in *England* in applying to the Improvement of their Country, creating Manufactures, employing the Poor, and propagating the Trade at Home, which they may see plainly has made their united Neighbours of *England* so rich. (*Tour* III, 237–38)

Nationhood is a fragile thing, and the creation of a truly united kingdom took generations and never attained a perfect state. As Linda Colley has shown, many decades passed before Scotland was properly integrated into a single commonwealth, and it retained distinctive religious, educational, and legal structures.[10] But at the start of the process, one prerequisite for the Union to gain acceptance (passive at least) was a clear argument on its behalf, setting out the political objectives, the economic potentiality, and the cultural benefits which might accrue. Defoe did as much as anyone to carry out this public relations exercise, and he was still promoting the agenda in his *Tour*, more than a decade after the Union came into being. In fact, the case gains much greater strength in 1726: partly because he could already point to hopeful signs that the programme was working, and partly because he was able to argue the case in detail with reference to particular places and trades he had encountered on his supposed journey. Above all, the contrast with English experience builds up over the course of the narrative. A truly united "whole island of Great Britain" will only emerge when the parts cohere, in a way that the design of the *Tour* brings them together in a single organic unit.

What Defoe was intent on creating had to do with something less than nationalism in the later sense. Nationalism "becomes pervasive and dominant only under certain social conditions, which in fact prevail in the modern world, and nowhere else."[11] His patriotism took the form of espousing an aggressive overseas trade policy, but he saw international trade as a mutually beneficial activity rather than an out-and-out struggle to the death, or simply war by other means. Internally, he wanted to see Scotland properly integrated into the Union. He saw Britain as evolving into a great world power, not just by military strength but by economic expansion. Trade, radiating out from its great power-house in London, would harness natural resources and, along with agriculture, take advantage of improvements devised by the innovating spirit of the people. As he went on his way round the country, his account was not quite accurate in every detail and not all his predictions came true. But, as history has shown, he was more often right than wrong. The author dipped his toes into the sea at the extreme corners of the nation, and the book left its own footprint on the English imagination.

NOTES

1. All references are to *Writings on Travel, Discovery and History*, ed. John McVeagh, vols. I–III, in *The Works of Daniel Defoe*, general eds. W. R. Owens and P. N. Furbank (London: Pickering & Chatto, 2001).

2. *Robinson Crusoe*, ed. John Richetti (London: Penguin Books, 2001).

3. G. M. Trevelyan, *Illustrated Social History*, vol. III, *The Eighteenth Century* (Harmondsworth: Penguin, 1964), pp. 18–19. The text is that of Trevelyan's *English Social History* (1944). Note that the map of "London in the Reign of George I" (pp. 276–77) appears to have been drawn at least in part on the basis of the information supplied by Defoe.

4. E. A. Wrigley, "A Simple Model of London's Importance in Changing English Society and Economy, 1650–1750," in *People, Cities and Wealth: The Transformation of Traditional Society* (Oxford: Blackwell, 1987), pp. 133–56.

5. Once the comparison goes the other way, when Defoe writes of Peterborough, "This is a little City, and indeed 'tis the least in *England*; for *Bath*, or *Wells*, or *Ely*, or *Carlisle*, which are all call'd Cities, are yet much bigger; yet *Peterborough* is no contemptible Place neither" (*Tour* III, 217–18).

6. *The Libraries of Daniel Defoe and Phillips Farewell*, ed. Helmut Heidenreich (Berlin: no pub., 1970), pp. xxi–xxii. This is a thorough and clear-headed edition, too little consulted by writers on Defoe.

7. Further confirmation comes from several books not listed in the sale catalogue which crop up regularly in the *Tour*. The most important include William Dugdale's *Monasticon Anglicanum* (1655–73), John Stow's *Survey of London* (1598, 1603), and Robert Plot's *Natural History of Oxfordshire* (1677).

8. Wrigley, "A Simple Model," p. 151.

9. Paul Langford, *A Polite and Commercial People: England 1727–1783* (Oxford: Oxford University Press), p. 396. Significantly, Langford discusses the turnpike system first in his section on "New Improvements," and devotes considerable space to the topic (pp. 391–410).

10. Linda Colley, *Britons: Forging the Nation 1707–1837*, 2nd edn. (New Haven: Yale University Press, 2005), p. 12. This is by far the most important study of the creation of the "united" kingdom.

11. Ernest Gellner's formulation, quoted by Gerald Newman, *The Rise of English Nationalism: A Cultural History 1740–1830* (London: Weidenfeld and Nicolson, 1987), p. 52.

7

JOHN RICHETTI

Defoe as narrative innovator

Defoe's fiction is traditionally labeled "realistic." But realism is a slippery notion. Once we move beyond basic biological circumstances, "reality" manifests itself as a historically variable entity that can be defined only tentatively according to prevailing philosophical, social, economic, and technological conditions. From antiquity onwards European literature had vividly represented many of those fundamental life events and physical needs – alimentary, sexual, and excretory for example – that readers immediately recognize and mark as "realistic." Traditionally, however, such representations were until relatively modern times relegated to the lower genres in the hierarchy of literary value that extended downwards from epic and tragedy, poetic genres that featured as their actors gods and heroes, to the lesser forms of mostly comic prose genres peopled by ordinary folk doing ordinary (and amusing) things.

Defoe's narratives certainly offer accounts of the lives of ordinary people, some of them socially marginal or even criminal, but his fiction is never realistic in the simple sense of representing basic human functions like sex or excretion or physical decay, although two of his novels, *Moll Flanders* (1722) and *Roxana* (1724), are about women who have many sexual partners (even if their descriptions of sexual acts are extremely reticent and even prudish). But the rendering of the particulars of experience, especially human biological facts, is not where his "realistic" originality lies. Defoe's "realism" as a novelist comes in his vivid evocation of individuals as they examine the conditions of their existence and explore what it means to be a person in particularized social and historical circumstances. Looking back on their lives, his characters discover the nature of *their* particular reality. They reveal how they adapted to their circumstances, how they modified actuality as they encountered it and constructed personal versions of "reality," all the while let it be said avoiding solipsism of the sort that Cervantes' Don Quixote exemplifies. So one should speak not of "reality" in some stable sense in Defoe's fictions but of shifting and multiple "realities." Indeed, "reality" (not a word that any of his narrators ever use) is itself in Defoe's narrative world a problem, often enough a realm full of uncertainties and even of mysteries. Robinson Crusoe, for example, is troubled by his strange fate and subject to disturbing and fanciful imaginings and dreams on his island; he wonders if God's Providence is behind all his troubles, just as he wonders after he finds the single footprint on the shore whether the Devil is after him. So he takes nothing for granted; he is a suspicious and careful observer, who sees clearly but recognizes the limits of his understanding. For example, after he and Friday see what appears to be an English ship in their harbor, he resolves on caution, trusting his intuition but interpreting his cautious hunch as proof of the reality of "an invisible world": "Let no man despise the secret hints and notices of danger which sometimes are given him, when he may think there is no possibility of its being real. That such hints and notices are given us, I believe few that have made any observations of things can deny; that they are certain discoveries of an invisible world, and a converse of spirits, we cannot doubt."[1]

Ian Watt called Defoe's innovation "formal realism," which he described as "the premise, or primary convention, that the novel is a full and authentic report of human experience, and therefore under an obligation to satisfy its reader with such details of the story as the individuality of the actors concerned, the particulars of the times and places of their actions, details which are presented through a more largely referential use of language than is common in other literary forms."[2] Formally realistic narrative highlights particularity; it locates events and persons in a specific time and socio-historical space. In doing so, novelistic narrative offers its readers what they will presumably recognize from their own daily experiences, just as it rejects or is deeply skeptical of events and explanations beyond the familiar and the quotidian. Realism is defined by its rejection of what it brackets as fantastic or romantic, an insistence on a disenchanted world where only empirical evidence counts as real. But Defoe's narrators like Crusoe and Roxana, especially, also try to hold on to a belief in the traditional world of providential arrangements and spiritual, non-material forces summed up in entities like God and the Devil. Even a hardened old sinner like Moll Flanders invokes the Devil as a factor in her life of crime. But in each case, reality with all its uncertainties arrives through the medium of individual perception and experience. Watt traced this new primacy of individual experience to the rise to prominence of the urban middle classes and the ideology of individualism, and also more generally to the theories of modern empirical philosophers like Locke, who ground truth in sense perception, and who assert that general or abstract truth derives from particular ideas and impressions.

But Defoe's characters are not lost in the bloom and buzz of primary impressions; their narrations are embedded in the context of exactly rendered circumstances. Defoe's clear-eyed fictions are novelistic precisely because their narrators evoke a shifting social and historical field of opportunity (and danger) rather than a hierarchical and settled order. Experience in such fiction thereby shapes or even determines identity and personality for better or worse. In dramatizing the exploratory and improvisatory careers of their characters, Defoe's narratives are part of a trend that undermines traditional status divisions and highlights individual actors who tend to move through those divisions rather than within them, who may be said to acquire identity instead of having it simply thrust upon them. Defoe's narratives dwell upon the material aspects of the world as it is experienced by characters conscious of their own unsettled and developing individuality, very much within a social and moral order but never entirely contained or fully explained by it. In short, Defoe's realism qualifies as such because it dramatizes the dynamic and historical essence of the "real" in the early modern period in Britain; his narratives evoke the actual as the inter-animation of the personal and the socio-historical. And, crucially, they exist in an effectively secular and material universe, where God and his Providence are powerful ideas but never actually or fully present as controlling concepts, even though individuals may (like Robinson Crusoe) spend a good deal of their time searching for religious meaning in their lives.

Despite this variegated nature of experience, this relativity of the "real" that they dramatize, Defoe's narratives claim aggressively to be literally true. They are fake autobiographies, life stories of supposedly actual people. These claims, doubtless, tell us what Defoe thought his readers wanted. Like all his subsequent fictions, *Robinson Crusoe* (1719) features a title page advertising the memoirs of a "real" person. Defoe's invention seems to have been inspired by journalistic accounts of a survivor on a deserted island off the coast of Chile. Alexander Selkirk, a Scottish sailor, was marooned for four and a half years on the island after a quarrel with his captain. After his rescue and return to England in 1711, he was interviewed by Richard Steele in 1713–14 in his periodical, *The Englishman*. From this germ, Defoe seems to have concocted his narrative, and the title page is careful to promise specific veracity among other distinctive features: "THE LIFE And Strange Surprizing ADVENTURES OF ROBINSON CRUSOE, Of YORK, Mariner: Who lived eight and twenty Years all alone in an un-inhabited Island on the Coast of America, near the Mouth of the Great River of Oroonoque; Having been cast on Shore by Shipwreck, wherein all the Men perished but himself. With an ACCOUNT how he was at last as strangely deliver'd by Pyrates. Written by Himself" (p. 1).

Although we can't be sure that Defoe rather than his printers composed the title pages for his fictions, they do offer enticing summaries of the books' events, and they all claim that their characters' lives are both true and fantastic, out-of- the-ordinary and thereby worth reading. Here's the title page of *Moll Flanders* (1722): "The Fortunes and Misfortunes of the Famous Moll Flanders, &c. Who was Born in Newgate, and during a Life of continu'd Variety for Threescore Years, besides her Childhood, was Twelve Year a Whore, five Times a Wife (whereof once to her own Brother) Twelve Year a Thief, Eight Year a Transported Felon in Virginia, at last grew Rich, liv'd Honest, and died a Penitent. Written from her own Memorandums."[3] As Lennard Davis has developed the idea, the early novel can be said to grow out of an increasing appetite in the late seventeenth and early eighteenth century in Britain for "news," representing what Davis calls the "news/novel" discourse. Defoe's novels are calculated for readers attracted to stories of actual and to some extent ordinary individuals (not kings or queens or divinities) who become extraordinary though experiencing those unusual but real events that we still call "news."[4] Thus, Defoe's final long fiction, *Roxana* (1724) offers sensational gossip about a former royal mistress and appeals to an already notorious historical actuality: "THE Fortunate Mistress: Or, A HISTORY OF The LIFE And Vast Variety of Fortunes Of Mademoiselle de Beleau, Afterwards Call'd The Countess de Wintselsheim, in GERMANY. Being the Person known by the Name of the Lady Roxana, in the Time of King Charles II."[5] But Defoe doesn't always strike the right balance. *Captain Singleton* (1720), an adventure story of a young urchin who becomes a pirate captain and African explorer, fails to combine successfully or seamlessly the ordinary and the fantastic. Bob Singleton and his mates trek across the entire African continent and embark thereafter upon a fantastically lucrative piratical career, so that Bob's humble origins rather quickly lose their relevance to his story. We forget that he is Bob and he becomes the quasi-legendary Captain Singleton, like many other romanticized pirate captains of the time.

Robinson Crusoe sets the pattern for Defoe's subsequent fictions in its rendering of the extraordinary tale of an ordinary man, from York in the north of England, a member of the lower middle classes who ignores his parents' advice to settle down and goes to sea as a trader to Africa. Defoe's accomplishment here and in the works to come is to reconcile those two trajectories. His narrators establish themselves as ordinary at the start, but their careers move them into the realm of the unusual and unexpected. In *Robinson Crusoe*, Defoe does this by grounding his hero's amazing adventures in a carefully evoked world of exactly observed phenomena and things. Here and in the novels that follow, the looseness of the plotting, the merely sequential form of a life as it is lived, helps to create a relatively unstructured train of events. Moreover, Defoe's invention of a personalized voice for each of his narrators offers a rambling, self-revelatory discourse that attempts to approximate a distinctive idiom for each of his characters that is equally artless – plain, simple, digressive, and thereby not "literary." Defoe's plain prose, which Watt calls "a more largely referential use of language than is common in other literary forms," is another means of making fiction look like "truth."

The word "realism" derives from the Latin word *res, rei*, a thing, object, matter, affair, circumstance; and Latin for the "nature of things" is *natura rerum*, the world, the universe, nature.[6] Defoe's narratives are attentive to "things" in all these senses, building up from particularized matters to a sense of a larger world, of nature, of society. There is one especially revealing moment in *Robinson Crusoe* that illustrates Defoe's attention to "things." Here is Crusoe's description of his first moments on the island and his summary of what he finds of his shipmates after the wreck:

> I walk'd about on the shore, lifting up my hands, and my whole being, as I may say, wrapt up in the contemplation of my deliverance, making a thousand gestures and motions which I cannot describe, reflecting upon all my comrades that were drown'd, and that there should not be one soul sav'd but my self; for, as for them, I never saw them afterwards, or any sign of them, except three of their hats, one cap, and two shoes that were not fellows. (pp. 38–39)

To some extent, Crusoe misses a golden opportunity for a full and accurate depiction of his panic after getting to shore; he "cannot describe" those manic "gestures and motions," although he asks readers to imagine them, thereby pointing to the contract between narrator and readers in which the latter do some of the crucial work of picturing reality. Crusoe is "reflecting" upon his drowned comrades, and this scene, like so much of the book, seeks to render his confused state of mind. But that subjectivity is suddenly matched by Crusoe's talent for exact objectivity as he enumerates the disturbing reality of those floating remnants of his shipmates: three hats, one cap, and two shoes that don't match. Defoe doesn't call any attention to its general implications, but this moment evokes a material world that is random, without purpose or pattern; his comrades have been reduced, as it were, to things, to miscellaneous items of clothing, just as Crusoe himself on the beach is in something like the same condition. In its exact bleakness, this enumeration prefigures Crusoe's attempts to order the objectivity of the island and to find meaning in his situation as isolated and bewildered survivor. This is the first of many such moments of empirical observation and exact enumeration. They produce the book's sharp factual focus, "that genius for fact," which, as Virginia Woolf observed, "achieves effects that are beyond any but the great masters of descriptive prose."[7]

Robinson Crusoe's isolation on the island, which takes up about three-quarters of the book, can be taken as a metaphor for how modern novelistic realism such as Defoe pioneered tends to operate. With only himself to talk to,

Crusoe has to depend upon his perceptions; he has by virtue of his isolation to establish and to order the world around him. His life depends upon getting all this right and making sense of things. In this regard, Crusoe's isolation is an intensified version of the enabling apartness and singularity his other narrators experience. Like all of Defoe's narrators, Crusoe tells his own story. So the first level of their realism is psychological; reality here is an individual's interior life under extreme and stressful circumstances. What does extended isolation and single-handed survival feel like? Defoe explores this question with an intensity that has almost no precedent in narrative fiction in English. The book's instant and perennial popularity thereafter marks the relevance of this image of the individual for eighteenth-century readers. The effect is to evoke an individual who is just and essentially himself; or to put it another way the narrative depicts Crusoe exploring his subjectivity, full of anxiety, wondering who he is and what he has done to earn his strange fate. Near the beginning of the island sojourn Crusoe looks back on his life:

> I had a dismal prospect of my condition … I had great reason to consider it as a determination of Heaven, that in this desolate place, and in this desolate manner I should end my life; the tears would run plentifully down my face when I made these reflections, and sometimes I would expostulate with my self, Why Providence should thus compleatly ruin its creatures, and render them so absolutely miserable, so without help abandon'd, so entirely depress'd, that it could hardly be rational to be thankful for such a life.
>
> But something always return'd swift upon me to check these thoughts, and to reprove me; and particularly one day walking with my gun in my hand by the sea side, I was very pensive upon the subject of my present condition, when reason as it were expostulating with me t'other way, thus: Well, you are in a desolate condition, 'tis true, but pray remember, Where are the rest of you? Did not you come eleven of you into the boat, where are the ten? Why were not they sav'd and you lost? Why were you singled out? Is it better to be here or there? and then I pointed to the sea. All evils are to be consider'd with the good that is in them, and with what worse attends them. (p. 53)

In these ruminations, Crusoe is not primarily a type or an allegory, not a representative of something larger or more comprehensive. He is simply himself. His moralizing is self-expressive, valuable not so much for its didactic usefulness as for its dramatizing of Crusoe's self-consciousness, his interior life. To be sure, he comes in the course of his narrative to embody a new sort of individualism, which is the general resonance that emerges out of his radically particularized story. But here and in the events that follow Crusoe is persuasively real because of his self-conscious uncertainty, his constant puzzlement as he seeks to extract a working truth from the flow of circumstances that constitute his particular and unique life.

That project of self-realization is furthered, brilliantly, by his resourceful-ness, his capacity for efficient action as he salvages supplies from the wrecked ship and establishes himself on the island, building shelter, hunting and gathering, mastering his environment and making it his own. Although he has retrieved many tools and materials from the shipwreck, Crusoe finds that he lacks crucial utensils such as pots for cooking and for storage, and he recounts how he managed to learn to make them, at first small and inade-quate: One night, "making a pretty large fire for cooking my meat," he finds a broken piece of earthenware in his fire and, ever alert, he notices that it is "burnt as hard as a stone, and red as a tile." So he experiments:

> ... I plac'd three large pipkins, and two or three pots in a pile one upon another, and plac'd my fire wood all round it with a great heap of embers under them; I ply'd the fire with fresh fuel round the out side, and upon the top, till I saw the pots in the inside red hot quite thro', and observ'd that they did not crack at all; when I saw them clear red, I let them stand in that heat about 5 or 6 Hours, till I found one of them, tho' it did not crack, did melt or run, for the sand which was mixed with the clay melted by the violence of the heat, and would have run into glass if I had gone on, so I slack'd my fire gradually, till the pots began to abate of the red colour, and watching them all night, that I might not let the fire abate too fast, in the morning I had three very good, I will not say handsome pipkins; and two other earthen pots, as hard burnt as could be desir'd; and one of them perfectly glaz'd with the running of the sand.   (pp. 96–97)

As Virginia Woolf observed in her essay on *Robinson Crusoe*, Defoe's adventure story of a man on a deserted island "is enough to rouse in us the expectation of some far land on the limits of the world," but instead what Defoe gives us is "nothing but a large earthenware pot." Reality is his subject, she says, rather than sunrises and sunsets, "fact and substance ... ruthless common sense," these are the substance of Defoe's novel.[8] In passages like this (and there are a good number of them), Defoe grounds his psychological realism in representations of the material world – the fine-grained observation of natural phenomena as Crusoe slowly learns to see them clearly and to manipulate them for his advantage. Necessarily, he is preternaturally alert from the beginning of his time on the island; he looks and listens for those animals or men who might attack him; he searches for edible flora and fauna, hunting and gathering; he scans the horizon for a sail and possible escape; he marks the growing and harvesting seasons as he masters agricultural techniques, and by trial and error he domesticates the island's goats for milk and meat. He makes himself master of various trades and techniques, from carpentry to baking and potting. And he explores his island, on foot and in a boat that he builds. Here is part of his first exploration:

At the end of this march I came to an opening, where the country seem'd to descend to the west, and a little spring of fresh water, which issued out of the side of the hill by me, run the other way, that is due east; and the country appear'd so fresh, so green, so flourishing, every thing being in a constant verdure, or flourish of *Spring*, that it it look'd like a planted garden.

I descended a little on the side of that delicious vale, surveying it with a secret kind of pleasure, (tho' mixt with my other afflicting thoughts) to think that this was all my own, that I was king and lord of all this country indefeasibly, and had a right of possession; and if I could convey it, I might have it in inheritance, as compleatly as any lord of a manor in *England*.   (p. 80)

This is not only exact as well as evocative of an exotic, non-European locale that is Europeanized ("like a planted garden"), but it also points to another aspect of the realism that *Robinson Crusoe* exemplifies. Let's call it ideological realism. Crusoe is by instinct an imperialist; he takes possession of his island as his property, partly in the sense that John Locke described by working on it, cultivating it and transforming it by his labor. He's also a member of the aspiring middle class, thrilled at the prospect of joining the land-owning gentry by acquiring this New World real estate. He emerges as a representation of the mentality of a European/Englishman of the early eighteenth century: resourceful, self-reliant, acquisitive. As James Joyce, a great admirer of Defoe, said in some lectures he gave in Trieste in 1911, Crusoe is "the true prototype of the British colonist," and in him one can find "the whole Anglo-Saxon spirit ... the manly independence; the unconscious cruelty; the persistence; the slow yet efficient intelligence; the sexual apathy; the practical, well-balanced religiousness; the calculating taciturnity."[9]

Crusoe's mapping and exploitation of his surroundings is a crucial aspect of Defoe's other narratives, where settings are often actual and (for his original audience) recognizable places. Three of his novels, *Moll Flanders* (1722), *Colonel Jack* (1722), and *Roxana* (1724) are set for long sections in London, and that urban scene is often rendered with what looks like pinpoint accuracy. Jack, for instance, spends his childhood as a homeless street urchin and pickpocket, part of a gang of young thieves, and he describes how they live in particular London streets and locales:

Thus we all made a shift, tho' we were so little, to keep from starving, and as for Lodging, we lay in the Summer-time about the Watch-houses, and on Bulk-heads, and Shop-doors, where we were known; as for a Bed we knew nothing what belong'd to it for many Years after my Nurse died, and in Winter we got into the Ash holes, and Nealing-Arches in the Glass-house, call'd *Dallows's* Glass house, near *Rosemary Lane*, or at another Glass-house in *Ratcliff-high-way*.[10]

And a bit later, with some of their ill-gotten gains, Jack and his comrade go to "a boiling Cook's in *Rosemary-Lane*," where they regale themselves with the following: "Three-penny-worth of boil'd Beef, Two-penny-worth of Pudding, a penny Brick, (as they call it, or Loaf) and a whole Pint of strong Beer, which was seven Pence in all. N.B. We had each of us a good mess of charming Beef Broth into the Bargain; and which chear'd my Heart wonderfully" (pp. 15–16). There is a documentary exactness about this rendition of the lives of young pickpockets, but of course for eighteenth-century readers such under-class urban subsistence is as exotic as Crusoe's deserted Caribbean island. Less exotic but equally exact is Jack's rendition of how he and his fellow pickpocket go about their business in the Custom House and find themselves, unexpectedly, with various bills of exchange, one worth three hundred pounds. Here is his description of their escape and their accounting of their take:

> … thro' innumerable narrow Passages, Alley's and Dark ways, we were got up into *Fenchurch-Street*, and thro' *Billiter lane* into *Leadenhall-Street*, and from thence into *Leadenhall-Market*.
> It was not a Meat-Market Day so we had room to sit down upon one of the Butcher's Stalls, and he bad me Lug out; what he had given me, was a little Leather Letter Case, with a French Almanack stuck in the inside of it, and a great many Papers in it of several kinds. (p. 20)

Readers thus participate in two realities – the objective world of the London streets and Jack's incomplete, naive view of it. That mysterious leather case with the "French Almanack" and papers in it marks the beginning of his discovery of a world of coherent events and institutions such as he will in due course enter as he matures through his experiences and expands his horizon. Defoe's documentary realism has, naturally, two purposes. Particularly in the urban settings of some of his novels, he evokes particular spaces, provides grounding that furthers the truth claims of the narratives. Equally important, such realism is linked to a verisimilitude, social and psychological, that promotes and complicates characterization, as it grows in relation to those vividly rendered specific circumstances. Consider Moll Flanders' account, worth quoting at length, of her initial descent into a life of crime, as she finds herself at the end of her resources, alone without a lover or a husband in London: "I sold off most of my Goods, which put a little Money in my Pocket, and I liv'd near a Year upon that, spending very sparingly, and eeking things out to the utmost; but still when I look'd before me, my Heart would sink within me at the inevitable approach of Misery and Want" (pp. 190–91). So she records how one evening, "being brought … to the last Gasp," she walks out, carried by "the Devil" to an apothecary shop in "Leadenhall street," where she commits her first theft, a bundle on a stool near the counter:

'twas like a Voice spoken to me over my Shoulder, take the Bundle; be quick; do
it this Moment; it was no sooner said but I step'd into the Shop, and with my
Back to the Wench, as if I had stood up for a Cart that was going by, I put my
Hand behind me and took the Bundle, and went off with it, the Maid or Fellow
not perceiving me, or any one else.

It is impossible to express the Horror of my Soul all the while I did it, When
I went way I had no Heart to run, or scarce to mend my pace; I cross'd the Street
indeed, and went down the first turning I came to, and I think it was a Street that
went thro' into *Fenchurch-street*, from thence I crossed and turn'd thro' so many
ways and turnings that I could never tell which way it was, nor where I went, for
I felt not the Ground I stept on, and the farther I was out of Danger, the faster
I went, till tyr'd and out of Breath, I was forc'd to sit down on a little Bench at a
Door, and then found I began to recover, and found I was got into *Thames-
street* near *Billingsgate*: I rested me a little and went on, my Blood was all in a
Fire, my Heart beat as if I was in a sudden Fright: In short, I was under such a
Surprize that I knew not whether I was a going, or what to do.

...

What the Bundle was made up for, or on what Occasion laid where I found it,
I knew not, but when I came to open it, I found there was a Suit of Child-bed
Linnen in it, very good and almost new, the Lace very fine; there was a Silver
Porringer of a Pint, a small Silver Mug and Six Spoons, with some other Linnen,
a good Smock, and Three Silk Handkerchiefs, and in the Mug wrap'd up in a
Paper Eighteen Shillings and Six-pence in Money.   (pp. 191–92)

Moll's recollections have two related aspects: she remembers a compulsion
verging on somnambulism, as she is driven by economic despair, a woman
with no husband and no profession, with absolutely no legitimate way of
supporting herself (not that Moll puts it this way, but readers recognize the
gendered social realities behind her despair), but she also remembers a number of exact particulars surrounding the act – her position vis-à-vis the shop
girl and the apprentice, that "little Bench at a door" on *"Thames street* near
Billingsgate," one of the streets she takes on her way home, the hour of her
arrival at home, and then a precise inventory of the contents and the value of
the basket she has stolen. Breathless and compulsive hurry and confused
apprehensions are linked to an exact accounting of places and things. The
necessity that drives Moll is as inexorable and unyielding as the urban maze she
instinctively negotiates; her rendering of her circumstances, from the overarching socio-economic situation to the particulars of that fateful evening, begins
her pushing back against a potentially destructive external world.

Defoe was a born and bred Londoner, so Moll's terrified escape from the
scene of her first crime is strikingly accurate in its rendering of her route home.
Moll's exactness has a narrative function; it balances the terror and moral
panic in her recollection with a preliminary form of control and her confusion

with a geographical specificity. The realistic rendition of Moll's movements, however provoked by despair and nearly involuntary as she recalls, begins at this point in her story to establish her mastery of a physical environment in which for five subsequent years as a thief, as she puts it, she "grew the greatest Artist of my time" (p. 241). And as she becomes an expert pickpocket and shoplifter this precision as Defoe renders it with consistent specificity becomes the key part of her modus operandi. Just as it is for Crusoe, the exact apprehension of the world is a technique for survival and not an end in itself.

Defoe was clearly drawn to the dilemma peculiar to a woman alone in his society. Like other socially marginal persons who feature largely in his fiction, such women face dramatic obstacles to survival. They are thus rich narrative material. Like Moll, Roxana is essentially alone and without resources; she confronts a bleak future after her feckless husband decamps and leaves her with five children and no means of support. On the advice of her maid, Amy, she sends for two women who may be able to help her, but when they arrive this is what they find:

> my Eyes were swell'd with crying, and what a Condition I was in as to the House, and the Heaps of Things that were about me, and especially when I told them what I was doing, and on what Occasion, they sat down like Job's three Comforters, and said not one Word to me for a great while, but both of them cry'd as fast, and as heartily as I did.
>
> The Truth was, there was no Need of much Discourse in the Case, the Thing spoke it self; they saw me in Rags and Dirt, who was but a little before riding in my Coach; thin, and looking almost like one Starv'd, who was before fat and beautiful: The House, that was before handsomely furnish'd with Pictures and Ornaments, Cabinets, Peir-Glasses, and every thing suitable; was now stripp'd, and naked, most of the Goods having been seiz'd by the Landlord for Rent, or sold to buy Necessaries; in a word, all was Misery and Distress, the Face of Ruin was every where to be seen; we had eaten up almost every thing, and little remain'd, unless, like one of the pitiful Women of Jerusalem, I should eat up my very Children themselves. (pp. 17–18)

A dramatically bleak rendition of a woman stripped, degraded, helpless, and hopeless, the scene illustrates Defoe's attraction to extreme, melodramatic situations as the impelling moments for his characters' lives. Scenes like this and Moll's (to say nothing of Crusoe on his island) illustrate the instability of modern identity, the fragility of communal bonds and support networks, the unforgiving economic laws of the market, the dangers of isolated individuality. Realism thus begins in extremity, and the material world is highlighted by the threat of inanition it poses. But lurking within Roxana's representation of her desperate circumstances is a talent for observation and self-dramatization that will eventually propel her into a hugely successful if guilt-laden career.

Of all Defoe's narrators, Roxana has the most turbulent inner life, although from *Robinson Crusoe* onwards all his fictions highlight moments of anxiety and instability for their protagonists, and the tension between an (eventually) controlled external world and a turbulent interiority is the imaginative heart of his realistic depiction of character. Because she is the most ruthless and successful of all his characters, Roxana comes to possess the most tortured and unresolved personality, which makes her to that extent the most realistically complex of his characters. Here is an episode, near the end of her story, that can serve as an especially powerful instance of this tension. One of her abandoned children, Susan, turns out to have been a "Cook-Maid" in Roxana's house in Pall Mall when she was the toast of high society and became the king's mistress. Roxana has retreated from high life and is posing as a Quaker, but upon visiting a friend, a ship captain's wife, she encounters Susan, her daughter, and in the course of the visit has to greet the young woman:

> I cannot but take Notice here, that notwithstanding there was a secret Horror upon my Mind, and I was ready to sink when I came close to her, to salute her; yet it was a secret inconceivable Pleasure to me when I kiss'd her, to know that I kiss'd my own Child; my own Flesh and Blood, born of my Body; and who I had never kiss'd since I took the fatal Farewel of them all, with a Million of Tears, and a Heart almost dead with Grief, when Amy and the Good Woman took them all away, and went with them to *Spittle-Fields*: No pen can describe, no Words can express, I say, the strange Impression which this thing made upon my Spirits; I felt something shoot thro' my Blood; my Heart flutter'd; my Head flash'd, and was dizzy, and all within me, *as I thought*, turn'd about, and much ado I had, not to abandon myself to an Excess of Passion at the first Sight of her, much more when my Lips touch'd her Face; I thought I must have taken her in my Arms, and kiss'd her again a thousand times, whether I wou'd or no. (pp. 276–77)

As she renders this scene, Roxana veers from instinctively devising strategies of evasion ("to feign a swooning, and faint away") to an evocation of an emotional intensity that she says was both unavoidable and inexpressible – control and compulsion are the twin experiences here. The transition from a slow-motion review of self-protective evasions that flashed through her mind at the time gives way to involuntary and overwhelming love and fear. Psychological necessity trumps evasive action. Defoe's art here lies in expanding a terrified few moments into a long, slow motion scene of mixed and intense emotions. Roxana exercises external self-control but asks readers to imagine an interior reality under tremendous pressure that shatters that control; the self she evokes is radically split.

And yet such explosive moments are relatively rare. More often, Defoe's characters cope with the world and maintain in the narrative of their lives an inner calm and competence, a controlling apartness and objectivity. Defoe's fiction exemplifies modern realism in its delineation of an individual's self-understanding and development within those socio-economic circumstances that are the ground of identity; but at moments of extremity like this he dramatizes how personality can begin to come apart, how emotions and urges take over from self-control. The modern individual, as Defoe imagines him and her, is not integrated into a community or a moral order. Rather, the social and the historical are encountered as shifting or mysterious realms that can in the best case offer opportunities for development. But more often for marginalized characters (or dispossessed like Moll and Roxana, disqualified as women from full agency), the socio-historical realm represents a massive, threatening opposition, a set of controlling or destructive forces that demand resistance or evasion for survival.

But at the same time, all of Defoe's narrators manage various forms of liberating and literal geographic movement of a spectacular and often enough fantastic sort. Young Crusoe trades in Africa, spends time in North Africa as a slave, then becomes a planter in Brazil before his shipwreck, and in the sequel, *The Farther Adventures of Robinson Crusoe* (1719), he travels to China and across Asia, through Russia and back to England. Colonel Jack achieves something like respectability and prosperity in Virginia and then in military service in Europe, where Roxana also prospers hugely as a courtesan in France and Italy. Moll goes to Virginia twice, and Captain Singleton leads a triumphant pirate band across Africa and amasses a fortune as a pirate. But despite these triumphant travels, the narrative perspectives of his characters/narrators are alienated or askew; circumstances such as Moll or Roxana or Jack or Crusoe encounter are both specific and strange, threatening in their inescapable objectivity, a problem to be solved, obstacles to be avoided, but also opportunities to be exploited and mastered.

Nowhere is this clearer than in *A Journal of the Plague Year* (1722), Defoe's extended evocation of the results of the bubonic plague that ravaged London in 1665 (an imaginative tour de force, by the way, since Defoe was five or six years old that year). The narrator is a London merchant, a saddler, who decides to stay in the city as the plague rages. That difficult decision is based on his pious trust in Providence: "casting my self entirely upon the Goodness and Protection of the Almighty ... and that as my Times were in his Hands, he was as able to keep me in a Time of the Infection as in a Time of Health; and if he did not think fit to deliver me, still I was in his Hands, and it was meet he should do with me as should seem good to him."[11] Such trust in Providence is not quite consistent with his distress and confusion as he describes the plague's horrific effects with a fascinated specificity. For one example among many, the narrator tells the story of a young woman and her mother. The daughter complains of violent pains and is put to bed. As the mother looks at her body, "with a Candle," she

> immediately discovered the fatal Tokens on the Inside of her Thighs. Her Mother not being able to contain herself, threw down her Candle, and scriekt out in such a frightful Manner, that it was enough to place Horror upon the stoutest Heart in the World; nor was it one Skream, or one Cry, but the Fright, having seiz'd her Spirits, she fainted first, then recovered, then ran all over the House, up the Stairs and down the Stairs, like one distracted, and indeed really was distracted, and continued screching and crying out for several Hours, void of all Sense, or at least, Government of her Senses, and as I was told, never came throughly to herself again: As to the young Maiden, she was a dead Corpse from that Moment; for the Gangren which occasions the Spots had spread her whole Body, and she died in less than two Hours: But still the Mother continued crying out, not knowing any Thing more of her Child, several Hours after she was dead. It is so long ago, that I am not certain, but I think the Mother never recover'd, but died in two or three Weeks after. (p. 55)

A Journal of the Plague Year alternates heartbreakingly detailed anecdotes from the plague with the narrator's attempts to gauge its larger depredations, as he reprints the tallies of the dead, the "Bills of Mortality," from the city's parishes. His horror mounts as the number of dead climbs steadily and as he roams the streets, recording terrible things with unsparing fidelity. But he also attempts to counter that horror by seeking to understand the origins and the meaning of the plague: is it, he wonders, a punishment from God? Popular preachers and the common people, he notes, make much of recent celestial phenomena: "a blazing Star or Comet appear'd for several Months before the Plague, as there did the Year after another" (p. 21). The narrator is uncertain, but in the end rejects simple providential explanations:

> I saw both these Stars; and I must confess, had so much of the common Notion of such Things in my Head, that I was apt to look upon them, as the Forerunners and Warnings of Gods Judgments; and especially when after the Plague had followed the first, I yet saw another of the like kind; I could not but say, God had not yet sufficiently scourg'd the City.
>
> But I cou'd not at the same Time carry these Things to the heighth that others did, knowing too, that natural Causes are assign'd by the Astronomers for such Things; and that their Motions, and even their Revolutions are calculated, or pretended to be calculated; so that they cannot be so perfectly call'd the Forerunners, or Fore-tellers, much less the procurers of such Events, as Pestilence, War, Fire, and the like. (pp. 21–22)

The narrator positions himself somewhere between the terrified credulity of the common people and the cool objectivity of material and scientific explanations. In taking this middle position, he is an empirical reporter who unflinchingly examines events (like the one above) as he sees them, and in the process dramatizes his varying and conflicted responses, from confusion and horror to the satisfactions of measuring and seeking to understand and as far as possible to order an almost unimaginable reality. Defoe's realism aspires to be a form of control and understanding of a world that is often mysterious or unresolved, larger than an individual can comprehend. *A Journal of the Plague Year* is a kind of laboratory experiment, an extreme instance of the problem of narrative realism: how to render a reality that escapes comprehension, that is multiple and shifting, subjective as well as more or less objective. The narrator's steady, descriptive gaze is a way to manage (or, at least, to stare down, to render exactly) what defies understanding.

Defoe's realism, however, lies not only in exact observations of his characters' environments. The renditions of various realities in *Moll Flanders*, for example, produce the larger entity that I have called "ideological realism," since Moll's whole career grows out of a specifically female destiny that Defoe imagines with great perspicacity. Little Moll, as she tells her story, is orphaned when her criminal mother is transported "to the Plantations" (Virginia), and at length she winds up in Colchester in Essex where the parish authorities board her with a poor spinster. Eventually, she draws the attention of various well-to-do families in the town, and she becomes a kind of servant in a wealthy household, brought up as essentially part of the family of two daughters and two sons. The elder of the sons, "a gay Gentleman that knew the Town, as well as the Country" (p. 19), takes a fancy to her when she is seventeen or eighteen. She is quickly seduced. One of her descriptions of her first sexual experience reveals a lot about Defoe's ability to render the intersection of sex, money, and class. She and the elder brother are alone one day, and he kisses her, "stoping my very Breath":

> tho' he took these Freedoms with me, it did not go to that, which they call the last Favour, which, to do him Justice, he did not attempt; and he made that self denial of his a Plea for all his Freedoms with me upon other Occasions after this: When this was over, he stay'd but a little while, but he put almost a Handful of Gold in my Hand, and left me; making a thousand Protestations of his Passion for me, and of his loving me above all the Women in the World ... as for the Gold I spent whole Hours in looking upon it; I told the Guineas over a Thousand times a Day. (pp. 24–26)

Old Moll looks back on her naive younger self and thinks about what she would have done then if she knew what she knows now after a long life of dealing in the marriage market where she has had a number of lovers and husbands before she is forced to turn thief. As she admits near the end of the story, Moll is not moralizing on her past, and in that recollection she dramatizes herself as a tough old veteran of the sex wars. Her book is in a sense one long dramatic monologue: "I leave the Reader to improve these Thoughts, as no doubt they will see Cause, and I go on to the Fact" (p. 337). In her retrospective account of her initial seduction, there is no romance, no sentiment, just the sexual and financial jockeying for pleasure and advantage between an upper-class male and a servant-class female. Sexual exploitation of the female servant class in early eighteenth-century England was a reality and perhaps so was the kind of hard bargaining that Moll wishes she had tried. Young Moll is caught up in sexual excitement, but her most intense recollection (who knows if she is remembering it the way it happened, since her narrative is told from the perspective of a hardened old age) is of the gold ("I spent whole Hours in looking upon it; I told the Guineas over a Thousand times a Day"). For all of her many amorous and marital relationships that follow, Moll is attuned to getting on in the material world, both as a mistress and wife several times over and then as a thief and pickpocket. Her relationships are almost exclusively economic.

Many modern readers, in fact, have found Moll coldly pragmatic, reducing all her relationships according to crassly materialistic terms. Like Crusoe and like H. F. (the narrator of *A Journal of the Plague Year*) and like Defoe's last creation, Roxana, Moll weighs and measures, quantifies just about everything. For example, early in her life as a young widow she grows disgusted with fortune-hunting men and resolves to change her "Station, and make a new Appearance in some other Place where I was not known." So she confides to a friend: "I made no scruple to lay my Circumstances open to her, my Stock was but low, for I had made but about 540 l. at the Close of my last Affair, and I had wasted some of that; However, I had about 460l. left, a great many very rich Cloaths, a Gold Watch, and some Jewels, tho' of no extraordinary value, and about 30 or 40 l. left in Linnen not dispos'd of" (pp. 76–77).

Moll is never rich, and her accountings are modest. Not so Roxana, who grows fantastically rich as a courtesan, and even as she looks back on what she regrets as a life of degenerative immorality she keeps a running total of her accumulating wealth, which grows steadily through shrewd investments and compounding interest. Here's one instance among many, as Roxana says she had the "common Vice of all Whores, I mean Money," so that "even Avarice itself seem'd to be glutted":

> ... including what I had sav'd in reserving the Interest of 1400ol. which, as above, I had left to grow; and, including some very good Presents I had made to me, in meer Compliment, upon these shining masquerading Meetings, which I held up for about two Years, and what I made of three Years of the most glorious Retreat, *as I call it*, [that is, when she was the king's mistress] that ever Woman had, I had fully doubled my first Substance, and had near 5000 Pounds

in Money, which I kept at home; besides abundance of Plate, and Jewels, which I had either given me, or had bought to set myself out for Publick Days.

In a word, I had now five and thirty Thousand Pounds Estate; and as I found Ways to live without wasting either Principal or Interest, I laid-up 2000 l. every Year, at least, out of the meer Interest, adding it to the Principal; and thus I went on. (p. 182)[12]

Such inventories may strike a modern reader as superfluous, but they are like the "Bills of Mortality" in *A Journal of the Plague Year*, Robinson Crusoe's tallies of cannibals killed and wounded in a battle on his island, or Colonel Jack's lists of his takings on the London streets, contributions to the project these narratives all share: to render as fully as possible the material circumstances of the protagonists and (implicitly but strongly) to project an objectivity from which they construct powerful subjectivities. The multimillionaire Roxana has the biggest triumph of all of Defoe's characters but also the most regret and painful retrospection. Roxana's financial accountings provide a stable and indeed a steadily productive alternative to her moral decline and psychological breakdown. From the material world they encounter, Defoe's characters largely construct themselves, often enough managing it to advantage, but thanks to Defoe's feel and eye for things and phenomena his characters are immersed in that world, always inseparable from it and to some extent produced by it. The more completely the material world is rendered, the implicit drive of these narratives suggests, the greater and deeper our sense of the characters' reality, which is measured as a resistance to the real, an attempt (not always successful or complete) to transform the actual by individual will.

NOTES

1. *Robinson Crusoe*, ed. John Richetti (London: Penguin Books, 2001), p. 197. All further references in parenthesis in the text are to this edition.
2. *The Rise of the Novel: Studies in Defoe, Richardson and Fielding* (Berkeley and Los Angeles: University of California Press, 1957), p. 32.
3. *Moll Flanders*, ed. G. A. Starr (London and New York: Oxford University Press, 1971), p iii.. All further references in parenthesis in the text are to this edition.
4. Lennard Davis, *Factual Fictions: The Origins of the English Novel* (Philadelphia: University of Pennsylvania Press, 1996; first published 1983), pp. 50–52.
5. *Roxana*, ed. Jane Jack (London and New York: Oxford University Press, 1964), p. iii. All further references in parenthesis in the text are to this edition.
6. *Cassell's New Latin Dictionary* (New York: Funk & Wagnalls, 1959), *res*, p. 517.
7. "Robinson Crusoe," in *The Common Reader* (second series) (London: The Hogarth Press, 1980; first published 1932), p. 57.
8. "Robinson Crusoe," pp. 54–55.
9. "Daniel Defoe," edited from Italian manuscripts and translated by Joseph Prescott, *Buffalo Studies*, 1 (December 1964), 24–25.

10. *The History and Remarkable Life of the Truly Honourable Colonel Jacque, Commonly Call'd Col. Jack*, ed. Samuel Holt Monk (London: Oxford University Press, 1965), p. 9. All further references in parenthesis in the text are to this edition.

11. *A Journal of the Plague Year*, ed. Cynthia Wall (London: Penguin Books, 2003), p. 15. All further references in parenthesis in the text are to this edition.

12. In terms of modern purchasing power, these are immense sums. One economic calculator estimates that £35,000 would be worth today nearly five million pounds or ten million dollars.

8

ELLEN POLLAK

Gender and fiction in *Moll Flanders* and *Roxana*

Defoe's multiple voices and the elusiveness of the unstable text

Defoe's novels – especially his five fictional autobiographies, *Robinson Crusoe, Captain Singleton, Moll Flanders, Colonel Jack*, and *Roxana* – can be an interpretive nightmare for those trying to locate in them a stable authorial voice or point of view. In these works, Defoe returns repeatedly to the same narrative experiment: the representation of a self in the process of narrative retrospection. To sustain the illusion that these representations are not in fact fictions but true accounts of real people, he deploys a distinctive and complex rhetorical strategy: in each case, he performs an authorial disappearing act by assuming the voice of a first-person narrator looking back at his or her life and attempting to make sense of it through the act of writing. The voices he impersonates in this way are neither simple nor internally unified. In fact, they have sometimes been called "double" because the temporal process involved in portraying an older consciousness reflecting on its own past errors and adventures simultaneously entails an act of distancing and identification; the perspective of penitent maturity from which these narrators "speak" is tempered by – if not at times in tension with – an intimate appreciation of the extenuating circumstances that prompted their actions and conditioned their personal choices along the way.

Into all but one of these "double-voiced" narratives, moreover, Defoe introduces yet another voice and another narrative frame: an impersonated editor who, in a preface to the memoir, promises profit as well as pleasure in setting the narrator's personal history before the public.[1] The diversions of narrative, these editors pledge, remain subordinate to religious application: "the best use is made even of the worst Story," writes the editor of *Moll Flanders*; or, as Robinson Crusoe himself testifies in the preface to his *Serious Reflections*, "The Fable is always made for the Moral," not the other way

around.[2] Publishing the recollected adventures of misguided and even criminal individuals who survive misfortune and sometimes thrive on vice but who
learn from experience and (at least ostensibly) repent the error of their ways
represents, for Defoe's fictive editors, an occasion to discourage immorality
by exposing it and to promote noble and religious principles.

The kaleidoscopic effect of shifting perspectives engendered by this play of
multiple "voices" that sometimes support and sometimes contest one another
is yet further intensified by the sheer variety of event and circumstance that
typically unfolds over the lifespan of a Defoe protagonist. This effect, along
with the profusion of factual detail and the numerous turns of plot and fate
that are so characteristic of Defoe's style, makes it exceedingly difficult, if not
impossible, to know with any security when (if ever) Defoe can or should be
identified with the characters he assumes. Where, for instance, is Defoe
positioned when Robinson Crusoe recounts that, upon finding a stash of
gold on his ruined ship, he first dismisses it as a seductive but worthless
"drug!" and then ("upon second thoughts") pockets it along with the other
provisions he salvages for survival on his "island of Despair"?[3] Is the author
here applauding the resourceful practicality of economic man or exposing
Crusoe's moral shallowness? The older Crusoe seems unfazed by what readers may experience as a curious tension in his account between the intensity
with which he insists upon the corrupting emptiness of money (its purely
symbolic value as an illusive cultural sign) and his supremely short-lived and
provisional adherence to that truth. But ultimately there is no way to know if
Crusoe's perspective from the hindsight of experience and old age is one of
bemused irony at his former lack of moral self-consciousness or of identification with his youthful acceptance of the uneasy coexistence of material and
spiritual exigencies. Similarly, when Moll recounts being laughed at for her
innocent childhood misconception that she could become a gentlewoman by
working for an honest livelihood, what if anything is being critiqued or
satirized? Is the older, more experienced Moll simply exposing her earlier
childish ignorance of social codes and prevailing gender asymmetries? Or is
she commenting on the callousness of those who laugh at her expense?
Perhaps the episode targets the gender asymmetries that make her youthful
aspirations so naïve a fantasy. Is it possible to determine whether Defoe is here
ultimately affirming or critiquing gender codes? Does he, in general, more
fully inhabit his characters in their often naïve youth or in their sometimes
cynical maturity? At some level, of course, it is the mark of Defoe's authorial
genius that he could be said to inhabit (or evacuate) all and none of these
positions equally. Although his writing might invite us to wonder where he
stands, it ultimately frustrates any effort to locate him stably or decisively
anywhere, suggesting that his authorial project may lie less in endorsing

particular moral or ideological truths than in using the device of the narrative frame to expose truth's always contested and circumstantial nature.

While moments of narrative instability pervade Defoe's novels generally, such textual elusiveness is especially pronounced in *Moll Flanders* and *Roxana*, the two novels in which he assumes the voice of female narrators. The following pages investigate the reasons for the intensification of interpretive instability in these novels by looking not only at how Defoe's narrative strategies are affected by the gender of his protagonists but also at how his female protagonists themselves become identified with the principles of textual unruliness and undecidability. To this end, I closely examine the prefaces to the two novels, focusing in particular on the relationships they construct between the novels' fictional editors and their female narrator-protagonists. I also consider Defoe's representations of women in light of the complex and contradictory position women occupied in the emerging capitalist economy of early eighteenth-century England. Ultimately, I want to illuminate Defoe's treatment of female fictional identity by exposing the underlying assumptions about women on which his novels rest; at the same time I seek to show how Defoe's unique strategies of narrative distancing, while designed to sustain the illusion of truthfulness, also work subtly and perhaps surprisingly to unsettle the very truths about gender that his plots seem to affirm.

Like Crusoe, the eponymous heroines of *Moll Flanders* and *Roxana* are exiles and survivors, though instead of confronting threats from natural forces, wild beasts, and cannibals on a desert island, the scene of their adventures is late seventeenth- and early eighteenth-century society where, as they both learn the hard way, their banishment as women from the privileges of economic independence puts their very lives in jeopardy. The two women differ markedly in their class origins: Moll, the daughter of a petty thief from the criminal underclass, is born in Newgate prison and orphaned when her mother is transported to America; Roxana is the daughter of economically comfortable French immigrants who have fled from France to England to escape religious persecution. But both heroines endure similar kinds of misfortunes as women on their own and, by coming to understand the societal codes that oppress them *as women*, eventually manage through various forms of trickery, disguise, and corruption to live prosperous (if not in both cases entirely happy) lives. After a series of sexual relationships (some outside the legal sanctions of marriage) and a career as a thief, Moll eventually becomes a rich plantation owner; Roxana accumulates and enjoys enormous wealth as a high-class courtesan, though by the end of her memoir she is tragically implicated in the suspected murder of her own daughter, and reports a series of ensuing calamities. As we shall see, both women ultimately reject their wicked practices, differing only in the apparent sincerity of their penitence. Although their narratives may be said to constitute elaborate confessions of their crimes, both also hide behind adopted identities: Moll uses an alias invented for her by her fellow thieves, and Roxana a name coined by the audience at a masquerade ball where she gains notoriety for a dance she performs in a dazzling Turkish dress.

Critics have long debated whether *Moll Flanders* and *Roxana* celebrate the resourcefulness and cunning of their proto-feminist heroines, provide cautionary lessons about the debasing and debilitating effects of female vice and debauchery, or simply exploit the titillating pleasures of representing female immorality under the pretense of exposing its wickedness. Nor do these options exhaust the critical possibilities. Some critics have argued that the two texts differ in important ways in their representation of female identity and that the transition from a comic vision in which Moll enjoys the fruits of her incestuous third marriage and substantial ill-gotten gain to the tragic portrait of Roxana's descent into paranoid obsession and melancholy marks a critical turning point in Defoe's disposition and development as a novelist. Most agree that *Roxana* signals a darkening of the author's vision and a "more 'novelistic' consciousness" than evidenced in his earlier work, and that it constitutes a *better* novel than *Moll Flanders* because it focuses more on the complexity of an inner life and, specifically, on a mind at odds with itself.[4] I shall have more to say about this assessment later on. For the moment, suffice it to say that, even acknowledging these important differences, few would dispute that *Moll Flanders* and *Roxana* offer particularly fertile ground for exploring the moral and interpretive instabilities produced by Defoe's distinctive narrative strategies. As we have seen, these strategies tend to generate competing interpretive possibilities that cannot be accounted for by any single, univocal, or totalizing reading. There always seems to be some destabilizing remainder or excess – some irony or other shift in perspective – that eludes assimilation by unitary interpretation and thus permeates such interpretation with an element of doubt.

Consider the pull of competing possibilities, for example, in the famous scene in which Roxana refuses a proposal of marriage from the Dutch Merchant. Having risen from destitution to independent wealth through her exploits as "a Lady of Pleasure" and become, as she puts it, "a Woman of Business" or "She-Merchant" in her own right, Roxana "will hear of no Matrimony, by any means."[5] Although she acknowledges that the Merchant had saved her from "the worst Circumstances," that she was carrying his child, and that she "loved him to an extraordinary Degree" (p. 185), she tells him that she has a "mortal Aversion" (p. 201) to marrying. Her experiences as an abandoned wife and later as a mistress, first to a jeweller and then a prince, have taught her that, while "a Wife is look'd upon, as but an Upper-Servant, a Mistress is a Sovereign" (p. 170). In an extended dispute with the Merchant in which she offers a radical critique of prevailing gender codes, Roxana argues that "the very Nature of the Marriage-Contract was ... nothing but giving up Liberty, Estate, Authority, and every-thing, to the Man" (p. 187), whereas a single woman "was Masculine in her politick Capacity ... had ... the full Command of what she had, and the full Direction of what she did ... was controul'd by none, because accountable to none, and was in Subjection to none" (p. 188). Any woman with an estate who would "give it up to be the Slave of a *Great Man*," she thus concludes, is a fool (p. 188). Knowing the sinister consequences of her ensuing life of scandal, the older Roxana brusquely repudiates these views as "many wicked Arguments for whoring" (p. 171) and calls herself a "standing Monument of the Madness ... which Pride and Infatuation from Hell" (p. 201) can bring about. But the powerful case she has already made against gender inequality and the compelling evidence she has brought to bear from her own experience to support it in her dialogue with the Merchant are neither easily ignored nor soon forgotten by the reader. Even the Merchant himself is "confounded by her discourse" and has trouble "answering the Force of ... [her] Argument" (p. 188–89). Although in his bewilderment he appeals at various points to the authority of nature, divine decree, and the general doctrine of female inferiority to argue against Roxana's view of marriage as a form of enslaved dependency for women, he also concedes that Roxana's logic is "right in the Main" (p. 192–93). In the end, Roxana calls herself a "thousand Fools" for having refused the security of marriage to her honest Merchant, regretting that she had "had a safe Harbor presented and no heart to cast-Anchor in it" (p. 202); but because she has so credibly and so "feelingly" (p. 190) demonstrated that women's "best Security in the World" is "the Staff in their own Hands" (p. 193), readers may distrust the wisdom of her remorse or lack the heart to condemn her for her choice. The episode resists tidy packaging; to read it with any finality as ultimately either condoning Roxana's outlaw existence or condemning her moral depravity would be equally reductive and equally precarious.

Tainted women: gender transgression and the ungovernable text

Interpretive instabilities trouble all Defoe's narratives, whether they feature male or female protagonists; but the moral uncertainties that riddle the novels about women are more intractable and defiling in their effects. One need only compare the level of contamination associated with the hoarding of needless capital (i.e., the accumulation of surplus or reserves) in, respectively, the scene where Crusoe pockets his supply of useless gold and the sequence in which Roxana, possessed of a surfeit of wealth, is tormented by the question, "What was I a Whore for now?" (pp. 243–45), in order to appreciate the gender differential operating for Defoe in representing the subject of early modern capitalism. It is as if the very quest for economic mastery and autonomy is itself fundamentally transgressive for a woman. The self-reliant man, to borrow words from James Joyce's commentary on *Robinson Crusoe*, "becomes an architect, a carpenter, a knife grinder, an astronomer, a baker, a shipwright, a potter, a saddler, a farmer, a tailor, an umbrella maker, and a clergyman."[6] The self-reliant woman becomes a whore and a thief. A woman on her own, uncontained by the neutralizing force of male authority, is spiritually and materially tainted.

Crusoe's spirituality may be somewhat tarnished by its material embeddedness, but it never enters the realm of depravity. He may find religion on his own terms; he may worship God on his own private Sabbath because he has unwittingly lost a day in his account of passing time; his readers may never know with certainty whether the providential meaning that Crusoe finds in life exists *in fact* or only in his head (when barley grows outside his fortifications or when he shrewdly engineers his own "delivery" from the island on an English ship, it is never absolutely clear whether we are witnessing the effects of divine intervention, human ingenuity, or random chance). But none of this does serious damage to Crusoe's spiritual essence because of the emphasis within Puritan ideology on both the salutary value of human works and the inherent meaningfulness of the individual's private relationship to God. For Moll Flanders and Roxana, on the other hand, to undertake the project of self-fashioning is to fall in some sense irredeemably into materiality. As her childhood confusion about the meaning of the term "Madam" makes clear, a woman in Moll's world can not "honestly" become a self-sustaining subject; the quest for prosperous self-sufficiency invariably defiles her sexually.[7]

What Roxana calls "the dirty History of [her] Actings on the Stage of Life" (p. 111) might find a gloss in anthropologist Mary Douglas's discussion of dirt as "matter out of place."[8] The female quest for autonomy is rendered abject in her case, as in Moll's, because autonomy is coded as male; for a woman to pursue it is already to transgress the very boundaries that constitute her as a gendered being. Filial disobedience may be Crusoe's original sin, but to vie with the father is exclusively a male privilege that ultimately affirms a man's masculinity. For a woman to disobey the father's law, on the other hand, is to usurp an authority denied her, to encroach upon a restricted cultural domain. Noting that "Liberty seem'd to be the Men's Property," Roxana is ready to be a "Man-Woman" (p. 212) rather than subject herself to the laws of marriage. But Crusoe's masculinity is never put in doubt, despite (if not indeed because of) the almost complete absence of women or evidence of heterosexual desire in his narrative. His dependence on the dependency of a feminized racial Other in the figure of Friday, and the strong homosocial dimension of that bond, are worthy of critical note; but they are aspects of the narrative that the text itself neither questions nor examines critically.

Interestingly, in their contaminating gender ambiguity, Moll and Roxana become embodiments of the very principles of undecidability and impurity that make their narratives so difficult to pin down. Not only is there doubt surrounding the sincerity and stability of each heroine's repentance (over time, Moll no longer seems to be "so extraordinary a Penitent, as she was at first" (p. 5); and Roxana struggles between ambition and conscience throughout her narrative), but the association of the heroines themselves with the seemingly intractable messiness of their texts comes to dominate the prefaces of their fictional editors. In fact, both editors use the same controlling image to represent the unruliness and uncontainability of the heroines' narratives: the figure of an elusive and ungovernable female body in need of sartorial rehabilitation. As we shall see, in contrast to the prefaces to the narratives of Defoe's male protagonists (who seem to need no introduction or apology), the prefaces to *Moll Flanders* and *Roxana* stage an anxious drama of textual re-dressing in which the excesses and indecencies of the female textual body threaten to undermine the performance of male editorial discipline.

The ostensible function of Defoe's fictional editors is generally two-fold: to promote the illusion of his narratives' truthfulness (their status as authentic and factual memoirs) and to bear witness to their salutary force. But depending on whether they are introducing works by male or female narrators, these editors perform their dual function with varying degrees of ease and confidence. In the prefaces to the memoirs of his male protagonists Robinson Crusoe and Colonel Jack, the task of the "editor" emerges as neither daunting nor difficult; the hero-narrator is presumed to be a reliable witness to his own existence and veracity. We are assured that, since Crusoe's story is already told by its hero "with modesty ... seriousness, and ... religious application" (*Robinson Crusoe*, preface), it requires only the briefest and most declarative of introductions; and the editor accepts its basis in fact with unquestioning confidence. The editors of *The Farther Adventures* (the sequel to *Robinson Crusoe*) and *Colonel Jack* are similarly unabashed and resolute. The first breezily dismisses as "abortive, and ... impotent" the endeavors of detractors to impugn the authenticity of the original memoir.[9] That the second has bothered to write a preface at all, he says, is a mere concession to the force of custom, as Jack's memoir "needs a Preface less than any that ever went before it" (a comment that may in turn explain the absence of any preface in

Captain Singleton).[10] Despite the thievery to which Jack (like Moll before him) is drawn by necessity, this editor affirms, the account of his life, with all its vicissitudes, poses no danger to the integrity of the reader; "The various Turns of [the hero's] Fortunes in the World," rather, "make a delightful Field for the Reader to wander in; a Garden where he may gather wholesome and medicinal Plants, none noxcious [sic] or poisonous" (p. 2).

In stark contrast, the editorial voices that frame the narratives of Moll Flanders and Roxana are plagued by doubt. The preface to each of these novels stages a drama of editorial insecurity in which a male editor is faced with the task of "re-dressing" a woman's story so as to make it presentable for public consumption. Neither editor sees this as an easy or uncomplicated task; on the contrary, they both figure the narrative before them as an indecently clad female body that, in performing a sort of anonymous strip-tease (i.e., revealing too much even as it hides the identity of its heroine under the mask of a pseudonym), threatens to overwhelm the editor's virtuous didactic aims. Thus, in contrast to the confident pronouncement of the editor of *Colonel Jack* that "Every wicked Reader [of the narrative] will here be encouraged to a Change" (p. 2), Moll Flanders' editor – who assumes responsibility for re-authorizing the heroine's narrative – dwells defensively on the challenges of his job:

> The Pen employ'd in finishing her Story, and making it what you now see it to be, *has had no little difficulty* to put it into a Dress fit to be seen, and to make it speak Language fit to be read. When a Woman debauch'd from her Youth, nay, even being the Off-spring of Debauchery and Vice, comes to give an Account of all her vicious Practices ... *an Author must be hard put* to wrap it up so clean, as not to give room, especially for vitious Readers to turn it to his Disadvantage.
>
> (p. 1) (emphasis added)

The editor worries on the one hand about being able to fit Moll's unruly textual body into a proper dress and on the other about the danger of leaving extra "room" between the body and the dress for error and indecency to enter. Despite his efforts, he seems painfully aware that the effects of reading "the History of a wicked Life repented of" will depend on conditions and contingencies outside his control – for example, on whether or not the work is enjoyed only by "those who know how to Read it" (p. 2). The goal of the editor may be moral edification, but the ungovernable female text may never-theless spawn unwanted readings, much as the promiscuous woman whose history it recounts produces so many unwanted births.

If the editor of *Moll Flanders* is locked in an anxious struggle with the narrator-protagonist for control over her story and its reception, Roxana's editor seems already to have ceded much of his recuperative authority.

Although he expressly represents himself and his female narrator as engaged in competing performances, he is so ready to accept responsibility for all the work's deficiencies – be it too diverting or not diverting enough – that one suspects he has himself been taken in by the lady's charms:

> The History of this *Beautiful Lady* is to speak for itself: If it is not as Beautiful as the Lady herself is reported to be; if it is not as diverting as the Reader can desire, and much more than he can reasonably expect; and if all the most diverting Parts of it are not adapted to the Instruction and Improvement of the Reader, the *Relator* says, it must be from the Defect of his Performance; dressing up the Story in worse Cloaths than the *Lady*, whose words he speaks, prepared it for the World.
> (p. 35)

The figure of a woman dressing up her story for a performance clearly echoes the famous episode in which Roxana dresses herself up to perform her dance in a Turkish costume. But the editor's project presumably is to put the story into plainer, less ostentatious clothes than Roxana at the height of her career is wont to wear – to dress it down, as the heroine for a time dresses in the story when, to disguise herself, she puts on Quaker garb. Such clothes – being more modest – would be *better* rather than "worse" than those with which the lady Roxana is likely to have prepared her story for the world. And yet, even as he hopes that the most diverting parts of the narrative will be adapted to moral ends, the editor feels compelled to apologize for the possibility that the clothes in which he adorns the story may be less dazzling or appealing than the lady's. In a way that anticipates Roxana's own self-division as both the most ruthlessly ambitious and the most conscience-stricken of Defoe's characters, this fictional editor himself seems divided by self-doubt and his own ambivalent attraction to the narrative performance he is ostensibly attempting to redeem.

There are moments in the preface, in fact, when the editor seems even *less* inclined to forswear the enticements of vice and ambition than the lady Roxana herself. Consider, for example, the following passage, whose mounting crescendo of pleasurable excitement suggests that, in spite of himself, the editor is reluctantly captivated by the very blandishments he tells his reader that the heroine has abjured:

> It is true, she met with unexpected Success in all her wicked Courses; but even in the highest Elevations of her Prosperity, she makes frequent Acknowledgments, That *the Pleasure of her Wickedness* was not worth the Repentance; and that *all the Satisfaction she had, all the Joy in the View of her Prosperity; no, nor all the Wealth she rowl'd in; the Gayety of her Appearance; the Equipages, and the Honours, she was attended with*, cou'd quiet her Mind, abate the Reproaches of Conscience, or procure her an Hour's Sleep, when just Reflections kept her waking.
> (p. 36; emphasis added)

Such evidence of the sustained allure of the lady's vices unsettles the narrator's assurances that only "Nobel Inferences" are to be drawn from her experiences and casts doubt on his expressions of hope that readers will find nothing in them "to prompt a vicious Mind" (p. 36).

The unstable power dynamics between editor and lady that complicate the preface to *Roxana* are of course already implicit in the figure the editor has chosen to represent his relation to the story: that of a maidservant dressing her lady. Casting him in the position of a subordinate, the metaphor seems to undermine his authority from the outset and to privilege that of the mistress-narrator. Once again, the figure mirrors the novel's plot, which revolves centrally around the relationship between a mistress (Roxana) and her maidservant (Amy) in which issues of agency and subordination become intensely problematic and the question of responsibility for vice and aggression in the matter of the disappearance of Roxana's daughter Susan remains painfully unresolved. Like the editor of *Moll Flanders*, this editor seems to acknowledge in his choice of controlling metaphors that – despite his best efforts – the proper relation of fable to moral can not be guaranteed.

Women, class, and kinship in early modern England

To a large extent, the aura of taint and abjection surrounding Moll Flanders and Roxana as women on their own is a product of deep contradictions inherent in the ideology of economic individualism that accompanied and helped to sustain the emerging market economy of early eighteenth-century England. In the largely agrarian economy that had traditionally prevailed in England, social status was mainly a function of lineage or birth. With the transition in the late seventeenth century to a more commercial economy characterized by increasing class mobility, however, capital accumulation and individual desire began to take precedence over kinship and familial obligation in the determination of social worth. Nevertheless, even within this incipiently mobile class structure, traditional forms of kinship (most importantly, the institution of marriage, with women and reproduction at its crux) continued to play an important role in the accumulation and transmission of property. As sexual objects and reproducers, women were expected to answer to *both* class and kinship imperatives – but to operate first and foremost as members of a family unit, not as independent productive agents. As Juliet Mitchell explains, "Men enter[ed] into the class-dominated structures of history, while women (as women, whatever their actual work in production) remain[ed] defined by the kinship patterns of organization ... harnessed into the family."[11]

Positioned at the site where individualism intersected with the residual operation of feudal structures within the family, women thus occupied a contradictory position within early modern capitalism. Moll is expected to become wealthy by marrying well, not by exploiting her independent productive capacity – hence the female laughter prompted by her innocent desire to acquire gentility through honest needlework. Indeed, as we shall see, when she comes to understand her value as a sexual object and tries to exploit it as an independent agent for her own benefit by circulating outside the constraints of marriage and familial obligation, she crosses over into outlaw territory.

When boundaries proliferate, transgressions multiply. The heightened transgressiveness of Defoe's heroines is in some sense a measure of the number of constraints under which they operate. Defoe's heroes are subject to the necessities of nature and Providence; his heroines are additionally subject to the codes of a society controlled by men. Critics have long understood Defoe's interest in exploring the problem of human freedom and necessity,[12] but his heroes and heroines live under very different cultural and biological imperatives. To an important extent, gender determines how the category of necessity is defined and imagined in his work.

The tension between the limits imposed by gender and the open-endedness of the project of self-fashioning that informs and shapes these heroines' stories manifests itself both structurally and thematically. It emerges thematically in the conflicts both heroines experience around questions of maternal responsibility and affection. Interestingly, the same culture that gave rise to the ideology of economic individualism also spawned the concept of natural maternal affection and the ideal of the loving mother.[13] Defoe's novels bear witness to the uneasy coexistence of these two principles in the lives of eighteenth-century women. Like Moll's dream of honest self-sufficiency, her dual wish on the one hand to free herself from responsibility for the child she has conceived by her Lancashire husband, Jemy Cole, so she can advantageously marry someone else and, on the other hand, to monitor the child's welfare from afar is represented as essentially unthinkable. As her midwife and Governess, Mother Midnight, observes, it is "impossible" for her to be "Conceal'd and Discover'd both together" (p. 175). Moll knows that she won't be assured of the child's safety unless she sees it, but she also understands, as she tells her Governess, that "to see it, would be Ruin and Destruction to me, as now my Case stands" (p. 175). That Mother Midnight manages to engineer this supposed impossibility for Moll by negotiating a special arrangement with the child's nurse evinces both the ingenuity of this veteran of the female underworld and the larger comic impulse of the novel.

More sinister is a comparable episode in *Roxana* when, after rising from a state of destitution to one in which she literally, as she puts it, "wallow'd in Wealth" (p. 230), the heroine decides to discover the fate of her grown children and to show them some anonymous kindness by sending Amy to look after their well-being. By inadvertently providing the clue that enables Susan to trace her mother's scandalous identity, this charitable venture ultimately triggers Roxana's final tragedy in the sequence of events that leads to the girl's disappearance and likely murder. Moll's words about "Ruin and Destruction" may thus apply more aptly even to Roxana's case than her own; but it is certainly true that, for both these women, the stakes of fleeing family ties are much higher than for the sometime father and husband, Robinson Crusoe.

Mother Midnight's conversion of the practice of mothering into a business in one sense resolves the contradictory pull of family and economics on women in Defoe's fiction; but it is also symptomatic of that very conflict in revealing, as Moll's own childhood also demonstrates, that mothers are not always in a position to provide maternal care and tenderness as effectively as hired surrogates. When Moll steals a necklace from a child whose mother she upbraids for a lack of parental care and vigilance, the competing values of self-preservation and maternal feeling once again collide. Does Moll's rationalization for preying on this helpless child – i.e., to warn its parents of the dangers of maternal self-interest and indifference – offer a critique of Moll's own hypocrisy, or of the hypocrisy of a society which, while it demands maternal solicitude generally, indulges maternal negligence in the privileged classes and makes such negligence difficult for single women living in poverty to avoid? Roxana's own experience as an abandoned wife suggests that such a society threatens to turn its women into savages when it leaves mothers with the impossible choice of abandoning their children, starving them, or worse; for as she recounts, when her children "had eaten up almost every thing ... little remain'd, unless, like one of the pitiful Women of Jerusalem, I should eat up my very Children themselves" (p. 51).

As if to insist that female agency will inevitably be delimited by the demands of kinship, both narratives enclose their dramas of class ascent within stories of kinship that work to neutralize or temper the subversive force of the heroines' transgressions, circumscribing the fates of both women within a range of narrative possibilities that seem to have the force of biological imperatives or to be built into the Providential order of the universe. In moments of apparent triumph when, having come to understand their compromised social status as women, the heroines take the reins of sexual power into their own hands and thereby transgress a gender boundary, their transgressions trigger the violent self-restitution of that boundary in the form of a menacing confrontation with their own familial pasts. Although both women remain anonymous to readers, at the level of plot their confrontations with the past threaten to expose their identities and thus jeopardize the power and authority each has acquired up to that point by having become untraceable. In both cases, ironically, Defoe's heroines are exposed by the very strategies of concealment that have also made it possible for them to survive and thrive.

The pivotal moment in Moll Flanders' kinship drama spans Moll's courtship of and marriage to her third husband, who also (as she learns after the fact) happens to be her half-brother. Having come to understand her status as a sexual object from her affair with the elder brother in the house where she is first employed as a servant, and having been betrayed by her own naïve inability to read appearances both in that affair and in her marriage to the Gentleman Draper, Moll determines to take control of her destiny by manipulating appearances herself. In her poetic courtship of her third husband, she perfects her skills in resourceful lying to obtain, at last, a good husband and economic security.[14] Later contemplating her success in landing this "best humor'd Man that ever Woman had" (p. 82), she reports thinking herself "the happiest Creature alive" (p. 85); but when she discovers that her mother-in-law is actually her own mother and that she has inadvertently entered into an incestuous marriage, she is reduced to "the most uncomfortable, if not the most miserable [creature], in the World" (p. 86). The moment of Moll's fullest realization of her agency as a woman – when refusing to be reduced to a mere object of exchange, she engineers her own marriage by successfully inserting herself as a subject into a masculine economy – is also the point at which she is most thwarted and defiled.

It may appear at the end of her narrative that Moll cashes in on her incestuous marriage by returning to Virginia to inherit her mother's estate, but we must not underestimate the importance of Moll's violent repudiation of her incest in the Virginia episode, for it has far-reaching implications for all the ensuing action of the novel – effectively establishing the conditions under which it becomes possible for Defoe to imagine the heroine's subsequent life of sexual transgression and hardened crime. While it is interesting enough that female self-determination here acquires a taint by association with a sexual crime, it is more striking still that Moll feels so powerfully compelled to reveal their unwitting incest to her brother and to flee her otherwise comfortable life to return to England. She could, after all, capitalize more profitably on her incest by keeping her own counsel and staying put. Although she is ready enough to lie or withhold information in the face of other sinful opportunities, in this case she is irresistibly moved to disclose her inadvertent crime, in spite of the fact that her own mother counsels secrecy. Why does Defoe choose to supply Moll with both an irresistible aversion to the consequences of her own agency and an implacable urge to reveal those scandalous consequences to her brother?

If one considers the logic and function of the incest prohibition which, according to anthropologists, is designed to ensure the circulation of women as sexual objects and reproducers among men, this narrative choice begins to make sense as a way of returning Moll to the very kinship imperatives that it is her original aim to either elude or undermine.[15] Figured at once as the product of her quest for power and as the one boundary that she refuses to cross over either wittingly or willingly, Moll's sibling incest becomes both a manifestation of her transgressiveness and its limit – a pivot around which her appropriation of independent subjectivity eventually gets harnessed or even cancels itself out. (Interestingly enough, in the earlier episode in which she is effectively handed between two brothers, Moll is forced to commit virtual incest "every Day in [her] Desires" (p. 59); here, in contrast, when she refuses to be circulated as a mere sign or object among men, she is fated to commit literal incest, which no one can persuade her to abide.)

By renouncing the fruits of her own desire in her repudiation of her third marriage, Moll triggers a countermovement or neutralizing subtext to the progress of her transgressive womanhood that propels her back from America and its possibilities for self-generation to the social hierarchies of the Old World. She will be able to return to America and economic security only after she has taken her place within those hierarchies and, through her marriage to a "gentleman" and the settlement of her estate upon her son, she is in a position to reenter the kinship economy in the "proper" role of wife and loving mother. By the end of the novel, we find Moll living with her husband in England on the profits of an American plantation managed by her son and sustained by the labor of servants and African slaves. She has, it would appear, traded the privileges of individual agency for the more collective gratifications of class and colonial supremacy indirectly attainable by women through the traditional course of marriage and reproduction. Only on these terms, it seems, can her life of crime and transgression become in the end both materially and spiritually "redeemable" and (despite some lingering doubt about the longevity of her repentance) her story maintain its basically comic character.

Like the incest episode in *Moll Flanders*, the familial drama in *Roxana* shows that, whether she works within the law or turns away from it, a woman's agency will ultimately be delimited by a kinship economy controlled by men. This logic, which unfolds over time in Moll's narrative, is epitomized in more concentrated form in *Roxana* in the scene in which the heroine performs her dance in Turkish dress. The episode distills within a single event the scope and limits of Roxana's quest for self-determination. Like Moll's initially triumphant courtship of her third husband, it emerges first as a moment of freedom for Roxana. But like Moll's incest, it is also a moment when the heroine's history turns back upon itself and confronts her with the ghosts of her own past. In Moll's case, this is the mother who had abandoned her in Newgate and with whom she is reunited in Virginia; in Roxana's case, it is the daughter she herself had been forced to forsake with four other children when her husband left her with no income to sustain them.

Having declined the suit of her Dutch merchant in order to avoid the "slavery" of marriage, and ambitiously aiming to become nothing less than mistress to the king himself, Roxana throws a masquerade ball at which she stages her "Turkish dance," wins the admiration and applause of a crowd of "Great Persons" (p. 222), and acquires the popular title of "Roxana." In recounting the thrill of the fame and attention generated by this performance, she describes herself as in her "Element" (p. 223). Her sense of power and control derives not simply from the liberating anonymity she enjoys in the midst of her public fame, but also from the artifice involved in the event. Only *she* knows that the diamonds on her costume are counterfeit (p. 215), that the dance she performs is really French though "the Company ... all thought it had been Turkish" (p. 216), and that, though she impersonates a Turkish princess, the dress she wears was purchased in Italy and only attainable there because the princess, who was also purchased for Roxana's use, had been taken as a slave (p. 215).

As if to replicate by a sinister irony the fate of this unfortunate princess, the exhilarating freedom and privacy associated with Roxana's performance becomes the occasion for her eventual entrapment by the threat of exposure. For at the moment when the heroine seems to hold sovereign control over the gaze of the crowd, her daughter and namesake, Susan – who happens to be a servant in her employ – is standing by. When Susan becomes obsessed with finding the mother who had abandoned her as a child, the dance witnessed at her mistress's masquerade becomes the key to her quest and the undoing of Roxana's coveted power and liberty; for as Roxana fears, she "must for-ever after have been the Girl's Vassal" were she "to let [Susan] into the Secret [of her scandalous career], and [trust] to her keeping it too" (p. 326).

Persecuted by Susan's dogged hunt for her mother's identity, Roxana descends into a state of melancholy and paranoia in which she projects her own tactics of deceit onto the figure of her daughter, worrying at points that the girl knows more than she actually does but has "artfully conceal'd her Knowledge ... till she might perhaps, [use] it more to [Roxana's] Disadvantage" (p. 328). These fears haunt the heroine's imagination, to be joined in time by bloody visions of Susan "with her Throat cut; sometimes with her Head cut, and her Brains knock'd-out; other-times hang'd up upon a beam; another time drown'd in the Great Pond at *Camberwell*" (p. 374). Thus, when Susan finally disappears after an outing with Roxana's servant,

Amy, who has all along been as "faithful to [her mistress] as the Skin to [her] Back" (p. 59), Roxana is convinced that the maid has executed her own murderous fantasies. Although the novel ends without absolute certainty as to Susan's fate, Roxana is left with no relief from the torment of guilt and misery resulting from her suspicion that, together, she and Amy are responsible for murder and infanticide. Like Moll's story of self-making, in which kinship returns powerfully and inescapably to delimit the quest for autonomy, Roxana's story is contained by a confrontation with family and fixed social identity.

Coda: the gender of fiction and the fiction of gender

Moll Flanders' and Roxana's liberating use of artifice to render themselves untraceable returns us rather conveniently to Defoe. Like Moll's mastery of disguise, which enables her to elude the law and become "the greatest Artist of [her] time" (p. 214), Defoe's authorial fondness for impersonation makes him, as we have seen, exceedingly difficult to locate or pin down. Like Roxana, who makes a spectacle of her unpainted face as proof that she is neither a prostitute nor a cheat (p. 108) and boasts that "not a Quaker in town ... look[s] less counterfeit" (p. 256) than she does when she adopts a Quaker dress, Defoe is a master at creating the pretense of naturalness.

But as we have also seen, the artistic freedoms of Defoe's heroines incorporate the seeds of their own undoing. Is there a parallel between author and characters here as well? Do the narrative strategies that free Defoe to disappear into his fictions also turn his texts back on themselves to expose him as well as the illusory nature of his narrative's "authenticity"? In *Moll Flanders* and *Roxana*, Defoe gives fiction a gender by figuratively identifying the seductive and elusive text with an alluring but deceitful and ungovernable female body. Might his distinctive narrative strategies also ultimately destabilize that gendering of fiction by exposing the fiction of gender that sustains it? If so, might Defoe's stories of female crime and immorality lend themselves to other than strictly religious didactic uses? Could they be redeemed, for instance, for a feminist or a postmodern reading? To pose the question another way: from the perspective of a twenty-first-century feminist reader, what might the *best* use of these worst of stories be?

We might gesture toward some answers to these questions by returning to the figure used in the prefaces to the two novels, in which a male editor puts a dress on a woman's story. The figure is of interest not just because it resonates with the themes of disguise and seduction in both plots but also because, in a manner of speaking, by impersonating a female narrator Defoe himself is, in each case, putting on a dress. Numerous clues in the prefaces suggest, moreover, that by also masquerading as the story's editor, Defoe may be *putting the reader on* as well.

Defoe cleverly distances himself from his own narrative truth claims by peeking out from behind the editorial mask to suggest that his editors themselves are naïve or overly credulous readers. For example, those who know *Roxana* are apt to chuckle when the editor invokes the authority of his friend the Brewer, the heroine's first husband, as witness to the truth of the first part of the lady's story, since this very Brewer is well established in the story as a fool, a scoundrel, and a liar. Within pages of the preface, we read of the Brewer "fraudulently … representing … Cases otherwise than they were" to his wife (p. 42); and later Amy will come to understand "that there was no depending on anything he said" (p. 129). When the editor subsequently acknowledges that the latter part of Roxana's history may "not be so well vouch'd as the first" because it takes place abroad, but that "as [the lady] has told it herself, we have less Reason to Question the Truth of that Part also" (pp. 35–36), we *know* we are on shaky factual ground. Similarly, when the editor of *Moll Flanders* invokes the argument made by advocates of the stage that "Plays are useful … and fail not to recommend Vertue" (p. 3) to support his claim that he has only virtuous designs in publishing Moll's story, that claim itself is subtly undermined by his own concession that much might be said in favor of such an argument in support of the theater *"were it true"* (p. 3; emphasis added). Over and over again, Defoe lifts the veil to show himself behind the ruse of both editorial innocence and narrative authenticity.

Thus, while Defoe's fictions may foster the illusion of an unmediated reality, that illusion is only as powerful as his own determination to efface himself as author by sustaining it; and Defoe, like Moll Flanders, ultimately would be "Conceal'd and Discover'd both together" (p. 175). Once the male author becomes visible beneath the dress and the privileged "reality" of his narrators becomes traceable to his deceptive artistry, the constructed and arbitrary character of that reality becomes plain. When the man behind the curtain comes into view, we are freed not just from the power of the illusion he has created but from the appearance of its inevitability. Such acts of unveiling may not release Defoe's heroines from the fiction of gender in the service of which they have been conceived, but they do free his readers to imagine the female subject otherwise, by opening the possibility of alternative ways to envision female identity.

These moments of unveiling may also prompt us to reflect on the implications of the prevailing critical consensus that *Roxana* is a more *evolved* novel than *Moll Flanders* – that it represents, in the words of one critic, "an important step in [the] direction [of] … the 'psychological' novel"[16] or, as another puts it, "is the closest Defoe comes to producing what deserves to be called a *novel* in very nearly the full, formal sense of the term."[17] By offering a sophisticated representation of its heroine's tortured inner life, these critics argue, *Roxana* anticipates the complexities of the emerging psychological novel. Such assessments suggest a certain teleology in the novel's development as a genre when they correlate the extent of novelistic success with a narrative's focus on the "moral self-consciousness" of its protagonist and the degree to which that protagonist has internalized external constraints as moral and psychological imperatives. But if Roxana is "Defoe's last and best character"[18] largely because she suffers, what does that tell us about the development of the novel as an institution in the eighteenth century with respect to its construction of the psychological and moral lives of women? Was what was *best* for the novel also best for women? These are difficult questions that need to be addressed if we wish to avoid reproducing the truths about women that Defoe's two novels about them elaborate, most seamlessly and successfully in *Roxana*. At the very least, it is clear that the formal development of the novel genre in eighteenth-century England, which is generally agreed to have come to fruition at mid-century with the publication of Samuel Richardson's novels *Pamela* (1740) and *Clarissa* (1749), was tied up with problematic norms of female interiority. It is a measure of the limit as well as the scope of Defoe's artistry that, even as he forcefully imagines such normative truths, his narrative strategies position him at a distance from them, as those strategies do from all his truth claims, thereby exposing such norms as neither absolute nor inevitable but as historical, constructed, and only provisional.

NOTES

1. The exception is *Captain Singleton*, which has no preface.
2. Daniel Defoe, *Serious Reflections during the Life and Surprising Adventures of Robinson Crusoe* (London, 1720), "Robinson Crusoe's preface." In an amusingly ironic move, Defoe frames the *Serious Reflections* with a preface in which Robinson Crusoe, by bearing witness to his own existence and to the authenticity and moral purpose of his writings, answers objections that the first two volumes of his memoirs, *The Life and Adventures* and *The Farther Adventures*, are mere fictions.
3. Daniel Defoe, *The Life and Adventures of Robinson Crusoe*, ed. Angus Ross (Harmondsworth and New York: Penguin, 1965), pp. 75 and 87. All future references to *Robinson Crusoe* are from this edition and page numbers will be given in parenthesis in the text.
4. James H. Maddox, "On Defoe's *Roxana*," *English Literary History*, 51 (1984), 684. See also John Richetti, *The Life of Daniel Defoe* (Oxford: Blackwell, 2005), ch. 9.
5. Daniel Defoe, *Roxana: The Fortunate Mistress or, a History of the Life and Vast Variety of Fortunes of Mademoiselle de Beleau, Afterwards call'd The Countess de*

Wintselsheim, in Germany. Being the Person known by the Name of the Lady Roxana in the Time of King Charles II (Harmondsworth and New York: Penguin, 1982), ed. David Blewett, pp. 169, 170, and 183. All future references to *Roxana* are from this edition and page numbers will be given in parenthesis in the text.

6. James Joyce, "Daniel Defoe," ed. and trans. Joseph Prescott in *Buffalo Studies* 1.1 (1964); reprinted in Daniel Defoe, *Robinson Crusoe*, ed. Michael Shinagel (New York and London: W. W. Norton, 1994), p. 323.

7. Daniel Defoe, *The Fortunes and Misfortunes of the Famous Moll Flanders, &c. Who was Born in Newgate, and during a Life of continu'd Variety for Threescore Years, besides her Childhood, was Twelve Year a Whore, five Times a Wife (whereof once to her own Brother) Twelve Year a Thief, Eight Year a Transported Felon in Virginia, at last grew Rich, liv'd Honest, and died a Penitent, Written from her own Memorandums*, ed. G. A. Starr (Oxford and New York: Oxford University Press, 1981), pp. 8–15. All future references to *Moll Flanders* are from this edition and page numbers will be given in parenthesis the text.

8. Mary Douglas, *Purity and Danger: An Analysis of the Concepts of Pollution and Taboo* (London: Routledge & Kegan Paul, 1966), p. 35.

9. Daniel Defoe, *The Farther Adventures of Robinson Crusoe; Being the Second and Last Part of his Life, and of the Strange Surprizing Accounts of his Travels Round three Parts of the Globe. Written by Himself* (London, 1719), preface.

10. Daniel Defoe, *The History and Remarkable Life of the Truly Honourable Colonel Jacque, Commonly Call'd Col. Jack*, ed. Samuel Holt Monk (London: Oxford University Press, 1965), p. 1. All future references to *Colonel Jack* are from this edition and page numbers will be given in parenthesis in the text.

11. Juliet Mitchell, *Psychoanalysis and Feminism* (New York: Vintage Books, 1975), p. 406.

12. See, for example, Richetti, *Life*, p. 299.

13. See, for example, Susan C. Greenfield and Carol Barash, eds., *Inventing Maternity: Politics, Science, and Literature, 1650–1865* (Lexington: University of Kentucky Press, 1999).

14. For a more detailed discussion of this episode and of Moll's incestuous marriage, see my *Incest and the English Novel, 1684–1814* (Baltimore and London: Johns Hopkins University Press, 2003), ch. 5.

15. On the role of the incest prohibition in the production of gender and kinship, see Gayle Rubin, "The Traffic in Women: Notes on the 'Political Economy' of Sex," in *Toward an Anthropology of Women*, ed. Rayna R. Reiter (New York: Monthly Review Press, 1975), pp. 157–210.

16. David Blewett, *Defoe's Art of Fiction* (Toronto: University of Toronto Press, 1979), p. 148.

17. Richetti, *Life*, p. 268.

18. *Ibid*, p. 271.

9

CYNTHIA WALL

Defoe and London

I BEGAN my Travels, where I Purpose to End them, *viz.* At the
City of *London* ...
(Defoe, *Tour* I, I)[1]

Daniel Defoe began and ended his own travels, so to speak, in London, and
the city of London is the implied or explicit setting, subject, or structuring
principle of just about every work he wrote, didactic or fictional, prosaic or
poetic. Cities in general fascinated Defoe, but he wrote most particularly of
London, its boundaries and buildings, streets and occupations, trade and
crime, strengths and vulnerabilities, ancient patterns and constant permuta-
tions. He knew it intimately and represented it vividly; however fictional the
plots and characters of his novels might be, London is always precisely real.
The streets are accurately mapped, the buildings reliably themselves. And yet,
for Defoe, there are many Londons overlapping in those precisely drawn
streets. There is the economically charged city, buoyant with trade, a city of
shops and houses and traffic and merchants and apprentices and servants. But
there are darker Londons with ragged children and forgotten elderly swept
into corners, thieves lurking in the underworld, stockjobbers corrupting
financial networks, watermen and hackney drivers imperiling the streets,
plague and fire ravaging the whole. Places of safety and prosperity are
simultaneously the spaces of danger and vulnerability. Defoe's London
teems with contradictions and ambiguities and peculiar linguistic, social,
and topographical codes – and he employs different genres to explore them.

The conflicting patterns Defoe finds in his city he formally replicates in
the patterns of his plots and even of his prose. His novels seem to take on the
shape of their subject: the narrator of *A Journal of the Plague Year* circles the city
and retreats into his house with the ebb and flow of the plague itself; Moll
Flanders circles Newgate prison in her attempts to escape it; Roxana hides events
beneath her frankness, to return to them later; Colonel Jack burrows into the
commercial and the secret spaces of London. All this nonlinearity, this circling
and concealing and connecting, is repeated syntactically. As George Starr puts it:
"Defoe uses active verbs where another writer might use copulative, favours
subordinate over co-ordinate clauses, and relies heavily on participial constructions; the resulting narrative style slights pictorial effects but conveys well the

sensations of bodies and minds in restless, obsessive motion."[2] That is to say, Defoe's prose tends to avoid verbs that record mere existence ("copulative") and tends towards verbs that point to particular acts; it strings together clauses without subjecting the actions they describe to strict relationships of cause and effect or equality, and in so doing his prose stresses process and continuity rather than static being. We can take the preface to the *Tour thro' the whole Island of Great Britain* (1724–27), Defoe's epistolary travelogue of the nation's physiognomy, as a sort of frontispiece example of the way his prose enacts his conceptions. Its bird's-eye-view of vast topographic change in the country as a whole is captured within one metonymic sentence:

> The Fate of Things gives a new Face to Things, produces Changes in low Life, and innumerable Incidents; plants and supplants Families, raises and sinks Towns, removes Manufactures, and Trade; Great Towns decay, and small Towns rise; new Towns, new Palaces, new Seats are Built every Day; great Rivers and good Harbours dry up, and grow useless; again, new Ports are open'd, Brooks are made Rivers, small Rivers [sic]; navigable Ports and Harbours are made where none were before, and the like. (1, 48)

As Pat Rogers has noted, the language and imagery of the *Tour* presume motion and change.[3] Cities, towns, houses, rivers, ports, rise and ebb "even while the Sheets are in the Press" (*Tour* 1, 49); one sentence swells with both decades and days, growth and destruction. Defoe's language – his sentences and his paragraphs – like his view of the country, is rarely straightforward, however clear and simple his diction. His language describing the city in his novels, pamphlets, journalism, and poetry replicates its urban web of commercial and social interdependence, of bright open possibilities and dark vulnerabilities, of streets leading into alleys and closes and back out again into main spaces, through commas, semi-colons, and colons before a full stop. Defoe represents the city so vividly because he writes its complexities into his very prose. Understanding the ways he sees his city helps us understand the digressive, repetitive way he writes – and the way he renders the city linguistically mirrors the way he and his characters experience it. In learning how to read Defoe's works, we learn how to read his London.

Defoe in London

What was Defoe's London like? Greater London comprised four main areas: the original medieval city bounded by the remnants of the Roman walls and gates – this was and is the commercial center, known as the "City"; Westminster lies to the west, home of king and court; the "Town" sits in between, center of law (the Inns of Court) and theater (Drury Lane and

1. "A New and Exact Plan of the Cities of London and Westminster." From *A Survey of the Cities of London and Westminster and the Borough of Southwark: containing the original, antiquity, increase, present state and government of those cities. Written at first in the year* MDXCVIII. *By John Stow, citizen and native of London ... Now lastly, corrected, improved, and very much enlarged ... by John Strype, MA a native also of the said city* (sixth edition, 1754–55).

Covent Garden); and Southwark is on the south side of the river Thames (see Figure 1). London was far and away the largest and most important city in England in the seventeenth and eighteenth centuries, as the *Tour* makes explicit, formally and factually:

SIR,
As I am now near the Center of this Work, so I am to describe the great Center of *England*, the City of *London*, and Parts adjacent. This great Work is infinitely

1. (cont.)

difficult in its Particulars, though not in itself; not that the City is so difficult to be described, but to do it in the narrow Compass of a Letter, which we see so fully takes up Two large Volumes in Folio, and which, yet, if I may venture to give an Opinion of it, is done but by Halves neither.   (*Tour* II, 65)

The "Two large Volumes in Folio" are presumably John Strype's 1720 version of John Stow's 1598 *Survey of London*, replete with ward maps and architectural analyses. The difficulty of describing London's "Particulars" lies in the city's rapid growth, as Defoe underlines in a long surging sentence:

> *London*, as a City only, and as its Walls and Liberties line it out, might, indeed, be viewed in a small Compass; but, when I speak of *London*, now in the Modern Acceptation, you expect I shall take in all that vast Mass of Buildings, reaching

from *Black Wall* in the *East*, to *Tot-hill Fields* in the *West* ... and how much farther it may spread, who knows? New Squares, and new Streets rising up every Day to such a Prodigy of Buildings, that nothing in the World does, or ever did, equal it, except old *Rome* in *Trajan*'s Time, when the Walls were Fifty Miles in Compass, and the number of Inhabitants Six Millions Eight hundred thousand Souls. (*Tour* II, 65)

London's population had been 400,000 in 1650 (8.2 percent of the total population of England); it jumped to 575,000 by 1700, and to 675,000 by 1750, when it comprised 11.6 percent of the total 5,800,000.[4] The city increasingly attracted people of all stations looking for jobs, fortunes, spouses, an upper rung on the social ladder. Even marking its boundaries is an open-ended job; like the brooks swelling into streams and rivers of the nation, the streets of London are proliferating prodigiously; the "Particulars" want watching and recording. The margins as well as the center constantly expand.

Defoe has various opinions about all this expansion, depending on where he's literarily standing. Defoe the urban planner finds the overall shape of the city aesthetically unpleasing:

It is the Disaster of *London*, as to the Beauty of its Figure, that it is thus stretched out in Buildings, just at the Pleasure of every Builder, or Undertaker of Buildings, and as the Convenience of the People directs, whether for Trade, or otherwise; and this has spread the Face of it in a most straggling, confus'd Manner, out of all Shape, uncompact, and unequal; neither long or broad, round or square; whereas the City of *Rome*, though a Monster for its Greatness, yet was, in a manner, round, with very few Irregularities in its Shape. (*Tour* II, 65)

But Defoe the novelist and economic observer will zoom in delightedly on the city's "Irregularities" to find its pulse, to watch the people negotiating its corners and shadows in business, love, and general survival, in an ultimate celebration (or at least vindication) of those straggling confusions and inequalities.

This paradoxical appreciation of London comes from Defoe's own complicated habitation within it. Daniel Foe (he added the aristocratic "de" later) was born in the center of the old City, in Broad Street Ward, to James and Alice Foe in about 1660; his father was a tallow chandler who practised his trade in Cripplegate. Defoe described the old City of his childhood as a place where

the Streets were narrow, and publick Edifices, as well as Private, were more crowded, and built closer to one another ... The Streets were ... narrow, and the Houses all built of Timber, Lath and Plaister ... [T]he Manner of the Building in those Days, one Story projecting out beyond another, was such, that in some narrow Streets, the Houses almost touch'd one another at the Top, and it has been known, that Men, in Case of Fire, have escaped on the Tops of the Houses, by leaping from one Side of a Street to another.   (*Tour* II, 75)

The streets that in his adult life were prosperous, were in his childhood "Lanes ... deep, dirty, and unfrequented, that Part now called *Spittlefields-Market*, was a Field of Grass with Cows feeding on it" (*Tour* II, 77). He grew up within a rapidly growing city.

During the first decade of Defoe's life London was charged with drama and change. The Act of Uniformity in 1662 required all Dissenters (including the Foes and their minister, Samuel Annesley) to subscribe to the Thirty-Nine Articles of the Church of England or be evicted from their churches; frequently the meeting houses were violently raided, the ministers escaping through secretly built passages in their pulpits. The Great Plague of 1665 killed over 97,000 people and the Great Fire of 1666 destroyed 13,200 houses (about three quarters of the old City) in four days. One of Defoe's most vivid urban images is of a city emptied: "Doors were left open, Windows stood shattering with the Wind in empty Houses," and "the great Streets ... had Grass growing in them."[5] Defoe's earliest perceptions of the city, then, were of instability, impermanence, insecurity.

Defoe's early education and experience also offered multiple and shifting perspectives, a sense of more-stories-than-one. As a Dissenter, Defoe was not allowed to attend the traditional schools and universities of England (including Oxford and Cambridge), and was instead educated at the Newington Green Academy (1674–79), where he studied the "modern" subjects of astronomy and geography in place of the usual Latin and Greek, and where free inquiry – "dissent," we might say – was encouraged. He originally planned to be a minister, but went into the hosiery business instead (1683–92), with a home and warehouse in Freeman's Yard, Cornhill (a center of well-heeled Dissenters) near the Royal Exchange, the building he thought "the greatest and finest of the Kind in the World" (*Tour* II, 80) (see Figure 2). In 1684 Defoe married Mary Tuffley, who brought a dowry of £3,700 (about £440,000 or near $900,000 in today's economy). As a wholesale merchant in increasingly various goods (including wine), he began to travel widely in Europe and to invest in "projects," or general schemes for urban and national improvement.

A description in the *Tour* of London's markets graphically reflects Defoe's admiration for the mercantile world. The text suddenly breaks away from simply verbal descriptions of buildings and opens into a sort of spatial plan that gives the vast variety of markets their own vastly respectable space on the page:

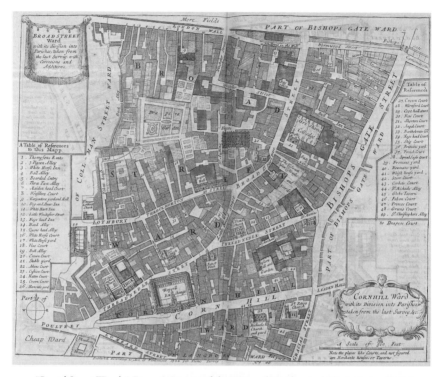

2. "Broad Street Ward." From *A Survey of the Cities of London and Westminster*, by John Stowe (sixth edition, 1754–55).

Fish Markets	*Billingsgate, Fishstreet Hill*, and *Old Fishstreet.*
Herb Markets	*Covent Garden, and Stocks Market.*
N. B. Cherry Market, and Apple-Market	At the Three *Cranes.*
Corn Markets	*Bear Key, and Queen Hith.*
Meal Markets	*Queen Hith, Hungerford, Ditch-Side*, and *Whitecross-Street.*
Hay Markets	*Whitechapel, Smithfield, South-wark*, the *Hay-Market Street, Westminster*, and *Bloomsbury.*
Leather Market	*Leaden Hall.*
Hides and Skins	*Leaden Hall*, and *Wood's Close.*
Coal Markets	*Billingsgate, Room Land.*
Bay Market	*Leaden Hall.*
Broad Cloath Market	*Blackwell Hall.*

N.B. The last Three are, without Doubt, the greatest in the World of those Kinds. (*Tour* II, 92)

Defoe manages a physical variety on the page that matches the spatial variety of London: as the earlier paragraphical sentences of colons and semi-colons mimic the physical crowding of buildings, so the extra-important function of markets is set apart in a special territory of its own.

The other city institution that gets the same spatial treatment in the *Tour* is the virtual counterpart of the markets: the prisons – which Defoe knew as intimately. By 1692 he found himself imprisoned in the Fleet for a debt of about £17,000. Defoe was imprisoned again for debt in the King's Bench Prison in 1693, and would be hounded by debt throughout his life. He found himself in Newgate in 1703 for the backfiring satire *The Shortest Way with the Dissenters*. Prison, we might say, shaped Defoe's life and imagination as much as the markets; in all his works he is as fascinated by what is open and offered as by what is caught and enclosed:

There are in *London*, and the far extended Bounds, which I now call so, notwithstanding we are a Nation of Liberty, more publick and private Prisons, and Houses of Confinement, than any City in *Europe*, perhaps as many as in all the Capital Cities of *Europe* put together; *for Example*:

Publick G A O L S.

The *Tower*.	The *Chink*, formerly the
Newgate.	Prison to the *Stews*.
Ludgate.	*Whitechapel*.
King's Bench.	*Finsbury*.
The *Fleet*.	The *Dutchy*.
Bridewell.	St. *Katherines*.
Marshalseas.	*Bale-Dock*.
The *Gatehouse*.	*Little-Ease*.
Two *Counters* in the City.	*New-Prison*.
	New-Bridewell.
One *Counter* in the Burrough.	*Tottil-Fields Bridewell*.
St. *Martin's le Grand*.	Five Night Prisons, called *Round-houses, &c.*

Tolerated P R I S O N S.

Bethlem or *Bedlam*.	The *Black Rod* Officers-Houses.
One hundred and Nineteen *Spunging Houses*.	
Fifteen private *Madhouses*.	*Cumaliis*.
The King's *Messengers-Houses*.	The *Admiralty* Officers-Houses.
The Serjeant at Arms's Officers Houses.	*Tip-staffs* Houses.
	Chancery Officers Houses.

(Tour II, 101)

The prisons in the *Tour* get the same sort of textual space as the markets because both are the institutional centers of the city, which would govern so much of Defoe's life and writing. But while the *Tour*'s list of prisons, at once extensive and spare, simply marks their names and categories, a novel can give them a more vivid reality: "*Newgate*; that horrid Place! my very Blood chills at the mention of its Name ... I look'd on myself as lost, and that I had nothing to think of but of going out of the World, and that with the utmost Infamy; the hellish Noise, the Roaring, swearing and Clamour, the Stench and Nastiness, and all the dreadful croud of Afflicting things that I saw there; joyn'd together to make the Place seem an Emblem of Hell itself, and a kind of Entrance into it" (*Moll Flanders*, pp. 273–74). Defoe's novels fill in the white spaces surrounding the *Tour*'s lists with personal experience; the Newgate of the topography overlaps in name with the Newgate of the novel, but the different texts present alternate spatial perceptions.

But like Moll, Defoe got out of prison and back into business. Before the Newgate experience, he had established a pantile factory in Essex and had become an accountant, a kind of clerical assistant for one of the commissioners, for the Glass Duty (bottles, dishes, and other glassware were taxed), giving himself the name "Defoe." By 1697 he was an agent for the king. After his two weeks in Newgate, he was convicted in July 1703 of seditious libel and sentenced to stand in the pillory in front of the Royal Exchange, not far from his house. But he fortunately if hastily penned *A Hymn to the Pillory*, which made him a hero, and the crowd pelted him with flowers instead of stones. Not so luckily, he was bankrupted again in 1703 and lost his pantile factory just before the Great Storm of 1703, which from 24 November to 3 December ravaged the British Isles with winds of up to 120 miles an hour (193 kilometers). Defoe rebounded again to become a political journalist, publishing the *Review* (1704–13) and reassuming his spy status for Robert Harley in Scotland to promote the union of Scotland and England (achieved in 1707, when the two countries became Great Britain). Under the name of Andrew Moreton he was a successful spy and propagandist. His variegated city life thus perfected his skills at multiple personalities, multiple perspectives, multiple energies.

In 1708 Defoe moved to the suburbs (Stoke Newington), and outside the city limits he expanded his range of voices and arguments as a political journalist (the *Review*), conduct book writer (*Conjugal Lewdness, The Family Instructor*), travel narrator (the *Tour*), business adviser (*The Complete English Tradesman*), and novelist (*Robinson Crusoe, Moll Flanders, Journal of the Plague Year, Captain Singleton, Colonel Jack, Roxana*). In all of these works, written from the edges of the city, London is intimately reinhabited, its markets and prisons, streets and houses, opportunities and dangers explored from every conceivable human experience. There is a blue plaque commemorating him at number 95 Church Street in Stoke

Newington, at the corner of Defoe Road – and appropriately, Stoke Newington is no longer the suburbs, but part of that "vast Mass of Buildings" of London, ever spreading that much farther (*Tour* II, 65).

Defoe's "travels" ended back in London proper when he died on 24 April 1731, "of a lethargy" (probably a stroke), in Ropemaker's Alley, another area of shopkeepers, hiding from creditors once again. He was buried on 26 April in Bunhill Fields, which had been made into a cemetery during the Great Plague of 1665. Bunhill Fields was often called "The Cemetery of Puritan England":[6] Defoe lies there in the excellent company of John Bunyan (1688), author of *The Pilgrim's Progress*; Susannah Wesley (1742), religious writer and mother of John and Charles; the hymnist Isaac Watts (1748); the poet William Blake (1827); and his own character H.F.: "N.B. The Author of this Journal, lyes buried in that very Ground, being at his own Desire, his Sister having been buried there a few Years before" (*Journal*, p. 223). His death record in the St. Giles, Cripplegate, General Registry declares him a "Gentleman"; his obituaries, "the famous Mr. Daniel De Foe" who was "well known for his numerous and varied Writings."[7] Defoe personally experienced *all* the lives of his city, its prosperity and poverty, respectability and criminality, its overworld and underworld: he knew it above and ended below its ground.

"Peculiar streets, and proper places": the prosperous city

Defoe was fascinated by the patterns of living and working in London and by the ways that different streets could actually determine different ways of life. He paid a great deal of attention to the topographical effects of the city's economic and architectural energy in the decades after the Great Fire and through the early eighteenth century. Maximillian Novak refers to Defoe's sense of "the economic sublime" in the "changing, pulsating nature of Britain,"[8] and the *Tour* certainly celebrates an economic sublime of domestic and commercial building in London, particularly in all the new buildings after the Great Fire, the new squares carving up old estates, and "fine large Houses ... inhabited by principal Merchants" taking the place of stableyards and inns, as in the King's Arms Yard in Coleman Street (*Tour* II, 76), home of H.F.'s brother and Defoe's father. The internal expansion is a sign of urban power, as is the external. Defoe celebrates the "Prodigy" of building in the houses going up just to the west of the City: "From hence we go on still *West*, and beginning at *Gray's Inn*, and going on to those formerly called *Red Lyon* Fields, and *Lamb's Conduit* Fields, we see there a prodigious Pile of Buildings; it begins at *Gray's Inn Wall* towards *Red-Lyon street*, from whence, in a strait Line, 'tis built quite to *Lamb's Conduit* Fields, *North*, including a great Range of Buildings yet unfinish'd, reaching to ... *King's Gate* in *Holbourn*, where it goes out" (*Tour* II, 78). Defoe's linguistic energy matches the urban pace of change; "we go on" and on and on, carried by the clauses of a sentence that unrolls steadily to the middle, from Gray's Inn to the gate in Holborn, "where it goes out" at a semi-colon (and then he pauses for breath to admire a particularly fine house). All the new building north and west, from Piccadilly to the village of Knightsbridge, and north to Cavendish Square, makes London "more in Bulk than the Cities of *Bristol, Exeter* and *York,* if they were all put together; all which Places were, within the Time mentioned, meer Fields of Grass, and employ'd only to feed Cattle as other Fields are" (*Tour* II, 79).

Who lives in these grand houses? Roxana, for one. She had been brought to London in 1683 as the daughter of Protestant refugees from Poitiers, and she liked the city immediately: "*London,* a large and gay City, took with me mighty well, who, from my being a child, lov'd a Crowd, and to see a great-many fine Folks."[9] Her first husband had been a foolish brewer in the City who lost all their money and disappeared; she then has an affair with her landlord in the house "about two Miles out of Town" (p. 10) – still close enough for "a *Leaden-Hall* Basket-Woman" to show up "with a whole Load of good Things for the Mouth" (p. 41). She spends several years abroad with a German prince, and then travels back to London, extremely wealthy and ready to conquer:

> [I took] handsome large Apartments in the *Pall-Mall*, in a House, out of which was a private Door into the King's Garden, by the Permission of the Chief Gardener, who had liv'd in the House ... and here I began to make a Figure suitable to my Estate, which was very great ...
>
> I paid 60 *l.* [today, about £6,895 or $14,000] a Year for my new Apartments, for I took them by the Year; but then, they were handsome Lodgings indeed, and very richly furnish'd; I kept my own Servants to clean and look after them; found my own Kitchen-Ware, and Firing; my Equipage was handsome, but not very great: I had a Coach, a Coachman, and Footman, my woman, *Amy,* who I now dress'd like a Gentlewoman, and made her my Companion, and three Maids ... And thus I appear'd, leaving the World to guess who or what I was, without offering to put myself forward. (pp. 164–65)

Roxana matches her address to her social desires, and creates a London persona of mysterious wealth in the center of its aristocracy. Her house is full of rich furniture, rich clothes, servants in rich livery; she has "a large Dining-Room in [her] Apartments, with five other Rooms on the same Floor" (p. 173), and she makes use of these to gather the "best" society and to arrange her rooms for lavish parties. She shows the gentlemen that she "understood very well what such things meant" (p. 173) – she knows the psychological patterns of London's social elite as well as she knows their addresses.

For a city address does, or at least *should*, in Defoe's opinion, define behavior. Roxana perches in fashionable Pall Mall and dangles her opulence in the height of her success, but when necessary she is fully capable of a chameleon change in another part of the city, donning sober Quaker dress when she lives in the Minories (named after a thirteenth-century abbey, in the eastern part of the City) to escape the reputation of "Roxana" and the stalking of her daughter:

> I was now in a perfect Retreat indeed; remote from the Eyes of all that ever had seen me, and as much out of the way of being ever seen or heard-of by any of the Gang that us'd to follow me, as if I had been among the Mountains in *Lancashire*; for when did a Blue Garter, or a Coach-and-Six come into a little narrow Passage in the *Minories*, or *Goodman's-Fields*? (p. 211)

Roxana knows the contours of her city, how to dress and behave within its different enclaves. Her London is a place simultaneously of exposure and concealment, depending on the circumstances; she matches her personae to different neighborhood requirements as a mode of survival.

Mapping Roxana onto the different social spaces of London is something Defoe does on a larger economic scale in *The Complete English Tradesman* (1725–27). It is crucial to know your streets and their firm patterns of expectation:

> In most towns, but particularly in the city of *London*, there are places as it were appropriated to particular trades, and where the trades which are plac'd there succeed very well, but would do very ill any where else ... as the orange-merchants and wet-salters about *Billingsgate*, and in *Thames-street*; the coster-mongers at the *Three Cranes*; the wholesale cheesemongers in *Thames-street*; the mercers and drapers in the high streets, such as *Cheapside, Ludgate-street, Cornhill, Round-court,* and *Gracechurch-street*, &c. ... Many trades have their peculiar streets, and proper places.[10]

The streets and spaces of London imply the boundaries of success or failure; the requirement for succeeding in London is reading its social and commercial spaces accurately:

> [A] particular trade is not only proper for such or such a part of the town, but a particular sortment of goods, even in the same way, suits one part of the town, or one town and not another; as he that sets up in the *Strand*, or near the *Exchange*, is likely to sell more rich silks, more fine hollands, more fine broad-cloths ... than one of the same trade, setting up in the skirts of the town, or at *Ratcliff*, or *Wapping*, or *Redriff*. (*Tradesman* I, 101)

The tradesman, just as much as any socially adept person, should know his territory – social, commercial, and topographic – and stay in it: "He that will be a tradesman should confine himself within his own sphere: never was the gazette so full of the advertisements of commissions of bankrupts as since our shopkeepers are so much engaged in parties, form'd into clubs to hear news, and read journals and politicks" (*Tradesman* I, 47).

The territory of trade tended to be closely compressed anyway; the tradesman's house was typically the floor above his shop, so the boundaries between domestic and economic were frequently blurred. You *must* pay attention to such details. Moll Flanders is finally caught in a house which "was not a Mercers Shop, nor a warehouse or a Mercer, but look'd like a private Dwelling-House, and was it seems Inhabited by a Man that sold Goods for the Weavers to the Mercers, like a Broker or Factor" (*Moll Flanders* 272). The whole family might be involved in the business; middle-class urban spaces were not particularly gendered. Indeed, Defoe encourages the tradesman to let his wife "into the knowledge of [his] business ... that she may be put into a posture to save him from ruin, if it be possible, or to carry on some business without him, if he is forc'd to fail, and fly; as many have been, when the creditors have encourag'd the wife to carry on a trade for the support of her family and children, when he perhaps may never shew his head again" (*Tradesman* I, 356). Family *is* business in London, and the architecture of business commingles the domestic with the commercial.

Defoe offers instructions for the appearance of the shop to enhance its commerciality, distinguishing between "furnishing" it (supplying it with goods) and "fitting up" it, or furbishing its appearance in unpuritan and wasteful "painting and gilding, fine shelves, shutters, boxes, glass-doors, sashes and the like" (*Tradesman* I, 312). The house and shop "should be ˙ decent and handsome, spacious as the place will allow," and there should be "something like the face of a master ... always to be seen in it" (*Tradesman* I, 316). The good shopkeeper has substance in his furnishings; the overreacher spends his capital on ornament. Though the shops and warehouses and houses of H.F. and his brother in *A Journal of the Plague Year* are never described, still, because those characters are successful and honest tradesmen, we can infer something decent, spacious, and handsome, without gilding and fine shelves.

The Complete English Tradesman as a text always has "something like the face of a master ... to be seen in it": without gilding or mirrors, every lesson is illustrated with a novelistic anecdote. Almost all of Defoe's didactic treatises are novelistically *peopled*; he gives his Londoners voices and habits in order to make the city immediate and real and readily reinhabited in the right way by his readers:

I have heard of a young Apothecary, who setting up in a part of the Town, where he had not much acquaintance, and fearing much, whether he should get into business, hir'd a man acquainted with such business, and made him be every morning between five and six, and often late in the evenings working very hard at the great mortar; pounding and beating, tho' he had nothing to do with it, but beating some very needless thing, that all his neighbors might hear it, and find that he was in full employ, being at work early and late, and that consequently he must be a man of vast business, and have a great practice; and the thing was well laid, and took accordingly; for the neighbors believing he had business, brought business to him; and the reputation of having a trade, made a trade for him. (*Tradesman* I, 316)

We move into a particular shop with a particularly ingenious young shop-keeper and see how he plies his trade in order to get his trade; we *live* in London in the anecdote. Defoe always connects the abstract to the concrete, giving us a line to the "real" by a particular fiction; the city never remains abstract for long.

The complicated architectural boundaries of houses-as-shops in London are further complicated by the interpenetrating social spaces of the city. The variety and hierarchy of servants inhabit the same houses, large and small, as the upper and middle classes. In *The Behavior of Servants in England Inquired into* (1725), Defoe presents an inventory of servant classes:

1. Apprentices, as well the Apprentices to Merchants, and more eminent Tradesmen, as the apprentices to meaner People; such as Shop-Keepers, Handicrafts Artificers, Manufacturers, &c.
2. *Menial Servants* such as Cooks, Gardeners, Butlers, Coachmen, Grooms, Footmen, Pages, Maid-Servants, Nurses, &c... .
3. Clerks to Lawyers, Attorneys, Scriveners, &c. and to Gentlemen in publick Offices, and the like ... [11]

Roxana, of course, often shared a bed with her maid/companion Amy (and once the same lover); Defoe's concern in this treatise is that some classes of servants were becoming too absorbed into the fabric of the house and family, so that apprentices will very rarely "condescend to open or shut the Shop-windows, much less to sweep the Shop, or Ware-houses; but their Masters are oblig'd to keep Porters or Footmen to wait upon the Apprentices," and it is difficult "to know the Chamber-Maid from her Mistress; or my Lady's Chief-woman from one of my Lady's Daughters" because they wear the same clothes "even to Patches and Paint" (*Servants*, pp. 12, 15, 14). The social hierarchy encounters the same blurring as the architectural; all the careful listing and sorting out of the levels of servants in this inventory is undermined by the narrative that watches their erosions in labor and dress. The list does one thing – sorting out – that is required by the ongoing cultural narrative of messing things up.

And that is part of Defoe's whole narrative ambivalence: sometimes the messing-up seems more interesting than the sorting-out. Though obviously anxious about the visible erosion of social distinctions, Defoe also celebrates them (finding himself a contender in the social and economic possibilities of change):

> Tradesmen in *England* live in better Figure than most of the meaner Gentry; and I may add than some of the superior Rank in foreign Countries ... [and those of] very ordinary Employments in *London*, such as *Cheese-mongers, Grocers, Chandlers, Brasiers, Upholsterers,* and the like ... are able to spend more Money in their Families, and do actually spend more than most Gentlemen of from 300 to 500 Pounds a Year, and that with this remarkable Addition, that the Tradesman shall spend it, and grow rich, and encrease under the Weight of the Expence; whereas the Gentleman spends to the Extent of his Revenue, and lays up nothing.[12]

In one casting of Defoe's verbal maps, everyone lives well in London – those in the great new houses and squares, the tradesmen in their houses and shops in the City, and the servants penetrating throughout the households. All bask in at least a bit of London's "economic sublime." Defoe in the end can celebrate the permeability of the city's social and commercial spaces because he often found room for himself in their eager latitudes. An erosion of hierarchy – deplorable – could simultaneously promise advancement for any Moll or Roxana or Jack or Dan with an eye to the main chance and an ability to read the city's spaces.

"Apoplexies, and suddenly": the dangerous city

But of course London wasn't simply full of the good, the true, the beautiful, and the prosperous; Moll and Roxana and Jack (and perhaps Daniel Defoe?) only *looked* – at times – trustworthy and respectable. The streets had to be known and navigated with as much skill by the thief as by the merchant; those paid to help you might just as easily cheat you; in the corners of the city skulked the ragged children; the private madhouses locked up unwanted wives and perversely lingering aged parents; the crowd could turn into a mob in a moment. And those are only the human threats; plague and fire and storm equally threatened the physical and haunted the psychological urban fabric.

The first class of urban threat is the thief, the one who rearranges the furniture of the city to her own advantage and who in the most successful cases looks just like you and me. When Moll glides into the silversmith's shop in Foster Lane (which the London historian John Strype described in 1720 as "a place of good resort for Silver Smiths, who forge and work Plate for the Goldsmiths, who sell it"[13]), she is charged (justly) by a neighboring goldsmith with attempting to steal the "loose Plate [that] lay in the Window." She resists her accuser, claiming: "I came in to buy half a Dozen of silver Spoons, and to my good Fortune, it was a Silver-smith's that sold Plate, as well as work'd Plate for other Shops" (pp. 269–70). (She also luckily happened to have an old spoon in her pocket to back up the pretense of matching.) Her "good Fortune" depends heavily on how well she knows the occupations of the streets. When she steals the gold necklace from the child in Bartholomew Close and runs in panic at being tempted to murder, she manages in that panic to map her exact route – which just happens to trace an arc around Newgate: "I went thro' into *Bartholomew Close*, and then turn'd round to another Passage that goes into *Long-lane*, so away into *Charterhouse-Yard* and out into *St. John's-street*, then crossing into *Smithfield*, went down *Chick-lane* and into *Field-lane* to *Holbourn-bridge*" (p. 194). Her financial survival – how well she steals – and her physical survival – how well she avoids getting caught – require an intimate knowledge of every street and every shop of London.

The good urban thief makes no distinction between public and private targets, though he must of course know which is which. *Colonel Jack* thus offers a rather different insider's view of the Custom House from that of the *Tour*, which notes that, when it is restored (by Thomas Ripley on Wren's foundations) after a nearby gunpowder explosion in 1714, it will "out-shine all the *Custom-Houses* in *Europe*" (*Tour* II, 81). (It was repaired 1717–1725, during the period of Defoe's novels and the publication of the *Tour*.) The *Tour* marks it as a *fixture*, something architecturally, commercially, conceptually, and necessarily stable: "As the City is the Center of Business; there is the *Custom-house*, an Article, which, as it brings in an immense Revenue to the Publick, so it cannot be removed from its Place, all the vast Import and Export of Goods being, of Necessity, made there; nor can the Merchants be removed, the River not admitting the Ships to come any farther" (*Tour* II, 85). But while in the *Tour*, that celebration of Britain's growth and prosperity, the Custom House is an immoveable object, for young Jack in the novel, that exploration of alternative Londons, it is a sitting duck, as he and his "new Instructor" work the room:

I Observ'd my Orders to a tittle, while he peer'd into every Corner, and had his Eye upon every Body; I kept my Eye directly upon him, but went always at a Distance, and on the other Side of the Long Room, looking as it were for Pins ...

but still my Eye was upon my Comrade, who I observ'd was very busy among the Crowds of People that stood at the Board, doing Business with the Officers, who pass the Entries, and make the Cocquets, &c.

At length he comes over to me, and stooping as if he would take up a Pin close to me, he put something into my Hand and said, put that up, and follow me down Stairs quickly: He did not run, but shuffl'd along a pace thro' the Crowd, and went down not the great Stairs, which we came in at, but a little narrow Stair-Case at the other End of the London Room; I follow'd, and he found I did, and so went on, not stopping below as I expected, nor speaking one Word to me, till thro' innumerable narrow Passages, Alley's and Dark ways, we were got up into *Fenchurch-street*, and thro' *Billiter lane* into *Leadenhall-street*, and from thence into *Leadenhall-Market*.[14]

Jack and his comrade go inside the Custom House, while the *Tour* looks on from the outside, unmindful (like its occupants) of rifling going on inside.

Another order of danger in the city lurks on its very surface, among those who wield its open, orderly services. Defoe recounts in *Every-Body's Business, is No-Body's Business* (1725) the particular egregiousness of watermen, those who carried passengers up and down the Thames:

A young Lady of Distinction, in Company with her Brother, a little Youth, took a Pair of Oars at or near the Temple on *April* Day last, and order'd the Men to carry them to *Pepper-Alley-Stairs*. One of the Fellows (according to their usual Impertinence) ask'd the Lady where she was going? she answer'd, *Near St. Olave's Church*. Upon which he said, she had better go through Bridge. The lady reply'd she had never gone through Bride [sic] in her Life, nor would she venture for an hundred Guineas; so commanded him once more to land her at *Pepper-Alley-Stairs*. Notwithstanding which, in spite of her Fears, Threats and Commands; nay, in spite of the Persuasion of his Fellow, he forc'd her through *London-Bridge*, which frighten'd her beyond Expression: And, to mend the matter, he oblig'd her to pay double Fare, and mobb'd her into the bargain.[15]

The nineteen arches of London Bridge churned the waters of the river into deadly rapids; people often died trying to pass through at high tide. And watermen could be frightening in their own right, always "a sturdy, rough breed with their own jargon and as quick with raillery and repartee as with their fists."[16] In general, travelers in boats and hackney coaches were at the mercy of their carriers; the simplest travel could be difficult and dangerous; those hired to serve could rework the city routes and rates as they pleased. The energy and independence of London was equally its threat.

Threats to the city's citizens came from the outside as well as from within – from plague, fire, and storm. Defoe concentrates most of his interest in natural disasters into the various pieces he wrote about the Great Plague, which decimated the city when he was about five years old. More than a decade before he published *A Journal of the Plague Year* (1722), he meditated on its ravages in his (usually politically oriented) journal, the *Review*. He reminds his readers that during the plague "the City was so thin of Inhabitants, that one might walk from *Aldgate* to *Ludgate*, and not meet, or see, 100 People; That the generality of the People were all fled, at least all such as had any Retreat; That above 70000 were dead at that Time of the Plague, and in their Graves, *Inclusive of this Week*; That Grass grew in the Streets, in the Markets, and on the Exchange; and nothing but Death and Horror was to be seen in every place."[17] He prints a copy of one of the Bills of Mortality for the week of 12–19 September 1665, listing all the many and unexpected ways people died:

From the 12th *of* September, *to the* 19th.
Anno *1665. Diseases* and *Casualties* this Week.

Abortive	5
Aged	43
Ague	2
Apoplexies, and suddenly	2
Bleeding	2
Burnt in his Bed at St. *Giles Cripplegate*	1
Canker	1
Childbed	42
Chrisoms	18
Consumption	134
Convulsion	64
Cough	2
Dropsie	33
Fever	309
Flox and Small-Pox	5
Frighted	3
Gout	1
Grief	3
Griping in the Guts	51
Jaundies	5
Imposthume	11
Infants	16
Kill'd by a Fall from the Bellfrey at *Allhallows* the Great	1
King's Evil	2
Lethargy	1
Palsie	1
Plague	7165
Rickets	17

Rising of the Lights	11
Scowring	5
Scurvy	2
Spleen	1
Spotted-Fever	101
Stilborn	17
Stone and Strangury	3
Stopping of the Stomach	9
Surfeit	49
Teeth	121
Thrush	5
Tympany	1
Tiffick	11
Vomiting	3
Wind	3
Worms	15

The plague deaths (7,165 of them) are tucked away inside the 1, 2, 3, or 101 ways you might die otherwise in London. Riddling the horrors of the plague itself are the reminders that you, too, could die suddenly of griping in the guts, burning in your bed, falling from a belfry, the stopping of your stomach, tympany, rising of the lights (a sort of lung congestion), grief, fright, and teeth. The official city documents – and the *Review* – put all this death and destruction into an orderly list, with numbers carefully attached and authoritatively added up. But the end sum is a disorderly world, a city unsafe in any moment: "The terrible Appearance of Death in so many dismal Shapes, must needs be very surprizing to many" (*Review* 1, 8, 16).

Trained by his education and his experience, and inclined by his temperament, to look at many sides of things simultaneously, Defoe could never render a city in a sound bite; he could never simply celebrate nor simply deprecate a London that had so many sides at once. The "sublime economics" was undermined by its underworld; the "great Center of *England*, the City of *London*" and its "Prodigy of Building" is faced with congestion and poverty and its own "straggling, confus'd Manner," its "uncompact, and unequal" shape; its commercial energy is matched by a criminal energy; its worldly stoutness available to attack by disease, fire, nature. And Defoe's city is matched, complication for complication, by his own representations of it.

"I will *let you into the Secret*": the ambiguous language of the city

Coal Markets	*Billingsgate, Room Land.*
Bay Market	*Leaden Hall.*

Broad Cloath	*Blackwell Hall.*
Market	

N.B. The last Three are, without Doubt, the greatest in the World of those Kinds.

Bubble Market	*Exchange Alley.*

(Tour ii, 92)

Right below the three *real* London markets ("greatest in the World") Defoe inserts the satirical "Bubble Market" in Exchange Alley (off Cornhill, near the Royal Exchange; see Figure 2), where stock jobbers lurked "to draw Innocent Families into their snares" by "Raising and Spreading False News to Ground the Rise or Fall of Stocks upon," propagating "Treasonable Rumours to Terrify and Discourage the People with Apprehensions of the Enemies to the Government," and trying "to make a Run upon the *Bank*, and Ruin publick Credit," among other nefarious schemes.[18] The Bubble Market was real enough, economically speaking, but it was not the sort of market to hang out a sign. Defoe disingenuously slips its code name into his list of legitimate markets to give the whole a sudden, ambiguous twist. And that rhetorical move, in fact, makes a good emblem of all Defoe's representations of the city. There is a *language* as well as a *space* of London that must be learned, which simultaneously records its duplicity and points to its sanctuaries. The language is both linguistic (learn the spoken codes) and architectural (find the alternative spaces). Understanding and decoding the linguistic and spatial secrets of London grants mastery of Defoe's city.

Just as certain streets are known or can be learned for certain properties in trade, so the very discourses of the city require some decoding. Defoe's *Anatomy of Exchange-Alley* (1719) is one of his many economic conduct books, on how to behave among and beware of sharpers. As with virtually all of his didactic works, Defoe populates its abstract corners with the particulars of immediate reality:

> If [stock-jobbers] meet with a Cull, a young Dealer that has Money to lay out, they catch him at the Door, whisper to him, Sir, here is a great piece of news, it is not yet publick, it is worth a Thousand Guineas but to mention it: I am heartily glad I met you, but it must be as secret as the black side of your Soul, for they know nothing of it yet in the Coffee-House, if they should Stock would rise 10 *per Cent.* in a moment, and I warrant you *South-Sea* will be 130 in a Week's Time, after it is known. Well, says the weak Creature, prethee dear *Tom* what is it? Why really Sir I will *let you into the Secret,* upon your Honour to keep it till you hear it from other Hands; why 'tis this, *The Pretender is certainly taken* and is carried Prisoner to the Castle of *Millan,* there they have him fast; I assure you, the Government had an Express of it from my Lord *St – s* within this Hour.

Are you sure of it, says the Fish, who jumps eagerly into the Net? Sure of it! why if you will take your Coach and go up to the Secretaries Office, you may be satisfied of it your self, and be down again in Two Hours, and in the mean time I will be doing something, tho' it is but a little, till you return.   (*Exchange*-Alley, pp. 4–5)

"Why really Sir I will *let you into the Secret*" – the City is almost always something to be decoded; in this case, the secret is that the "*Secret*" is a trap. All the displays of transparency – "go and check with the secretary" – are simply extra layers of obliquity in obloquy. For Defoe's characters (and by implication his readers), things are seldom what they seem. It is Defoe's moral obligation to attempt transparency, while it is his literary talent to craft ambiguity.

"Shop rhetorick" is another language requiring proper translation, for both sides of the transaction. In an entertaining little scene in *The Complete English Tradesman*, Defoe substitutes what is really meant, when a shop-keeper and customer haggle, for what is actually said:

LADY.   I like that colour and that figure well enough, but I don't like the silk, there's no substance in it.
MERCER.   Indeed, Madam, your Ladiship [sic] *lies*, 'tis a very substantial silk.
LADY.   No, No, you *lie* indeed, Sir, 'tis good for nothing, 'twill do no service.
MER.   Pray, Madam, feel how heavy 'tis; you will find 'tis *a lie*; the very weight of it may satisfy you that *you lie*, indeed, Madam.
LADY.   Come, come, shew me a better piece; I am sure you have better.
MER.   Indeed, Madam, your Ladiship *lies*; I may shew you more pieces, but I cannot shew you a better; there is not a better piece of silk of that sort in *London*, Madam.
...

I might make this dialogue much longer, but here is enough to set the mercer and the Lady both in a flame, and to set the shop in an uproar, if it were but spoken out in plain language, as above; and yet what is all the shop-dialect less or more than this? The meaning is plain; 'tis nothing but *you lie*, and *you lie*; downright *Billingsgate*, wrap'd up in silk and sattin, and deliver'd dress'd finely up in better cloaths, than perhaps it might come dress'd in between a Carman and a Porter.   (*Tradesman* I, 307–8)

"You lie" replaces, perhaps, "you jest" – "the meaning is plain," though not quite plain enough until someone like Defoe says it out loud. The real language is a Billingsgate fishwife dressed up in lady's clothes – and perhaps this "lady" is not much more "real" in terms of her natural temperament than, say, Moll or Roxana are quite the ladies their dresses proclaim.

But some of the city's secrets are more benign. If you know where to look, even the dark treacherous city offers unexpectedly comfortable corners. Over and over again, Defoe is eager to uncover the small safe spaces of refuge. Young waifish, thievish, semi-honest Jack, for example, finds sanctuary in the midst of mercantility – in London's glass-making houses:

> Those who know the Position of the Glass-houses, and the Arches where they Neal the Bottles after they are made, know that those Places where the Ashes are Cast, and where the poor Boys lye, are Caveties in the Brick-work, perfectly close, except at the Entrance, and consequently warm as the Dressing-room of a *Bagnio*; that it is impossible they can feel any Cold there, were it in *Greenland*, or *Nova Zembla*, and that therefore the Boys lye not only safe, but very comfortably. (*Colonel Jack*, p. 16)

Jack's narrative lights up the dark corners of the city, domesticating them; throughout Defoe's urban novels London is riddled with the kinds of underground refuges that don't make it into the *Tour* and other didactic celebrations of the city. Here, unlike poor Jo in Dickens's *Bleak House*, even the riffraff of London can find – if they are "those who know" – some place not only safe, but really rather nice.

Less surprisingly, perhaps, finding unexpected refuges in the city is also open to the middle and upper classes. In *Due Preparations for the Plague*, for example, two merchant brothers carry their families into a new little world inside a ship on the Thames:

> The Vessel they were in, was a Ship of Force, carrying 16 Guns, but could carry 24; so that they liv'd at large and had room enough; the Merchant and his Family had the great Cabbin and Steerage to themselves, with some Cabbins built on purpose for his Maid-Servants and Children in the Gun-Room; an Appartment was built up out of the great Cabbin for his *Sister*, and her Nurse and Maid, and himself and his *Brother* had each of them a large Cabbin built in the Steerage, so the rest of the great Cabbin was their Dining Room: The *Captain* had the Round-House and the little Room before it, which they call the Cuddie, for his Family, and the Quarter-Deck was their Parade or walking Place; over which the *Captain* had caus'd an Auning to be built, and cover'd it so close, both Top and Sides, that it was like a great Hall.[19]

The details of the ship's cabins are as replete as those Crusoe gives of his "fortifications," the endlessly repeated descriptions of the increasing invisibility he creates for himself. Those smart people evading plague in the ship manage to create for themselves dining rooms, walking spaces with awnings, separate apartments, and a whole system of comfort food, with "fresh Butter, some Eggs and a great Quantity of Garden Stuff, such as the Season afforded, with Apples in abundance … [and] fresh Meat, as Veal and Pork" (*Due*

Preparations, p. 251). As Katherine Matson observes, "The people on the boats are agents who steer their own courses, without relying on the government or the aristocracy for help ... Defoe takes obvious delight in explaining how the ship has gone from commercial or military use to a home away from home ... This new ark is both spacious and snug."[20]

There is more "snugness," generally, in *Due Preparations*, than there is in the novelistic *Journal of the Plague Year*; as with other parallel treatments of urban spaces in Defoe's didactic and fictional works, the didactic tends to work towards resolution, reassurance, or celebration, while the fictional often tips into unsteadiness and uncertainty. This family escapes happily because they took due preparations. The parallel story in the *Journal* is that of the three men – "two Brothers and their Kinsman," a soldier, a sailmaker, and a "Joiner or Carpenter by Trade, a handy Fellow" (*Journal*, p. 57) – who also succeed in crafting a safe space in England's plague-ridden wilderness, taking due preparations and emerging unscathed, but their tale is embedded in the center of the novel, surrounded by hundreds of shorter, darker, or more ambiguous stories. (In *Due Preparations* the spotlight focuses on the characters at the end.) The didactic work suggests pragmatic possibilities; the novel investigates darker choices and endings – although it, too, ends resoundingly with "*an Hundred Thousand Souls / Away; yet I alive!*" (*Journal*, p. 238).

Yet H.F. is not, strictly speaking, alive at the end; not only is he fictional, he is pre-embedded in Bunhill Fields (*Journal*, p. 223). He is the perfect emblem of Defoe and the city: what is above ground is at the same time buried there. All of his Londons jostle with each other in his cross-pollinated genres: "Defoe and London" ought to be renamed "Defoe and His Londons," reflecting his habit of overlaying multiple viewpoints, of presenting a picture of London that is inherently unstable, but inherently interesting. There is no one "City"; Defoe writes many Londons.

NOTES

1. *A Tour thro' the whole Island of Great Britain*, p. 51, in *The Works of Daniel Defoe*, general eds. W. R. Owens and P. N. Furbank, *Writings on Travel, Discovery and History by Daniel Defoe*, ed. John McVeagh, vol. 1 (London: Pickering & Chatto, 2001). All further references in the text are to this edition.
2. Daniel Defoe, *The Fortunes and Misfortunes of the Famous Moll Flanders, &c.* (1722), ed. G. A. Starr (Oxford and New York: Oxford University Press, 1971), Introduction, p. xx.
3. Pat Rogers, "Literary Art in Defoe's *Tour*: The Rhetoric of Growth and Decay," *Eighteenth-Century Studies*, 6, no. 2 (Winter 1972), 153–85.
4. See J. Paul Hunter, *Before Novels: The Cultural Contexts of Eighteenth-Century English Fiction* (New York: W. W. Norton, 1990), p. 112; the numbers are based on the researches of the Cambridge population group.

5. Daniel Defoe, *A Journal of the Plague Year* (1722), ed. Cynthia Wall (London: Penguin, 2003), pp. 164, 98.

6. Ben Weinreb and Christopher Hibbert, *The London Encyclopaedia* (London: Macmillan, 1983), pp. 107–8.

7. Quoted in Paula R. Backscheider, *Daniel Defoe: His Life* (Baltimore: Johns Hopkins University Press, 1989), p. 527.

8. Maximilian E. Novak, *Daniel Defoe: Master of Fictions* (Oxford: Oxford University Press, 2001), p. 632.

9. Daniel Defoe, *Roxana, The Fortunate Mistress* (1724), ed. John Mullan (Oxford and New York: Oxford University Press, 1996), p. 5. All further references in parenthesis in the text are to this edition.

10. Daniel Defoe, *The Complete English Tradesman, in Familiar Letters*, 2 vols. (London, 1726–7), I, 98–99.

11. Daniel Defoe, *The Behavior of Servants in England Inquired into. With a proposal containing Such Heads or Constitutions as would effectually Answer this Great End, and bring Servants of every Class to a just Regulation* (London, 1725), p. 8.

12. Daniel Defoe, *A Plan of the English Commerce* (London, 1728), p. 99.

13. Quoted in Starr's notes to the Oxford edition of *Moll Flanders*, p. 388.

14. Daniel Defoe, *The History and Remarkable Life of the Truly Honourable Col. Jacque* (1722), ed. Samuel Holt Monk, intro. David Roberts (Oxford: Oxford University Press, 1989), pp. 19–20.

15. Daniel Defoe, *Every-Body's Business, is No-Body's Business; Or, Private Abuses, Publick Grievances* (London, 1725), p. 32.

16. Weinreb and Hibbert, *London Encyclopedia*, p. 960.

17. Daniel Defoe, *Review* (1704–1713), Tuesday, 26 August, 1712, I, 8, 15.

18. Daniel Defoe, *The Anatomy of Exchange-Alley: or, A System of Stock-Jobbing* (London, 1719), title page.

19. *Due Preparations for the Plague, As well for Soul as Body. Being some seasonable Thoughts upon the Visible Approach of the present dreadful Contagion in France; the properest Measures to prevent it, and the great Work of submitting to it* (London, 1722), pp. 249–50.

20. Katherine Matson, in a commentary for my graduate seminar ENEC 982, "Georgian Spaces" (Spring 2007), 25 April 2007.

10

MICHAEL SEIDEL

Robinson Crusoe: varieties of fictional experience

Island supplements

The story of the castaway merchant-adventurer, Robinson Crusoe, is among the most widely recognized in world literature, and even those who have never read the book seem to know something of what is in it. The island *isolato* belongs to the culture as an archetype – a man cast away on a deserted island – and all the speculation attached to that scene constitutes a kind of fictional parlor game. How would any man or woman react? What tools and materials would one want? What books would one wish to bring? What kind of company would prove most desirable, if company were to arrive at some time? How would one pass the hours, days, months? How would one dispose space? As Elizabeth Bishop remarked in her wonderful poem "Crusoe in England," Crusoe's "brain breeds islands." The island is a supplement to Crusoe's (or anyone's, for that matter) imagination. Bishop puts it this way:

> ... But my poor old island's still
> un-rediscovered, un-renamable.
> None of the books has ever got it right.[1]

I have titled this essay "Varieties of Fictional Experience,"[2] because in the three hundred years since Defoe published *The Life and Strange Surprizing Adventures of Robinson Crusoe* the most fertile reader of the Crusoe story is Robinson Crusoe himself. Whether he speculates on the meaning of what happens to him (as he does in a subsequent volume, *Serious Reflections* [1720]), or on things that might have taken place on his island but did not, Crusoe's imagination generates many more fictions than the one he experiences. Part of his imaginative life derives from the perfectly natural fears of exposure on his island – paranoia, after all, is a fiction-producing obsession. Crusoe worries about all sorts of things, the worst of them sudden annihilation: being devoured by wild beasts or cannibals, being swallowed up by enormous waves, or being buried alive by the debris from landslides. He seems afraid inside his cave (earthquakes) or outside it (animals): "The fear of being swallow'd up alive, made me that I never slept in quiet, and yet the Apprehensions of lying abroad without any Fence was almost equal to it" (p. 66).[3]

On his island, Crusoe does much more than build, organize, store, labor, and relax. He engenders fantasies that never materialize and conjures wild plans he never puts in practice. He also supposes, imagines, ponders, speculates, projects, and fictionalizes. Crusoe begins his imaginative life early in his stay when he spends days portraying to himself in great detail what his life would have been like on the island had he not removed so much material from the shipwreck offshore: "I spent whole Hours, I may say whole Days, in representing my self in the most lively Colours, how I must have acted, if I had got nothing out of the Ship" (p. 103). This is an extraordinary sentence because Defoe tells us that inside the fiction there are other unwritten fictions, fictions that might test circumstantial reality if circumstances were represented differently. To represent in "most lively Colours" is precisely what writers of fiction do, or should do. Not only does Crusoe begin his island stay by supplementing the facts of his own story with an array of other possible stories, but he ends his stay the same way. In his twenty-fourth year he pulls what he can from the second wreck of a European ship, a Spanish one, and spends his remaining time carefully living on the island filling his head "all this two Years … with Projects and Designs, how, if it were possible, I might get away from this Island" (p. 151).

The bizarre appearance of a single footprint on the beach in the fifteenth year of Crusoe's island stay is the strongest instance of Crusoe spinning off yarns beyond those ever actually accredited to the action. He offers himself and the reader a host of explanations – without ever resolving the matter – for who might have made the impression. His "dismal Imaginations" (p. 121) are more fearful than the actual footprint, and he spends a good deal of time conjuring a full body for the partitive print, even factoring in the possibility that the Devil made it. He finally assumes that the print is that of a cannibal, and for years after he projects in his mind the satisfaction of ambushing an unsuspecting party of man eaters: "I went so far with it in my Imagination, that I employ'd my self several Days to find out proper Places to put my self in Ambuscade" (p. 132). Crusoe then says of his scheme that he "in my Imagination put it in Practice" (p. 133) just as he also puts in practice what might have happened to him if, instead of the print, he had come upon live walking cannibals. The detail of Crusoe's projected scene is almost indistinguishable from the scenes that he describes as real, and he gets so carried away with his made-up narrative that he adds precisely the kind of detail he does when describing the actual events that happened to him.

> I look'd back with some Horror upon the Thoughts of what my Condition would have been, if I had chop'd upon them, and been discover'd before that, when naked and unarm'd, except with one Gun, and that loaden only with small Shot, I walk'd every where peeping, and peeping about the Island, to see what I could get: what a Surprise should I have been in, if when I discover'd the Print of a Man's Foot, I had instead of that, seen fifteen or twenty Savages, and found them pursuing me, and by the Swiftness of their Running, no Possibility of my escaping them. (p. 136)

It is only when a reader actually begins paying close attention to Crusoe's language that he or she realizes how much of what happens on the island exists in the supplemental or projected realm. Here is Crusoe, for example, trying to figure out what happened to the crew of a ship he sighted in distress off the coast of his island in his twenty-fourth year. He sees almost nothing and has to imagine almost everything, but spares little detail in conjuring up scenes. I have placed what amount to Crusoe's own fictions in bold face to illustrate just how riddled his prose can be with imagined recreations within the fiction that Defoe gives us.

> Had they seen the Island, **as I must necessarily suppose they did not**, they must, **as I thought** have endeavor'd to have sav'd themselves on Shore by the Help of their Boat; but their firing of Guns for Help, especially when they saw, **as I imagin'd**, my Fire, fill'd me with many Thoughts: First, **I imagin'd** that upon seeing my Light, they **might have** put themselves into their Boat, and **have endeavor'd** to make the Shore; but that the Sea going very high, **they might have** been cast away; other Times **I imagin'd**, that they **might have** lost their Boat before, **as might be the Case many Ways**; as particularly by the Breaking of the Sea upon their Ship, **which many Times** obliges men to stave, or take in Pieces their Boat; and **sometimes** to throw it over-board with their own Hands: **Other Times I imagin'd**, they had some other Ship, or Ships in Company, who upon the Signals of Distress they had made, had taken them up, and carry'd them off: **Other whiles I fancy'd**, they were all gone off to Sea in their Boat, and being hurry'd away by the Current that I had been formerly in , were carry'd out into the great Ocean, where there was nothing but Misery and Perishing; and that **perhaps they might by this Time** think of starving, and of being in a Condition to eat one another. (p. 146)

Defoe uses the term *imagined* here to chart a parallel narrative universe that exists in the mind at all times as potential. At other points in the narrative, he even imagines experiences beyond the time that he actually stays on the island, as when he comes upon an old goat dying in a hollow and projects his own end as if he "had laid me down and dy'd, like the old Goat in the Cave" (p. 141) or when he points out that the parrot he had trained to speak his name might well live to a hundred "still, calling after *Poor Robin Crusoe*" (p. 141). In a more sustained and complicated version of the same process, Crusoe at the end of the narrative tries to predict what the English mutineers suddenly arrived on his island will do and think, and guesses that they will leave before collecting their lost comrades. Crusoe congratulates himself on his insight, and, in the process, explains something about Defoe's conception of realistic narrative: "As soon as I perceiv'd them go towards the Shore, I imagin'd it to be as it really was" (p. 205). Here the imagined projection encounters the imagined actuality, and both modes exist comfortably for Defoe in terms of what human beings are likely do and how they are likely to think. To put perceptions together with imagination is to produce fiction.

The situation gets even more interesting. In order to get the mutineers back so that he might ambush them, Crusoe sets up a series of feigned shouts from their supposed comrades. That is, he creates a contrived action within the presumably real fiction to make something actual happen. But his stratagem is only the start of it. After Crusoe's entourage manages to kill, disarm, and capture the party of mutineers on shore, the ship's original captain explains to those mutineers begging for mercy that the governor of the island (Crusoe) "might hang them all there, if he pleased" (p. 208). The narration then concludes: "Though this was all a Fiction of his own, yet it had its desired Effect" (p. 208), the point being that the threat followed the laws of probability even if Crusoe had never proposed such a thing and had no intention of executing it. But to believe Crusoe capable of such a sentence the mutineers must also believe he has the force behind him to carry it off. The English captain therefore creates the fiction that Crusoe as governor commands a garrison of fifty troops, a number made up out of whole cloth. Moreover, Crusoe himself appears to the mutineers as an emissary of the fictional (or, better, strategic) governor, therefore a duplicate of himself "so that as we never suffered them to see me as Governour, so I now appear'd as another Person, and spoke of the Governour, the Garrison, the Castle, and the like" (p. 210). Indeed, Crusoe will not appear to the mutineers as actual governor of the island until the English sea captain brings him a complete and elegant change of clothes from the ship in the harbor so that instead of looking like a rag-tag castaway on a desert island he looks like a modern gentleman: "After some time, I came thither dress'd in my new Habit, and now I was call'd Governour again" (p. 213).

All of Crusoe's designs, schemes, and projections add up during the course of the island adventure and provide a kind of Prospero-like finale near the end when Crusoe as forest wizard directs the pageant that takes place when Europeans come ashore. And the question might occur to an average reader: why does Defoe go to all the trouble he does to intensify and supplement the fictional action on Crusoe's island? The answer has to do with the innovative nature of the form in which Defoe wrote, a form that he virtually invented himself in the early decades of the eighteenth century. The way that Defoe tells the Crusoe story becomes a kind of primer on the new art of realistic novel writing in the period.

Defoe was an enormously inventive writer, and he discovered many years before *Crusoe* that the adaptation of a "situational" voice was the best way to engage readers in a subject. Defoe's mind was such that imagining circumstances and contriving plots came to him almost naturally. The masks he wore through his life as a revolutionary, a business man, a correspondent, a ministerial spy, and an anonymous newsmonger elided the divide between experience and fiction. It was in his journalism in the first decade of the eighteenth century that Defoe cultivated the various seeds for his later novels. He would nurture any subject for its narrative qualities, and his work presented a sequence of imagined dialogues, from made-up conversations on the streets and coffee houses of London to reported testimonies of ghost sightings, to domestic squabbles within the families of England's middle class to discussions of projects and schemes to alter the very substance of social life and commerce. He invented probable settings for subjects of interest to him and invited his readers to engage in his fictions by the force of a believable and exciting story. The circumstances he most liked to imagine – storms, crimes, bankruptcies, rebellions, plagues, wrecks, supernatural visions – gave fictional form to catastrophes and personal dilemmas.

Defoe's contemporary, Colley Cibber, claimed that *Robinson Crusoe* was "written upon a model entirely new," but it is crucial to recognize that the *new* for Defoe was always an amalgam of narrative forms that already existed in the literary marketplace. When Defoe's journalistic career was temporarily stymied by finances and a change of political ministries, he and his publishers cultivated a very profitable notion for longer books: it was easier to invent "true" stories than to actually uncover them. *The Life and Strange Surprizing Adventures of Robinson Crusoe* refined Defoe's practice of fabricating material that could be conveyed in recognizable forms, in this case travel literature, captivity narrative, personal memoir, and religious confession. And the immense success of the *Crusoe* story made Defoe think of his project as something of a franchise. He tried to capitalize on the publication of the first volume, Crusoe as captive and castaway, with a second, Crusoe as world traveler, and third, Crusoe as moral and practical philosopher. The second and third volumes were not nearly as popular as the first, but each suggested that Defoe was adjusting Crusoe's fictional venue to the market for true-to-life experiences and personal commentaries.

The eighteenth-century reading audience in England had a hunger both for the circumstantial details of lives lived and for the remote and exotic, and Defoe was prepared in *Robinson Crusoe* to satisfy that hunger with tales of slave trading, harrowing sea escape, shipwreck, island exile, cannibal adventure, and (back in Europe) wolf attack. Crusoe's almost boiler-plate explanation of his life to the English sea captain on the island at the end of his island stay confirms what Defoe knew about his reading audience: "my Story is a whole Collection of Wonders" (p. 209). Defoe is very deliberate with his use of terms in describing his enterprise. In the preface to the second volume, *The Farther Adventures of Robinson Crusoe* (1719), he insists that his work is not a romance, by which he means a narrative remote from probability. Though he admits that his work contains a "Part that may be call'd Invention," he means only that a narrator fabricates material in such a way that its contents reflect the real experiences and decisions facing human beings in a world of recognizable prospects and necessities. In romance, one might perhaps fall ill of a fever; in Defoe's fiction the detailed course of the illness itself becomes the force field for narrative.

> *June 19.*   Very ill, and shivering, as if the Weather had been cold.
> *June 20.*   No rest all Night, violent Pains in my Head, and feverish.
> *June 21.*   Very ill, frighted almost to Death with the Apprehensions of my Sad Condition, to be sick, and no Help: pray'd to GOD for the first Time since the Storm off of *Hull*, but scarce knew what I said, or why; my Thoughts being all confused.
> *June 22*   A little better, but under dreadful Apprehensions of Sickness.
> *June 23.*   Very bad again, cold, shivering, and then a violent Head-ach.
> *June 24.*   Much better.
> *June 25.*   An Ague very violent; the Fit held me seven Hours, cold Fit and hot, with faint Sweats after it.
>
> (p. 69)

Defoe meticulously tracks the course of disease in the midst of imitating the kind of journal that travelers often employ to record experience. No romance writer in his or her right mind would spend so much time on the flu, but Defoe does so with relentless composure because Crusoe would think it appropriate for the day-to-day writing in which he was then engaged. Furthermore, if Crusoe decides that a mixture of rum and tobacco might work to ease his ague symptoms, sure enough, Defoe sees no difficulty in spending half a page explaining how Crusoe mixes the concoction.

> I first took a Piece of Leaf, and chew'd it in my Mouth, which indeed at first almost stupify'd my Brain, the Tobacco being green and strong, and that I had

not been much us'd to it: then I took some and steeped it an Hour or two in some Rum, and resolv'd to take a Dose of it when I lay down; and lastly, I burnt some upon a Pan of Coals, and held my Nose close over the Smoke of it as long as I could bear it, as well for the Heat as almost for Suffocation. (p. 75)

At the heart of Defoe's theory of fiction is the notion that the mind expands upon circumstance to engage reader interest only if the "wonders" described do not depart from the temporal and spatial laws of nature and are perceived as probable. Defoe never tired of advancing just such an argument for the power of narrative, and he finds himself particularly pressed to do so for *Crusoe* when shortly after its publication it was challenged as a tissue of lies. A dyspeptic critic, Charles Gildon, wrote a long critical exposé of the story in which he insisted that Defoe was simply allegorizing his own troubled life in England through the memoir of Crusoe, mariner of York. A year later, in *Serious Reflections*, Defoe responded to Gildon's charges of falsity by defending fiction in Crusoe's own fictional voice, and by adding a veneer of legal reality to the invented subject in the same way the Portuguese captain in the first volume made Crusoe attest to his survival in order to retrieve his money from Brazil: "he made me enter my Name in a Publick Register, with his Affidavit, affirming upon Oath that I was alive, and that I was the same Person who took up the Land for the Planting the said Plantation at first" (pp. 219–20). In his sequel, Defoe has Crusoe again affirm his identity, as if a phony testament will legitimize a made-up character.

> I *Robinson Crusoe* being at this Time in perfect and sound Mind and memory, Thanks be to God therefore; do hereby declare, their Objection is an Invention scandalous in Design, and false in Fact; and do affirm, that the Story, though Allegorical, is also Historical, and that it is the beautiful Representation of a Life of unexampled Misfortunes, and of a Variety not to be met with in the World, sincerely adapted to, and intended for the common Good of Mankind, and designed at first, *as it is now farther apply'd*, to the most serious Uses possible.　　　　　　　　　　　　　　　(Preface to *Serious Reflections*)

Rather than deny Gildon's premise, Defoe brilliantly absorbs it, and in the bargain offers one of the earliest and most profound defenses of the art of fiction. Defoe's answer to those who maligned his faction by maligning its authenticity was a simple one: fiction does its job best when its imagined situations (allegories) bear on potentially real ones (histories). To defend the bases upon which he constructs *Crusoe*, Defoe sets up a sequence of possible psychological reactions that a human being may have to experience in life – to, as he phrases it "one whole Scheme of a real Life of eight and twenty Years, spent in the most wandring desolate and afflicting Circumstances that ever Man went through" – and then argues that his story represents that process in "whatever borrow'd Lights they may be represented by."

If one looks closely at what Defoe says about Crusoe's twenty-eight years of desolation and affliction, the circumstances need not only refer to island life. (In that Crusoe's twenty-eight years virtually overlap the first twenty-eight years of Defoe's own life and the twenty-eight years of what he saw as the political oppression of the Restoration period in England, there are indeed other readings possible for the sequence.) The psychological pattern of isolation can, as Defoe says, present itself in a populous city as well as a remote island. He could not be more forceful about the processes involved in fiction writing than when he has Crusoe claim that his island experience is a "just History of a State of forc'd Confinement, which in my real History is represented by a confin'd Retreat in an Island: and 'tis as reasonable to represent one kind of Imprisonment by another, as it is to represent any Thing that really exists, by that which exists not." Defoe both repeats and trumps his critic, Charles Gildon, when he says that Crusoe's represented history takes place on an island, but as a fiction the story is applicable to circumstances that, as Defoe puts it, "had its original so near Home." This is the case precisely because the island narrative is a believable representation of a set of particular circumstances from which lessons, morals, exempla can be extracted by readers living in the very places they inhabit when they read the book.

To reinforce this point about the nature of fiction, Defoe has Crusoe live fictionally inside the story; that is, Crusoe reflects on the relation between what he experiences and what he imagines, dreams, or hallucinates. At one point, he comments on the power of the imagination to register experience both apprehensively and speculatively. What enters the mind stays there, whether an actual reality or not. In many of the scenes of *Robinson Crusoe*, Defoe hints at a theory of the imagination developed more fully a few generations later by Hazlitt and Wordsworth. Crusoe ponders on the nature of experiences that project powerfully upon the mind.

> There are some secret moving Springs in the Affections, which when they are set a going by some Object in view; or be it some Object, though not in view, yet rendered present to the Mind by the Power of Imagination, that Motion carries out the Soul by its Impetuosity to such violent eager embracings of the Object, that the Absence of it is insupportable. (p. 147)

Perhaps the best take on the power of imagination – aside from the footprint in the sand episode – comes when in the midst of his raging ague-induced fever Crusoe dreams of an Avenging Angel confronting him for the miserable life he has led, not miserable in his accomplishments but in his disconnections from humanity. Crusoe is in a way like Everyman or like K in Kafka's *The Trial*; he does not do any one thing that is demonstrably bad, but he does not live a thoughtful life. The Angel says to him, "Seeing all these Things have not brought thee to Repentance, now thou shalt die" (p. 70). Crusoe knows before he writes up this evocative dream in his journal that it is the product of his fevered imagination, but he still claims the impression made upon him does not go away no matter how fictional it is:

> No one, that shall ever read this Account, will expect that I should be able to describe the Horrors of my Soul at this terrible Vision, I mean, that even while it was a Dream, I even dreamed of those Horrors: nor is it any more possible to describe the Impression that remain'd upon my Mind when I awak'd and found it was but a Dream. (p. 70)

Defoe again offers an implicit defense of fiction here, especially fiction that *seems* true. If the impression is great enough, the truth is measured more by its power than its verification.

Island replicates

The lure of the narrative establishes itself early when the young Crusoe, not particularly fit for any profession or trade in England yearns to travel by sea, whereas his father, beset by age and gout (clearly a stay-at-home condition) insists he establish himself locally. The impetus to adventure – Crusoe's "wandring Inclination" (p. 5) – serves for the reader as much as for the character. It opens vistas in this particular fiction, as it will in so many others over time, and it allows for a character trait to presage plot. Defoe not only makes the adventure of Crusoe speak to a range of impulses and states of mind and being, but he literally tells the story over and over again in various forms and sequences. Crusoe in Brazil turns a profit on his sugar and tobacco plantation, but worries that he has few friends and lives in relative isolation "just like a Man cast away upon some desolate Island, that had no body there but himself" (p. 30). Soon enough Defoe sets his hero in motion again until he actually becomes a man cast away upon some desolate island. The narrative predates itself here just as it does again in one of Crusoe's dreams before the Carib, Friday, arrives on the island: "I dream'd, that as I was going out in the Morning as usual from my Castle, I saw upon the Shore, two *Canoes*, and eleven Savages coming to Land, and that they brought with them another Savage, who they were going to kill in Order to eat him" (p. 155). In both these instances – one a metaphoric projection that comes true and the other a dream that comes true – Crusoe replicates his story before he experiences it.

In so many ways, replication is the name of Defoe's fictional game. As an almost obsessively driven individual, Crusoe performs on his island spaces what many captives in remote places imagine during the lonely years of isolation: the elaborate, detailed, and time-consuming projection of a dream home and compound down to the most precise details. And what he transforms he feels obligated to protect. In his later years he makes sure all he has built remains natural to the eye as a measure of protection against potential invaders (presumably, cannibals). So we get all the ingredients of a magical place, with enumerated passages, tunnels, hidden gates, secret points of entry and egress.

The worlds Crusoe builds on his island extend to the fabricated nature of the language he uses to describe his places. It is crucial that Crusoe names things that pertain to his condition in such a way that he builds a replicate universe in isolation. So instead of saying to himself (and, presumably, to his readers, in that by the time we apprehend his experience he has already written it up) that he climbs out of the tree he slept in, he says "When I came down from my Apartment" (p. 40). Or, instead of merely deliberating about what to do next, he says that "then I called a Council, that is to say, in my Thoughts" (p. 44). Such phrasing is very important to Crusoe. It gives him a civilized veneer in so natural a place. He is very conscious about how his language determines him, often referring to things in verbal doublets that key the actual and mental status of his environment. So when he digs out the rock behind his tent to place his powder for shot he says, "I plac'd it in my new Cave, which in my Fancy I call'd my Kitchin" (p. 50), just as he soon calls additions to his cave his "Dining-room" (p. 60) and his "Cellar" (p. 60). When he plans to collect citrus fruits from the lush side of the island he spends three days away from "Home, so I must now call my Tent and my Cave" (80). When he is frightened by the footprint he runs home to "my Castle, for so I think I call'd it ever after this" (p. 121). When he shows his perfectly camouflaged habitation to the English sea captain at adventure's end he calls it "my Castle, and my Residence" (p. 201).

All of this verbal doubling is not idle. As Crusoe's places become more familiar they become, of needs, less remote and less threatening. The verbal doubling extends to Crusoe's psychological condition, first represented as a two-columned account of miseries and hopes he reproduces as a balance sheet (pp. 53–54), and then in paired phrasings that continue throughout the narrative. Crusoe's replicate sentences are a stylistic reinforcement of the actions Defoe's narrative constructs for him. He refers to the island experience as "my Reign, or my Captivity, which you please" (p. 108). More to the point, he drifts into longer sentences that reflect in their structure the reflective quality of his experience: "I learn'd to look more upon the bright Side of my Condition, and less upon the dark Side; and to consider what I enjoy'd, rather than what I wanted" (p. 102). In his very words and in their cadences Crusoe replicates his island status: "I take Notice of here, to put those discontented

People in Mind of it, who cannot enjoy comfortably what God has given them; because they see, and covet something that he has not given them: All our Discontents about what we want, appear'd to me, to spring from the Want of Thankfulness for what we have" (pp. 102–3). He continues, "In a word, as my Life was a Life of Sorrow, one way, so it was a Life of Mercy, another" (104). The balancing of clauses reproduces the state of Crusoe's mind as a castaway and social being. When he sights the distressed ship in stormy seas in his twenty-fourth year he despairs over the imagined fate of the crew: "In all the Time of my solitary Life, I never felt so earnest, so strong a Desire after the Society of my Fellow-Creatures, or so deep a Regret at the want of it" (p. 147).

The doublets extend to the naming of the island itself, which he cannot help but think of as his point of ultimate exile and, at the same time, his new home. He begins by first calling the place his "Island of Despair" (p. 56), but the same place soon enough becomes "my beloved Island" (p. 110). The island almost serves as the locus for all one's failures and one's comforts, a very metaphor for life itself. The stylistic doublets also reflect the duality of Crusoe's inner life, his insecurity and his adventurism. We see the doublets again at the end when he shifts from fearing cannibals who might eat him to anticipating cannibals who might save him: "But the longer it seem'd to be delay'd, the more eager I was for it; in a Word, I was not at first so careful to shun the sight of these Savages, and avoid being seen by them, as I was now eager to be upon them" (p. 156).

Doubling up in the narrative extends not only to Crusoe's phrasings during the course of island life, but also to the very narrative forms in which Defoe presents his material. One of the more blatant narrative replicates is the journal buried within the memoir in which Defoe itemizes material he later has Crusoe narrate at his retrospective leisure. The first year of island life therefore appears in two literary forms, and Defoe melds those forms together inside the text, having the memoirist comment on the journalist in the midst of reproducing the journal's text. Had Crusoe possessed enough ink to continue his day-to-day journal composed in island time, we can assume there would be less need for the account that Crusoe composed later in a more reflective (and, for the reader's sake, fictionally disposed) time. But Defoe did not wish to give up the physical look on the page of a journal written to the moment because its appearance in his text would lend credence to Crusoe's story. Diary entries and journals were the means by which actual travelers and adventurers recorded their experiences: "I began to keep my Journal, of which I shall here give you the Copy (tho' in it will be told all these Particulars over again)" (p. 56). Fortunately, Crusoe's ink supply ran out and he never could find the ingredients to restore it: "A little after this my Ink began to fail me, and so I contented my self to use it more sparingly, and to write down only the most remarkable Events of my Life, without continuing a daily *Memorandum* of other Things" (p. 83).

Crusoe has his own doubts about the literary quality of the actual journal, which he tells the reader "would ha' been full of many dull things" (p. 56); indeed, many more dull, repetitious, and inconsequential things than are already there if the diary had lasted for more than one year. Crusoe is so sure the diary itself is insufficiently interesting as fiction that even while presenting it he interrupts as a narrator, adding notes and other longer elaborating passages. The memoir writer takes precedence over the diarist because a diary cannot look back on present activity from the prospect of the future, exactly as Crusoe does when he interrupts his diary with extended commentary. Only a memoir, for example, could have the following sentence, a sentence that would be impossible as a daily diary entry because the course of time would not allow it: "While this Corn was growing, I made a little Discovery which was of use to me afterwards" (p. 84).

The inclusion of replicate forms and even replicate documents in the body of *Robinson Crusoe* does not stop with the journal. For the calculating reader, Crusoe produces in his double-entry account sheet a list of the deficits and benefits of island life. The list appears as a double column on the page under the categories "EVIL" and "GOOD," which allows the reader to proceed in any number of ways, each producing an accurate but differently disposed island fiction. To read the first column from top to bottom is to accrue despair in a kind of manic depressive state: "I am cast upon a horrible desolate Island, void of all Hope of Recovery" ... "I have no Soul to speak to, or relieve me" (pp. 53–54). To read the second column top to bottom is to be almost buoyant: "But I am alive and not drown'd" ... "I have gotten out so many necessary things [from the wreck] as will either supply my Wants, or enable me to supply my self even as long as I live" (pp. 53–54). These are, indeed, the extreme scenarios for Crusoe, but the artifact of the double columns printed on the page also encourages a third reading, a horizontal reading where one adjusts from evil to good, from deficits to benefits, a procedure that Crusoe sustains in the many years of his island experience: "there was scarce any Condition in the World so miserable, but there was something *Negative* or something *Positive* to be thankful for in it" (p. 54). If one measures Crusoe throughout the narrative, he is most sure of himself when making contingent adjustments and least sure when he sinks too deeply into what might be termed a column of despair or rises too effusively on a column of hope.

Defoe is not done yet. There are other replicating documents in the narrative that serve as addenda beyond journals and double-entry accounts. There are charts, lists, contracts, memoranda, affidavits. Even bits of the island experience seem accountable as writing replicates, such as the immovable canoe hacked out of a log, which Crusoe calls a "*Memorandum* to teach me to be wiser next Time" (p. 107). He also calls his own memory of events an "Abridgement" or "the whole History of My Life in Miniature" (p. 153). And he finds himself practising for the account he will later write when he provides the English seamen who arrive on the island with "the whole History of the Place, and of my coming to it" (p. 215). Moreover, there are scenes within the fiction whose design seems to replicate the whole of the narrative or, at least, pose questions that reflect on the whole. We learn in the sixth year of the adventure that Crusoe has kept a parrot with him in what he calls his seaward or original bower compound. After a harrowing attempt to circulate the island by a small canoe he fabricated, he lands in an inlet and walks a good distance back to his "Country House," or bower, considerably removed from his compound. Exhausted, he falls asleep only to be awakened by a voice: "*Robin, Robin, Robin Crusoe*, poor *Robin Crusoe*, where are you *Robin Crusoe*? Where are you? Where have you been" (p. 112). He is startled, but soon enough recognizes that the voice belongs to his parrot, which has flown to the bower from the seaward compound miles away.

Once Crusoe recovers from the shock, he realizes the voice he hears is a version of his own, "for just in such bemoaning Language I had used to talk to him, and teach him" (p. 112). We hear in the parrot's mimicry something that had been sounded before on the island but whose precise articulation we, as readers, had never heard before in the narrative; that is, the actual bemoaning voice of Crusoe from an earlier time on the island. We know the parrot – with Crusoe's voice imprinted – has made the same journey from the seaward to the coastal side of the island. We know that the bird is a time capsule of sorts, a replica of an earlier Crusoe. We know that Crusoe referred to himself by his familiar name and that he asked himself a double question. Where is he? And where has he been? These very questions, of course, constitute the frame of the narrative for both reader and Crusoe in a much more crafted and complicated way when the story finally achieves written form. Of course, these questions could well be addressed to Crusoe at any time in the narrative – they are the generic questions for the traveler, the exile, the castaway, the convert – and that is precisely Defoe's point in creating this sequence as a replica of the adventure's thematic and structural design.

The parrot sequence introduces other crucial matters for the narrative. What is the nature of intrusion on the island and what the nature of companionship? And what is the nature of homecoming? Crusoe says of the parrot at the end of the scene, "and so I carry'd him Home along with me" (p. 113). He does the same when he domesticates Friday, almost as a member of his island family. And his very understanding of "home" is what the castaway adventure experience addresses in its totality, as when Crusoe begins to refer to his island as his new home, his settled place. In one instance, when Crusoe returns from a long mini-journey around the island, Defoe repeats the narrative pattern of the whole in the language he uses to describe the part.

> I cannot express what a Satisfaction it was to me, to come into my old Hutch, and lye down in my Hammock-Bed: This little wandring Journey, without settled Place of Abode, had been so unpleasant to me, that my own House, as I call'd it to my self, was a perfect Settlement to me, compar'd to that; and it rendered every Thing about me so comfortable, that I resolv'd I would never go a great Way from it again, while it should be my Lot to stay on the Island.   (p. 88)

As content as Crusoe seems here, he cannot resist giving in to his wandering inclination again, partly because Defoe thinks of fiction in terms of impulses that characters cannot repress. All his life Defoe was fascinated with such urges, and his famous literary characters answer to one or another version of this very principle. Crusoe is risk-driven; Moll Flanders seeks emotional warmth; Roxana responds to a fierce sense of domestic independence. No doctrine or code of conduct can subvert these impulses in these characters. There are two almost contradictory impulses at work in Crusoe – his need for the new and different and his sense of deep insecurity at a remove from the familiar. He recognizes the pull of his nature, which dominates all safer choices, as "a secret overruling Decree that hurries us on to be the Instruments of our own Destruction" (14). So Crusoe sets out again in his sixth year on the island by constructing a small boat to tour the coast. Predictably, he gets carried out on currents and his ensuing panic serves to reverse the conditions of castaway and home comer: "Now I look'd back upon my desolate solitary Island, as the most pleasant Place in the World, and all the Happiness my Heart could wish for, was to be but there again" (p. 110).

Island allegories

In his defense of his novel against the charges of the critic Charles Gildon, Defoe claimed that the Crusoe story was both allegorical and historical. The most obvious allegorical properties of the island experience make Crusoe a kind of Everyman in space and time. What happens on the island is not that Crusoe abjures the comforts of middle-class life initially promised him by his father for the insecurity of an adventurer, but that by a kind of centripetal force Defoe pulls all normative human experience into Crusoe's sphere. At various times in the narrative Crusoe calls himself a seafarer, a merchant, a slave, a prisoner, a commander, a master, a planter, a governor, a king, a lord, an emperor, a *Generalissimo* (he even uses the inflated and ironic Spanish term), a trapper, a herdsman, a breeder, an estate owner, a gentleman, a household manager, a carpenter, a tailor, a canoe-builder, a cook, a basket-weaver, and a pipe-maker. Crusoe accumulates stock; he possesses estates; he labors endlessly for the production of goods he then consumes or utilizes, becoming a dedicated, if indifferent, master of all trades.

Upon his wider survey of the island, Crusoe finds himself struck by the status his domain gives him: "it was a secret Kind of Pleasure, (tho' mixt with my other afflicting Thoughts) to think that this was all my own, that I was King and Lord of all this Country, indefeasibly, and had a Right of Possession; and if I could convey it, I might have it in Inheritance, as compleatly as any Lord of a Mannor in *England*" (80). Precisely because Crusoe is alone he is sovereign, standing with his livestock where he was "my Majesty the Prince and Lord of the whole Island; I had the Lives of all my Subjects at my absolute Command. I could hang, draw, give Liberty, and take it away, and no Rebels among all my Subjects" (p. 116).

Why does it matter that Crusoe absorbs class strata in his person and takes on sovereignty as subject? One possibility is that Defoe was doing exactly what he said he was doing when he reflected on the fictional opportunities implicit in the narrative – he was developing an allegorical history in which Crusoe becomes a kind of conglomerate "man." The island scene then offers Defoe a chance to recreate and speed up the story of the race without the encumbrances of sexual reproduction. Crusoe even literally pulls the ages of mankind out of the wrecked ship when he first begins his island stay, taking on his various raft trips material consisting of gold, silver, iron, and lead. That Defoe was thinking of Crusoe as a kind of time capsule is clear enough from the way he refers to his habitat. His second night's lodging is a kind of hut made from the chests and boards he has carried to land from the wrecked ship. Next, he fabricates a tent from sails, and soon enough he is talking about his "Settlement" (p. 48), his "Habitation" (p. 53), his "Storehouse" (p. 55), his "Camp" (p. 66), his "Home" (p. 79), his "Country-House" and "Sea-coast House" (p. 81), and his "Fortress" (p. 49).

The idea of the island experience as speeding the development of the species and cataloguing the occupations of humankind makes *Robinson Crusoe* a kind of modern encyclopedia, a role that novelistic narrative generally grows to take over from the older epic forms of narrative. The idea of the encyclopedia was a relatively new phenomenon in the eighteenth century and the most famous would be the later mid-century multi-volume work of Denis Diderot and others in France, the goal of which was to include in its articles the history of arts and sciences in human civilization. Crusoe does not write an encyclopedia on his island, but he performs one, commenting at one point that with or without the proper tools "by stating and squaring every thing by Reason, and by making the most rational Judgment of things, every Man may be in time Master of every mechanic Art" (p. 55). Many pages of the island account are mini-articles on a myriad of subjects, practices, crafts, from agriculture to herding, from design to construction, from the weather to the tides, from cannibalism to theology. Defoe is always making analogies to island life that place Crusoe, one way or another, back in the larger world from which he departed. When he ponders how to grind his tools it "cost me as much Thought as a Statesmen would have bestow'd upon a grand Point of Politicks, or a Judge upon the Life and Death of a Man" (p. 66). The result is that Crusoe's world in exile seems just at the point of absorbing all the processes of a culture that his castaway status abjures.

At the most secure moment in the narrative, fifteen years into his adventure, Crusoe surveys his island estate in a way that reflects its relative vastness and variety. His property becomes domain, and it takes him two pages to describe his "two Plantations" (p. 119) and his plots for planting, his enclosures for goats, his storage points and camouflaged safe havens. It is, ironically, at this very point that Defoe unmakes the man and his estate. One day at noon on the shore where Crusoe moored his small boat, he comes upon a single footprint on the beach. The print is, in effect, a new consignee for the territory Crusoe has just so laboriously inventoried for the benefit of the reader. A man cast on a desert island without human company is now distraught that someone else sets foot upon his land and at once rivals and threatens his sovereignty, a sovereignty that by Defoe's very careful elaboration of roles had made Crusoe an entity unto himself. Naturally, Crusoe considers the possibility that the particular someone else is a cannibal, in which case he has something more than his metaphorical status to worry about. He loses his composure and comes apart "like a man perfectly confus'd and out of my self," and "terrify'd to the last Degree" (p. 121). Indeed, Crusoe runs "Home to my Fortification, not feeling, as they say, the Ground I went on" (p. 121); that is, he moves so fast that his feet make no impression on the ground in contrast to the print that so frightens him.

No more is Crusoe the image of reconstituted "man" and the master of all crafts. He has just enough wherewithal to recognize that his fear of the print is ironic, that he who is "banished from human Society" as a castaway "should now tremble at the very Apprehensions of seeing a Man, and was ready to sink into the Ground at but the Shadow or silent Appearance of a Man's having set his Foot in the Island" (p. 123). But irony is no salve to apprehension. Crusoe's next few years are difficult; he spends his time carefully, cutting down the free range of his movements, checking the rate of gunfire to virtually nil, turning the inventive cast of his mind away from practical improvements or experiments towards schemes for slaughtering as many cannibals as he could should he ever encounter them. He also subtly erases the visible signs of his island construction and reproduces its naturalness. Even much earlier in his stay for reasons of security he needed to mask all his craft and craftiness: "if any People were to come on Shore there, they would not perceive any Thing like a Habitation" (pp. 61–62). Camouflage is an instinct that serves Crusoe's sense of vulnerability, a part of Crusoe attendant upon his risk mentality. Crusoe may take chances, but he does not feel particularly heroic about them. Indeed, the chances he takes seem to petrify him.

Toward the end of the island adventure, the notion of Crusoe as the conglomerate man gives way to a series of renegotiated status roles. The rescued Carib, Friday, dramatically announces himself as subservient by placing Crusoe's foot on his bowed head. It takes Crusoe about a page and a half of prose before he appropriates the as yet unnamed Friday possessively as "my Savage" (p. 159). He makes the distinction because Friday is running from two other savages who plan to eat him, and Crusoe at least has the decency to help Friday before he enslaves him. Of course, Crusoe never does consult with Friday about the abrogation of rights involved in servitude or slavery. It is enough for Crusoe that the pronoun "my" does that for him. Crusoe even offers readers a model for the colonial subjugation when he displays Friday in such awe of the killing power of a musket that "if I would have let him, he would have worshipp'd me and my Gun" (p. 165). After Friday shows Crusoe the proper signs of obeisance, Crusoe teaches him two words, the first being his new name, "Friday" (for the day Crusoe saved him), and the second, "Master" (p. 161) for the relation that seems to have come down upon him fully formed. This puts Friday from the very first at a some-what lower rank than Crusoe's parrot, which got to call its master by his first name.

At the end of his adventures on the island, Crusoe becomes more a master of ceremonies than a sovereign entity or emblem. He is at once manifest and hidden, and his island virtually allegorizes itself out of existence, as when the English sea captain marvels at what he can barely see:

> but above all, the Captain admir'd my Fortification, and how perfectly I had conceal'd my Retreat with a Grove of Trees, which having been now planted near twenty Years, and the Trees growing much faster than in *England*, was become a little Wood, and so thick, that it was unpassable in any Part of it, but at that one Side, where I had reserv'd my little winding Passage into it   (p. 201)

Here, at the very end of a long stay on a deserted island, Crusoe's spaces and his experiences answer to the needs of culture and nature, and to all the variety of fictions the mind produces to survive, to fill time, and to endure.

NOTES

1. Elizabeth Bishop, *Poems, Prose, and Letters*, ed. Robert Giroux and Lloyd Schwartz (New York: The Library of America, 2008), p. 151.
2. The turn, of course, is on William James's *Varieties of Religious Experience*, a title that even unchanged might also work perfectly well for a different sort of essay on *Robinson Crusoe*.
3. I have used the Norton Critical edition, *Robinson Crusoe*, ed. Michael Shinagel (W.W. Norton: New York and London, 1975) because it employs (with some emendations) the first-edition text. Page references cited in the body of my text are to this edition.

11

JOHN McVEAGH

Defoe: satirist and moralist

It could be argued that more or less everything Defoe wrote involved some moral evaluation of human behavior and that this evaluation was generally ironic. But this does not mean that his writing is all of a piece. At first the opposite seems true, as different works written in different contexts produce a few contradictions in his examination of character and conduct. But a recognisable moral outlook still emerges, in which Defoe's stern ethical code jostles with a generally sympathetic interest in human beings under pressure. To discuss the subject we must interpret "satirical" in a broad sense which includes much of Defoe's later journalism, novels, and etiquette manuals as well as the verse satires proper which preceded them.

Defoe names as "Satyrs" seven early poems: *A New Discovery of an Old Intreague* (1691), *The True-Born Englishman* (1701), *The Mock Mourners* (1702), *Reformation of Manners* (1702), *More Reformation* (1703), *The Dyet of Poland* (1705), and *Jure Divino* (1706). Their dates remind us that verse satire occupied him intensively for several years after he began writing, but in 1708 he drew a line under serious poetic composition by declining to compose a poetic tribute to Prince George of Denmark, who had died recently. In his periodical *The Review* Defoe explained to an imaginary questioner that his "Rhiming Days" were "almost done" and that he no longer thought himself "quallify'd for such a Subject."[1] Instead he had already begun concentrating on less aggressive satire in prose. Thus, whereas in his early verse Defoe projects himself as a moral champion or modern Juvenal rebuking powerful public men, and naming names, he later tackles broader targets in a more ambivalent way – the High Church clergy or the Jacobite party rather than individuals, and abstract topics, such as political ambition, crime, war, and social and family life. In some books in his last decade he strikes a cantankerous note under the pen name of "Andrew Moreton." His novels and instructional manuals from his latter years also show a more complex moral view of human behavior.

In early verse satire Defoe employs the Juvenalian convention of indignant rage to bear down his victims in a torrent of invective. A similar anger inspires some early prose, such as the *Poor Man's Plea* (1698), which stingingly rebukes magistrates who punish vice in the poor but overlook it in themselves. Defoe in this angry mood can suggest a radical quality. W. P. Trent saw in his bold delivery of *Legion's Address* to Harley, the speaker of the Commons, "something of the uncalculating love of liberty that marks the true tribune of the people."² But verse, not prose, is the commoner satiric vehicle. It would seem from a judgement on himself in the *Pacificator* (1700) that Defoe was willing to be known for his aggression. He recommends writers to stick to what they do best and claims the lampoon as his mode:

> To their own Province let him all confine,
> Doctors to Heal, to Preaching the Divine;
> D[ryde]n to Tragedy, let C[reec]h Translate,
> D[urfe]y make Ballads, Psalms and Hymns for T[at]e:
> Let P[rio]r Flatter Kings in Panegyrick,
> R[atclif]f Burlesque, and W[ycherle]y be Lyrick:
> Let C[ongrev]e write the Comick, F[o]e Lampoon,
> W[esle]y the Banter, M[ilbourn]e the Buffoon.³

The lampoon, a popular Restoration form, simplified and exaggerated human failings and specialized in vituperative personal attack (The *Oxford English Dictionary* defines a lampoon as "a virulent or scurrilous satire upon an individual"). It projected men and women as (in Harold Love's words) "material bodies engaged in a Hobbesian pursuit of material objects of desire" – whether those objects were other bodies or "such tangibles as money, land, white staffs, letters patent, and coronets."⁴ Love relates lampoon to a public life dominated by Stuart political absolutism and Hobbesian materialism and traces to the same cause the mode's eventual decline as Dryden championed irony over vituperation.⁵ Thus when Defoe in 1700 claimed the lampoon as his field he was linking himself with a style already yielding to the opposite ideal of sophisticated mockery. This may help to explain his demise as a satirical poet after 1706 – which is not to deny that other pressures also came into play. While for him the move from aggressive verse to milder prose was the discovery of his true métier, and he saw it as a specific result of the abolition of censorship in 1695,⁶ it exemplifies a general shift which Michael McKeon has termed a "growing transgeneric consensus" in literary style in the period.⁷

Defoe's early verse satire bears out McKeon's suggestion that a simpler name for the lampoon might be "personal abuse."⁸ Before he began, in the *Pacificator*, to urge moderation (which later became a principal theme in his moral and satiric writing),⁹ and rapprochement with those on the opposing political side from his own, he expressed strong hostility towards public figures with deficient morals and shows them little mercy. *A New Discovery of an Old Intreague* (1691) heaps insulting reproach on city dignitaries both for being hypocrites and for being jurymen at the trials of the Whig martyrs Cornish and Russell. Good manners do not hold Defoe back in these lines. He calls the woollen draper Sir William Dobson, or Dodson, ineradicably stupid:

> In Whigg-Plot days have you not seen the *Beau*,
> With Martial Bagpipe to the Main Guard go;
> With many a Blunderbuss, and Musquetoon,
> Compleatly arm'd, with Cane, and Pantaloon:
> Equipp'd with his Hereditary Pride,
> And his Inheritance of Brains beside:
> Nature has wisely blazon'd on his Face,
> The Escutcheon of his Family, an Ass. (507–14; p. 52)

In the same poem he jokes tastelessly about Sir Ralph Box's name, the Master of the Grocer's Company, terming him "a very Ralph, a very piece of Wood" (that is a blockhead) as well as a stupid fool:

> Some hid accomplishments he may contain,
> That do for Speculation still remain;
> Or to be known, when th'art, to understand
> Without the drudgery of speaking's gain'd,
> At present, if we judge by what is known,
> As to the species of a Fool, he's one. (528–33; pp. 52–53)

Defoe mocks the physical infirmity as well as the name of the linen draper Sir William Withers, who "hobbl'd" with his "*wither'd* Face and Foot" to "abhor" the Petitioners, before hobbling back again after the wind had changed to "recant" his act of abhorring. He seems to gloat over Sir William's possible death from gout:

> Besides some change attends him that he knows,
> Inform'd by his prognosticating Toes. (551–2; p. 53)

Sir Thomas Vernon attracts cruel ridicule for both his politics and his physical ailments together. He is condemned for his "Fiery Zeal" in furthering James II's attack on London, when, as Defoe imagines it, "Frigidated by Distemper'd *Hams*," he had pushed his "Gouty Corps" along to vote for the surrender of the charters (lines 602–5; p. 54). Scoffing at an old sick man is not subtle. But Defoe lowered the tone even further on the Tory woollen draper Sir Robert Bedingfield, well known in the city for his coarse manners:

> Now if you'd hear some Loyal City Farce,
> Hear *Bed — d*, hee'l bid you kiss his Ar —

Nor Sherriffs, nor Mayor, nor Common Halls excus'd,
But his Posteriors are alike expos'd:
Nay, if *Bow* Bells for Whiggish Joys are rung,
The jangling Mettal must salute his Bung;
The Parliament he hopes will hear him now,
If not, his common Compliment they know.   (553–60; p. 53)

Such rough blows in rough rhyme show Defoe's commitment as an early satirist to the mode of personally injurious polemic. This style he rejected in later years, when he became a remarkably decent controversialist, but here he adopts scurrility as part of the convention. The lampoon legitimated coarseness. It was named from the French *lampons*, first person plural of the verb to drink ("let's get pissed"), signifying that the restraint of civilized discourse was being laid aside.

Defoe's move towards moral and linguistic restraint is marked. Although *Reformation of Manners* (1702) still attacks individual persons, most of them Tories, he now replaces mere insult with a more complex, considered moral reproof. Take the lines on Sir Salathiel Lovell, Recorder of London. Defoe accuses Lovell of atrocious lapses in morality and taste, such as selling justice, running protection rackets and jeering at criminals on their way to execution. But he is silent about infirmity and flexible enough to acknowledge Lovell's abilities, including his power over an audience:

Sometimes he turns his Tongue to soft Harangues,
To banter Common Halls, and flatter Kings:
And all but with an odd indifferent Grace,
With Jingle on his Tongue, and Coxcomb in his Face;
Definitive in Law, without Appeal,
But always serves the Hand who pays him well:
He Trades in Justice, and the Souls of Men,
And prostitutes them equally to Gain:
He has his Publick Book of Rates to show,
Where every Rogue the Price of Life may know;
And this one Maxim always goes before,
He never hangs the Rich, nor saves the Poor.   (125–36; pp. 160–61)

The notorious financier Sir Charles Duncombe also receives unexpectedly restrained treatment despite (or because of) his mauling in the earlier *True-Born Englishman* (1701), and when Defoe widens his field in Part II of the present poem from city to country, with clerics, poets, and pamphleteers among the targets, his handling is even milder than in Part I. This change of style, he acknowledged in the Preface, was deliberate. He now disavows attacks on *"private Infirmity, or … Personal Vices"* but criticizes those who, "*pretending to suppress Vice, or being vested with Authority for that purpose, yet make themselves the Shame of their Country, encouraging Wickedness by that very Authority they have to suppress it*" (p. 155). There is typical ambivalence in Defoe's position. In the *Pacificator* he had kept one foot in the "Sense" camp and one in the "Wit" camp. Here he criticizes wit but also aims at wit, and while encouraging reform puts the reformers on his list of targets.

Traces of lampooning aggression remain in Defoe's energetic attack on chauvinistic Englishmen in his most famous satire, the *True-Born Englishman*. Though his target is a nation, not a single person, it is the nation seen as an individual – he seeks to capture the English national character. Equally prominent is the moral ambivalence already noted, for instance in the poem's intermixture of contempt with reverence. Satire is intrinsically hostile, but here a fervent patriotism overlays the negative theme, producing a double-tiered or marbled effect typical of Defoe though not easily matched in other writers. Thus in reply to John Tutchin's xenophobic *The Foreigners* (1700) Defoe ridicules, or lampoons, the English as foreigners of the worst kind, namely the spawn of robbers and refugees. The nation is dunghill-bred.

> We have been *Europe*'s Sink, *the Jakes* where she
> Voids all her Offal Out-cast Progeny.   (249–50; p. 92)

To substantiate this charge (and give the poem its structure) Defoe describes how waves of looters land-grabbed England from the native inhabitants and founded the ruling families who now cheekily despise immigrants. The English, he says, are

> A horrid Crowd of Rambling Thieves and Drones,
> Who ransack'd Kingdoms, and dispeopl'd Towns.
> The *Pict* and Painted *Britain* [*Briton*], Treach'rous *Scot*,
> By Hunger, Theft, and Rapine, hither brought.
> *Norwegian* Pirates, Buccaneering *Danes*,
> Whose Red-hair'd Offspring ev'ry where remains.
> Who join'd with *Norman-French*, compound the Breed
> From whence your *True-Born Englishmen* proceed.   (237–44; p. 91)

Once his lever is in place, Defoe can almost let this satire write itself. He only needs to run through history and Tutchin is demolished. But there is the question of development. How will he take the poem forward?[10] One answer would have been to close it after the history lesson. But for Defoe the debunking and affirming impulses were strangely interwoven and under the latter he now moves away from invective into panegyric by addressing William III, Tutchin's target, as a saviour, and celebrating England's destiny.

The Mock-Mourners (1702), a tribute to the recently deceased king, is similarly mixed. Defoe calls it "a Satyr, by Way of Elegy." He damns and eulogizes in equal measure, even assuming a different personality for each purpose. As "Satyr," he reviles the hypocritical mourners with sarcastic relish. As "Britannia" he praises the dead king in words lacking irony.

Perhaps Defoe felt a little less keen on compromise when he came to write the *Dyet of Poland* (1705) – the title means "the Parliament of England" – because of the strong indignation roused in him by the "Tack" of 1704. (By this piece of parliamentary trickery the Tory administration had tried to compel the Lords to pass a law against Dissenters by "tacking" it to a money bill which constitutionally the upper house could not block.) Defoe draws a complicated analogy between Poland, recently forced by Charles XII of Sweden to dump their old king and accept a new one, and England, risking the Williamite settlement by faction fighting while France got ready to pounce. Defoe remained a lifelong defender of the Williamite or Revolution settlement, which had guaranteed religious toleration for Protestant Dissenters, subjected royal power to parliamentary power, and fixed the succession in the Protestant line. But the imaginative charge of this poem comes from the old rage of the lampoon as it lays into the Tory leaders Nottingham and Rochester, Seymour and Rooke, Mackworth, Pakington, and others. Lord Nottingham, for example, who had been secretary of state when Defoe was pilloried, gets buffeted through sixty or seventy lines as "Finski," a secret Jacobite, a malign and tedious politician and an empty man.

> Envy and awkward Spleen sit on his Face,
> In Speech precise, but always thinks apace;
> In *Earnest Nonsense* does his Hours divide,
> Always to *little* Purpose, *much* employ'd.   (301–4; p. 353)

Rochester ("Lawrensky") with his "*Janus* Face" (375; p. 355) foments civil war under his talk of unity. Sir Edward Seymour ("Seymski") wants nobody else to "Cheat us but himself" (433–34, 408; pp. 356–57). The Tory Admiral Rooke ("Rokosky") is "never Beaten" because he would "*seldom Fight*" (514–15; p. 359). Such flailing abuse makes the poem seem backward-looking even for Defoe. It holds out none of the compromise which he made room for in other polemical writings such as the *Pacificator*, where he had asked the gods at the close to "Mediate Peace" between the warring factions (332; p. 73). Of interest for Defoe's development as a writer is the *Dyet*'s sister-work, *The Consolidator* (1705), which preceded it into print by four months. This also deals with the Tack, but in prose, not in verse, and by means of fantasy not political allegory; and if Defoe's verse lampoons look backwards this narrative of a trip to the moon by way of China looks forward, perhaps anticipating *Gulliver's Travels*. As satire the *Consolidator* may not quite succeed but its bizarre inventions convey Defoe's restlessly allegorising imagination at work on stubborn material. Some sections of it seemed telling enough to his first readers to attract pirate publishers.[11]

By the early eighteenth century Defoe was clearly ready to turn from verse to prose, having already shown in *The Shortest Way with the Dissenters* (1702) how effective a prose satirist he could be. For a while he maintained his poetic ambitions in *More Reformation* (1703), *A Hymn to the Pillory* (1703), and *Elegy on the Author of the True-Born Englishman* (1704) – all of them meditations on his shattered career which re-defined his relationship with the literary and political world. Thus *More Reformation* ironically advises writers against irony, for which the world will punish them, saying that "*he that writes any thing that may be misunderstood*, Ought to expect to be misunderstood."[12] Genuine rather than assumed rage fuels the satiric-Pindaric *Hymn to the Pillory*, and something more like desperation the *Elegy on the Author of the True-Born Englishman*, where Defoe warns wrongdoers that although he is now legally dead (being bound over not to write) his ghost will rise against them if they merit reproof. He dared much in promptly ignoring the legal ban.

Defoe's transference from poetry to prose during these years, with a hint as to why it happened, is strikingly illustrated in *Jure Divino* (1706), in particular in his reliance upon the many exegetical footnotes added to the lines of poetry. A critic has called some of these annotations "sharper and more eloquent than his verse."[13] But though interesting, they obscure the effect of the lines they serve, like camp followers slowing down an army's advance. Defoe might have conveyed his message in verse alone, or simply implied it in the portraits of tyrants, but instead he hammers it into the reader's head by means of the superadded notes to avoid any possibility of mistake. Sometimes these notes refer not to the subject of tyranny but to Defoe's meaning in a particular word or line, betraying a lack of poetic confidence. Thus in Book x he writes that Egbert, the first English monarch, was made sacred "By his *Almighty Sword*" (x, 20; p. 294), then adds in a note that the word "Almighty" refers to "the Power he had to subdue all this Nation, too mighty for all join'd together: And 'tis hop'd the Reader cannot think it prophanely intended" (Note (a), p. 294).

This explanation is surely too cautious. Or take Defoe's denunciation of writers who have praised the divine right theory in the past. He exclaims of them, "*Perish those Poets* and be *Damn'd* the Song" (II, 349; p. 112) – intelligible enough for any reader, one might think, but evidently not for Defoe. In a footnote he asks us to be sure not to misunderstand the word "Damn'd." It is used, he explains, in the Language of the Poets, who use it when any of their Works are generally dislik'd, or condemn'd and censur'd; and not in the vulgar Acceptation of the Word; and therefore 'tis ascrib'd to the Song, not to the Poets, and I should have inserted none of this Note, but for the captious Distemper of the Age, which is apt to condemn a Work for a Word; and that Word, not because it merits the Censure, but because they do not understand it. (Note (b), p. 112)

One can see why Defoe wanted not to be misread. In 1703 a misreading of *The Shortest Way* had landed him in jail. But spelling out every nuance in each line weakens the effect.

In *Jure Divino*'s twelve books Defoe seeks to disprove the "divine right" theory of kingship which the 1688 Revolution had overturned, but not destroyed, and does so in two ways. He first demonstrates from history that as no unbroken line of kings could be proved to extend from Adam to modern times, no living king could claim divine right. Secondly he argues philosophically, and in Lockean terms, that true authority derives from a contract between ruler and ruled, implying mutual obligation, and not from the subjection of one to the other. These disruptive and constructive aims pulling in opposite directions perhaps explain the poem's split between satire and celebration – the ambivalence noted earlier. Defoe mingles a fierce attack on divine right with a passionate defence of the Williamite settlement. He summarizes kingly crimes with impressive scorn,[14] but surrenders to reverential panegyric when he turns from them to King William and Queen Anne. P. N. Furbank argues that there may be some classical precedent for this mixing of modes.[15] But it is not so much a development from one mode to another as a juxtaposition. Both satire and panegyric run through the work. In Book I a passage against tyrants is followed by a lengthy eulogy of William III (I, 469–96; pp. 99–100). In Book XII Defoe scoffs at some modern aristocrats before flattering others and Queen Anne (XII, 400–14 and 519–652; pp. 356 and 360–63). If a hatred of bad kings was one originating impulse, another was Defoe's reverence for good ones, and of the two modes, satire and panegyric, to which these emotions give rise, panegyric would have ended up the dominant one if Defoe's original intentions had been followed. We know this from the statement he lets fall near the end of the poem that he had planned a second volume of eulogy on William III and Queen Anne. This second volume, as he puts it, would

> By Foils present, and make a new Essay;
> And try our Vice, by Vertue to display:
> Learn by the soft and milky Way to soar,
> A Path that SATYR never trod before;
> By just Antithesis illustrate Crime,

And see how strangely Vice and Vertue Chime:
Let gentler Scenes guild thy aspiring Verse,
And *Britain*'s Pride, in *Britain*'s Queen rehearse;
Let the Reverse of Tyranny be known,
And *ANN*'s inlighten'd Character be shown;
Her Panegyrick stabs a Tyrant's Praise,
As Hell's long Night's described by Heav'n's long Days.

(XII, 472–83; p. 358)

It seems that Defoe's publishers advised against this sequel and it never got written. But his sketch of the concept offers an insight into his make-up. He had planned a verse diptych of satire against bad rulers on the one side and "soft and milky" praise of good rulers on the other. This in turn suggests that he had too much reverence to be a cynic – despite the apparent evidence to the contrary in the poem's Hobbesian opening lines:

Nature has left *this Tincture in the Blood*,
That all Men *would be Tyrants* if they cou'd:
If they forbear their Neighbors to devour,
'Tis not for want of *Will*, but want of *Power*;
The General Plague infects the very Race,
Pride in his Heart, and *Tyrant* in his Face;
The Characters are legible and plain,
And perfectly describe *the Monster, Man*.

(Introduction, 1–8; p. 71)[16]

Certainly Defoe begins with the categorical principle that tyranny is universal. "All Men *would be Tyrants* if they cou'd," he writes, adding: "We'd all be Emperors, *'tis in our Blood*" (10). Yet when he gets to William III he drops this theory. William had the chance to be a tyrant, so why did he not become one? Defoe remains silent. Elsewhere he affirms that William was no tyrant because he was a redeemer, and that was that.

You could not *with all your brutish Skill* provoke him to be a Tyrant – He abhorr'd Oppression, and scorn'd to practise it – and he that had Fire enough to assault all your Oppressors, and a Hand strong enough to wrestle with an establish'd and confirm'd Tyrant – had yet Meekness enough to *let you* oppress him, because he would not *oppress you*.   (*Review*, 5 November 1709)

It seems that William at least had no tincture in his blood. The law was not a law.

Defoe's publication problems with *Jure Divino* included delays, quarrels with subscribers, and press piracy, and it may be that these experiences, along with his sense that he had to annotate the poem to make it understood, led to his decision about this time to abandon verse satire. Another reason may have been that Defoe was finding less of the old material available to him as the Revolution settlement became more firmly established and the Jacobite threat (after 1715) ceased to be of serious concern. He abandoned poetry just as Alexander Pope was beginning to make his mark, and perhaps for the same reason. Whereas Pope found in "the arrogance of a Whig hegemony" that was consolidating in his lifetime a satiric seam of endless provocation,[17] the opposite was the case for Defoe, who broadly supported that same development. His major targets were being removed.

For the last twenty years of his life Defoe's moral and satirical writings appear particularly ambiguous and teasing, partly because of their range of subject and varied contexts but also because of his increasing use of impersonation. He had been drawn to this device from the first, exploiting it in poetry in Duncombe's speech in the *True-Born Englishman* (which may owe something to Oldham's *Satires Upon the Jesuits*), and, in prose, in *The Shortest Way with the Dissenters*. In both these works his method had been to let his enemies condemn themselves out of their own mouths. This was a dangerous tactic. But despite the danger his response to opposition and abuse was to keep on stirring the wasps' nest by multiplying the satiric impersonations further. In the *Review* he is protean, adopting the High Church language of a Tory bigot, advising France how to beat Britain, probably composing many a letter to himself in the "Scandal Club" section as vain coquette or spurned lover, trader or madman or drunk. One of Defoe's favourite impersonations was that of the plain man offering plain truth unadorned by rhetoric, as when he warns his *Review* readers that "If a dark Way of ambiguous doubtful speaking, will open the Poor People's Eyes, *I am not your Man*, Gentlemen, you must turn another Way – When this Paper ceases to speak *plain English*, and *apply it Home* to the very Persons, you may conclude this Author has laid it down."[18] But of course ambiguous doubtful speaking was another of his methods. When the Commons debated copyright he composed a booksellers' petition begging Parliament to let them continue robbing authors as they always had done, not being able to write books themselves.[19] He wrote against the Hanoverian succession in *And What if the Pretender Should Come?* (1713) and *An Answer to a Question that No Body Thinks of* (1713). He praised the admirable traits of James Butler, the Jacobite Duke of Ormond, in his *Account of the Great and Generous Actions* [1715], listing his extravagance and pomp and his natural talent for wasting the queen's money and incurring debts. Discussing schism in *The Layman's Vindication of the Church of England* (1716), he pulled the rug from under the Nonjurors' feet by taking on the character of a Church of England man and explaining that all Anglicans knew the Dissenters were the Church's true friends. A favorite impersonation was of Quaker speech, which Defoe used several times when tackling antagonists who lacked any significant connection with the Society of Friends.[20] His interest in Quaker language resurfaces in the character of William in *Captain Singleton* (1720). When Defoe had a real Quaker antagonist to deal with he was straightforward and dispensed with irony.[21]

In ironic publications like these Defoe replaces his old lampooning aggression with a cultivated indeterminate ambiguity, as if taking pleasure in emptying the text of his own presence and leaving the reader to guess what connection, if any, the author has with the words on the page. It is tempting to see in his many pamphlets by imaginary people, though written with an eye on a specific political situation, anticipations of the fiction of his last decade. In the first place these pamphlets exhibit a spirit of satiric mischief analogous to that of the novels. Secondly they testify to Defoe's curiosity about how another person might argue or feel and what would make them tick – almost in itself a definition of what novels do. But there are differences. The novels are distinguished from the preceding pamphlets and poems by their more pervasively ironic and ambiguous morality, which is to say they are richer texts. For instance, none of Defoe's pamphlets (despite mistakes made by readers at the time) is hard to interpret. We do not doubt that the writer of *And What if the Pretender Should Come?* supports the Hanoverian succession and is trying to help make it happen. But disagreements do exist about what a text like *Robinson Crusoe* or *Roxana* "really" means, or whether the moral judgments offered in Defoe's fiction can be laid at the writer's door. For one reader *Robinson Crusoe* may seem to undercut religion because the protagonist's worldly obsession contradicts his pious claims. This is the opinion of many commentators, including Karl Marx or Ian Watt. For another reader Defoe's concern with moral rebirth outweighs the odd flash of irony.[22]

The celebrated crux of Crusoe and the money he finds on the ship brings this issue to a point. As Crusoe at the time needs only useful equipment he rejects the money with a moralistic harangue, only to add, "however, on second thoughts, I took it away." Whether in this incident Defoe intended to reflect satirically on human conduct or merely intended to describe conduct is something we can never settle. But it is Defoean to play with a moral attitude by lodging a satirical implication about it, like this, in the reader's mind and then not resolve the issue either way. His fiction seems designed to keep the reader guessing about the proper estimate of behavior by allowing both negative and positive interpretations to be made. Indeed in part of his mind Defoe must have felt when he invented those long narrative fictions we have come to think of as the earliest novels in English that he had discovered the ironist's heaven – the kind of text in which no reader could finally pin the author down.

Few readers would disagree that in Defoe's writing generally the spirit of a cynic and of a moralist, a pessimist and an optimist, are at play. But are the novels really satires? Gilbert Highet offers a distinction between genuine satire, which offers an "aftertaste of derisive bitterness" based on a moral judgment, and non-satirical narrative, which does not. He writes:

> Hatred which is not simply shocked revulsion but is based on a moral judge-ment, together with a degree of amusement which may range anywhere between a sour grin at the incongruity of the human condition and a delighted roar of laughter at the exposure of an absurd fraud – such are, in varying proportions, the effects of satire. When they are absent from a piece of fiction, it is not satirical.[23]

If we apply such a distinction to Defoe's fictional narratives, where does it leave them? Sometimes they seem to come into the satire category and some-times not. They still elude categorization. Perhaps his accessibility to other ways of looking and feeling, while it made for ambivalence, also led Defoe to break through from allegory into modern prose fiction. (Compare the single-minded Bunyan.) Another view might stress his quick-changing imagination, raising him above the rigors of a creed.[24]

In some late sociological writings Defoe resurrects the aggression, though not the personal invective, of his early lampooning verse. The tone varies: vituperative in *The Anatomy of Exchange-Alley* (1719), comic in *Every-Body's Business Is No-Body's Business* (1725), genial in the *Political History of the Devil* (1726), flippant in *A System of Magick* (1726). Both *Augusta Triumphans* (1728) and *Second Thoughts Are Best* (1728) sustain Defoe's "captious old-gentleman persona"[25] convincingly enough to per-suade some readers to read them as the genuine outpourings of a grumpy old man. And perhaps they are this. But more likely Defoe impersonates geriatric ill-humor for rhetorical purposes. The old optimism still runs through the *Compleat English Gentleman* (written 1728–29?), with its fer-vent celebration of material and moral improvement.

Defoe as moralist is often categorical on specific issues. But to sum him up in the round appears less easy. He tends to undercut any given idealistic position with a sardonic admission that the opposite is also true. Furthermore, few writers have so carefully covered their tracks with anonymous and pseudonymous publications. He was a Protestant Dissenter who saw life as a pilgrimage to better things under a providential creator, and this optimism influenced his writings on economics and politics and shaped the novels into fables of spiritual growth. But a negative strain partly drawn from Defoe's own obsession with sin and partly from his unpuritanical delight in the witty cynics of the Restoration – particularly Rochester, Butler, Marvell, and

Dryden – tempted him in a different mood to dismiss morality as a sham. He can appear to be a devout Christian and a cynic even in the same text. Thus, early in his *Complete English Tradesman* (1725–27) Defoe insists that no tradesman must mix up honest and dishonest action:

> the rectitude of his soul must be the same, and he must not only intend or mean honestly and justly, but he must do so; he must act honestly and justly, and that in all his dealings; he must neither cheat or defraud, over-reach or circumvent his neighbour, or indeed any body he deals with; nor must he design to do so, or lay any plots or snares to that purpose in his dealing, as is frequent in the general conduct of too many, who yet call themselves *honest* tradesmen, and would take it very ill to have any one tax their integrity.[26]

Later, though, he candidly admits that a tradesman facing ruin might find the moral injunction too hard to follow:

> It is true, strictly speaking, he ought to sink, he ought to perish, rather than do it: When he has his Neighbour's Bread in his keeping, he ought to starve, and see Wife and Children starve and perish, rather than touch it; but where is the Man?, or, who is the Man that can resist the absolute Necessity? (II, Part I, p. 193)

This pessimistic perception is frequent in Defoe, and not just regarding matters of commerce. Any hungry man will steal his neighbor's loaf and eat it rather than die, and eat his neighbor with it, and, Defoe adds, "crave a Blessing to the Food too" (II, Part I, p. 194). In *Jure Divino*, we have seen, he defines human relationships as aggressive stand-offs, in which destruction is averted only because "my Neighbor's *just as proud as I*" and "his *Abortive Envy* ruins mine" (Introduction, 16, 18; p. 71).

In *The Family Instructor* and *The Complete English Tradesman* Defoe's idealism and cynicism battle it out on the page, sometimes one spirit dominating, sometimes the other. In *The Family Instructor* (1715–18) the cynical view takes over as Defoe recommends that daily prayers be established to protect family life but then describes the "upheaval and disruption" the new regime causes. We cannot doubt his stated moral aim, nor that his text highlights the violent consequences of setting up family worship, including "catastrophic illness, madness, or even a temptation to murder."[27] Ten years later, when he wrote *The New Family Instructor* (1727), his fictional family was less torn between tyranny and irreligion and "in an altogether more hopeful state."[28] *The Complete English Tradesman* also moves towards moral optimism. In this work Defoe begins sternly, threatening destruction if the tradesman spends, borrows, marries, or indulges in pleasure, but the family dialogues in the later part are more humane. Here he shows how the tradesmen's wives tend to save their families after the husbands' mistakes have all but ruined them. As if to underline the redemptive qualities that women possess, Defoe closes the dialogue between husband and wife in Letter XI with the comment: "His wife very well argues the injustice and unkindness of such usage, and how hard it was to a wife, who being of necessity to suffer in the fall, ought certainly to have the most early notice of it; that if possible she might prevent it."[29] (In the brewer episode in *Roxana* Defoe in a gloomier mood reworks this subject from the woman's viewpoint.) Although Defoe cynically stipulates that interest will pull apart all human relationships and mourns subordination broken down, apprentices lacking care and morality in decline in his late lifetime, the optimist in him counters with a defense of luxury as also capable of bettering human life by supplying social and moral needs. As he puts it, "the people grow rich by the people" and "one hand washes the other hand, and both hands wash the Face" (II, Part II, p. 118). In the novels too, again and again, Defoe's Hobbesian cynicism is counter-balanced by the idea of redemption, not always convincingly.[30] As a moralist Defoe reserved a special value for gratitude, and dislike of ingratitude, which in his most celebrated and influential satire, *The True-Born Englishman*, he nominated as the English vice (lines 159–64). He repeated the same judgment elsewhere, personal experience giving it a bitter sound: "if you carry an *English* Man twenty Mile upon your Back, and set him down HARD, he'll curse you to your Face."[31] For all Defoe's reserves of scorn the primacy he gives to gratitude may be the moral centre of his baffling personality. It would explain the mixture of anger and reverence in his writing.

Satire is inherently ambiguous. It claims to be reformative but is actually aggressive and often unfair. Defoe declared somewhat narrowly in *More Reformation* that he wrote solely to convert the guilty, saying that "Satyr ceases when the Men Repent" (Preface, p. 212). This implies that, for him, generalized satire on the human condition, such as Juvenal's Satire X on ambition, or Horace on country living, held little appeal. But the purely aesthetic motive cannot be cast out. Defoe's tailor in the *Review*, asked to explain his reasons for mocking people with his satirical coat, replies, "What do you tell me of Designs, my Design was to make the *Coat*."[32] Swift offered two motives for the writer of satire: the "private Satisfaction and Pleasure of the Writer; but without any View towards personal Malice" and "a public Spirit prompting Men of genius and Virtue to mend the world as far as they are able."[33] We might add a third in the thrill of the chase. Defoe as an early verse satirist might claim the second and third of these motives, but possibly not the first. In his later writing he could claim all three. Impersonation became his chief weapon, though after the bitter experience of *The Shortest Way with the Dissenters* he must have known that using it would have the opposite of a calming effect. Wayne Booth considered that work a problem because Defoe captured in it the mind-set of a High Church bigot with "masterful impersonation" but "too much consistency of tone and sincerity of purpose."[34] Perhaps we might think the political climate of 1702–3, not the writer's ineptitude, was the real cause of his mauling by the government.[35] Defoe himself called *The Shortest Way* a "plain-dealing Piece"[36] and thought its extreme tone gave the reader adequate warning of his satirical intent. As Ronald Paulson puts it: "The most effective satire (given its generic aims) would be the one that passed as something else."[37]

NOTES

1. *Review*, 16 December 1708, *Defoe's Review*, ed. John McVeagh, 9 vols. (London: Pickering & Chatto, 2003 – ongoing) vol. v, part 2 (2007), p. 527. All subsequent references are to this edition.

2. W. P. Trent, "Defoe – the Newspaper and the Novel," in *The Cambridge History of English Literature*, ed. A. W. Ward and A. R. Walter, 15 vols. (Cambridge: Cambridge University Press, 1907–27), vol. ix, p. 8. Defoe defends his satiric style in the *Review*, 7 April 1709 (Edinburgh edition); see *Defoe's Review*, vol. vi, part 1 (2008), p. 29. Juvenal references appear in the *Review* of 26 August 1704, 25 March 1707, 17 June 1708; *Defoe's Review*, vol. i, part 1 (2003), p. 322; vol. iv, part 1 (2006), p. 96, vol. v, part 1 (2007), p. 175 and frequently elsewhere in Defoe's writing.

3. *The Pacificator*, lines 415–22, in *The Works of Daniel Defoe*, general eds. W. R. Owens and P. N. Furbank, *Satire, Fantasy and Writings on the Supernatural*, vol. 1; *The True-Born Englishman and other Poems*, ed. W. R. Owens (London: Pickering & Chatto, 2003), pp. 75–76. Subsequent line and page references incorporated in the text are to this edition.

4. Harold Love, *English Clandestine Satire 1660–1702* (Oxford: Oxford University Press, 2004), p. 27.

5. See John Dryden, *A Discourse Concerning the Original and Progress of Satire* (1693). Love calls the lampoon both a product of the older culture and "one of the means by which it was reformed" (*English Clandestine Satire*, p. 147).

6. Defoe in 1711 warned against a newspaper tax that "What is wanting in Pamphlet, will be made up in Lampoon" (*Review*, vol. vii, "Preface"). He developed the same point on 29 March 1711 (vol. viii).

7. Michael McKeon, "Recent Studies in the Restoration and Eighteenth Century," *Studies in English Literature*, 45, 3 (Summer, 2005), 738.

8. McKeon, "Recent Studies," p. 737.

9. In the poem Defoe praises Cowley, Milton and Rochester, poets of the past, as "*Giants* ... of Wit and Sense together" (line 131; *True-Born Englishman and other Poems*, p. 68), implying that rapprochement is achievable again.

10. David Macaree finds Defoe in the *True-Born Englishman* "too busy marshalling the facts to consider the effect of their presentation"; *Daniel Defoe's Political Writings and Literary Devices* (Lewiston, NY: E. Mellen Press, 1991), p. 41.

11. See Rodney M. Baine, "Daniel Defoe's Imaginary Voyages to the Moon," *PMLA*, 81 (1966), 377–80.

12. *True-Born Englishman and other Poems*, p. 209.

13. *Jure Divino*, ed. P. N. Furbank, in *Satire, Fantasy and Writings on the Supernatural By Daniel Defoe*, vol. II, p. 4.

14. See Defoe's survey of the bad kings of history in Book VIII of *Jure Divino*, pp. 240–71.

15. See *Jure Divino*, p. 3.

16. Similar statements will be found in Books IV and V, and had appeared in Defoe's *History of the Kentish Petition* (1701). See *Jure Divino*, p. 368, note 51.

17. Stephen N. Zwicker, "Satiric Inheritance," *Studies in English Literature*, 44, 3 (Summer, 2004), 658.

18. *Review*, 18 July 1710, in *Defoe's Review*, vol. VII.

19. *Review*, 21 February 1710, in *Defoe's Review*, vol. III, part 1 (2005), pp. 88–92.

20. For Defoe's Quaker impersonations see *A Friendly Epistle by way of Reproof* (1715), *A Trumpet Blown in the North* (1715), *A Sharp Rebuke from one of the People called Quakers* (1715), *A Seasonable Expostulation with ... James Butler* (1715), and *A Friendly Rebuke to one Parson Benjamin* (1719).

21. *Review*, 5 February 1706, in *Defoe's Review*, vol. III, part 1 (2005), pp. 88–92.

22. For a discussion of critical responses to *Robinson Crusoe* see Pat Rogers, *Robinson Crusoe* (London: Allen and Unwin, 1979), pp. 51–53.

23. Gilbert Highet, *The Anatomy of Satire* (Princeton, NJ: Princeton University Press, 1962), p. 150.

24. John Richetti pinpoints Defoe's "elusive intelligence which somehow kept functioning brilliantly through disaster" in *Defoe's Narratives: Situations and Structures* (Oxford: Clarendon Press, 1975), p. 4.

25. P. N. Furbank and W. R. Owens, *A Critical Bibliography of Daniel Defoe* (London: Pickering & Chatto, 1998), p. 235.

26. Defoe, *The Complete English Tradesman*, 2 vols. (1725–27), vol. I, Letter XVII, pp. 274–75. Subsequent references to this work are incorporated into the text.

27. *The Family Instructor*, ed. P. N. Furbank, in *Religious and Didactic Writings of Daniel Defoe*, 8 vols. (London: Pickering & Chatto, 2006), vol. I, p. 21.

28. See *The New Family Instructor*, ed. W. R. Owens, in *Religious and Didactic Writings of Daniel Defoe*, vol. III, p. 1.

29. *Complete English Tradesman*, vol. I, p. 175.

30. Peter Earle likens the redemption theme in Defoe's novels to the note of "a very cracked bell" in *The World of Defoe* (Newton Abbot: Readers' Union, 1977), p. 228.

31. *Review*, 12 March 1709, in *Defoe's Review*, vol. V, part 2 (2007), p. 699.

32. *Review*, 29 April 1710, in *Defoe's Review*, vol. VII.

33. Quoted in Macaree, *Defoe's Political Writings*, p. 56. The passage is taken from Swift's *The Intelligencer*, no. 3 (1728); see *Prose Works of Jonathan Swift*, ed. Herbert Davies, 16 vols. (Oxford: Blackwell, 1939–74), XII, p. 34.

34. Quoted in E. Anthony James, *Daniel Defoe's Many Voices* (Amsterdam: Rodopi, 1971), p. 101.

35. See James, *Many Voices*, p. 111.

36. *Review*, 5 January 1710, in *Defoe's Review*, vol. VI, part 2 (2008), p. 562.

37. Ronald Paulson, *The Fictions of Satire* (Baltimore, MD.: Johns Hopkins University Press, 1967), p. 152.

12

J. PAUL HUNTER

Defoe and poetic tradition

To modern eyes, Daniel Defoe does not look much like a poet. He seems temperamentally wrong for the role: practical and matter-of-fact in his outlook, prosaic in his language, always concerned with getting and spending, very seldom meditative or even deeply thoughtful about his own feelings. His writing is almost always rambling and loose rather than concise, analytical and argumentative rather than sensitive or reflective; he piles up facts, details, and rationales rather than depending on nuance, allusion, or subjective association. When he does write poetry (and there is a period in his life when he wrote verse voluminously), he demonstrates an ability to reason articulately and rhyme readily but seldom creates smooth, satisfying harmonic lines or verse paragraphs with pleasures for the ear or eye: his lines vary between utter metric predictability and a rough and rugged uncertainty of rhythm that seems to result from impatience or haste.

And so almost no one except his biographers bothers to read his poetry today – in spite of the fact that he was arguably the most-read poet in England for some years in his middle age, wrote more than a dozen long poems totaling some 20,000 lines, and for much of his lifetime was far better known as a poet than a novelist. Even though he is now one of the three or four most written-about writers of the eighteenth century (and quite possibly the most-often read), there is very little critical analysis of, or even commentary on, his poetry.[1] And the poems themselves are hard to find; until the late twentieth century, almost all of them had been out of print for more than 250 years, and even now most are available in print only in scarce and expensive editions that even many research libraries do not own.[2] Yet for much of his early writing career Defoe seems to have thought of himself *mainly* as a poet and to have imagined that any literary posterity he might have would depend on his poetry.

OK, it happens. History, as years pass, seldom sees people as they saw themselves or even as their contemporaries saw them, and a "historical perspective" develops. Times, values, emphases, and directions change. Changing standards – both because of fads and fickleness and because times and cultures do genuinely hold different assumptions, values, and interests that lead to different tastes – explain why a lot of writers and works have either substantially lost or dramatically gained acclaim after the writers' deaths. But in the case of Defoe's poems, historical considerations apply especially strongly because of changed ideas of what poetry is supposed to be and do. Defoe was by no means the most talented poet of his time, but he was prolific, timely, widely read, and in many ways representative of his time in what he wrote and how he wrote it: his poems are very helpful in understanding how and why poetry was written and read in the early eighteenth century. Readers then, like poets, were different from you and me, and it is historically and intellectually useful to articulate the differences. Thinking of Defoe's poems as a body – their preoccupations, tones, and rhetorical strategies – provides a convenient way to see how poetry relates to public issues and cultural practices of the time, and, at the same time, the poems themselves offer their own pleasures when they are seen within the interests, values, and expectations of their audience.

Defoe's reputation and *The True-Born Englishman*

Defoe's most famous poem, *The True-Born Englishman*, can almost be said to have ushered in the English eighteenth century, and it did so with a bang. It was published in either the early days of 1701 or the waning days of 1700, was widely read and popular, and quickly made a sensational reputation for its author. W. R. Owens calls it "an immediate and unprecedented best-seller," and claims that it was to become "the most frequently reprinted poem of the early eighteenth century."[3] Defoe was then forty years old but as yet hardly known for his writing; until the late 1690s he had made his living primarily as a merchant and entrepreneur, and only recently had he begun to get some public attention for his pamphleteering, social commentary, and literary projecting. Defoe claimed proudly (but misleadingly and possibly inaccurately) that the poem's publication brought him the personal attention of the king, William III, and he also made broad claims about its sales and popularity, pointing to nine authorized and twelve pirated editions by 1705 and complaining that 80,000 unauthorized and inferior copies were sold at reduced prices. If his numbers are anywhere near correct and if the authorized editions had even modest print runs, copies of the poem must have been ubiquitous in London. Defoe's claim (if true) would mean that one out of every three or four adult Londoners not only read but *owned* a copy of the poem in a time when print ownership was very expensive indeed.[4] And the claim, with its emphasis on cheap, crude copies democratizing print and reading practices, also underscores the social range of poetry's readership at the time.

What made *The True-Born Englishman* so popular? In the first place, the poem was very much about public matters, issues that were on the minds and tongues of English readers and talkers everywhere but especially in London, where increasing percentages of England's populace lived and where consciousness of England's rising international status centered. Poetry then was a common vehicle for airing issues of wide public interest; it is hard to appreciate today – when poetry accounts for a truly minuscule portion of print output – how much contemporary poetry was available from booksellers and how many poets threw themselves into the public fray in verse; about one in ten print publications then was a poem or collection of poems.[5] Writing about public affairs – whether matters of state, commerce, or social interaction – often took poetic form, for poetry was thought of more as a species of rhetoric than of self-expression, and the serious strategies of dialogue, discourse, and persuasion characterized poetry as well as prose. Moreover, the relationship between reading and conversation was more fluid then than in more modern times, so that coffee-house or tavern conversation was in many ways an extension of the reading matters of the moment – and vice versa. Writing poetry about issues that dominated public conversation was very much the thing to do for varieties of men in public functions or places or stances (though just beginning to be so for a few prominent women). Nearly as many Englishmen shared an itch to versify as to offer their public opinions more generally in prose or talk, and it is quite astonishing how many people were at least competent versifiers and published their poems (often of some magnitude) on public topics. The climate of reception for poetic narrative or philosophy or politics, while often hostile to new views, was eclectic, and the habitual use of the pentameter couplet form for serious explanation or argument meant that audiences generally had a tuned and attentive ear for formal verse. Not all those who attempted to write poetry were talented or even knowledgeable, but the rhythms and sounds of verse were familiar to contemporary ears and could be triggered readily by the eye-catching print of poetry which looked, in its space-wasting, conspicuous-consumption formats, less fearsome than dense prose and seemed to promise some relaxed pleasure as well as information and edification – delight as well as profit. Poetry was common reading for those who could and did read (in a time when perhaps two thirds of the men and only a third of the women were literate), and often poetry was a major source of news and opinions about matters of public concern, not just leisure entertainment.

The True-Born Englishman clearly touched a nerve with Defoe's contemporary audience. It was, first and foremost, a tribute to the beleaguered king and a defense of his character, attitudes, aims, and Whig-friendly policies (as well as his Dutch, European Protestant heritage), but the praise is mostly indirect, refracted from a teasing but insistent complaint about the national character of the English people. Every nation, Defoe posits stereotypically, has some sort of characteristic weakness or "sin." For Spain it is pride, for Italy lust; the Germans drink, and the French indulge "ungoverned passion." And so on. He sketches some scathing caricatures that resonate well in the xenophobic English consciousness – famously suspicious of "foreigners," especially other Europeans. France, for example is a place "Where mankind lives in haste, and thrives by chance" and is said to be "A dancing nation, fickle and untrue ..." (lines 118–19). But the poem does a quick U-turn (and this is the source of its ironic power) on these English stereotypes and national prejudices, isolating and stressing England's own national characteristic – "ingratitude," according to Defoe. It attacks especially the English public's failure to appreciate that their deliverance from constitutional crisis (and possible enslavement to popery) in 1689 had been due to the grace of "foreign" influence; William had in fact been imported from Holland, in a legal move that was dubious at best, as part of the Glorious Revolution to preserve the Protestant monarchical succession.[6] In Defoe's rendering, the national distrust of "foreigners" thus quickly turns against the English themselves, and the characterization of historic (and contemporary) ingratitude is unrelenting, appealing to both the English pride in their own fairness of judgment and the equally characteristic (but less attractive) English tendency toward self-suspicion and even self-loathing.

The crucial part of the poem's argument involves English history. Who, Defoe asks, is a "true-born" Englishman? We are all, he goes on to demonstrate, "foreigners" of some kind in some not-too-distant period of history, coming or descending from all the places and groups we like to stereotype and poke fun at. He then lists a series of invasions and assimilations in English history – Romans, Saxons, Danes, Scots, Picts, Irish, Normans, etc. – to delineate what a mixed breed any "true-born" Englishman represents:

> From this amphibious ill-born mob began
> That vain, ill-natured thing, an Englishman.   (lines 187–88)

As a spirited and funny, if somewhat overly ingenious, defense of William's foreignness, the poem worked very well as propaganda and social balm in a volatile public atmosphere. The rough justice of the defense of a "foreign" king whose reign had successfully beaten back traditional Catholic European rivals appealed to English pride (even while it exposed and chided the national character) and defused or at least muted some of the persistent public grumbling about William that had spawned the poem in the first place. The year or so just previous to the poem's appearance had been characterized by especially nasty clashes between William (and his Dutch advisers) on the one hand, and Parliament on the other, with the general murmuring complaint narrow-mindedly registering widespread disaffection. Thus, in quieting some of the furor, the poem can be said to have at least partially accomplished a pragmatic, propagandistic, rhetorical mission; certainly – whether or not it actually "persuaded" individual readers to different self-analysis – the poem addressed a volatile issue in teasing terms that exposed the excessive binary simplification in thinking of "foreign" vs English attitudes and characteristics. In an important sense it undermined the very stereotypical conception that sponsors the poem. And it not so subtly reminded readers of the vexed and arbitrary history of English kingship and the fragile nature of national identity, effectively making it almost impossible to use the term "foreigner" without irony and at least some consciousness of context and history.

The poem thus amounts to a direct intervention in ongoing conversation about the nature of the nation, the monarchy, and both governing and social practices. Its immediate occasion was the publication of another poem, *The Foreigner*, by John Tutchin, which was a direct attack on the king's foreignness, his dependence on Dutch advisers, and his reluctance to trust the natives of his adopted kingdom. Most of Defoe's poems are "occasional" in this sense; that is, they result from, or are triggered by, a specific event or situation or occasion; often they get into direct dialogue with points that have been made elsewhere – in conversation or print, prose or poetry, and sometimes all of the above. But the occasional-ness is mainly contextual in the sense that the position argued by Defoe evokes the whole larger context of discussion and debate, usually framed by a specific reading of contemporary events that manifest larger political, social, or philosophical issues. Much of that detail is interesting now only to historical specialists (though watching how it is worked out with cleverness and wit can be a fruitful reading experience for any reader), but Defoe's great art as a writer, in poetry or prose, is in personalizing and illustrating issues poignantly, finding ways to make them lively, vivid, and relevant to concerns of readers in a specific political or cultural moment.

The poem in its first edition runs to seventy-one pages; it is 1216 lines long – half again as long as Pope's expanded version of the *Rape of the Lock* and almost ten times as long as Gray's *Elegy Written in a Country Church Yard*. It is divided into sections that, in part, help to clarify its organization: after a prose preface of seven paragraphs, there is a short poetic introduction, two main sections (labeled simply Parts I and II), and then two shorter inserts before the "Conclusion" – one of the inserts a rousing patriotic section labeled "Britannia" and the other a parody of a "fine speech" in which Defoe lets a contemporary public figure speak in the first person and expose his devious motives. The title page helps set expectations of the poem's rhetorical stance, announcing it as "A Satyr." That label, like most generic claims in poems of the eighteenth century, helps set general expectations of content and tone for readers without necessarily giving much away about exactly how the poem is going to enact its appeal; here and elsewhere in Defoe's titling, "Satyr" suggests rigorous critical commentary and an attack on contemporary mores, claiming an urgent need for social reformation and implying a vigorous, direct, and rugged way of arguing for improved behavior. Critical orthodoxy of the time, besides emphasizing the Roman precedent of a satiric mode in such figures as Horace and Juvenal, often claimed some very early, primitive, almost feral origins of the form, and Defoe (in adopting that archaic, suggestive spelling) seems to ally himself with the roughshod, punitive impulses of the tradition. The opening lines suggest the urgency of the situation:

> Speak, Satyr, for there's none can tell like thee,
> Whether 'tis folly, pride, or knavery,
> That makes this discontented land appear
> Less happy now in times of peace, then war:
> Why civil feuds disturb the nation more
> Than all our bloody wars have done before.　　　(lines 1–6)

Here, as elsewhere, Defoe addresses "Satyr" directly, almost as if it were a pugnacious muse, asking this figure to declare and discriminate directly the causes and issues behind a serious contemporary crisis. Polite and urbane satirists of the time (and some not so polite) often ask their muse to "sing" – in praise or blame, as the needs may be – but Defoe seems to invoke the cruder, harsher, less melodic voice of an older generation of rough-hewn English satirists like Skelton or Gascoigne: "Speak, Satyr ..." he begins more flatly: "none can tell like thee." And in some ways the poem *is* direct, brutal, and unbending in delineating flaws in the character, institutions, and habits of the English nation at the start of the eighteenth century.

But satire as a mode also can imply more analysis and critical commentary than attack as such, and often (as here) incorporates praise (in this case, of William III) with blame (in this case, the national character of ingratitude and complaint). Generic identification at the time, in poetry or prose, gave readers a sense of what was to come but didn't necessarily mean sticking close to classical or neo-classical definitions and prescriptions. The poem offers serious analysis and commentary and is hard-hitting at times; Defoe himself once described his own talent as that of a lampooner (that is, someone who directly and deliberately attacked specific, identifiable figures). But there is also a teasing, almost playful quality about the poem that seems designed to laugh readers out of their foibles more than to chastise them. There are snarling but not biting moments, and there is no Drydenian swordplay, Swiftian finesse, or Popean fireworks. The subjective poet combines with the choral "Satyr" into a communal voice that is, as Spiro Peterson remarks, "a voice very close to the people or folk."[7] Defoe is clearly enjoying himself immensely in creating such a table-turning pose. If the poem is unrelenting in its insistence on national self-analysis and the need for more tolerant and good-natured collaboration with well-meaning and benevolent leadership, its observations are often bemused, and they seem understanding of human weakness; the poem is more pleading than caustic in its ethical demands and exposures and finally rather comic about the contrariness and contradictory character of Defoe's fellow Englishmen. In both prose and poetry, Defoe can often be read as insistent, vituperative, angry, and extreme – or equally as teasingly ironic, humorously hyperbolic, genially corrective, and coolly rational. This is the set of contradictory tonal qualities that quickly got him in trouble two years later when he wrote the widely misunderstood prose piece, *The Shortest Way with the Dissenters*, for which he had to stand in the pillory as punishment for his ambiguities.

Irony, mockery, wit, humor, irritation, deprecation, scolding, frontal attack, patient explanation, historical review, rational argument, appeal to self-knowledge and self-interest – all these have a part in Defoe's rhetorical method in *The True-Born Englishman* and contribute to its composite methods, which reflect audience expectations of the time. The poem has much in common – in subject, aim, tone, and direction – with most of Defoe's other poems and with many other poems of the period. Before glancing at other, less prominent Defoe poems, let me enumerate ten aspects of *The True-Born Englishman* that typify features of eighteenth-century poetic practice more generally.

1. It is in aim and mode a *public* poem, concerned with public events and public issues that are under public discussion in the culture of England more generally, but especially in cosmopolitan London. It involves participatory writing, with the poetic voice deeply involved in – and concerned about – contemporary events: the speaker is within – a part of – the society he examines, and the criticism comes from *within* the culture rather than being an outsider's view.

2. Its style and method are designed to attract market attention; it is designed to make a profit for the bookseller by competing robustly with other discussions, in prose *or* poetry, on the same or similar topics.

3. It is substantial in size and scope. Most poems on public affairs that were separately published were designed for sixteen- or twenty-four-page formats (sometimes larger) and sold competitively, usually for a shilling or

less. *The True-Born Englishman* is longer than the average separately published quarto or folio poem, but is conceived in much the same terms of magnitude and reach.

4. Its method involves argument and elaborate discourse, quite similar to argument in prose, and its rhetorical strategies make a plain and direct appeal for response and reformed thinking.

5. It has an obvious, plainly stated didactic intent, and proposes or implies, beyond attitude changes, behavioral results on the part of its readers.

6. Readers are addressed directly in a tone that is at once personal and hortatory, often seeming to be an extension of conversation. The oral quality of the poetry acknowledges virtues associated with artful conversation – wit, compactness, sententiousness, and clever, pithy verbal constructs.

7. The rhetoric is phrased primarily in terms of persuasion but also sometimes implies threats of public consequences if its advice is not heeded.

8. It is written in the era's dominant verse form for longer poems – the pentameter couplet, sometimes called the "heroic" couplet because it is used primarily for serious, ambitious, and sustained projects. A vast majority of longer poems – and a large percentage of shorter ones – were written in couplets, and the couplet was generally regarded as the most dignified and serious of poetic forms.

9. It shows a consciousness of other poets (and often prose writers) concerned with similar issues. Sometimes poems are written as direct "answers" to other texts, and sometimes they implicitly or explicitly argue (as here) with other texts.

10. There are gestures toward abstraction and generalization (and a general invocation of "universal" principles of fairness, decency, public good, etc.), but the primary attention is to the details and ramifications of a particular contemporary issue or situation. Poetry of the time tends to be timely, local, and particular.

Earlier and later poems

Over the next six years Defoe capitalized on his signal popular success by publishing a flood of other poems on contemporary public issues. Most of these poems announced on their title pages that they were "by the Author of the *True-Born Englishman*": that single poem had become Defoe's public identity, and he claimed, exploited, and extended it.[8] And it was over these years – between 1701 and 1706 – that Defoe pursued most vigorously his career as a poet, publishing more than 18,000 lines of verse during that span – more than 85 percent of his lifetime's poetic output. In many ways, the structure of those years builds toward the publication in 1706 of his longest and by far most ambitious poem, the much-delayed and long-awaited *Jure Divino*, an epic-like accomplishment divided into the classical pattern of twelve formal "books" and consisting of more than 8,500 lines. It was promised long in advance, printed in expensive folio format, and offered by prepaid subscription for 15 shillings, fifteen times the price of *The True-Born Englishman*. Like just about all of Defoe's other poems, *Jure Divino* deals with issues prominent in public discussion, and (as P. N. Furbank notes) it "constitutes the fullest account of his political philosophy."[9]

As its title suggests, *Jure Divino* is about the idea of the "divine right" of kings to rule, a doctrine under severe scrutiny in the century of rebellions and regime-changes between the 1640s and the 1740s. Elaborately, emphatically, and characteristically, Defoe opposed the divine-right doctrine, arguing both philosophically and practically, and as events played out over the next decade (when the Hanoverian line of kings was brought in from Germany in 1714 to once again preserve the Protestant succession rather than bowing to the rule of primogeniture), the insistently Protestant process of English history agreed with his pragmatic analysis.[10] But despite its virtues – it is Defoe's most polished and perhaps most formally successful work – *Jure Divino* was not a popular success: except for two pirated editions, both launched early when the poem was expected to be a popular bestseller, it was not reprinted in Defoe's lifetime or indeed for many generations thereafter. *Jure Divino* was much ballyhooed before publication, and Defoe seems to have had high hopes of its reception and lasting cultural success. Clearly *Jure Divino* had been designed to culminate the public poetic career that Defoe's signature poem had in effect announced, but instead it seems to have virtually ended Defoe's engagement with verse. Later in the year, Defoe (who was then intensely engaged in completing negotiations for England's formal Union with Scotland) did publish one ambitious and lengthy poem, *Caledonia ... A Poem in Honour of Scotland and the Scots Nation*, and at least two other satirical poems on Scottish politics, but then there was almost nothing: the poetic chapter of his life had come to a close by the end of the year. After 1706 Defoe turned almost exclusively to prose. The only major poem we know to be his was published in 1715, *A Hymn to the Mob*, and even that "late" poem seems to have been mostly written years before. Otherwise, Defoe later in his career wrote (or at least published) only bits and fragments of verse; quite a few short verse passages are scattered throughout his journalistic, political, and social writings, and some even found their way into the novels, but the poetic "career" was over.[11]

However, in the first six years of the new century, Defoe (besides being an active pamphleteer) was a very busy poet indeed. Prominent in the poems early on were the kinds of public behavioral issues he raised in *The True-Born Englishman*; his mode was always didactic and primarily satirical, though often mingled with panegyric when he could find heroes – such as William III or the Duke of Marlborough – worthy of praise. The king died only a year after the success of *The True-Born Englishman*, and Defoe's poem memorializing his death (*The Mock Mourners*, 1702) is in effect a sequel, continuing to pursue the central issues of national character, leadership, loyalty, and patriotism, but leaving the spotlight on the character and accomplishments of William himself. Defoe's now retrospective praise of the late king honors his military prowess, heroic European leadership, and accomplishments in nation-building, but it also ostentatiously honors his successor as sovereign, Queen Anne, a lone Protestant from the waning Stuart line. Like its predecessor, *The Mock Mourners* mixes praise and blame – the title page labels it "a Satyr by way of Elegy" – and it was widely read and often republished, going through a dozen or so editions or printings in the early months of its existence: it proved to be Defoe's second most popular poem. Though superficially not as witty or ranging as its predecessor, *The Mock Mourners* is more compact and more tonally coherent, and still reads very well today as an encomium on national leadership and a critique of graceless grumbling. Defoe here is especially conscious of historical and literary predecessors, citing classical and biblical models and touchstones and alluding gracefully to Dryden's example as a political defender of royal power.

Like an earlier poem of his, *A New Discovery of an Old Intreague* (1691), some of Defoe's poems in these years are so aggressively occasional that they are difficult to follow today without extensive footnotes explaining events, contexts, and personalities; they are characterized by what John Richetti calls "intense topicality."[12] (Modern readers will find the footnotes of Defoe's editors, especially W. R. Owens and Frank Ellis, indispensable in sorting out historical references and details in several of these poems.) *The Spanish Descent* (1702), for example, celebrates a major English naval victory, the capture at Vigo of the whole Spanish fleet, and *The Dyet of Poland* (1705) launches a violent attack on Tory politics through an elaborate allegory about "Poland", which is of course code for England.[13] And other poems of these years repeatedly deal with domestic and foreign issues of note, putting the stress on public awareness of international, especially European, leadership issues and their implications for domestic attitudes and morality. But the emphasis is always behavioral and local. For Defoe, the constant issue is the attitudes, manner, and character – collective and personal – of the English people, and their responses to issues of social and cultural import, and he quickly turns interpretation of any event, foreign or domestic, to moral issues involving attitudes and conduct in daily life. As he had said succinctly in the very first words of the preface to *The True-Born Englishman*, "The end of Satyr is Reformation."

"Reformation" might be said to be the guiding theme of all of Defoe's poems in these years, and if, first, that term signals attention to correctable attitudes and personal conduct, it also calls special attention to its crucially Protestant historical roots in Luther's reformation agenda and their flowering in seventeenth-century Puritan programs in England. Sometimes Defoe seems to use the term, in addition to its literal meaning as correction and atonement, as a conscious historical alternative to "Restoration" – implying the near-arrival of a hoped-for new era that might reverse cavalier excesses and the narrow intolerance of religious difference. What was once unbridled revelry and persecution of dissidents, Defoe seems to suggest, might now convert into responsibility and toleration, though he quickly discovered that the cultural spotlight was actually more on would-be reformers (like himself) than actual targets of the reformative impulse.

All Defoe's poems of this period rail against improper behavior of one kind or another, recommending higher moral standards in line with the "reform" urges of Williamite rule, which means more demanding ethical judgments, better leadership models, and more responsible everyday behavior. But Defoe is not a knee-jerk crime-in-the-streets reformer, and his emphasis is on patterns of behavior and responsibility (rather than individual lapses). His attack focuses on causes, influence, and leadership. He saw through the superficial social analysis that punished poor and ordinary people for minor infractions and follies while ignoring worse abuses among the leadership classes. One of his most powerful reformist poems, *Reformation of Manners* (1702), took on the issue directly. The contemporary urban ethical societies that went under the general title of Societies for the Reformation of Manners (founded in the 1690s under the reformist agenda of William III), seemed to Defoe to have aimed too narrowly and too low, pursuing personal vices and minor "manners" issues in quite superficial ways – going after drunkenness, swearing, Sabbath-breaking, and other everyday behavioral offenses as if they constituted the sinister core of moral deterioration – whereas Defoe believed that corruption and depraved habits in higher, more influential social classes were the true culprits, representing a more fundamental and far-reaching danger. The opening lines of *Reformation of Manners* call attention to "Shams of Reformation" and place blame upon judicial, ecclesiastical, and political officials and cultural models:

> Superiour Lewdness Crowns thy Magistrates,
> And Vice grown grey usurps the Reverend Seats;
> Eternal Blasphemies, and Oaths abound,
> And Bribes among thy Senators are found.　　　　(lines 99–102)

Defoe gets quickly to particulars in these poems, and one recurrent feature makes them quite readable today in spite of their detailed historical particularity. He fleshes out his satirical analysis of events and issues by peopling his poems with type-characters, often based on contemporaries who figured prominently in the actual events and issues of the time but then transformed to general, almost allegorical types whose character is dominated by a single characteristic or obsession, which Alexander Pope later popularized as a "ruling passion." The referentiality of these portraits – though still recoverable by social and political historians – is largely lost on modern readers. But still appreciable is the portraiture itself, with its emphasis on witty summation and a few telling details that in effect stand for the whole person. Most of the figures have, like the nations stereotypically described in *The True-Born Englishman*, one dominating character flaw and thus become representative types interacting in his social psychodramas. Defoe creates scores of such characters – Spiro Peterson counts thirty-nine in *Reformation of Manners* alone[14] – and they remain, despite their now obscure local referents, vivid analytical representations of human behavior. One early prototype for Defoe's creation of character portraits is a poem he wrote in 1697 eulogizing a dissenting clergyman, *The Character of the Late Dr. Samuel Annesley by Way of Elegy*. This poem, more than three hundred lines long and a bit rambling, is somewhat roundabout and general in asserting the virtues of the man who had been Defoe's pastor in his formative years: Annesley is portrayed as incorruptible, unselfish, unpretentious, uncontentious, and unworldly, not guilty of the besetting sins of his generation which Defoe would go on to detail in later poems. But the positive qualities seem mostly the effect of the absence of negatives: Defoe is almost always better at depicting flaws and weaknesses than at making positive qualities convincing – that is, he is (like most of his contemporaries) better at satire than panegyric, in spite of his attempts to balance his judgmental rhetoric.

Defoe's best portraits, however truthful or exaggerated historically, are very good examples of the popular "character" literary subgenre in the late seventeenth to early eighteenth century, associated earlier with Overbury, Halifax, and Butler and later popularized journalistically by Addison and Steele and in poetry by Dryden and Pope. Writing "characters" was quite common at the time in both poetry and prose, sometimes as part of some larger analytical or narrative frame, and sometimes produced as independent texts; the periodical *Spectator* depended for much of its social analysis on repeated examples of character portraits, and a little later Pope made it a staple of his poetic satires. And later Defoe himself adopted related strategies in prose, recalling or creating type-figures to illustrate and flesh out his commentary not only in journalistic pieces but in his later novelistic fictions.[15]

Here, from a poem called *More Reformation* (1703), is an example of the concentrated energy Defoe manages to compress into a telling portrait:

> K — 's a Dissenter and severe of Life,
> Instructs his Household, and *Corrects his Wife;*
> Reproves a Stranger, if he hears him Swear,
> For Vice and he ha' been some Years at War;
> But Sins of Inclination will remain,
> Eclipse the Christian, and Expose the Man:
> For Wine's the darling Devil of his Life;
> This reconciles the Anti-Christian strife
> Betwixt the Convert and his former Friends,
> And for his Reformation makes amends.
> Religion seems to have possest his Soul,
> But Vice Corrupts the Parts, and Taints the whole,
> Infects his painted Piety and Zeal,
> And shows the Hypocrite he'd fain conceal.
> The Bottle Conquers all his Reformation,
> And makes Religion stoop to Inclination.
> Lectures and Sermons he frequents by Day,
> But yet comes home at Night too Drunk to Pray;
> Yet too much Piety is his Disease,
> Thank Heaven! there's few such Hypocrites as these;
> That wipes his Mouth, and acts without remorse,
> Sins and Repents, Repents and sins in course.   (lines 248–69)

Typically, Defoe gets interested here in perhaps more details than he needs, and there isn't the crispness or the quick thrust found in the very most memorable characters of the period – such as Pope's "Atticus" and "Sporus" or Dryden's "Zimri," "Og," and "Achitophel." But Defoe shares the same telling eye for the pertinent fact, a desire to summarize a definition of character in a single gesture or moment, and sponsoring notion that a single dominant characteristic can "explain" the thrust of an individual's impact on a situation, event, episode, pattern, or idea. And he often finds the apt phrase or homely summary detail that creates a memorable edge as in the vividly conceived contrast of "Lectures and Sermons he frequents by Day" with "But yet comes home at Night too Drunk to Pray." Not always but often, Defoe finds in his "characters" the virtue of concision and pointedness that eludes him in historical and situational description or in broader satirical attacks. And sometimes without quite imitating classical figures of rhetoric he finds the resources of the antithetical couplet adaptable to his needs, as when he summarizes the garrulous character of "Finski" in *The Dyet of Poland*:

> Polite in Words, a stiff and formal Tongue,
> *And speaks to little Purpose, very long.*   (lines 319–20)

Many of the poems in the latter part of the 1701–6 period introduce, extensively, another form of "character" – a portrait of Defoe himself – who is not described separately or concisely or crisply at all but whose hovering presence as a consciousness haunts poems such as *More Reformation, Hymn to the Pillory* (1703), and *An Elegy on the Author of the True-Born Englishman* (1704). The first of these poems Defoe subtitles "A Satyr upon Himself" and (besides employing the revered subgenre of "the satirist satirized") rehearses the pitfalls and fears that seem to attend being a public commentator and critic in his time. He was beginning to understand those consequences in quite dramatic and highly personal terms. The immediate occasion for his confinement in Newgate prison and condemnation to stand three days in the pillory – a kind of public announcement of national shame – was the publication of a prose pamphlet, *The Shortest Way with the Dissenters*. But Defoe believed, quite possibly correctly, that his punishment was not solely due to that single pamphlet – that it was a legacy of his satirical social analysis more generally (most of which up to this point in his career had been in his poetic satires), and in *More Reformation* he elaborately defends the function and methodology of public satire. Part of the price of his release from Newgate was that he had to promise seven years of good behavior, and these poems reveal a Defoe contemplating the end of his "career" as he then knew it, hence the "elegy" for himself. In fact, the pillory episode did not end Defoe's outspokenness, and his life as a poet continued without abatement for three full years. *A Hymn to the Pillory* became one of his most successful poems, celebrating as it did both the central public vehicle of his punishment and the fact of his public recognition as an influential writer and popular hero. The whole pillory episode can be seen as a kind of defense of Defoe's career to this point and, far from ending his public role, extended its scope and enabled the final three years of his poetic voice. And certainly the celebratory pillory poem represents one of Defoe's most triumphant public moments; there is no other place in Defoe's writing that shows him so fully and authentically displaying and explaining himself for his attitudes and public function or so genuinely joyous. Defoe does seem somewhat more subdued in his subsequent poems – or at least somewhat more prone to find things to cheer rather than attack (*A Hymn to Victory, The Double Welcome*) – but the fears of silence that Defoe expresses turn out to be unfounded, and his later flight from poetry cannot be explained by either the punishment itself or threats of more. *More Reformation*, in fact – self-righteous and self-indulgent as it is – is Defoe's strongest defense of the idea of satire and is one of the more eloquent, if perhaps too personally inflected, apologies of the time for the public role of the poet.

One final note on the range and chronology of Defoe's poetic career. Early on, Defoe had flirted with two kinds of poetry that he did not later pursue. The first involved brief youthful experiments with private meditations: they exist only in a manuscript dated when Defoe was about twenty-one years old, and not published until the middle of the twentieth century. These poem drafts – there are seven short poems or fragments preserved in a notebook in which Defoe also recorded, nearly word for word, several sermons he had heard preached by a dissenting divine – represent intense, devout effusions of piety perhaps inspired by the precarious threats Dissenters feared in the late 1670s when Defoe was a teenager. They are compact verses (Defoe labeled them "Meditacons") marked by humility, anxiety, and solemnity. The following lines briefly suggest his fervent but rather unsure voice:

> Let Me Not Go, But Flee,
> My God,! To Hide my Burthened Soul wth Thee.
> Swift be my Steps, & Swifter my Desyre,
> To Such a refuge to Retyre,
> Teach Me from what, and whom,
> With Eager hast it is I Come.
> From Sin,
> And Legions of Strong Lusts within;
> From a base heart,
> That Eagerly wth Hell Takes Part,
> From Fatall, and Accurst Desyres,
> That Bursts From Thence wth Too Uncertain fires:
> From all my Pride,
> And all the Lusts That have my Soul Betraid:[16]

There may be suggestions of the style of George Herbert or John Donne here (or Thomas Traherne or Edward Taylor), though more in terms of temperamental and formal likeness than direct stylistic imitation. Defoe is certainly conscious of the metaphysical mode with its elaborate conceits and craggy lyrical style. But his experiments are more meditative than dramatic and more plaintive than calculated or constructed. These verses are only exercises, of course, and very youthful ones at that, and it would be a mistake to think of them as prototypes of any kind of serious direction. But the interesting thing about them is that they show Defoe in a private posture unlike anything he tried in his public career as a poet. This is the inquisitive, thoughtful, sincere, and devout mode, and in these exercises we see a young writer working much harder at his craft and more carefully with his words and music than he ever demonstrated as a more mature public poet. Even though they are just drafts, evidently never intended for publication, the poems here show a meticulous care for word choice and an attention to meter and rhythm that are missing from most of Defoe's published poetry. The earnest play here does not become poetic power as in the best of metaphysical poetry (and no one would, from these examples, expect Defoe to develop into a great devotional poet), but a careful reader would have been able to glimpse the rhetorician, word-lover, wordsmith, and self-preoccupied figure that Defoe became in his public role not many years after.

The other trial mode is represented by *The Pacificator* (1700), where Defoe writes as a public figure but a very different one from the political analyst, social critic, and satiric scourge he shortly became. This poem is about debates and stances within the world of poetry itself, and Defoe is here concerned to describe the literary rather than the political state of public affairs. He characterizes the various contemporary poets contending for the leadership role and reviews the issues that divide them; Defoe is writing in the wake of a specific poem – Sir Richard Blackmore's *A Satyr against Wit* – but the full context involves decades-old debates about not only the nature of poetry and its cultural role but the contributions that individual poets – with individual styles, biases, and loyalties – can make.

What Defoe has to say here about moral responsibility is of course relevant to the satiric role he goes on to play in the coming years, but the focus in *The Pacificator* is totally different: about the landscape of poetry itself at the end of the century and the nature of individual poets. Defoe literalizes the battle imagery that often characterized poetic debate in the 1690s especially, and represents the poets as using crude weapons on each other: his account is almost as concrete and literal-minded (though not as clever) as Swift's in *The Battle of the Books*, probably written by this time but not published until 1704. The Defoe voice here is witty, urbane, and bemused; and Defoe clearly was a close reader of literary directions and individual styles, but the stakes for him here are nothing like those argued by Pope when he recorded and fueled the culture wars a quarter century later. The literary issues Defoe articulated in 1700 are, to be sure, closely related to the social and political issues he helps define in the coming years, but his subsequent career choices took him into the thick of political battle itself rather than refining or sorting out the literary accounts of it. And Defoe was more at home creating distinctions and mounting arguments than in the role of chronicler or "pacificator."

Formal issues: accomplishments and limitations

Defoe seems mostly to have thought of his poetry as utilitarian, that is, as an artful means to attain specific results in his time – much the way he thought about all of his writing, fact or fiction, poetry or prose: he was very much a man *in* the world and determined to move it or change it in specific ways, and words were his main means. He was interested in how the world ran and how to make it run better, and throughout his life he always had the projector's sense of what work in the world was like, a world of doing that was informed and moved by ideas and thought, but not a world *of* ideas. And although literary craft was thus always on his mind – finding the right way to gain attention and be persuasive about a particular matter – it was never the primary driving force in his work. His poems, even more than his prose works perhaps, seem to expose Defoe more clearly as a man at work in a world-in-progress – boasting, fearful, struggling, emotional, celebratory, calculating, struck both by how magical words are when they go right and how treacherous they can turn out to be even when uttered in the most honest, thoughtful, and carefully calculated way. He was very much a figure in present time, anxious to employ his cautionary love affair with language in fruitful, practical ways but not bothering overmuch about methodology or self-analysis.

Defoe's preoccupation with the present and its directions perhaps automatically meant that he was deeply conscious of the past as both guide and cautionary example; perhaps it was his background and early deep immersion in a religion of dissent that pushed him toward this cautious, pragmatic way of relating to tradition. Defoe seems to have felt deeply the doubtful, suspicious, individualist Protestant thrust in relating to habits and the "givens" of history and tradition, and he certainly brought to his engagement with poetry a relationship with history that was different from that of writers more traditionally and classically trained. He was extraordinarily *well* read in some ways (and perhaps more able than most of his contemporaries to apply the relevance of recent vernacular traditions), but he was not *widely* or *deeply* read in the predictable-titles sense that most of the other male poets of his generation – Swift, Prior, Halifax, Pomfret, Garth, Dennis, Congreve – were. His own education and experience were not so firmly rooted in a sense of past accomplishment and harmony. And so his sense of tradition was different: he wore it lightly, perhaps somewhat suspiciously, and saw no special need to rehearse his literary or intellectual allegiances, though sometimes he did boast a bit by allusion or echo. He shared his age's sense that poetry had public duties and responsibilities, and he knew about the various traditions of appropriateness of forms to functions, but he did not begin with either habituation or devotion to a particular literary creed.

Defoe, then, both was and was not a "traditional" poet. He was born solitarily into a poetic moment when poetry was public and confrontational, grew up when much political poetry circulated privately and often surreptitiously, and came into his own as a poet when much of this "coterie" poetry was making its way into public print.[17] He inherited from Restoration poets – Cowley, Marvell, Dryden, Rochester, Behn – the expectation that many, perhaps most, readers went to poetry for analysis and opinion and argument and that they expected to be informed, challenged, and possibly convinced to see their social and political world anew – at the same time that they were being amused and entertained. He inherited, too, a sense that the swirl of controversy and disagreement was the stuff of which poetry was made, and held himself to high standards of observation and persuasion. About formal issues he was perhaps (as in his prose) more ambivalent, and he seems to have adopted practical habits of competence and workability rather than formal exactitude or excellence. He sometimes heard rhythms imperfectly (or at least did not discipline his voice always to achieve satisfying metrical patterns), and he conformed to the then-prevailing genial acceptance of consonance – in which final consonants repeat themselves in "rhyming" lines but preceding vowels do not, so that he rhymes "appease" with "skies," "town" with "own," and "appear" with "there" rather than following the newer standard (which was developing in the very early years of the eighteenth century and exemplified by the "correct" Pope), which insisted on the tougher, more precise test of "full" or "exact" or "perfect" vowel-plus-consonant rhyme.

Defoe wrote mainly in two poetic styles, both typical of his time, working predominantly in pentameter couplets in his satires and longer poems, and using a variation on ode stanzas when celebrating some glorious moment or achievement or when moving into effusive praise or emotional outburst, often calling poems in that mode "hymns" (thinking of them perhaps in the classical sense of abstract praise rather than the religious one of worship and faith). His contemporaries (and poets over the next two or three generations in the eighteenth century) followed the same general strategy – and predictably wrote four or five times as often in couplets as in the ode-like stanzas. Those odic structures were designed to accommodate freer expression and give both poets and readers a sense of liberation from convention and pattern (sometimes even associating freedom of sound pattern with political "liberty"). In contemporary practice, "odes" allowed for irregular stanzas of varied magnitudes and tolerated all sorts of mixed line lengths from two to fourteen syllables or even more. Still, Defoe – when writing ode-stanzas – was at one with his contemporaries in regularly and repeatedly lapsing into couplet-like consecutive-rhyme patterns, even after deliberately freeing themselves from couplet expectations: the habit of rhyming consecutive lines was that deeply engrained. (Look, for example, at the meditation quoted on p. 230, a good example of formal metrical freedom in tension with habitual rhyming practice.) Even so, the perceived freedom of ode-stanzas provided an illusion of fitful, emotional outpourings, and the fact that there was no *predictable* pattern of rhyme, line length, or stanza shape offered a sense of improvisation and liberty.

Like his contemporaries, Defoe also paid homage to the neoclassical idea of genre-labeling and genre frameworks, though in actual practice calling most of his poems satires, hymns, or elegies (not the dominant classical genres). But, also like his contemporaries, he employed the labels loosely and allowed himself freedom from generic rules while staying within broad genre expectations. His hymning effusions were sometimes self-indulgent, but he genuinely (unlike many of his contemporaries) seems to have valued and enjoyed (or even wallowed in) the greater structural freedom of unpredictable stanza and line lengths, and there is almost a giddy abandon, an above-it-all nose-thumbing, in his triumphant celebration in *A Hymn to the Pillory*, written to memorialize the humiliation-turned-triumph when the crowds of bystanders gathered to honor Defoe's integrity and public courage.

There is, I think, no *great* poem in the Defoe canon: even when he is at the top of his form (as in, for example *The True-Born Englishman* and *A Hymn to the Pillory*) he composes flabbily and sometimes carelessly and seldom bothers to revise or edit carefully. He seems to be telling the truth when he says that he expects to be "cavilled at about my mean style, rough verse, and incorrect language: things I might indeed have taken more care in."[18] And he is regularly prolix and certainly does not harvest the full, intense possibilities of wit, brevity, and symmetry in couplets in the same way that exemplary contemporaries such as Prior and Pope do. Still, he plainly understands the structural assets of the couplet idea – based on balance, equipoise, antithesis, challenge, and the interplay of double and triple parallelisms – and the subtleties of the caesura (that is, mid-line pause). Defoe does not follow classic formulas or exploit traditional practice in constructing his couplets, but he does seem to think his own way toward such structural exploitations without working from models or textbooks. Generally speaking, he constructs better, more crafted and effective verse paragraphs than couplet units, though he is sometimes repetitious and flaccid in both units of construction.

Sometimes Defoe carves out quite memorable aphoristic lines:

> Wherever God erects a House of Prayer
> The Devil always builds a Chappel there:
> And 'twill be found upon Examination,
> The latter has the largest Congregation:[19]

But usually (even when he was consciously working with tight comparisons and contrasts) he refuses to follow compression to its logical limit. His talent lies in accumulation and piling up rather than concision, precise word choice, and musical sensitivity, and even when he makes a pithy observation (as in the opening lines of *The Mock Mourners*: "Such has been this Ill-Natur'd Nations Fate / Always to see their Friends and Foes too late") he seldom points, hones, or polishes the lines smoothly and sharply. Look again, for example, at the opening lines of *The True-Born Englishman*, quoted on p. 221, where the idea is crisply bipolar (times of war, times of peace) but the execution takes six lines. Pope would have done it in two.

Defoe was not a "great" poet, and he is unlikely to be read again in our time with the same attention he got for some years in his. But he is an instructive poet, and modern readers can learn a lot about how couplets work (and what makes their demands so complicated) by watching Defoe struggle, without extensive training or classical vocabulary, with formal intricacies. The seams are visible here, the work still in process. So there is aesthetic pleasure, if of occasional and fleeting sorts, in confronting Defoe's poems, and almost anyone can enjoy them in small doses. And if you want to fathom the politics, social issues, and attitudinal formations of the turn of the eighteenth century – from Williamite to Stuart Anne's England and then to the "forging" of England into Britain, the movement from *The True-Born Englishman* to *Caledonia* – you have to read, with real attention and care, Defoe's poetry, all of it.

NOTES

1. The primary exceptions are Spiro Peterson, whose essay "Daniel Defoe" in the *Dictionary of Literary Biography*, vol. xcv surveys and places all the major poems: *Eighteenth-Century British Poets: First Series*, ed. John Sitter (Detroit: Gale Research, 1990), pp. 7–35, and Paula R. Backscheider, who offers a full critical evaluation (chapter 2 in her *Daniel Defoe: Ambition and Innovation* (Lexington: University of Kentucky Press, 1986)), pp. 12–41, and also a lengthy discussion of Defoe as political philosopher, "The Verse Essay, John Locke, and Defoe's *Jure Divino*," *English Literary History*, 55 (Spring 1988), 99–124.
2. Most of the poems are edited and annotated by W. R. Owens in volume I (*The True-Born Englishman and Other Poems*) of *Satire, Fantasy and Writings on the Supernatural by Daniel Defoe* (gen. eds. W. R. Owens and P. N. Furbank), 4 vols. (London: Pickering and Chatto, 2003). Volume III in that series, edited by Furbank, is devoted to *Jure Divino*; and three other poems are included in vol. IV (*Union with Scotland*, ed. D. W. Hayton) of *Political and Economic Writings of Daniel Defoe*, ed. Owens and Furbank (London: Pickering and Chatto, 2000). Nine of Defoe's most prominent poems are included in vols. VI and VII (edited by Frank Ellis, 1975) of *Poems on Affairs of State*, 7 vols. (New Haven: Yale University Press, 1963–75), with helpful annotations.

3. Introduction to *The True-Born Englishman and Other Poems*, ed. Owens, pp. 16–17. Owens counts "some fifty editions" by 1750. The other standard "candidate" for most reprinted poem of the century is Samuel Pomfret's "The Choice" (1701).

4. Calculation based on population and backward projections of demographics in E. A. Wrigley and R. S. Schofield, *The Population History of England 1541–1871: A Reconstruction* (London: Edward Arnold, 1981); see especially p. 218.

5. For a fuller account of poetry's place in early eighteenth-century culture, see my "Political, Satirical, Didactic and Lyric Poetry (1): From the Restoration to the Death of Pope," in *The Cambridge History of English Literature 1660–1780*, ed. John Richetti (Cambridge: Cambridge University Press, 2005), esp. pp. 160–62.

6. The crown was offered to William and Mary jointly, even though the lineage claim via the Stuart line was through Mary; when Mary died in 1697 William became sole monarch.

7. Peterson, "Daniel Defoe," p. 17.

8. Quite a few poems definitely *not* by Defoe also claimed on their title pages to be "by the author of *The True-Born Englishman*."

9. Introduction to *Jure Divino*, ed. Furbank, p. 28.

10. For a convenient book-by-book summary of the poem's argument, see Furbank's Introduction to his edition of the poem, pp. 4–15.

11. In the *Review*, Defoe said in 1708 that he had given up poetry.

12. Richetti, *The Life of Daniel Defoe: A Critical Biography* (Oxford: Blackwell, 2005), p. 110.

13. For a brief account of the contents of individual poems of this period, see Peterson "Daniel Defoe," and for explanations of the many contemporary references in the poems see the annotations of Owens and Ellis listed in note 2.

14. Peterson "Daniel Defoe," p. 21.

15. John Sitter usefully distinguishes between characters like Defoe's that represent "static sketches" as opposed to "character progresses" like Hogarth's, which depend on narration and development over time. See *Arguments of Augustan Wit* (Cambridge: Cambridge University Press 1991), pp. 7–8.

16. *The Meditations of Daniel Defoe*, ed. George Harris Healey (Cummington, MA: Cummington Press, 1946), p. 4.

17. See Harold Love, *English Clandestine Satire 1660–1702* (Oxford: Oxford University Press), 2004.

18. Preface to *The True-Born Englishman*.

19. *The True-Born Englishman*, lines 56–59.

GUIDE TO FURTHER READING

Collected Editions of Defoe's Works

Novels and Miscellaneous Works, 20 vols. London: 1840–41, rpt. New York: AMS Press, 1973

Romances and Narratives by Daniel Defoe, ed. George A. Aitkin, 16 vols. London: J. M. Dent, 1895

The Works of Daniel Defoe, ed. G. A. Maynadier, 16 vols. Boston: Old Corner Bookstore, 1903

The Shakespeare Head Edition of the Novels and Selected Writings of Daniel Defoe, 14 vols. Oxford: Basil Blackwell, 1927–28, rpt. in 9 vols. Totowa, NJ: Rowan and Littlefield, 1974

Defoe's Review. Reproduced from the original editions, with an introduction and bibliographical notes by Arthur Wellesley Secord, 9 vols. Published for the Facsimile Text Society in 22 vols. New York: Columbia University Press, 1938

The Stoke Newington Daniel Defoe Edition, ed. Jim Springer Borck, *et al.* (in progress). New York: AMS Press, 1999–

The Works of Daniel Defoe, general editors W. R. Owens and P. N. Furbank, 44 vols. (in progress). London: Pickering & Chatto, 2000–8

Bibliographies

Moore, J. R. *A Checklist of the Writings of Daniel Defoe*. Bloomington, Indiana: Indiana University Press, 1960

Novak, Maximillian E. "Daniel Defoe." In *The New Cambridge Bibliography of English Literature*, ed. G. Watson. Cambridge: Cambridge University Press, 1971, vol. II, 880–917

"Defoe." In *The English Novel: Select Bibliographical Guides*, ed. A. E. Dyson. London: Oxford University Press, 1974

Owens, W. R., and P. N. Furbank. *Defoe De-Attributions: A Critique of J. R. Moore's Checklist*. London and Rio Grande, Ohio: The Hambledon Press, 1994

Owens, W. R., and P. N. Furbank. *A Critical Bibliography of Daniel Defoe*. London: Pickering & Chatto, 1998

Peterson, Spiro. *Daniel Defoe: A Reference Guide*. Boston: G. K. Hall, 1987

Stoler, John. *Daniel Defoe: An Annotated Bibliography of Modern Criticism, 1900–1980*. New York: Garland Press, 1984

Biographies of Defoe

Backscheider, Paula R. *Daniel Defoe: His Life*. Baltimore and London: Johns Hopkins University Press, 1989

Bastian, Frank. *Defoe's Early Life*. Totowa, NJ: Barnes & Noble, 1981

Chalmers, George. *The Life of Daniel Defoe*. London, second edition, 1790

Healey, George Harris, ed. *The Letters of Daniel Defoe*. Oxford: Clarendon Press, 1955

Lee, William. *Daniel Defoe: His Life and Recently Discovered Writings*, 3 vols. London, 1869; rept. New York: B. Franklin, 1969

Moore, J. R. *Daniel Defoe: Citizen of the Modern World*. Chicago: University of Chicago Press, 1958

Novak, Maximillian E. *Daniel Defoe: Master of Fictions*. Oxford: Oxford University Press, 2001

Owens, W. R. and P. N. Furbank. *A Political Biography of Daniel Defoe*. London: Pickering & Chatto, 2006

Richetti, John. *The Life of Daniel Defoe: A Critical Biography*. Oxford: Blackwell, 2005

Sutherland, James R. *Defoe*. London: Methuen & Co., 1937

Watson, Francis. *Daniel Defoe*. Port Washington, NY and London: Kennikat Press, 1969

West, Richard. *Daniel Defoe: The Life and Strange, Surprising Adventures*. London: Harper Collins, 1998

Wilson, Walter. *Memoirs of the Life and Times of Daniel Defoe*, 3 vols. London: 1830

Critical studies

Alkon, Paul K. *Defoe and Fictional Time*. Athens, GA: University of Georgia Press, 1979

Alter, Robert. *Rogue's Progress: Studies in the Picaresque Novel*. Cambridge, MA: Harvard University Press, 1964

Backscheider, Paula R. *A Being More Intense*. New York: AMS Press, 1984
   Daniel Defoe: Ambition & Innovation. Lexington, Kentucky: University Press of Kentucky, 1986
   Moll Flanders: The Making of a Criminal Mind. Boston: G. K. Hall, 1990
   A Journal of the Plague Year: A Norton Critical Edition. New York: W. W. Norton, 1992

Baine, Rodney M. *Daniel Defoe and the Supernatural*. Athens, GA: University of Georgia Press, 1965

Bell, Ian. *Defoe's Fiction*. London: Croom Helm, 1985

Bender, John. *Imagining the Penitentiary: Fiction and the Architecture of Mind in Eighteenth-Century England*. Chicago: University of Chicago Press, 1987

Birdsall, Virginia Ogden. *Defoe's Perpetual Seekers: A Study of the Major Fiction*. Lewisburg, PA: Bucknell University Press, 1985

Blewett, David. *Defoe's Art of Fiction*. Toronto: University of Toronto Press, 1979
   The Illustrations of Robinson Crusoe 1719–1920. Gerrards Cross: Colin Smyth, 1995

Bloom, Harold, ed. *Daniel Defoe: Modern Critical Views*. New York: Chelsea House, 1987

Boardman, Michael. *Defoe and the Uses of Narrative*. New Bruswick, NJ: Rutgers University Press, 1983

Byrd, Max, ed. *Daniel Defoe: A Collection of Critical Essays*. Englewood Cliffs, NJ: Prentice-Hall, 1976

Curtis, Laura. *The Elusive Defoe*. Totowa, NJ: Vision Press and Barner & Noble, 1984

Damrosch, Leopold. *God's Plot and Man's Stories: Studies in the Fictional Imagination from Milton to Fielding*. Chicago: University of Chicago Press, 1985

Davis, Lennard J. *Factual Fictions: The Origins of the English Novel*. New York: Columbia University Press, 1983

Dijkstra, Bram. *Defoe and Economics: The Fortunes of Roxana in the History of Interpretation*, Basingstoke: Macmillan, 1987

Downie, J. A. *Robert Harley and the Press: Propaganda and Public Opinion in the Age of Swift and Defoe*. Cambridge: Cambridge University Press, 1979

Earle, Peter. *The World of Defoe*. New York: Atheneum, 1977

Ellis, Frank, ed. *Twentieth-Century Interpretations of Robinson Crusoe: A Collection of Critical Essays*. Englewood Cliffs, NJ: Prentice-Hall, 1969

Erickson, Robert. *Mother Midnight: Birth, Sex, and Fate in Eighteenth-Century Fiction*. New York: AMS Press, 1986

Faller, Lincoln B. *Crime and Defoe: A New Kind of Writing*. Cambridge: Cambridge University Press, 1993

    Turned to Account: The Forms and Functions of Criminal Biography in Late Seventeenth- and Early Eighteenth-Century England. Cambridge: Cambridge University Press, 1987

Flynn, Carol Houlihan. *The Body in Swift and Defoe*. Cambridge: Cambridge University Press, 1990

Furbank, P. N., and W. R. Owens. *The Canonisation of Daniel Defoe*. New Haven and London: Yale University Press, 1988

Gladfelder, Hal. *Criminality and Narrative in Eighteenth-Century England*. Baltimore and London: Johns Hopkins University Press, 2001

Green, Martin. *Dreams of Adventure, Deeds of Empire*. London: Routledge & Kegan Paul, 1980

    The Robinson Crusoe Story. University Park and London: Penn State University Press, 1990.

Greenfield, S. C. and C. Barash, eds. *Inventing Maternity: Politics, Science, and Literature, 1650–1865*. Lexington: University of Kentucky Press, 1999

Hammond, J. R. *A Defoe Companion*. Basingstoke: Macmillan, 1993

Hulme, Peter. *Colonial Encounters: Europe and the Native Caribbean 1492–1797*. London and New York: Routledge, 1992

Hunter, J. Paul. *The Reluctant Pilgrim: Defoe's Emblematical Method and Quest for Form in Robinson Crusoe*. Baltimore: Johns Hopkins University Press, 1966

    Before Novels: The Cultural Contexts of Eighteenth-Century English Fiction. New York: W. W. Norton, 1990

Ingrassia, Catherine. *Authorship, Commerce, and Gender in Early Eighteenth-Century England: A Culture of Paper Credit*. Cambridge: Cambridge University Press, 1998

James, E. Anthony. *Daniel Defoe's Many Voices*. Amsterdam: Rodopi, 1971

Joyce, J. "Daniel Defoe," ed. and trans. Joseph Prescott, *Buffalo Studies* 1.1 (1964); in *Daniel Defoe, Robinson Crusoe*, ed. Michael Shinagel. New York and London: W. W. Norton, 1994, pp. 320–23

Kahn, Madeline. *Narrative Transvestism: Rhetoric and Gender in the Eighteenth-Century English Novel*. Ithaca and London: Cornell University Press, 1991

Kay, Carol. *Political Constructions: Defoe, Richardson, and Sterne in Relation to Hobbes, Hume, and Burke*. Ithaca, NY: Cornell University Press, 1988

Lund, Roger, ed. *Critical Essays on Daniel Defoe*. New York: G. K. Hall, 1997

Lynch, Deidre Shauna. *The Economy of Character*. Chicago: University of Chicago Press, 1998

Macaree, David. *Daniel Defoe's Political Writings and Literary Devices*. Lewiston, NY: E. Mellen Press, 1991

Maniquis, Robert, and Carl Fisher, eds. *Defoe's Footprints: Essays in Honor of Maximillian E. Novak*. Toronto: University of Toronto Press, 2008

Mayer, Robert. *History and the Early English Novel: Matters of Fact from Bacon to Defoe*. Cambridge: Cambridge University Press, 1997

McKeon, Michael. *The Origins of the English Novel: 1600–1740*. Baltimore and London: Johns Hopkins University Press, 1987; rpt. 2002

McKillop, Alan D. *The Early Masters of English Fiction*. Lawrence, KS: University of Kansas Press, 1975

Meier, Thomas Keith. *Defoe and the Defense of Commerce*. Victoria, British Columbia: English Literary Studies, University of Victoria, 1987

Novak, Maximillian E. *Economics and the Fiction of Daniel Defoe*. Berkeley and Los Angeles: University of California Press, 1962
Defoe and the Nature of Man. Oxford and London: Oxford University Press, 1963
Realism, Myth, and History in Defoe's Fiction. Lincoln, NE: University of Nebraska Press, 1983

Pollak, Ellen. *Incest and the English Novel, 1684–1814*. Baltimore and London: Johns Hopkins University Press, 2003

Richetti, John. *Popular Fiction before Richardson: Narrative Patterns, 1700–1739*. Oxford: Clarendon Press, 1969; reprinted with a new introduction by the author, 1992
Defoe's Narratives: Situations and Structures. Oxford: Clarendon Press, 1975
Daniel Defoe. Boston: G. K. Hall, 1987
The English Novel in History, 1700–1780. London and New York: Routledge, 1999

Richetti, John, ed. *The Cambridge History of English Literature 1660–1780*. Cambridge: Cambridge University Press, 2005

Rivero, Albert J., ed. *Moll Flanders: A Norton Critical Edition*. New York: W. W. Norton, 2004

Rogers, Pat. *Robinson Crusoe*. London: Allen & Unwin, 1979
The Text of Great Britain: Theme and Design in Defoe's "Tour." Newark, DE and London: University of Delaware Press, 1998

Rogers, Pat, ed. *Defoe: The Critical Heritage*. London: Routledge & Kegan Paul, 1972

Roosen, William. *Daniel Defoe and Diplomacy*. Selinsgrove, PA: Susquehanna University Press; London and Toronto: Associated University Presses, 1986

Schmidgen, Wolfram. *Eighteenth-Century Fiction and the Law of Property*. Cambridge: Cambridge University Press, 2002

Schonhorn, Manuel. *Defoe's Politics: Parliament, Power, Kingship, and Robinson Crusoe*. Cambridge: Cambridge University Press, 1991

Secord, Arthur Wellesley. *Studies in the Narrative Method of Defoe*. Urbana, IL: University of Illinois Press, 1916

Seidel, Michael. *Exile and the Narrative Imagination*. New Haven: Yale University Press, 1986

"Robinson Crusoe": Island Myths and the Novel. Boston: G. K. Hall, 1991

Sherman, Sandra. *Finance and Fictionality in the Early Eighteenth Century: Accounting for Defoe*. Cambridge: Cambridge University Press, 1996

Shinagel, Michael. *Defoe and Middle-Class Gentility*. Cambridge, MA: Harvard University Press, 1968

Shingael, Michael, ed. *Robinson Crusoe: A Norton Critical Edition* (second edition). New York: W. W. Norton, 1994

Sill, Geoffrey. *Defoe and the Idea of Fiction 1713–1719*. Newark and London: University of Delaware Press and Associated University Presses, 1983

Spearman, Diana. *The Novel and Society*. London: Routledge & Kegan Paul, 1966

Starr, George. *Defoe and Spiritual Autobiography*. Princeton: Princeton University Press, 1965

Defoe and Casuistry. Princeton: Princeton University Press, 1971

Sutherland, James. *Daniel Defoe: A Critical Study*. Cambridge, MA: Harvard University Press, 1971

Thompson, James, *Models of Value: Eighteenth-Century Political Economy and the Novel*. Durham, NC: Duke University Press, 1996

Trent, W. P. *Defoe: How to Know Him*. Indianapolis, IN: Bobbs-Merrill, 1916

Vickers, Elsa. *Defoe and the New Sciences*. Cambridge: Cambridge University Press, 1996

Warner, John M. *Joyce's Grandfathers : Myth and History in Defoe, Smollett, Sterne, and Joyce*. Athens, GA: University of Georgia Press, 1993

Warner, William. *Licensing Entertainment: The Elevation of Novel Reading in Britain, 1684–1750*. Berkeley and Los Angeles: University of California Press, 1998

Watt, Ian. *The Rise of the Novel: Studies in Defoe, Richardson, and Fielding*. Berkeley and Los Angeles: University of California Press, 1957

Zimmerman, Everett. *Defoe and the Novel*. Berkeley and Los Angeles: University of California Press, 1975

Zweig, Paul. *The Adventurer*. New York: Basic Books, 1974

Essays

Aikins, Janet, "Roxana: The Unfortunate Mistress of Conversation." *Studies in English Literature 1500–1900* 25 (Summer 1985): 529–56

Backscheider, Paula, "The Verse Essay, John Locke, and Defoe's *Jure Divino*." *English Literary History* 55 (Spring 1988): 99–124

Baine, Rodney M. "Daniel Defoe's Imaginary Voyages to the Moon." *PMLA* 81 (1966): 377–80

Bell, Ian. "Narrators and Narrative in Defoe." *Novel: A Forum on Fiction* 18 (Winter 1985): 154–72

Blewett, David, "Roxana and the Masquerades." *Modern Language Review* 65 (July 1970): 499–502

Boulukos, George E. "Daniel Defoe's Colonel Jack, Grateful Slaves, and Racial Difference." *English Literary History* 68 (Autumn 2001): 615–31

Brown, Homer Obed. "The Displaced Self in the Novels of Daniel Defoe." In *Institutions of the English Novel: From Defoe to Scott*. Philadelphia: University of Pennsylvania Press, 1987

"The Institution of the English Novel: Defoe's Contribution." *Novel: A Forum on Fiction* 29 (Spring 1996): 299–318

Castle, Terry, "'Amy, Who Knew my Disease': A Psychosexual Pattern in Defoe's *Roxana*." *English Literary History* 46 (Spring 1979): 81–96

Chaber, Lois A. "Matriarchal Mirror: Women and Capital in *Moll Flanders*." *PMLA* 97 (March 1982): 212–26

Damrosch, Leopold, "Defoe as Ambiguous Impersonator." *Modern Philology* 71 (November 1973): 153–59

Griffin, Robert J. "The Text in Motion: Eighteenth-Century Roxanas." *English Literary History* 72 (Summer 2005): 387–406

Hume, Robert D. "The Conclusion of Defoe's *Roxana*: Fiasco or Tour de Force?" *Eighteenth-Century Studies* 3 (Summer 1970): 475–90

Jack, Jane F. "*A New Voyage Round the World*: Defoe's 'Roman à Thèse.'" *Huntington Library Quarterly* 24 (August 1961): 323–36

Kibbie, Ann. "Monstrous Generation: The Birth of Capital in Defoe's *Moll Flanders* and *Roxana*." *PMLA* 110 (1995): 1023–34

Kim, Sharon. "Puritan Realism: *The Wide, Wide World* and *Robinson Crusoe*." *American Literature* 75 (Dec. 2003): 783–811

Knox-Shaw, Peter. "Defoe and the Politics of Representing the African Interior." *Modern Language Review* 96 (October 2001): 937–51

Latta, Kimberly. "The Mistress of the Marriage Market: Gender and Economic Ideology in Defoe's *Review*." *English Literary History* 69 (Summer 2002): 359–83

Liu, Lydia H. "Robinson Crusoe's Earthenware Pot." *Critical Inquiry* 25 (Summer 1999): 728–57

Maddox, James H. "On Defoe's *Roxana*." *English Literary History* 51(1984): 669–91

"Interpreter Crusoe." *English Literary History* 51 (Spring 1984): 33–52

Markley, Robert, "'So Inexhaustible A Treasure of Gold': Defoe, Capitalism, and the Romance of the South Seas." *Eighteenth-Century Life* 18 (November 1994): 114–28

Marshall, David. "Autobiographical Acts in *Robinson Crusoe*." *English Literary History* 71 (Winter 2004): 899–920

McDowell, Paula. "Defoe and the Contagion of the Oral: Modeling Media Shift in *A Journal of the Plague Year*." *PMLA* 121 (2006): 87–106

McVeagh, John. "Rochester and Defoe: A Study in Influence." *Studies in English Literature, 1500–1900* 14 (Summer 1974): 327–341

Novak, Maximillian, "Defoe and the Disordered City." *PMLA* 92 (March 1977): 241–52

O'Brien, John F. "The Character of Credit." *English Literary History* 63 (1996): 603–31

Peterson, Spiro. "Daniel Defoe." *Dictionary of Literary Biography*, vol. xcv, *Eighteenth-Century British Poets: First Series*, ed. John Sitter. Detroit: Gale Research, 1990: 7–35

Richetti, John. "Writing About Defoe: What is a Critical Biography?" *Literature Compass* 3 (March 2006), doi:10.1111/j.1741-4113.2006.00302.x65-79, 76

Rogers, Pat. "Literary Art in Defoe's *Tour*: The Rhetoric of Growth and Decay." *Eighteenth-Century Studies*, 6, no. 2 (Winter 1972): 153-85

Schellenberg, Betty A. "Imagining the Nation in Defoe's *A Tour thro' the Whole Island of Great Britain*." *English Literary History* 62 (Summer 1995): 295-311

Schonhorn, Manuel. "Defoe and the Limits of Jacobite Rhetoric." *English Literary History* 64 (Winter 1997): 871-86

"Defoe's *Journal of the Plague Year*: Topography and Intention." *Review of English Studies* 19 (November 1968): 387-402

Scrimgeour, Gary J. "The Problem of Realism in Defoe's *Captain Singleton*." *Huntington Library Quarterly* 27 (November 1963): 21-37

Seidel, Michael. "Crusoe in Exile." *PMLA* 96 (1981): 363-74

Starr, G. A. "Defoe's Prose Style: I. The Language of Interpretation." *Modern Philology* 71 (February 1974): 277-94

Turley, Hans. "Piracy, Identity, and Desire in *Captain Singleton*." *Eighteenth-Century Studies* (Winter, 1998): 199-214

Wheeler, Roxann. "'My Savage,' 'My Man': Racial Multiplicity in *Robinson Crusoe*." *English Literary History* 62 (Winter 1995): 821-61

Cambridge Companions to ...

AUTHORS

TOPICS